ATLAS *of* EMPIRES

Weber del. Lith. de Marlet & Cie, r. du Bouloi, No. 19.

Cipayes.

ATLAS *of* EMPIRES

The World's Great Powers *from* Ancient Times *to* Today

PETER DAVIDSON

For my mother
who wanted to read this book but didn't get the chance

Atlas of Empires

CompanionHouse Books™ is an imprint of Fox Chapel Publishers International Ltd.

Project Team
Vice President–Content: Christopher Reggio
Editor: Jeremy Hauck
Copy Editor: Laura Taylor
Design: Justin Speers
Index: Elizabeth Walker

ISBN 978-1-62008-287-4

Library of Congress Cataloging-in-Publication Data

Names: Davidson, Peter (Peter Bruce), 1963- author.
Title: Atlas of empires / Peter Davidson.
Description: Mount Joy, PA : CompanionHouse Books, [2018] | Includes index.
Identifiers: LCCN 2017048739 | ISBN 9781620082874 (pbk.)
Subjects: LCSH: Imperialism--History. | Imperialism--Maps.
Classification: LCC JC359 .D29 2018 | DDC 909--dc23
LC record available at https://lccn.loc.gov/2017048739

Fox Chapel Publishing
903 Square Street
Mount Joy, PA 17552

Fox Chapel Publishers International Ltd.
7 Danefield Road, Selsey (Chichester)
West Sussex PO20 9DA, U.K.

www.facebook.com/companionhousebooks

We are always looking for talented authors. To submit an idea, please send a brief inquiry to acquisitions@foxchapelpublishing.com.

Printed and bound in Singapore
21 20 19 18 2 4 6 8 10 9 7 5 3 1

***Frontispiece:** Three sepoys, Indian soldiers serving Western powers interested in colonizing their country: the British (in red) and French (in green). Empire usually requires the cooperation of parts of a subject population and brings with it cultural fusion. From a French ethnography of 1827, taken from a 1794 watercolor by a British officer.*

CONTENTS

INTRODUCTION

"Murder, incest, and the wearing of expensive jewelry." That is the definition of "empire" a friend gave me when I said I was writing this book. It covers the basics of how to seize power, how to keep it in the family, and what to do with the spoils. But beyond this, what is *"empire"?*

For the Romans, the Latin word *imperium* meant simply the power to rule. *Imperator*, from which we get our word "emperor," was a title given to a military commander after a particularly great victory on the battlefield, allowing him to parade through the streets of Rome in triumph. Later, it became a title reserved for the one man who ruled Rome and all its possessions.

There is the image here both of glorious conquest and of power held over far-flung lands, and indeed this captures something of what we have come to mean by the term "empire." But how, then, does empire come about, what forms can it take, and does it have a defining characteristic?

Early in the 20th century, explanations of empire in terms of international finance capitalism were put forward by both English political scientist J. A. Hobson and Russian revolutionary V. I. Lenin. They each wanted to explain the sudden race of Western powers to carve up Africa and Asia from the 1870s onward and believed the root cause to be huge concentrations of money created by the growth of monopolies. There was too much money to bring continued returns at home so investment opportunities were sought abroad, safeguarded by political and military intervention. This was imperialism: for Hobson, a perversion of capitalism; for Lenin, its inevitable final stage.

Back in the mid-19th century, however, Karl Marx had seen empire not so much as a development of capitalism but rather as its underlying foundation. According to him, gold and silver plundered from the newly discovered Americas led to a buildup of capital in 16th-century Europe, without which capitalist economies could not have emerged in the first place.

But economics can only be part of the story. During the late 19th century, France grabbed vast yet economically worthless tracts of West Africa. Writing at the end of the First World War, Austrian-American economist Joseph Schumpeter thought military expansion expressed a primitive urge unrelated to economic interests. He suggested that wherever a military class influences government, a "war machine" is produced that seeks conquest as an end in itself. Schumpeter's first example was New Kingdom Egypt.

These are all particular descriptions of a general phenomenon: the domination of one state by another. This idea lies at the heart of the common use of the term "empire" and is as old as state-building itself. The earliest city-states tried to grow by taking over their neighbors. Where they succeeded, a single larger state might form, but more often the aggressor became a core state holding sway over a number of semi-independent peripheral states—a halfway stage to a larger state.

This core state became more than merely the strongest in the region. Ancient Sparta was the leader of a league of states but had little interest in interfering with their domestic politics. Athens, by contrast, also led a league but forced a supervised

Athenian-style democracy on its supposedly independent members. Sparta was a hegemonic state, the strongest of a group, while Athens was interventionist and thereby imperial. The fact that Athens replaced tyrants with democratic government did not lessen the imperial nature of this relationship.

This book, then, defines "empire" as an unequal relationship between a core state and a periphery of one or more states controlled from the core. On the simplest level, control means military occupation or other formal political intervention, but it can also cover informal economic or cultural influence. Economic pressure by itself has frequently been enough to manipulate governments. Religion, ideology, or other cultural forces have habitually accompanied political or economic persuasion.

The culture of the colonized, however, can exert its own pull and threaten to absorb a conquering power, most famously in the case of the Mongol conquest of China. As such, the imposition of an imperial culture is not a necessary feature of empire. More often than not, a cultural cross-fertilization develops. The rise of national independence movements in recent centuries might imply otherwise, but

The Via Appia running from Rome to Brindisi, begun in 312 BCE to supply troops across mountains and marshes. As Rome colonized the Italian peninsula, the need for efficient communications between core and periphery grew, and a web of highways radiating out from Rome developed.

national identity is itself a weaving together and never easy to rely on, here producing a hybrid, there masking regional identities that tell a truer story about how people see themselves. In the end, the acid test for cultural identity has remained solidarity in the face of a common enemy, and this is a test most empires have at some stage passed.

To tell the story of how empires, thus defined, have risen, persisted, and fallen over the millennia, the imperial core, the colonized periphery, and the international situation each need to be examined.

The core state is the place to look to find various motives for expansion, from the dream of imposing an imperial peace on squabbling states to desire for economic exploitation, lust for the glory of conquest, or evangelical zeal, whether religious or ideological.

The periphery is the place to look for crucial resistance or collaboration. The fates of many empires have hinged on leaders of colonized states deciding where their best interests lay. Often, the core can provide an account of an empire's rise, while the periphery better explains its persistence.

Decline and collapse may come from internal decay, but usually the international situation plays a part. Some empires have been able to exist pretty much in isolation, but the threat of war from other powers has been more common. In this context, a bipolar world has often been more stable than one composed of several rival empires. On the other hand, an international situation dominated by two rivals tends to leave no place for neutral states, so provides an additional motive for expansion.

In the background lies technology. Who acquires an empire, what form it takes, and how long it lasts have always been inseparable from the kinds of weapons empire-builders wield, the kinds of transport and communications technology they possess, and the kinds of finance they have access to.

As changing motives, changing structures, and changing technology have produced different empires, so this book is organized as a roughly historical progression of themes. This is not meant to suggest watertight categories, but simply to offer ways of looking at various empires. There is in any case a good deal of overlap between sections.

Nonetheless, different themes have come and gone over the centuries. The first empires, born from endemic war, gave way to empires espousing social and political ideals, which in turn gave way to empires fired by religion. Land empires won on horseback gave way to maritime empires won by seapower. Industrialization, the most profound revolution since the introduction of farming, brought new kinds of imperial relationships. Each empire furthered an inexorable movement toward wider integration.

Such a short book can be only the briefest introduction to a handful of the more influential empires of the last 5,000 years or so. All have involved murder, incest by one definition or another, and the wearing of extremely expensive jewelry.

Statues depicting Genghis Khan's warriors, near the capital of present-day Mongolia, Ulaanbaatar. During the 13th century Temüjin, the Genghis Khan *("supreme ruler"), and his descendants used the horse to establish the Mongolian Empire, at a cost of up to 40 million lives.*

KEY TO MAPS

PHYSICAL FEATURES

Coastline
Rivers
Seasonal lakes
Coastline (interpolated/modern)
Lakes
Salt lakes
Mountains
Small Islands

GRATICULE FEATURES

Lines of longitude/latitude
Tropics
20°N Degrees of longitude/latitude

TYPOGRAPHIC KEY

Indian Ocean — Geographical features/areas
Chaldeans — Group of people/tribe
ASSYRIA — Political region
Tarentum — Settlement
Rome — Important settlement

SYMBOLS

Gold	Silver	Copper	Tin	Diamonds
Pearl	Carnelian	Lapis lazuli	Obsidian	Turquoise
Coal	Oil	Pine tar	Timber	Rubber
Sugar	Grain	Spices	Salt	Tea
Tobacco	Textiles	Hemp	Cotton	Pottery
Slaves	Fur	Ivory	Meat/dairy products	Opium
Machinery	Steel	Iron	Battle	Uprising

Following page: main map:

THE CONTEXT IN WHICH THE FIRST EMPIRES AROSE
3000–2000 BCE

Irrigation agriculture produced centrally organized states, expanding trade networks, and a competitiveness fiercest along the Tigris and Euphrates.

1 WAR *and* PEACE

Sumer and Akkad / Egypt / Assyria and Babylonia / Persia

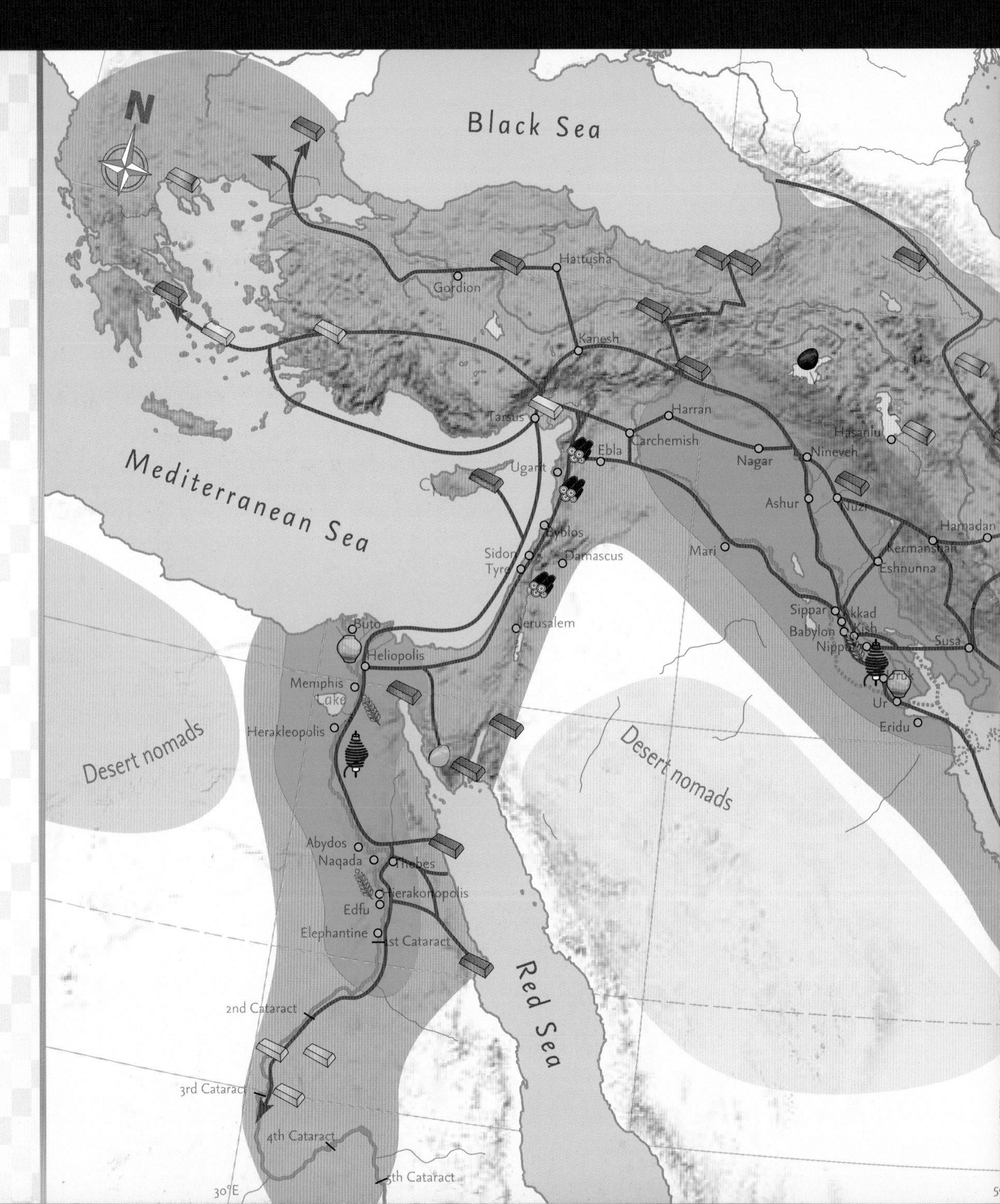

The first empires were attempts to keep the peace. The great river valleys of the Nile, Tigris–Euphrates, and Indus all gave rise to wealthy farming civilizations able to produce crops, pottery, and textiles. Lacking minerals, timber, and other raw materials, however, these societies had to trade with people who lived in the less fertile lands beyond.

Competition for natural resources led to war, which became a struggle to impose peace and stability over an ever-wider area so economic life could flourish. But maintaining peace required more than force. Communications systems were necessary. Some form of local administration for conquered territories was needed. In the long run, a way to win hearts and minds had to be found—the more so the larger empires grew.

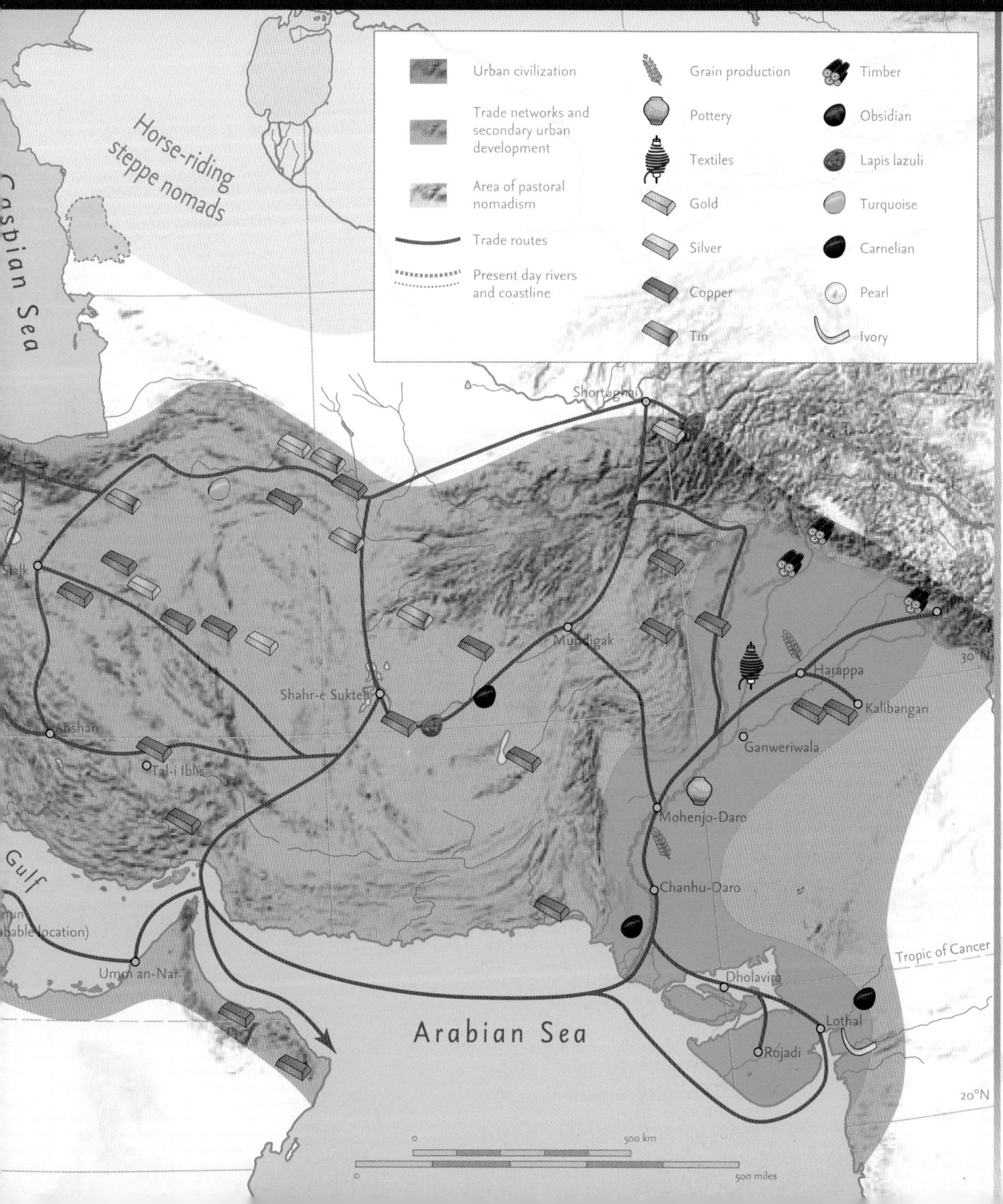

SUMER *and* AKKAD

The first experiments in empire-building emerged from the evolution of city-states in Mesopotamia. Each city-state concentrated wealth and power into the hands of one person as never before, but there was competition between them. The result was war, to which the only answer seemed to be more war, driven by the dream of a supreme victor imposing peace. But waging war and imposing lasting peace were two different things.

INVENTING THE STATE

Before about 6000 BCE, no one had settled the delta created by the Tigris and the Euphrates, which the Greeks were later to call *Mesopotamia*, "the land between the rivers," and which is now Iraq. There was little here to attract hunters and gatherers of wild food and even less to attract the first farmers working the surrounding hillsides. They needed rain for their crops but in the Mesopotamian valley there was hardly any rain. Instead, there were two rivers that flooded the region every spring, creating a temporary swampland destined only to bake dry and crack in the scorching heat.

But the silt from the two rivers produced a light soil that was easy to work in a time before metal tools, so gradually people began to come down from the hills until, by around 5000 BCE, the riverbanks of the far south had become dotted with villages. The villagers shared a common culture and named the region "Sumer."

What made life in Sumer possible was cooperation. There was more than enough water in the rivers to make up for the lack of rainfall, but to make cultivation possible it had to be controlled. Dikes were needed to prevent flooding, then a network of irrigation channels had to be dug to bring river water to the crops. Constructing and maintaining dikes and ditches was a huge undertaking that demanded a great and ongoing collective effort. But irrigation yielded big enough harvests for stores of surplus food to be built up, which made taxation possible.

An administrator was chosen to oversee a single irrigation system connecting several villages. He organized work teams and collected taxes to pay for maintenance work in the form of a percentage of agricultural produce. The administrator's village grew larger and more wealthy than its neighbors, becoming the center for local trade as well as taxation. It became a city-state, controlling a group of satellite villages and their fields. Between 4000 and 3000 BCE, dozens of such city-states established themselves throughout Sumer.

Eannatum of Lagash leads his troops against the city of Umma in a border dispute concerning irrigation ca. 2450 BCE. Eannatum was one of several Sumerian rulers who moved toward controlling the whole of Sumer in the period between Gilgamesh and Sargon.

These were societies of a size and complexity hitherto unknown, brought into being by efficient management. Without keeping track of who owed what to whom, the latticework of relationships supporting the economy would collapse. Luckily, the land between the rivers had no shortage of clay and a series of marks made by the end of a reed pressed into a wet clay tablet created a permanent record when the clay dried. From these beginnings the Sumerians invented writing and recorded history.

WAR

As Sumer prospered, so its agricultural wealth enticed the nomads of the western desert and the hill-tribes of the Zagros Mountains to mount raids. Each city-state responded by choosing a war-leader, who used the public coffers to equip and train an army and build a city wall behind which everyone could hide.

But the raiding parties kept coming. It became obvious that collective action beyond city-state level was called for, so the war-leaders of several cities met in the city of Nippur and formed a league to defend all of Sumer against outsiders. Impromptu raids by scattered tribes were no match for the combined powers of a developed civilization, and after the formation of the Nippur League, they largely died away.

Deprived of a common enemy, however, Sumer's city-states found cooperation more difficult. Each of the big cities now had a wall, a well-equipped army, and a military commander reluctant to hand power back to a peacetime administrator. There was always an excuse for conflict in Sumer because land and water had to be so carefully managed. There was also more to be gained from going to war against a wealthy city than a raiding party, especially because they now contained stashes of luxury goods.

The surplus produced by irrigation farming was able to support new social classes. Incessant raiding had pushed many to leave the land for a safer life within the city walls where they became potters and weavers in the employ of a new business class. These merchants were keen to trade pots and textiles upriver for the materials Sumer lacked, in particular copper and gold from Anatolia. So the rich became richer and Sumer's cities acquired expensive jewelry, precious artifacts, and weapons made of bronze. And now Sumer's war-leaders began to fight each other for booty, using the spoils of war to increase their personal power.

For hundreds of years Sumer was torn apart by endemic warfare. Out of the exploits of its warrior kings grew the epic stories of Sumer's "Age of Heroes" (ca. 2650–ca. 2550 BCE), the most famous of whom was Gilgamesh of Uruk. After sacking Kish, foremost city of the time, Gilgamesh took the title "King of Kish," though he was still king of Uruk. This began a tradition of the title "King of Kish" being claimed by the most powerful king in Sumer at any one time.

Now the object of these intercity wars began to shift. Plunder became less attractive than the goal of subduing enough cities to put an end to fighting in the interests of peace and prosperity.

Around 2400 BCE, the king of Ur succeeded in uniting his city with its rival, Uruk, and then taking Kish, thereby bringing pretty much the whole of the lower Euphrates under his control. A later king of Umma, Lugal-zage-si (ca. 2295–ca. 2271 BCE), conquered Lagash, Umma's old rival on the Tigris, inherited control of Ur–Uruk, and sacked Kish once more, making almost all the cities on both rivers his. Sumer seemed to be edging toward the formation of a larger state.

But Lugal-zage-si had not reckoned with Sargon.

ENFORCED PEACE

Sumer ended where the Tigris and Euphrates neared each other. Close to both rivers and a pass in the Zagros Mountains, this region became a crossroads for trade. The people who lived here and as far afield as Mari were descendants of Sumer's early desert raiders. They were heavily influenced by Sumerian culture, but they looked different and spoke their own Semitic language called Akkadian.

Sargon I (ca. 2270–ca. 2215 BCE) was Akkadian. According to Sumerian records, he was the son of a date farmer who became cup-bearer to the king of Kish—though, like many empire-builders, Sargon's origins are clouded by several rags-to-riches stories. It seems he somehow escaped Lugal-zage-si's sacking of Kish to become the first king of Akkad, a city he founded near where the two rivers come together.

Sargon's rise to greater power began in reaction to further aggression from Sumer. Lugal-zage-si led a coalition of numerous cities against Akkad, little expecting its young king to resist such force, let alone that he would take Lugal-zage-si and 50 other rulers prisoner. Knowing he had to press his surprise victory, Sargon immediately advanced south, taking the cities of Ur, Umma, and Lagash and claiming the title of "King of Kish" for himself.

But Sargon had concerns beyond imposing peace on the squabbling cities of Sumer. The trade on which Akkad relied was all too vulnerable to disruption by bandits or by rival cities charging tolls to allow goods to pass. Sargon embarked on a further round of conquests designed to create a single, stable zone of trade stretching all the way to the copper mines of Anatolia, the cedar forests of the Mediterranean coast, and into the Zagros to the kingdom of Elam.

For a time, Sargon's imperial peace bore fruit. He used his monopoly of power to enforce business contracts, settle disputes, and provide a constant police presence. Farmers returned to their land and merchants traveled in safety. Ships from the cities of the Indus valley could sail all the way up to Akkad, which soon became the richest city yet known.

Sargon's idea of how to govern his assembled conquests, however, remained crude. Local rulers were left to run their own affairs but any whiff of disorder was immediately pounced on by Sargon's imperial forces. It was both too little and too much and, inevitably, revolts broke out. Realizing he needed to pay more attention to regional administration, Sargon replaced local rulers with his own men from Akkad. At the same time, he tore down the walls of the cities he stormed to make rebellion harder—a measure which only reinforced the feeling of living in a police state.

Sargon was able to get away with this because he provided the strong and charismatic leadership an empire run by force alone requires, but neither of his sons had his talents.

His daughter Enheduanna became a famous poet and high priestess of the moon god Sin at the temple of Ur, where Sin was the city's protector god. Her standing may have gone some way towards ameliorating Akkadian rule in the south of Sumer, but if so neither of Sargon's twin sons had the leadership qualities to build on it. Rimush managed to alienate pretty much the whole of Sumer by an obsessively bloodthirsty mania in his punishment of rebelling cities, Manishtusu tried to calm things down, and both died at the hands of their courtiers in palace intrigues. As a result, the empire quickly unraveled, leaving Sargon's grandson Naram-Suen (ca. 2190–ca. 2154 BCE) with only the city of Akkad itself and Elam.

Naram-Suen, however, was cut from the same cloth as Sargon and his achievements in battle were even more spectacular. The major Sumerian cities plus Mari and several

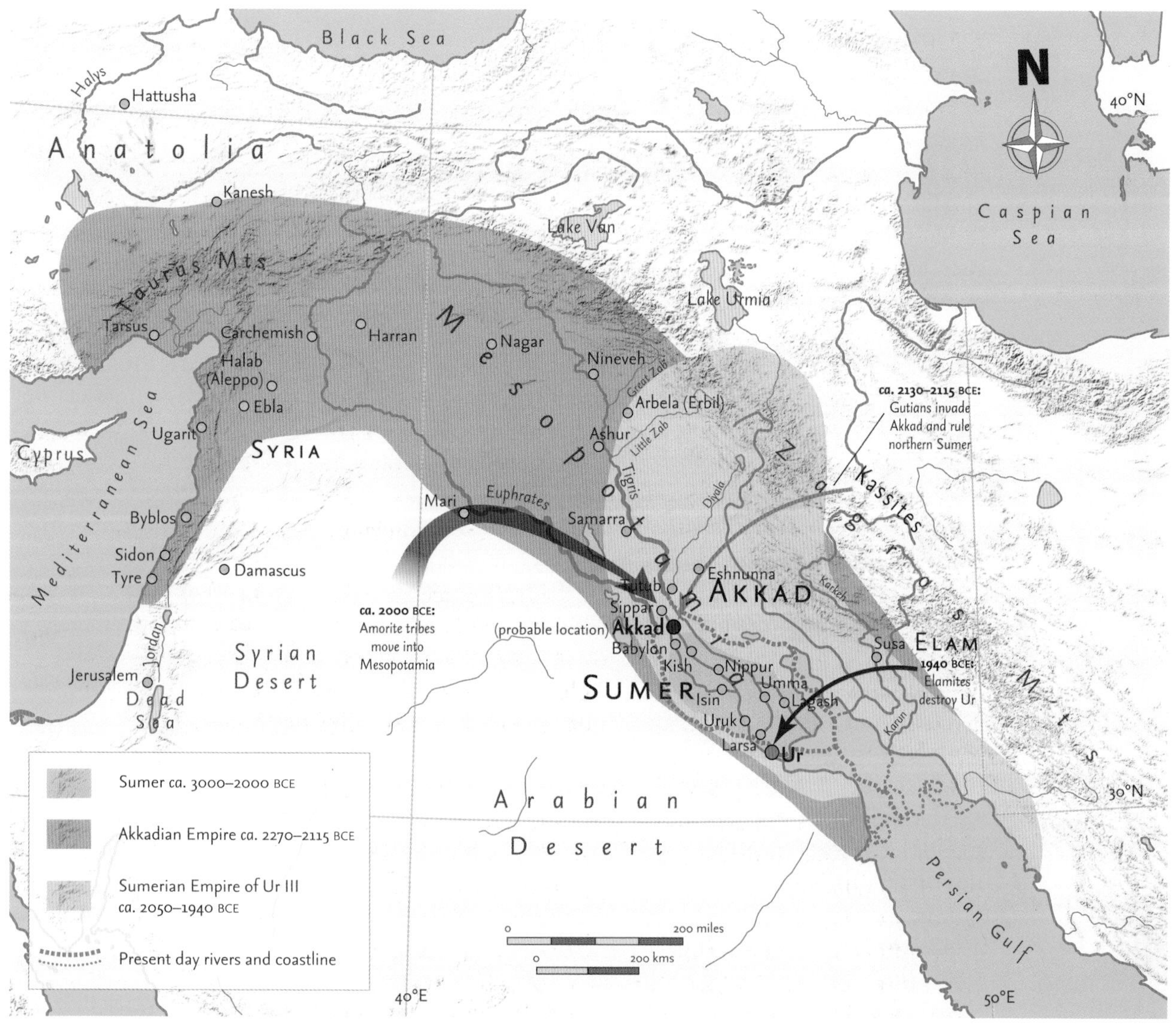

THE FIRST EMPIRES OF MESOPOTAMIA
ca. 2270–ca. 1940 BCE

Sumer was finally brought under single rule by Sargon of Akkad. His empire reached the Mediterranean, but relied simply on force. The later Sumerian empire built by the Third Dynasty of Ur was smaller but brought with it the beginnings of bureaucracy.

others all attacked Akkad together, forcing Naram-Suen to fight nine defensive battles in one year. He won them all and went on to reconquer his grandfather's empire.

The people of Akkad were so astounded by Naram-Suen's feats they decided he must be more than human. After consulting the gods on the matter, they made him the patron god of their city and built a temple to him. A leader able to inspire this type of personality cult was exactly what Sargon's administratively primitive empire needed. Unfortunately, there were no more Naram-Suens and by 2115 BCE, Akkad had been overrun by Gutians, hill tribes from the Zagros, who laid waste to all but the far south of Sumer.

BUREAUCRACY

Spared the worst of the Gutian devastation, the cities of Uruk and Ur soon rose again to develop a new Sumerian empire based more on bureaucracy than force.

Utu-hegal of Uruk (ca. 2055–ca. 2048 BCE) took the first step by driving the Gutians out of Sumer, after which agriculture and river trade began to revive. At the time, the city of Ur was run by a military governor from Uruk called Ur-Nammu, who succeeded Utu-hegal to take charge of both cities around 2047 BCE. He took the next step in the creation of a new empire by annexing Lagash and its surrounding countryside.

There Ur-Nammu stopped. Any conquests farther afield would be too expensive to hold on to and would only distract from more important reconstruction nearer home, such as building a safe harbor for seagoing ships and restoring temples fallen into disrepair under the Gutians.

Ur-Nammu turned to figuring out how best to keep control of his modest empire. He divided it into a core area around the cities of Ur and Uruk and a peripheral area toward Lagash and beyond from which to exact tribute. He appointed regional governors whom he shuffled from post to post lest they build up their own power base. Sumer's pioneering of writing enabled him to introduce standard laws to apply across his empire—replacing violent punishment with fines for many offenses provided an extra source of revenue. Ur-Nammu's conservative and bureaucratic empire provided enough wealth for him to build the great Ziggurat at Ur, the largest temple yet built.

Shulgi (ca. 2029–ca. 1982 BCE) further developed his father's infrastructure, having main roads measured and rest houses built along them for traveling merchants. Subsequently, he tried to expand his territory, but the later part of his reign saw waves of Semitic tribes, the Amorites, pressing in from the desert. Sumer's wealth had long attracted immigrants, such as the Akkadians, but the scale of the new influx was too much to absorb, so Shulgi began building a massive fortified wall along Sumer's northwestern border to keep the Amorites out.

The wall was not enough to save Sumer, however. Centuries of over-irrigation had made the soil around Ur so salty the area had become dangerously dependent on food imports. With trade and communications disrupted by social upheaval, the result was famine. Finally, seeing its age-old foe weakened, Elam sacked the city of Ur around 1940 BCE.

Sumer had fallen, yet its influence lived on. By digging ditches along the riverbank, it had produced taxation, war, and empire, together with a literate culture destined to underpin new societies formed by the very Amorite tribes whose arrival spelled its downfall. The empire of Ur-Nammu, with its law code and bureaucratic bent, formed the blueprint for the future rise of Babylon.

Sumer had also established the pattern for one route to empire, that of a dynamic, competitive society trying to transcend local rivalries. A different route, charted by a state more centralized from the outset, first emerged in Ancient Egypt.

EGYPT

While the city-states of Sumer were trapped in an endless cycle of war, Egyptian society found peace. Here, the stable larger realm that eluded the Sumerians was achieved early on and regarded as a single, unified country for a thousand years. Subsequently, Egypt remodeled itself as a military state and became an aggressive imperial presence on the stage of the ancient world.

UNIFICATION

What sets a unified state apart from an empire is often less a question of structure than of whether central rule is accepted as legitimate.

Around 3100 BCE, farming communities in the Nile Delta (Lower Egypt) and further upstream (Upper Egypt) came together under single rule from the city of Memphis. All the farmers along this stretch of the Nile shared elements of a common culture but it seems that what precipitated unification was an invasion of Lower Egypt by a ruler of Upper Egypt, known as Narmer or Menes (most likely two names for the same person).

During the fourth millennium BCE, the settlements of Upper Egypt had gradually become walled towns, perhaps in response to skirmishes with Nubian tribes from further upriver. In time, these towns formed themselves into three groups centered on Hierakonopolis, Naqada, and Abydos, until Narmer brought all three under his control. From this power base, Narmer seems to have embarked on a conquest of the less centralized delta, and an overall capital at Memphis followed.

Egyptian religious ideas enabled the Memphis rulers to present themselves as offspring of the gods, able to control the ebb and flow of the Nile itself. While the leaders of Sumer's jostling city-states were having to prove themselves in battle, the *pharaohs* of Egypt had found a way to put their authority beyond question. Their real power, however, lay largely in the hands of the *nomarchs*, local rulers of the 42 independent states, or *nomes*, of the Nile. The decision of the nomarchs to accept the authority of Memphis transformed what might have been seen as imperial subjugation into a unified Egypt, of which the nomes became districts.

The cooperation of the nomarchs led to 500 years of stable rule under the Old Kingdom (ca. 2686–ca. 2181 BCE), expressing itself most clearly in the building of the pyramids, which required the mobilization of huge workforces across the country. After about 2180 BCE, however, famines brought on by climate change made the pharaohs' ability to mediate with the gods look suspect, and the authority of Memphis crumbled.

After a century and a half, central control was reestablished by the nomarchs of Thebes, who became the first pharaohs of the Middle Kingdom (ca. 2040–ca. 1650 BCE), ruling from a new capital upriver and ushering in a second 500-year period of stability. In reviving Egypt's economy they began to look outwards, establishing maritime trade with Lebanon and along the Red Sea, as well as opening the first mines in Nubia and the Sinai Desert.

Nonetheless, the pharaohs of both the Old and Middle Kingdoms ruled a largely insular society defined by a desert boundary that kept external threats to a minimum

THE UNIFICATION OF EGYPT *ca. 3100 BCE*

From Upper Egypt Narmer invaded Lower Egypt to create a unified state along the Nile. Hemmed in by the desert, Egypt under the Old Kingdom did not seek further expansion.

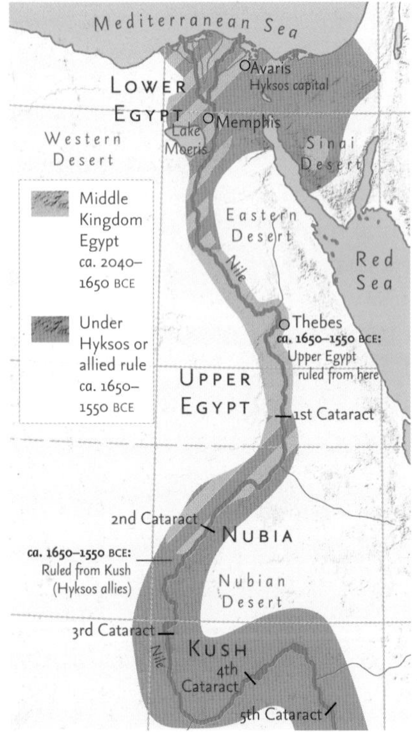

EGYPT UNDER THE HYKSOS *ca. 1650–ca. 1550 BCE*

The Middle Kingdom ended with Lower Egypt falling to incomers from the Levant. In Upper Egypt, a resistance movement grew, imitated Hyksos warfare, and after a century reconquered Lower Egypt.

and within which their rule was, for the most part, accepted as legitimate. For over a thousand years there was little incentive for aggressive expansion.

OCCUPATION AND EXPULSION

Then, around 1650 BCE, a people known as the Hyksos gained control of Lower Egypt, setting themselves up as Egyptian pharaohs in a new capital at Avaris. They formed an alliance with the Nubian kingdom of Kush in the south, but kept only indirect control of Upper Egypt, which continued to be ruled from Thebes.

Who the Hyksos were and how they came to power remains obscure. Historical accounts have them storming across the Sinai Desert into Egypt on horse-drawn chariots armed with small, high-tensile bows that could be fired on the move, none of which equipment the Egyptians had seen before. Archaeological evidence, however, suggests the Hyksos may have been one of many immigrant populations in the delta region that gradually grew in size and influence as central authority waned.

What is beyond dispute is that Hyksos rule provoked a reaction from the native royal family at Thebes. Egypt does not seem to have suffered under the Hyksos, not least because the Hyksos imitated Egyptian rule and adopted Egyptian traditions. But this did not prevent them being seen as foreign usurpers.

So at Thebes, a resistance movement developed. The new military hardware was adopted, a series of campaigns fought, and, eventually, Ahmose I, the Theban ruler, succeeded in driving the Hyksos out of Egypt and back across the Sinai Peninsula. Ahmose then reunited his country under native rule, founding the 18th Dynasty, the first dynasty of the New Kingdom (ca.1550-ca.1069 BCE), under which Egypt asserted itself for a final 500 years.

EMPIRE

Egypt under the New Kingdom was a changed society. The demands of taking on the Hyksos had produced a centralized military state with nomarchs appointed from the capital, agricultural production streamlined, and the organization of the armed forces closely linked both to the structure of government and to the social hierarchy.

Generals now wielded as much power as priests. A military class had been created, with the ear of the country's rulers and a vested interest in campaigning. The army moved beyond Egypt's borders to create buffer zones. The plan was to prevent another Hyksos experience but, with a new military establishment, campaigning soon developed a self-sustaining dynamic.

Under Thutmose I (ca.1506-ca.1493 BCE) Nubia was effectively annexed. His troops pushed up beyond the fourth cataract of the Nile. In their wake came miners, merchants, and civil servants to exploit the region's gold reserves, as well as priests who all but stamped out indigenous Nubian culture.

Across the Sinai Peninsula, Egyptian forces reached up the Levant as far as Carchemish on the upper reaches of the Euphrates, threatening the kingdom of Mitanni. Thutmose III (ca. 1479–ca. 1425 BCE), most militaristic of all the pharaohs, fought almost annual campaigns against Mitanni in the first 20 years of his reign before accepting he had to stay south of Carchemish.

Thutmose III expanded Egyptian rule to its farthest extent, turning Canaan into tribute-paying provinces overseen by Egyptian officials and policed by the army. In the larger cities, local princes were left as puppet rulers, their loyalty guaranteed by taking their sons hostage.

Egypt was drawn into the world of Middle Eastern rivalries, exchanging gifts with Babylon, arranging a marriage alliance with Mitanni, and conducting diplomatic correspondence with all its neighbors. The cosmopolitanism and vastly increased wealth of the New Kingdom, with its gold mines and tributary provinces, brought Egyptian cultural influence to a peak under Amenhotep III (ca. 1388–ca. 1351 BCE), who built Egypt's largest temple at Luxor.

Amenhotep III's son, also named Amenhotep, took Egypt in a different direction, changing his name to Akhenaten and moving the

New Kingdom Egypt was transformed into a military power by adopting the horse, the two-wheeled chariot, and a light and powerful bow made by laminating strips of wood together. Here Tutankhamun (ca. 1333–ca. 1323 BCE) fights Nubians from upriver.

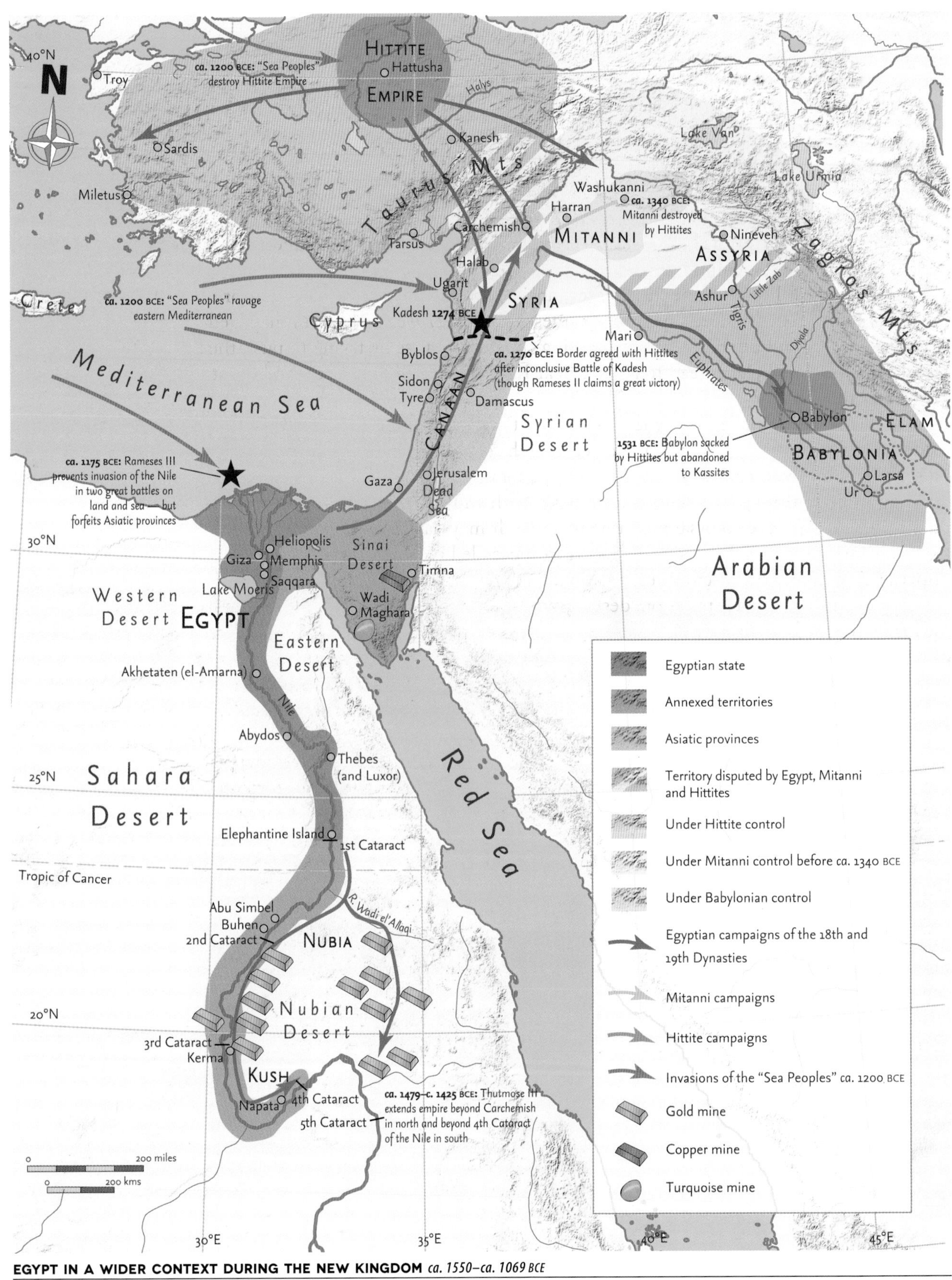

EGYPT IN A WIDER CONTEXT DURING THE NEW KINGDOM *ca. 1550–ca. 1069 BCE*

After expelling the Hyksos, the pharaohs of the 18th Dynasty continued expanding north and south, creating a larger Egyptian state with provinces in Asia.

capital downstream to Amarna, where he practiced a reworked religion centered on the sun god Aten, which exchanged traditional concern over the afterlife for focus on the here and now. Sculpture became more naturalistic, ceasing to show the pharaoh as all-powerful, and Akhenaten's rule became unpopular.

His own son, the boy king Tutankhamun (ca.1332-ca.1323 BCE), moved back to Thebes and began to undo all this but died young, whereupon his widow asked to marry a prince from the Hittite kingdom in Anatolia. When he was murdered en route to Egypt, the Hittites became a new and aggressive enemy and Canaan was soon lost to them. The dynasty died out and the early pharaohs of the 19th Dynasty found themselves trying to claw back the empire.

Faced with hostility from the Hittites, expansion was harder than it had been for Thutmose I and III and more expensive. Rameses II (ca.1279-ca.1213 BCE) managed to retake Canaan but after 15 years of draining the public purse by trying to push the Hittites farther north, he agreed to a truce near Kadesh in 1274 BCE, after the largest chariot battle in history.

What he may have failed to achieve on the battlefield, however, Rameses II more than made up for through the advertising power of architecture. Peace, the provinces restored, plus a reign of 67 years allowed him to pursue a continuous program of monumental building projects throughout the lands he ruled with an accent on size and quantity rather than quality. The colossal monuments he built may have lacked a refinement known in the days of Amenhotep III, but they succeeded in stamping the image of imperial Egypt on the consciousness of all who laid eyes on them for three thousand years and winning him a reputation, deserved or otherwise, as greatest of the pharaohs.

But by the 20th Dynasty and the reign of Rameses III (ca.1186-ca.1155 BCE), last of the great New Kingdom pharaohs, new and terminal stresses had arrived. Successive waves of seafaring raiders known collectively as the Sea Peoples swept down across the eastern Mediterranean, wiping out the Hittites and pushing Egypt back to the Nile. Here Rameses III held the Sea Peoples at bay in two epic battles fought in one year, in addition to fighting off invasions from the western desert. But the cost of warfare on such a scale was producing food shortages and even led to a strike by the royal tomb builders. After Rameses III the provinces slipped away and climate change brought years of famine, weakening the treasury further and exposing once more the inability of the pharaohs to control the Nile. Now Egypt entered a slow decline set to continue until the arrival of Alexander the Great in 331 BCE.

Egypt's New Kingdom demonstrated the dynamic for expansion that a government tied to a military career structure can deliver. It stood in stark contrast to the Egypt of earlier times, whose rulers had kept to a zone in which they could rely on religion and a common culture to provide legitimacy.

Farther east, this contrast between military power and cultural authority had, by the time of the New Kingdom, become the focus of the ongoing battle for control of Mesopotamia.

ASSYRIA AND BABYLONIA

Sargon's attempt to control the whole of Mesopotamia was only the first act in a drama that would take almost 2,000 years to play itself out. After the fall of Akkad and Sumer, two new powers appeared: one militaristic, the other a largely cultural force. It became increasingly clear that only a partnership of the two would create an empire of any stability.

SIBLING RIVALRY

The years around 2000 BCE brought ethnic change to the whole of Mesopotamia as Amorite tribes came to settle and mix with indigenous populations. When the dust began to settle, ruling Amorite clans had taken hold over much of the region and the cities of Mesopotamia were held in a new web of rivalries.

One area that fell under Amorite sway was Assyria, centered around the city of Ashur on the upper reaches of the Tigris. Ashur imported copper from beyond the Taurus Mountains through a trading outpost in the northwestern city of Kanesh. Shamsi-Adad of Ashur (ca. 1749–ca. 1717 BCE) began to take control of this trade route and by the end of his rule, all of northern Mesopotamia down to Mari was in his grip. But Assyria fell afoul of a neighboring Amorite clan headed by Hammurapi (ca. 1728–ca. 1686 BCE).

Hammurapi ruled Babylon, a city not far from Akkad. Where Shamsi-Adad was a warrior, Hammurapi was a politician. He had already outmaneuvered another Amorite ruler, Rim-Sin, who ran a mini-empire based around the southern cities of Isin and Larsa. Rim-Sin helped Hammurapi take Elam only to have Hammurapi turn the tables on him, after which southern Mesopotamia, now controlled from Babylon, became known as Babylonia.

Hammurapi then smoothed the way for a northern takeover by exchanging ambassadors with both Assyria and Mari. By now, Shamsi-Adad was dead and Hammurapi was able to persuade Mari to help invade a weakened Ashur before turning on Mari itself.

Having won an empire by manipulation, Hammurapi used bureaucracy to hold on to it. He was heir to the empire of Ur-Nammu as well as more generally to the literate culture of Sumer. His government was staffed by teams of scribes and he kept abreast of developments hundreds of miles away through letters, the cutting-edge communications technology of the day. He also disseminated written laws, adding the Amorite custom of "an eye for an eye" to Ur-Nammu's code. Written laws allowed Hammurapi, like Ur-Nammu, to extend centralized administration throughout his realm while giving his subjects a sense of benefiting from his rule by having rights.

Beyond this, inheriting the Sumerian tradition made Babylon the guardian of Mesopotamian culture, now a fusion of Sumerian, Akkadian, and Amorite elements. The Babylonians spoke and wrote a dialect of Akkadian, but Sumerian remained the language of priests and scholars. Sumerian literature was carefully copied out and Marduk, Babylon's city god, joined Sumer's pantheon.

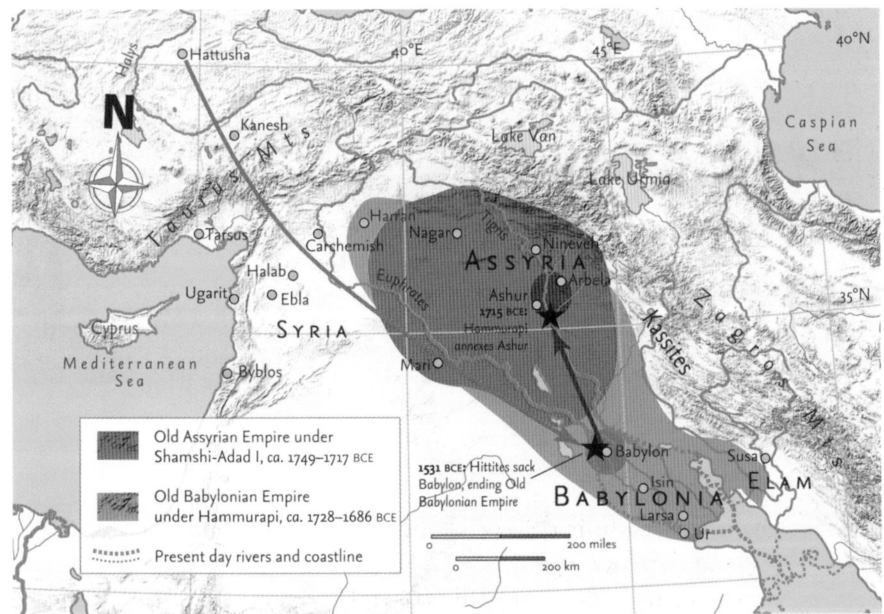

THE FIRST ASSYRIAN AND BABYLONIAN EMPIRES
ca. 1749–ca. 1531 BCE

After the fall of Sumer, the Assyrians and Babylonians gained control of Mesopotamia. Assyria soon fell to its southern neighbor, then, in 1531 BCE, Old Babylonia itself fell. But Assyrians and Babylonians remained rivals for a millennium.

CONQUEST AND INFLUENCE

Hammurapi's Babylon was sacked by Hittites around 1531 BCE, after which the Middle East entered centuries of turbulent power play, barbarian raiding, and large-scale movement of peoples. Assyrians and Babylonians fought, made alliances, and broke them off to fight again. Underneath the confusion, however, a pattern was emerging. Assyria was defining itself as a warrior society eager to subdue its neighbors while Babylonia was demonstrating its growing ability to exert a widespread cultural pull.

The Kassites of the Zagros Mountains were the first to feel this pull. They took over Babylon in the wake of the Hittites and simply became Babylonian themselves. Their first act was to retrieve the statue of Marduk from the Hittites. Since Sumerian times, carrying off a city's protector god from its temple had been a standard ploy to ensure a sacked city remained broken in spirit. Kassite Babylon was to be confident.

Meanwhile, Assyria had come under the grip of Mitanni and had to wait until around 1340 BCE when the Hittites sacked Washukanni, Mitanni's capital, before it could regain its independence. Under Ashur-uballit I (ca. 1353–ca. 1318 BCE), Assyria began 300 years of flexing its own military muscle, largely thanks to new technology. The Assyrians became masters in the use of the new two-wheeled chariot. Later on, as metalworkers in the nearby mountains improved smelting, they were the first to use iron weapons as standard equipment.

But Assyria's rise served Babylon's interests too. Ashur-uballit married his daughter to Babylon's king, who then died in a revolt, at which Ashur-uballit stepped in to restore the monarchy. Under the new king, Kurigalzu II (ca. 1332–ca. 1308 BCE), Kassite Babylon's influence reached its full extent. Ashur adopted Babylon's Marduk cult and a subsequent outbreak of war only brought more Babylonian customs to Assyria.

Around 1155 BCE, a joint Assyrian–Elamite operation finally brought Kassite Babylonia down, but under the new dynasty of Nebuchadnezzar I (ca. 1125–ca. 1104 BCE), Babylon rose yet stronger. Bringing Marduk back from Elam, Nebuchadnezzar I elevated him to head the Mesopotamian pantheon. He also began collating texts from Hammurapi's time to create a Babylonian literary canon.

Assyrian military might also reached a high point at this time under Tiglath-pileser I (ca. 1115–ca. 1076 BCE). The raids of the Sea Peoples had destroyed the Hittites and left a power vacuum along the Mediterranean coast which Tiglath-pileser I was able to fill. Shortly afterward, however, Mesopotamia was once again overrun by Semitic migrants from the west who would alter its ethnic makeup—this time tribes of Aramaeans and Chaldeans. Assyria shrank back to its heartland and waited.

A NEW ASSYRIA

Surrounded by mountains, the Assyrians had always been vulnerable to sudden raids from nearby hill tribes. In order to survive, they themselves became a warlike raiding people. But under Ashurnasipal II (883–859 BCE) a tribe of warriors became a military empire.

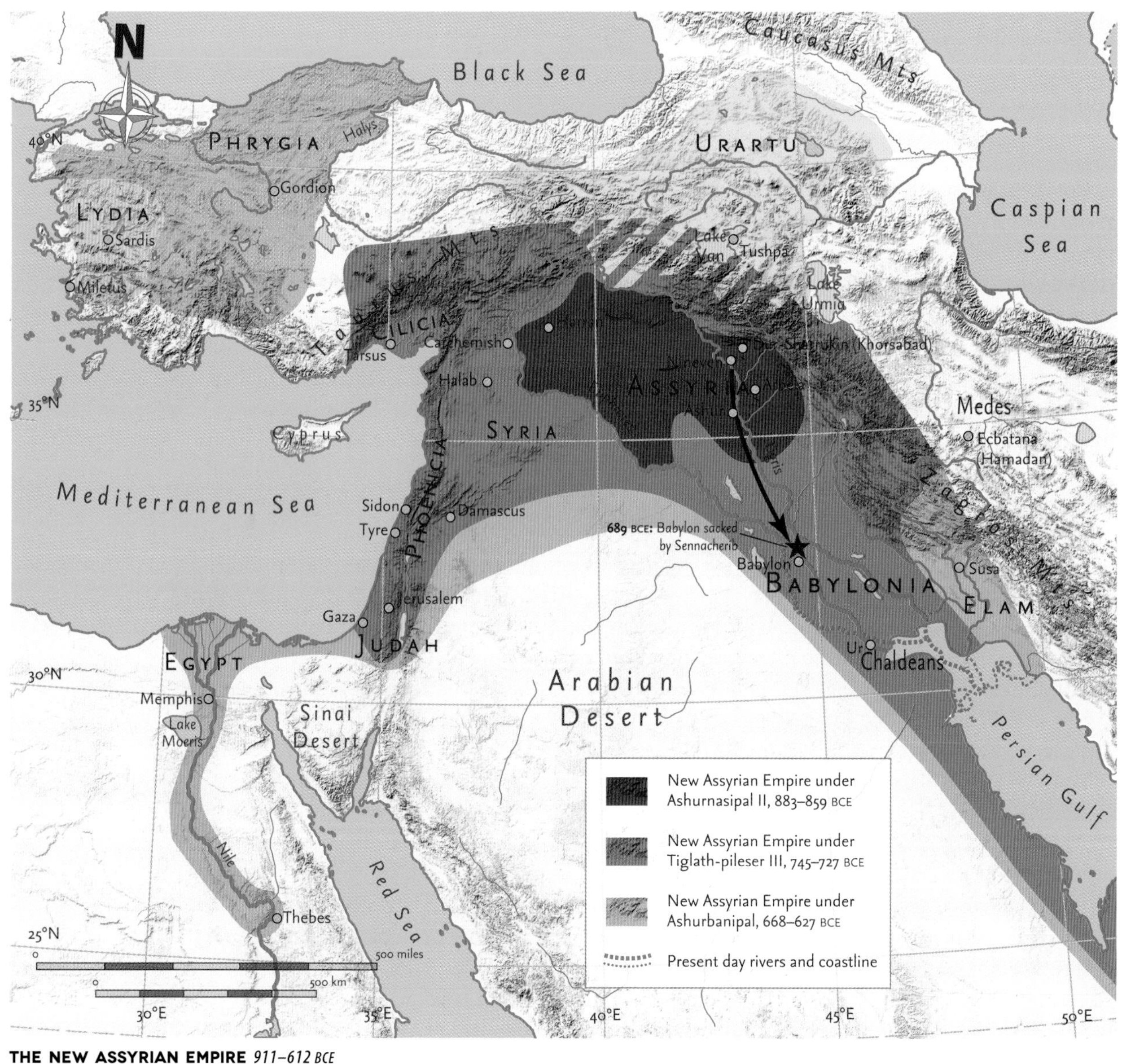

THE NEW ASSYRIAN EMPIRE *911–612 BCE*

Assyria came under Mitanni rule until ca. 1340 BCE, after which it began to expand. Expansion was checked from about 1100 by tribes arriving from the west, before a remodelled Assyria emerged during the reign of Ashurnasipal II.

Assyrian forces under Tiglath-pileser III use a siege engine to storm a city, impaling inhabitants on wooden stakes outside the walls to dissuade others from resisting. From Ashurnasipal II's capital at Kalhu (Nimrud), ca. 730 BCE.

Previously, Assyrian campaigns in the west had really been giant raiding parties, periodically repeated. Now they became annual tribute-collecting processions through conquered lands. As these processions journeyed farther afield, Ashurnasipal built local depots to store grain and other tribute. In time, these depots formed the nuclei of provincial capitals run by Assyrian officials.

This system relied on continuing military dominance. Now cavalry was adopted as well as new hardware such as the siege engine, a kind of wooden tank fitted with a battering ram. Assyria's makeover was completed by Tiglath-pileser III (745–727 BCE), who created the first paid standing army, one of the subsequent hallmarks of any strong state.

Tiglath-pileser III used his new professional army to check Urartu, a successor state to Mitanni threatening access to the Mediterranean. He then pushed down the coast all the way to Sinai, regaining the lands his namesake had conquered 350 years earlier. Assyria was now the greatest military power the world had yet known and was ready to play a new part in the fortunes of Babylon.

In the far south of Babylonia, Chaldean tribes had settled around the old city of Ur. The Babylonians had mixed feelings toward these outsiders who had taken over part of their country but adopted Babylonian ways. The Assyrians, however, saw them simply as a new rival power. So, when the Chaldeans made a bid for the Babylonian throne in Tiglath-pileser III's time, he stepped in and took it for himself.

From now on, Babylon became a prize held by Assyria, sometimes snatched by Chaldea. Caught in a tug of war, the loyalties of the Babylonians wavered until Sennacherib (704–681 BCE) sowed what may have been the seed of Assyria's eventual downfall.

Sennacherib spent his time making Nineveh a sumptuous Assyrian capital, leaving one of his sons to rule in Babylon. When Babylonian rebels kidnapped this son and handed him to the Elamites in 689 BCE, Sennacherib vented his fury by opening Babylon's dikes and flooding the city. Any other city could have expected worse but this was Mesopotamia's religious mother city. The shock of its desecration was never forgotten by Babylonians or Assyrians alike.

Despised by all, Sennacherib was assassinated a few years later, probably by another of his sons. His successor Esarhaddon (680–669 BCE) became obsessed with making amends by rebuilding Babylon's temples. Hoping to avoid future trouble, he split Assyria and Babylonia between his two sons, but this only produced a four-year war, after which one of the brothers, Ashurbanipal (668–627 BCE), claimed both crowns.

Ashurbanipal was almost more Babylonian than a Babylonian. Taught to read as a child, he was steeped in Babylonian literature and, like his father, acutely aware of how politically sensitive religious matters were. He knew the importance of having the gods on his side and would publicly consult priests and astrologers before making big decisions.

All of this found expression in the great project of Ashurbanipal's life, the creation of the world's first organized library at Nineveh—much larger than the later library at Alexandria. Ashurbanipal employed teams of scribes to collect, edit, copy, and translate all manner of texts from the 1,000-year-old Babylonian literary tradition. There were medical works, mythologies, guides to religious ritual, and a large section devoted to astrology, designed to help Ashurbanipal achieve stability throughout his 40-year reign. It seems to have worked quite well.

A NEW BABYLON

But no one had forgotten Sennacherib. After Ashurbanipal, Assyrian authority in Babylon collapsed and the Chaldeans came to power under Nabopolassar (625–605 BCE). Nabopolassar wanted more than Babylon. He made a pact with the Medes from across the Zagros Mountains to attack Assyria and divide the spoils. Together they took Nineveh in 612 BCE. Nabopolassar then pursued the last Assyrian king, who had fled west to seek protection from an Egypt eager to keep Babylon away from the coast. But Nabopolassar could not be stopped, and his son, Nebuchadnezzar II (605–562 BCE), eventually pushed all the way down to Egypt itself.

The only persistent trouble Nebuchadnezzar met with was in the little kingdom of Judah. When this irksome state finally fell, he demolished its capital, Jerusalem, and deported its people to Babylon to prevent further problems. Most of them intermarried and became assimilated like others before them, but a hardened core was radicalized by exile, nurturing its cultural identity and keeping alive the dream of a future homecoming.

Under Nebuchadnezzar II, Babylon became fabulously rich, displaying its wealth in wonders such as the Hanging Gardens and the gorgeously tiled Ishtar Gate at the city's main entrance. It owed all this to the Assyrians—it was their empire Nebuchadnezzar had usurped. In another sense, however, Babylon had simply taken administrative control of a region over which it had long wielded spiritual authority. By ignoring this authority, Sennacherib had seriously weakened Assyria. In the end, the same mistake would bring down Babylon itself.

In 556 BCE, Nabonidus came to the throne in Babylon. He was a religious man, but of the wrong sort. His mother was a priestess from Harran, a city where the moon god Sin was worshipped, and Nabonidus pressed this cult on Babylon. He made the further mistake of moving to an Arabian oasis for ten years, leaving Babylon in the hands of his son, Belshazzar. All this time, the New Year festival of Marduk, which guaranteed the city's well-being, could not take place because Marduk could only make the journey from his temple to the New Year's house accompanied by the king.

The religious divide between Nabonidus and his subjects was a gift to Cyrus the Great of Persia. Persuaded that Cyrus would better respect tradition and perform the necessary rites to protect their city, the people of Babylon opened their gates to him in 539 BCE. Once again, Mesopotamia's natural imperial capital had exchanged one leader for another, exposing the fragile status of power without authority.

But in Cyrus the Great the upholders of tradition had met their match. He would perform their ceremonies for them, but within an altogether larger vision of his own.

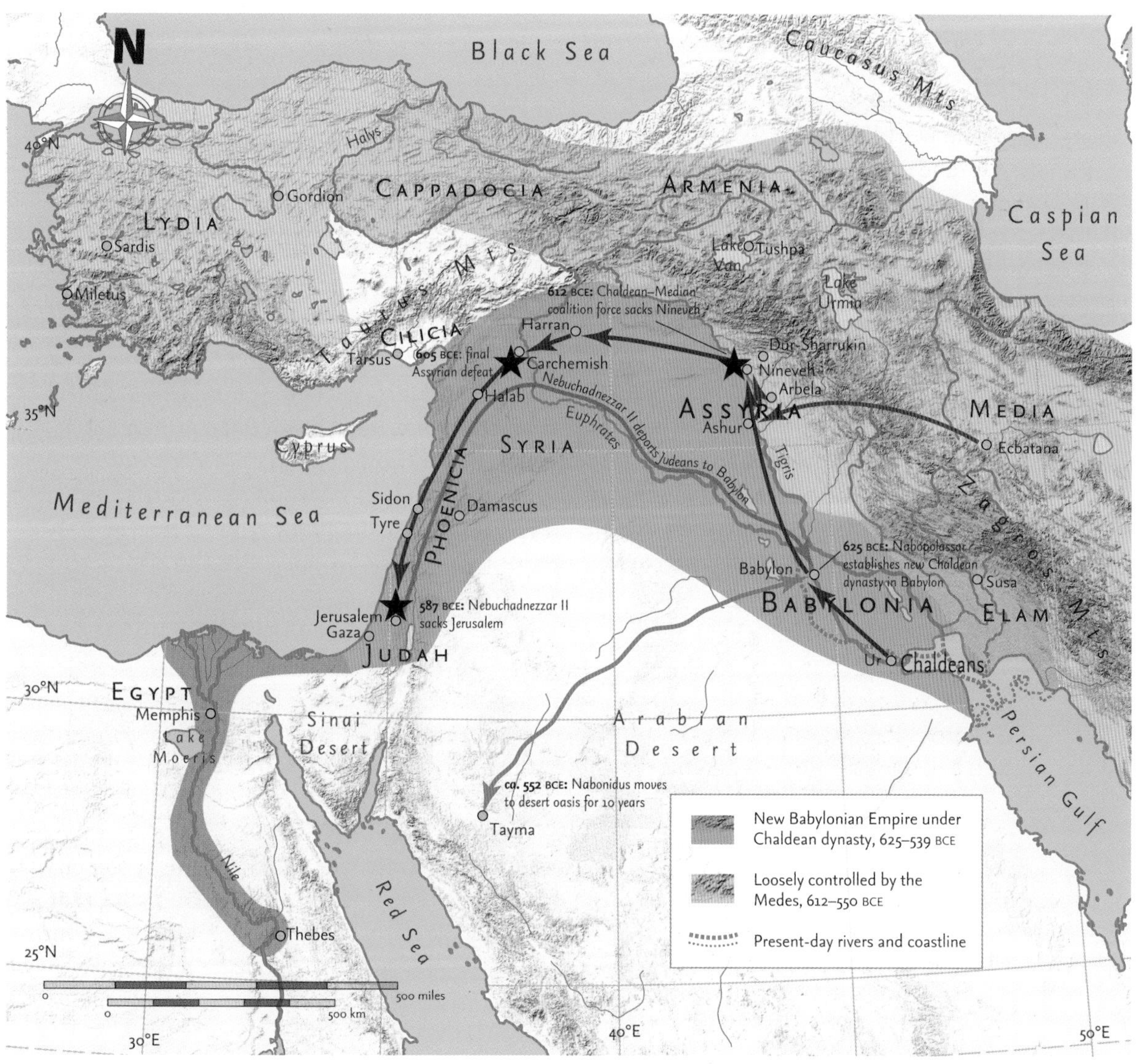

THE NEW BABYLONIAN EMPIRE *625–539 BCE*

Chaldeans and Assyrians vied for Babylonia and in 625 BCE, Nabopolassar set up Chaldean rule in Babylon. In 612 BCE he sacked Nineveh with the Medes, beginning a takeover of the Assyrian Empire completed by his son Nebuchadnezzar II.

PERSIA

As the powers of the ancient world battled to build empires, they came up against a series of requirements. An empire needed a monopoly on the use of force, a communications system, and a method for administering outlying regions. But if an empire were to avoid continual unrest, it also needed the consent of conquered peoples. The first to find solutions to all these requirements were the Persians.

THE RISE OF PERSIA

East of the Zagros Mountains, a high plateau stretches off toward India. While Egypt was rising up against the Hyksos, a wave of pastoral tribes from north of the Caspian Sea was drifting down into this area and across into India. By the time the Assyrians had built their new empire, a second wave had covered the whole stretch between the Zagros and the Hindu Kush. Some tribes settled, others retained their seminomadic lifestyle. These were the Iranian peoples.

Like all nomadic peoples lacking police and law courts, a code of honor was central to the Iranian tribes, and their religious beliefs differed from those of farming people. Whereas the farmers of Egypt and Mesopotamia had converted nature gods into city guardians, the Iranians had begun distilling them into a few universal principles. Zoroaster, who lived sometime around 1000 BCE, drove this process. For him, the only god was the creator, Ahura Mazda, bringer of *asha*—light, order, truth; the law or logic by which the world was structured. Even those who were not practicing Zoroastrians grew up shaped by a culture that valued simple ethical ideas such as telling the truth.

In some areas, one tribe would manage to gather a collection of other tribes under its leadership. The Medes were one such tribe. They built a capital at Ecbatana ("meeting place") in the eastern Zagros from where they extended their power. In 612 BCE, Cyaxares, king of the Medes, stormed Nineveh with the Chaldeans, after which he pushed into the northwest. In 585 BCE, the Medes were fighting the Lydians on the Halys River when a solar eclipse frightened both sides into making peace. Soon afterwards, Cyaxares died leaving an empire of sorts to his son Astyages (585–550 BCE).

The walls of Persepolis were adorned with tribute-bearers from across the empire, distinguished by their dress. Here Babylonians bringing pottery and textiles are led by a Median guard. Below, a Persian guard leads a party from Lydia.

One of the regions whose tribes paid tribute to the Medes was Persia, which lay southeast of Ecbatana, beyond Elam. There were around 10 or 15 tribes in Persia, one of which was the Pasargadae. The leader of the Pasargadae always came from the Achaemenid clan, and, in 559 BCE, a new leader was chosen: Cyrus II ("the Great").

We are told that Cyrus was the grandson of Astyages on his mother's side, but that did not keep him from wanting to shake off the Median yoke. By 552 BCE, he had formed the Persian tribes into a federation and begun a series of uprisings. When the inevitable showdown with his grandfather came in 550 BCE, the Medes mutinied and joined Cyrus to march on Ecbatana.

Cyrus took the title "*Shah* (King) of Persia" and built a capital on the site of his victory, which he called Pasargadae, after his tribe. Winning over the Medes, however, had landed Cyrus with a vague, sprawling empire of countless different peoples. He faced cultural diversity, suspicion, and outright hostility. Lydia and Chaldean Babylon had had agreements with the Medes; neither felt comfortable about a Persian takeover.

Lydia was won because Cyrus did not play by the rules. After an indecisive battle near the Halys River one autumn, King Croesus (ca. 560–ca. 546 BCE) returned to Sardis, expecting to resume fighting in the spring according to custom. But Cyrus followed him home and captured Sardis itself, Lydia's capital and richest of the Ionian cities. A century earlier, Lydia had minted the first coins, making Ionia a hub of commerce. Now all this fell to Cyrus.

As for Croesus himself, it seems Cyrus may have spared his life, again against all precedent. Cyrus developed a reputation for sparing conquered rulers so he could ask their advice on how best to govern their lands. How much of this reputation was warranted is hard to know, but before Cyrus no one would have wanted it anyway; it would have been a sign of weakness.

EMPIRE OF MANY NATIONS

Cyrus, by contrast, saw cooperation as a strength, particularly when it came to securing the main prize: Babylon. Rather than trying to take the world's greatest city by force, Cyrus fought a propaganda campaign to exploit the unpopularity of its king, Nabonidus. Babylon's traditions would be safer with Cyrus, was the message. It worked: in 539 BCE, the gates were opened and palm fronds were laid before him as he entered the city.

Once in Babylon, Cyrus performed the religious ceremonies Nabonidus had neglected and returned confiscated icons to their temples around the country. These acts enabled Cyrus to claim legitimate rule in Babylon; rule sanctioned by the Babylonian gods. He then explained what place this would take in his empire: his would be an empire based, in effect, on a kind of contract between himself and the various peoples in his care. They would pay their tribute and he would ensure all were free to worship their own gods and live according to their customs.

The exiled Jews were allowed to go home and given money toward the building of a new temple in Jerusalem. This earned Cyrus a glowing write-up in the Old Testament as well as providing him with a useful buffer state against Egypt.

Cyrus's multiculturalism made an enduring imperial peace a real possibility at last and defined the way later empires sought to achieve stable rule. It was obvious to Cyrus that this was the only way he could hope to hold on to his conquests, but his was a vision only someone from outside the civilizations of the river valleys, with their intense attachments to local gods, could have conceived.

KING OF KINGS

Cyrus's son and successor Cambyses II (530–522 BCE) added Egypt to the Persian Empire, but then a revolt broke out at home, led, it seems, by a Median priest posing as Cambyses's brother, whom Cambyses had secretly murdered. Cambyses hurried back but died on the way, leaving one of his generals, a distant relative, to step in. His name was Darius.

Darius I ("the Great") killed the pretender to the throne, but uprisings were now breaking out all over and he found himself having to reestablish Cyrus's conquests. Backed by the army and the noble clans of Persia grown rich from imperial rule, Darius regained the empire and extended it into the Indus Valley, a prize worth several times more in tribute than Babylon.

Darius realized that if the empire were to work it needed efficient organization. He divided it into 20 *satrapies*, or provinces, each paying a fixed rate of tribute to Persia. Each *satrapy* was run by a centrally appointed *satrap*, or governor, often related to Darius. To prevent the satrap from building a power base, Darius appointed a separate military commander answerable only to him. Imperial spies known as the "king's ears" kept tabs on both and reported back to Darius through the postal service—the empire was connected by a network of roads along which couriers could change horses at stations spaced a day's travel apart.

Darius took much of this structure from the Assyrians, simply applying it on a larger scale, but his use of tribute was something new. Previously, tribute had been essentially protection money paid to avoid trouble, but Darius treated it as tax. He used it to build a navy and embarked on massive public-spending programs, pumping money into irrigation works, mineral exploration, roads, and a canal between the Nile and the Red Sea.

He also established a common currency, which made working far from home much easier. Darius now brought together teams of craftsmen from all over the empire to build, under the direction of Persian architects, an imperial capital at Persepolis. Here he could keep his gold and silver in a giant vault (which soon became too small) and show off the multiethnic scope of his empire. Persepolis became a display case for the artistic styles of just about every culture within the empire, held in a frame of Persian design. It was a visualization of Cyrus's idea of empire.

But Darius never acknowledged Cyrus. He seems to have had a chip on his shoulder about not belonging to Cyrus's branch of the Achaemenid clan. As he outstripped Cyrus's achievements, he began to carry himself in an ever more exalted manner, dropping the title Shah for the grander *Shahanshah* ("King of Kings"). Like Persepolis, however, this followed directly from Cyrus's vision. Cyrus had played the part of Babylon's king when he entered the city, but his concept of empire demanded a ruler who stood above all kings linked to the interests of any one community. It required a king of kings.

Following pages: main map:

THE ACHAEMENID PERSIAN EMPIRE *ca. 550–ca. 331 BCE*

The empire of Cyrus and Darius covered the entire region from the Nile to the Indus over which powers had fought for 2,000 years. A network of roads linked the 20 satrapies into which the empire was divided, each paying a set rate of tribute to Persia.

Inset map:

THE CREATION OF THE EMPIRE

Cyrus won an empire largely in two moves: the Medes joining him with their empire in 550 BCE and the Babylonians handing him theirs in 539 BCE. Keeping it was harder. Cyrus died in 530 BCE fighting steppe tribes in the northeast and Darius had to reconquer the empire after internal rebellion.

HUMILIATION AND DECADENCE

Darius's later rule saw trouble in the Mediterranean. In 499 BCE there was a Greek revolt in Ionia. After eventually quashing it, Darius's fleet sailed to punish Athens for backing the rebels, only to encounter a surprise defeat. If the Persian administrative machine were not to look dangerously weak, the Greeks would have to be taught a lesson. But when Darius raised taxes to fund a rearmament drive, he provoked unrest in more important areas such as Egypt.

It fell to Darius's son Xerxes I (486–465 BCE) to restore order in Egypt and take up the Greek question. Xerxes carried himself more loftily still than Darius and, with two great empire-builders to follow, had even more to prove. But he lacked their cultural sensitivity. When tax increases produced riots in Babylon in 482 BCE, Xerxes sacked the city, destroyed the temple, and melted down the solid gold statue of Marduk, three times the size of a man. With it went Babylon's greatness.

Marduk's gold allowed Xerxes to begin assembling his forces to crush the Greeks in 480 BCE. Forced into battle too soon, however, he suffered a worse humiliation than his father. After that, Xerxes seems largely to have withdrawn into the luxury of his court and harem. When Cyrus entered Babylon he had aped the behavior of a Mesopotamian king for public consumption, but now the private lives of Persian rulers took Mesopotamian form. Shut up in opulent isolation, the later Achaemenids played out an increasingly gaudy pantomime of harem intrigue and palace assassination.

The empire Cyrus and Darius had built was strong enough to weather this slide into decadence for 200 years, but gradually it took its toll. Satraps carved out their own islands of power. Inflation began to bite as taxes kept rising. Even the multiculturalism of the empire, initially its great strength, had its drawbacks; the huge army was a bewildering grab bag of troops all trained and equipped according to their own traditions, all speaking different languages.

In 401 BCE, Cyrus the Younger, Satrap of Lydia, Phrygia, and Cappadocia, staged a coup against his brother Artaxerxes II (404–358 BCE) with the help of 10,000 Greek mercenaries who returned home when the coup failed. The information they brought back paved the way for the triumphant arrival of Alexander the Great in 334 BCE.

Persia had been the first real empire, an empire with an organizational structure developed from a realistic idea of how to govern different subject peoples. Later Irans would look back on this Persia, and when Alexander arrived he held the example of Cyrus in the front of his mind. Cyrus defined the role of an emperor and set a template for future empires from the Romans to the British.

The Persian daric, *struck from the time of Darius by the Lydian mint at Sardis. Lydia had pioneered the use of money a century before Cyrus's arrival and its conquest greatly boosted commerce across the empire.*

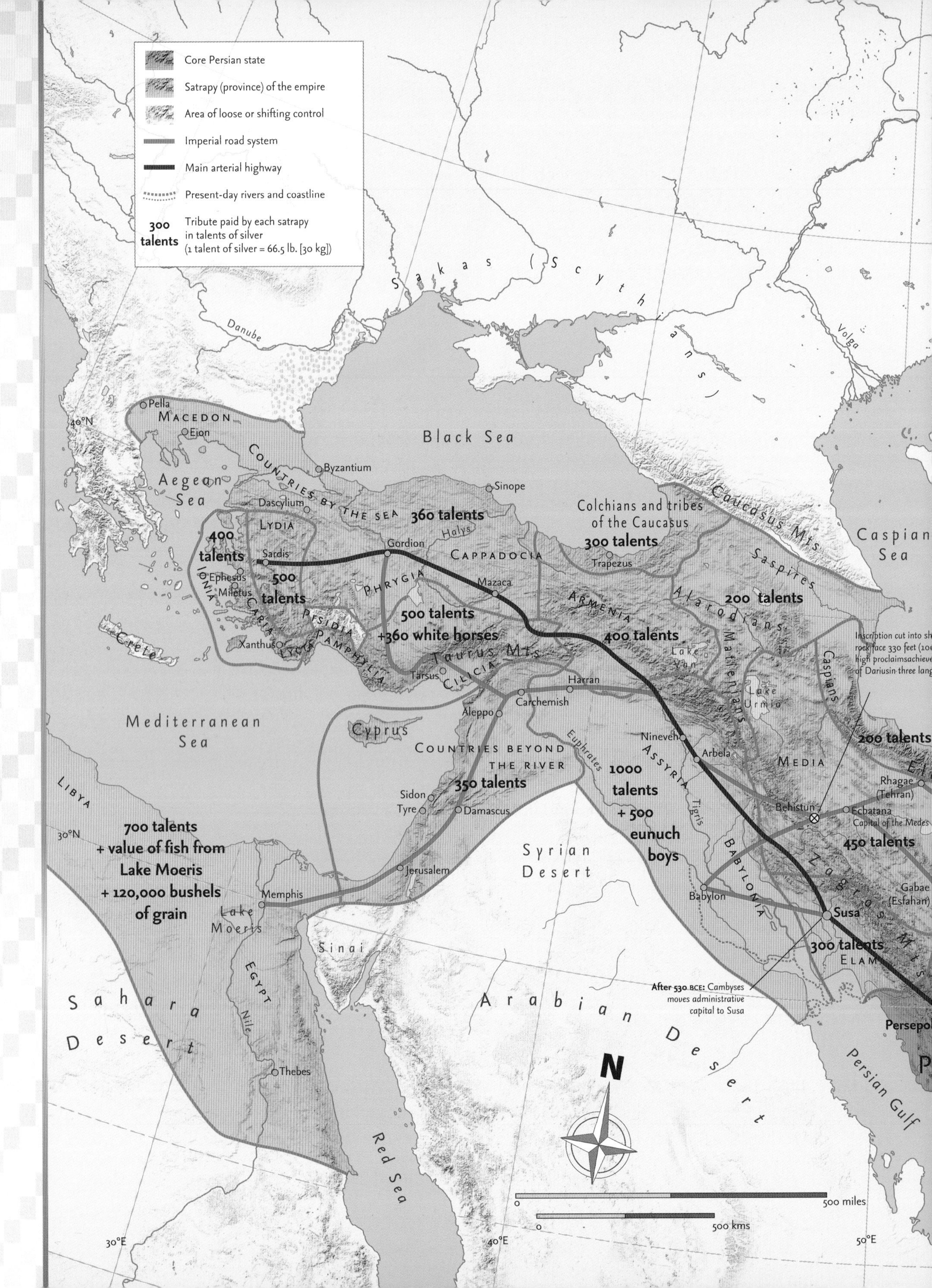

Core Persian state
Satrapy (province) of the empire
Area of loose or shifting control
Imperial road system
Main arterial highway
Present-day rivers and coastline
300 talents
Tribute paid by each satrapy in talents of silver (1 talent of silver = 66.5 lb. [30 kg])
Sakas (Scythians)
Danube
Volga
Pella
Macedon
Ejon
40°N
Black Sea
Countries by the Sea
Byzantium
Aegean Sea
Sinope
Dascylium
360 talents
Colchians and tribes of the Caucasus
300 talents
Caucasus Mts
Caspian Sea
Lydia
400 talents
Sardis
Gordion
Halys
Cappadocia
Trapezus
Saspires
Ionia
Ephesus
Miletus
500 talents
Phrygia
Mazaca
Armenia
Alarodians
200 talents
Caria
Pisidia
500 talents +360 white horses
400 talents
Crete
Xanthus
Lycia
Pamphylia
Taurus Mts
Lake Van
Matienians
Caspians
Tarsus
Cilicia
Harran
Carchemish
Lake Urmia
Aleppo
Mediterranean Sea
Cyprus
Countries beyond the River
Euphrates
Nineveh
Arbela
Assyria
Media
200 talents
1000 talents +500 eunuch boys
Sidon
Tyre
350 talents
Damascus
Tigris
Rhagae (Tehran)
Behistun
Ecbatana Capital of the Medes
Libya
30°N
700 talents + value of fish from Lake Moeris + 120,000 bushels of grain
Syrian Desert
Babylonia
450 talents
Jerusalem
Memphis
Lake Moeris
Babylon
Susa
Zagros Mts
Gabae (Esfahan)
Sinai
300 talents
Elam
Egypt
Nile
Sahara Desert
Arabian Desert
After 530 BCE: Cambyses moves administrative capital to Susa
Persian Gulf
Thebes
N
Red Sea
0
500 miles
500 kms
30°E
40°E
50°E

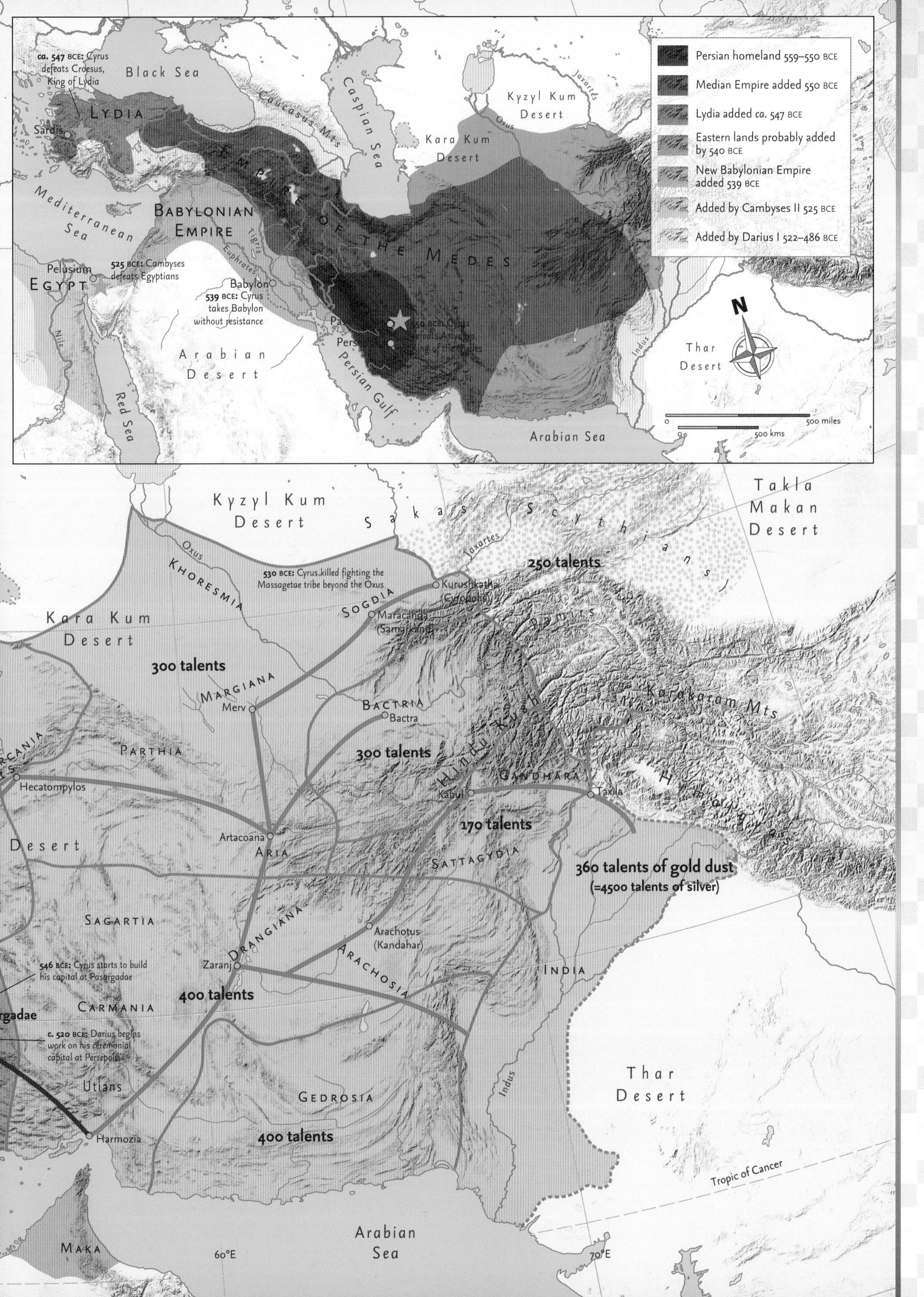

Persian homeland 559–550 BCE
Median Empire added 550 BCE
Lydia added ca. 547 BCE
Eastern lands probably added by 540 BCE
New Babylonian Empire added 539 BCE
Added by Cambyses II 525 BCE
Added by Darius I 522–486 BCE
ca. 547 BCE: Cyrus defeats Croesus, King of Lydia
Black Sea
Lydia
Sardis
Caucasus Mts
Caspian Sea
Kyzyl Kum Desert
Jaxartes
Oxus
Kara Kum Desert
Mediterranean Sea
Babylonian Empire
Empire of the Medes
Tigris
Euphrates
Pelusium
525 BCE: Cambyses defeats Egyptians
Egypt
Babylon
539 BCE: Cyrus takes Babylon without resistance
Nile
Arabian Desert
Red Sea
Persian Gulf
Indus
Thar Desert
N
Arabian Sea
500 miles
500 kms
Kyzyl Kum Desert
Sakas (Scythians)
Takla Makan Desert
Oxus
Khoresmia
Jaxartes
250 talents
530 BCE: Cyrus killed fighting the Massagetae tribe beyond the Oxus
Kurushkatha (Cyropolis)
Sogdia
Maracanda (Samarkand)
Pamirs
Kara Kum Desert
300 talents
Margiana
Merv
Bactria
Bactra
Karakoram Mts
Parthia
300 talents
Hindu Kush
Gandhara
Himalayas
Hecatompylos
Kabul
Taxila
170 talents
Artacoana
Desert
Aria
Sattagydia
360 talents of gold dust
(=4500 talents of silver)
Sagartia
Drangiana
Arachotus (Kandahar)
546 BCE: Cyrus starts to build his capital at Pasargadae
Zaranj
Arachosia
India
400 talents
Carmania
c. 520 BCE: Darius begins work on his ceremonial capital at Persepolis
Indus
Thar Desert
Utians
Gedrosia
Harmozia
400 talents
Tropic of Cancer
Maka
60°E
Arabian Sea
70°E

EMPIRES OF THE CLASSICAL WORLD

Athens / Rome / Alexander / Iran / India / China

The Achaemenid Persian Empire built a bridge to straddle the ancient and classical worlds. On one bank stood the people of Babylon, anxious to restore the sacred rituals that safeguarded their city. On the other stood the Greeks, confident in their own abilities. Between the two, Persia both preserved and transcended tradition, accommodating the ancient world of Egypt and the Middle East while fitting it into a framework that looked forward to the classical world of Greece and Rome.

But the classical world was not just a European phenomenon. The thousand years or so from around 500 BCE saw new kinds of society develop across the four great zones of Eurasian civilization: Europe, the area covered by the Persian Empire, India, and China. Each of these zones produced empires that brought people together within a social and political vision.

Athens and Rome each built an empire around a democracy, creating problems only Rome managed to solve. Alexander the Great cast himself as bringer of cultural fusion. In Iran, the new order he brought produced a mounting desire to revive what had been swept away. India tried to anchor a unified culture in an overarching system of spiritual thought. China developed an all-inclusive bureaucracy.

The classical empires extended their influence by combining military conquest with the dissemination of ideas, bound up with the wider spread of literacy. In Rome, it became fashionable for the comfortably off to commission portraits of themselves as suitably cultured individuals. Fresco from a house at Pompeii, ca. 50 CE.

ATHENS

What Athens left to the world was achieved in little more than a half century between war with Persia, out of which the city-state arose, and war with Sparta, which brought it down. During this time, Athens blossomed as a democracy but its growing hold over the Aegean as policeman, educator, and exploiter also made it an empire.

A COMMON ENEMY

The Greece of 500 BCE resembled the Sumer of 2500 BCE. Both were collections of city-states, fiercely independent yet sharing elements of a common culture. Like the Sumerians, the Greeks had their gods and epic poems—they had developed the alphabet in the 8th century BCE largely to write down the *Iliad* and the *Odyssey*. Since at least 776 BCE they had also had the Olympic Games through which to express the mixture of fraternity and competition they felt toward each other. Beyond this world there were merely *barbarians*—people whose speech met Greek ears as "bar bar bar."

The most advanced Greek cities were in Ionia, on the Anatolian coast. They had benefited from Lydia's economic boom but then fell under the control of first Lydia, then the Persian governor at Sardis, which they found deeply insulting. In 498 BCE, Ionian Greek rebels stormed Sardis and set it on fire.

By 493 BCE, the Persians had restored order in Ionia, but two western cities, Eretria and Athens, had helped the rebels, so Darius, the Persian king of kings, sent his fleet across the Aegean. Eretria was sacked, but, in 490 BCE, the Persians were driven back by Athenian infantry at Marathon.

Surprised and humiliated, Darius and his successor Xerxes spent the next decade preparing a far larger invasion. When it became imminent, the Greeks met at Corinth to plan a response. Age-old rivalries prevented a common front forming, some cities remaining neutral, others siding with the Persians, but eventually an alliance of several cities emerged under Sparta, a militaristic society from the Peloponnesian plain with the strongest army in Greece.

Against all odds, the Persians were routed a second time. For a week in 480 BCE, a small Spartan-led force held back a Persian army of over 200,000 at Thermopylae, a narrow pass guarding the way south to Athens. A year later, Spartan troops spearheaded a final victory at Plataea.

The Greek triumph, however, was really a naval one. In 483 BCE, a large seam of silver had been discovered in the Athenian mines at Laurium. The Athenian statesman Themistocles (493–471 BCE),

Athena, city goddess of Athens. As goddess of wisdom but also of war, Athena represented a city that dominated the Aegean both culturally and militarily in the 5th century BCE.

having constructed a naval base at Piraeus, argued it should be used to build a fleet of 200 warships; however vast an army Xerxes might march into the Greek mainland, it would depend on supplies brought by sea.

After Thermopylae fell, Themistocles drew Xerxes's huge fleet into the narrow straits of Salamis, just outside Piraeus, where its size advantage counted for little. The Persian ships were outmaneuvered, rammed, and sunk, and most of their crews could not swim. The following year, Themistocles's fleet ferried Athenian and Spartan troops to Ionia, where they began a renewed Ionian revolt.

A COMMON DEFENSE POLICY

Athens and Sparta now found themselves at a fork in the road. Athens wanted to finish the job of clearing the Aegean of Persian influence. Sparta felt it had done its part to push Persia back from the mainland and wanted to go home. Each had sound economic motives.

Athens was a city built on poor, rocky soil whose people could not feed themselves without trade. They survived by exporting wine, olive oil, and pottery and by importing food, in particular grain from the Black Sea. The need to keep trade routes open made continuing the war a natural idea.

By contrast, Sparta lay in highly fertile land and was self-sufficient. Produce was distributed according to a quota system. Sparta used no money and trade was outlawed, so it had no economic reason to cultivate ties with other cities. In addition, all Sparta's agricultural work was done by *helots*, enslaved prisoners captured as Sparta took over its neighbors. About 80 percent of the population were slaves, compared to about 30 percent in Athens, so when the army was away Sparta lived in fear of a helot uprising.

So it was left to Athens to form the Delian League in 478 BCE, an association of cities, each contributing toward a common defense force under Athenian direction. Athens and a few others provided ships, the rest paid a fixed rate of tax (much less than Persian tribute), and the money was kept on the centrally placed island of Delos.

It sounded like everyone would benefit, but from the start Athens had the most to gain. One of the first actions Athens took on behalf of the League in 475 BCE was to colonize Skyros, an island lying along the Black Sea route, the main artery of Athenian trade. The people of Skyros were enslaved and their island resettled by Athenians, reducing overcrowding in Athens as well as protecting its economy.

That same year, the Persians were ousted from Eion, a city at the mouth of the Strymon River in Thrace. The forests inland from Eion contained abundant timber for shipbuilding and the mountains were home to the richest gold mines around the Aegean. In 465 BCE, Athens tried to colonize this area, too, but met stiff opposition.

The common defense force, swollen with Delian League funds, was in practice the Athenian navy, a fact that was becoming clearer and more worrying as the Persian threat receded. Concerned about its own access to the gold mines of Thrace, the nearby island of Thasos tried to stop its payments and secede. This action revealed how Athens really viewed the League; Thasos was beseiged for three years before being forced back into the League with its walls torn down and its ships and mainland possessions taken by Athens.

Naxos, in the central Aegean Sea, had already had a similar experience and others followed as Athenian control of the League grew more self-interested. Athens began using the League's money not just to build ships but also to beautify Athens with buildings such as the Parthenon, into which the Delian treasury was moved in 454 BCE. Now there was no longer any pretense.

REPUBLIC AND EMPIRE

The profits from its domination of the Delian League paid for the golden age of Athens, an intellectual and artistic explosion that laid the foundation for European civilization. Inseparable from both its cultural output and its imperialism was its democratic tradition.

The development of the Greek *polis*, or city-state, had everywhere been part of a progression toward representative government, usually pushed by the rise of a business class, but Athens had progressed farthest down this road. In 753 BCE, *archontes*, or magistrates, elected from the *eupatridae*, or noble class, replaced the king. By 594 BCE, power had passed to the *boule*, a council of 400, chosen on the basis of property ownership, not nobility. By 508 BCE, the boule had become a council of any 500 citizens representing Athens's districts—the *demes* (hence "democracy"). The boule was elected by the *ekklesia*, a general assembly of all 50,000 or so citizens.

By 462 BCE, the ekklesia passed law, judged all cases except murder trials, and chose public officials, including ten annual *strategoi*, or military leaders. Themistocles had been a *strategos*, as was Pericles (461–429 BCE), whose popularity led to him being reelected every year. As the navy moved from fighting Persians to controlling the Delian League, the strategoi found themselves orchestrating Athenian imperialism.

The navy was as tied in to democracy as it was to imperialism. The rise of the polis had brought a change in warfare; noble warriors in single combat gave way to *hoplites*, or infantrymen, who worked together by locking shields to hold the line. As hoplites paid for their own equipment, this was war fought by the new men of property given access to the boule in 594 BCE. An Athenian warship, however, needed about 200 rowers to power it, none of whom required equipment. Crews could be recruited from the *thetes*, citizens who owned nothing.

It was the thetes who had routed the Persians and enabled Athens to control the Delian League. They had been allowed to sit in the ekklesia for over a century but seldom did so because they could not afford to take a day off work—not until 451 BCE, when Pericles paid them to attend. Now they joined nobles and businessmen in feeling they benefited themselves by extending Athens's power.

In addition, the very nature of Athenian democracy fed an appetite for glory. The ekklesia was a stage on which anyone had the chance to sway a decision. It released an enormous competitive energy, encouraging ambition and bringing skilled orators such as Pericles to the top.

Pericles saw his city as an education to all, a cause for intense civic pride and evangelical zeal. When Athens tore down the walls of a resisting city-state, it was only natural for it to dismantle the political system and introduce democracy. To Pericles, sending *hellenotamia*, imperial tax collectors, to oversee the running of these imposed democracies was a public service.

REVOLT

However, while Athens felt it had a superior culture to impart, other Greek cities did not quite see it that way. They each had their own proud and independent histories. Athens was no Persia, able to overawe with its wealth and splendor. It was not even the only Greek city to have colonies.

As the Persian menace faded, therefore, resentment of Athens coalesced into a rival league under Sparta. A bipolar Greece emerged, making it all the more important for Athens to prevent secession from the Delian League.

Main map: **THE DELIAN LEAGUE** *478–404 BCE*

A common defense organization for the Greeks soon became a de facto Athenian empire, especially after the treasury was moved to Athens in 454 BCE. In 404 BCE, after two wars of rebellion led by Sparta, the League was dissolved.

Inset map: **WARS WITH PERSIA** *498–479 BCE*

Athenian aid during the Ionian Revolt provoked Darius to attack Athens, but he was held off in 490 BCE. Xerxes launched a larger invasion in 480 BCE but was chased back across the Aegean, after which the Delian League was formed.

At a meeting of the Spartan League in 432 BCE, Corinth pressed for war because Athens had been helping Corfu, one of its colonies, to break away. Aegina complained that Athens had interfered in its government, and Megara that it had been barred from trading with Delian League cities. To top it all, there was Potidaea, another Corinthian colony but one tied into the Delian League. Sparta had promised to help it revolt against Athens, and now Athens had sent the troops in.

So the first Peloponnesian War began in 431 BCE. Every year, Sparta marched north to destroy Athenian crops, and every year Athens just imported more goods by sea. In 457 BCE, it had completed an enormous wall that ran around the city and all the way down to its port at Piraeus, sealing it off from attack by land. The best Sparta could hope for was a truce in 421 BCE.

During the war, however, plague had struck Athens. Corpses piled up and increasingly radical proposals were put forward in the ekklesia.

Alcibiades (421–415 and 411–406 BCE), strategos and nephew of Pericles, won support for a daring plan to take the Sicilian city of Syracuse from Corinth, main economic rival of Athens. The loss of Sicily's huge grain harvests would destroy Corinth. But once the fleet set sail, Alcibiades was called back to face trial on charges trumped up by his political enemies. He defected to Sparta and persuaded it to help Syracuse resist his own invasion. The whole Athenian fleet was lost and a second Peloponnesian War began in 413 BCE.

Subsequently, Sparta made a deal with Persia, allowing Persia to retake Ionia in return for help against Athens, which resulted in Sparta capturing a new Athenian fleet and using it to blockade Piraeus. Besieged by land at the same time, Athens was starved into surrender in 404 BCE.

Athens had shown that a democracy is just as likely to create an empire around itself as any other form of government, if not more so. Democracy opened up opportunity and convinced Athens of its moral superiority, both of which encouraged a spiraling imperialism that ended in its downfall.

By then, another proud republic, one that would try to avoid the fate of Athens, had appeared at Rome.

Ordinary thetes powering a three-tiered Athenian warship, or trireme. *Only the upper row of oarsmen can be seen, but oars from two more rows show through below. From a marble relief ca. 410 BCE.*

ROME

The story of Rome is one of adaptation. Rome lasted as an imperial power for about 800 years, but only because it kept changing. The early growth of Roman power sprang from a zealous and rapacious republicanism that eventually threatened to destroy the republic itself. Unlike Athens, however, Rome restructured to resolve the tension between republic and empire. Subsequently, Rome began to resemble the Persia of Cyrus and Darius in the measures it took to cope with its increasing size and multiculturalism. In the end, the extension of Roman citizenship made it hard to continue speaking of an empire at all.

CITIZENS

After 1200 BCE, the eastern Mediterranean entered a dark age and tribes from around the Danube overran both Greece and Italy. Much of central Italy became settled by Latins. In the 8th century BCE, as a new Greece was forming, three Latin tribes came together in the hills around a crossing point on the River Tiber. These were the Romans. Here they farmed pigs and traded salt from the mouth of the river. They had a king, who was advised by a council of 300 elders known as the senate (from *senex* "old man").

To the north were the Etruscans. From their heartland in Tuscany they gained control of a string of cities and, around 625 BCE, became kings of the Romans. They built a sewage system to drain the valley and created the Forum, an area where the hillside villagers could meet to trade and discuss matters. Scattered villages now became a city.

Trade between the Etruscans in the north and *Magna Graecia* ("Greater Greece") in the south brought Greek civilization to the Romans and drew attention to a bridge they had built across the Tiber. To defend this bridge, an army of all those able to arm themselves was created, with soldiers organized into ranks depending on the equipment they could afford. The first rank equipped themselves like Greek hoplites, with swords, spears, heavy armor, and shields they would lock together to create a solid barrier.

By 509 BCE, the nobility of Rome was largely Etruscan, but this did not stop them from throwing out their Etruscan king, Tarquin the Proud, following his son's rape of Lucretia, a well-known noblewoman. The Roman kingdom now became a *res publica*—a "concern of the people."

To prevent a return to absolute rule, the new republic strengthened the senate. It received the power to pass law and oversee the appointment of government. Rome was now led by two *consuls*, professional civil servants elected annually by the senate after climbing a ladder of promotion. In practice, however, creation of a strong senate was a gradual process.

The senate was staffed by the *patrician* class, the old nobility, and two hundred years of the *plebeians* (the rest of Rome's citizens) pushing for political representation kept it weak. General strikes won the plebeians their own assembly—and, moreover, access to the senate for the wealthy among them (as senators were not paid). Eventually, political agitation faded as a new senatorial class of nobles and rich businessmen came to dominate government.

The republic was based on an idea that resonated far beyond the senate, however: the idea of the Roman citizen, a free man of property. Since all property was owned by male heads of families, there was only one citizen for each household, whatever its size.

The property requirement had its roots in the formation of the army; citizenship meant having the means to help defend the republic. With this came the right to vote and other privileges, but most citizens were farmers for whom cooperating to protect and extend their homesteads meant having a stake in society in and of itself. The citizen army was the basis of Roman identity.

With the Etruscan kings gone, trade with the south declined and Rome turned to its Latin neighbors, leading a league of cities to take territory and open trade. Peeved at not sharing equally in the spoils, the other cities rose up against Rome in 340 BCE, only for Rome to abolish the Latin League, absorb its possessions, and continue its own expansion.

Roman expansion within Italy was nevertheless a subtle matter. Most of the defeated Latins were made Roman citizens and this became a general pattern. Territory was seized, garrisons were stationed in key locations, roads were built radiating out from Rome, but conquered peoples were often given citizenship or else classed as allies with at least partial rights. Rome benefited from both; citizens paid tax and served in the army, allies paid tribute and supplied their own troops. Beyond this, the different peoples of Italy were becoming used to Roman institutions and Roman culture.

THE REPUBLIC ABROAD

Carthage was a Phoenician city on the coast of Africa, capital of a great trading empire. It had long had outposts in nearby western Sicily but when, in 270 BCE, trouble with pirates provoked it to garrison the city of Messina, closest crossing point to Italy, Rome took notice. When the pirates of Messina asked Rome for help against Carthage, the first of three wars began which ended with the Mediterranean in Roman hands.

The First Punic (*Punicus*—"Phoenician") War made Rome a new kind of naval power. Carthage possessed huge five-tiered warships, designed for ramming. Rome copied these but added grappling hooks to pull enemy ships alongside so troops could board them and fight hand to hand. This technique brought victory in 240 BCE plus Sicily with its vast grain production.

Checking Carthage's expansion had been rewarding and a Second Punic War in 218 BCE was provoked by Rome's own advance into Spain. The Carthaginian general Hannibal pushed the Roman legions back and took his elephants over the Alps into Italy. But with his supply lines cut at Massilia (Marseilles) and Carthage facing a Numidian revolt, he had to sail for Africa. Followed by the Roman general Scipio Africanus, Hannibal met defeat in 202 BCE.

A final Punic War in 149 BCE was engineered by Rome and ended with it annexing Carthaginian north Africa and leveling Carthage.

Rome had now changed. After the First Punic War, Sicily became neither an extension of the republic nor an ally but a province carved up into large estates worked by an enslaved population. There were no Sicilian citizens. At home, the smaller farmers who had fought for their republic for 24 years had been away so long their farms had fallen into debt and they now found they could not compete with cheap slave-produced grain flooding the market from Sicily. One by one, their farms were taken over, and the republic of proud citizen farmers became a society of rich slave-owners.

Now other provinces were sought outside Italy, not least because the growth of large estates was producing a shortage of land at home. The businessman looking for new opportunities, the farmer looking for a new homestead, the soldier looking for somewhere to retire to; each drove expansion abroad, as did the extension of citizenship in 89 BCE to everyone in Italy, all of whom wanted a piece of the pie.

This was an empire in all but name, though imperial control took different forms in the developed east and the less developed west. Meager trade networks in the west kept tribes isolated and unable to unite against the Roman legions. Once conquered, a dearth of political institutions both allowed and forced Rome to impose direct rule, installing garrisons and governors and enslaving the population. In the east this was both difficult and unnecessary. Here were complex societies watched by powerful neighbors and containing various social classes and interest groups. A governing elite was nearly always only too eager to collaborate with Rome for the protection it offered. In 133 BCE, for example, the king of wealthy Pergamum simply offered Rome his kingdom.

THE INEVITABLE CRISIS

Within the republic, imperial expansion had unleashed forces hard to contain. Rome had swollen with upper classes from around Italy, grown rich from Rome's rise and now hungry for political power. Then there was the threat of mob rule. Many who lost their farms had come to Rome looking for work, creating a large class of urban poor.

In addition, the economy now depended on a slave labor force that might revolt at any time. In practice, the only slaves able to pose a threat were those trained as gladiators, but, in 73 BCE, one such called Spartacus led a wider slave rebellion, holding out for two years on Mount Vesuvius outside Naples. It was serious enough for Spartacus and 6,000 rebels to be crucified as an example along the Appian Way, the main road south from Rome.

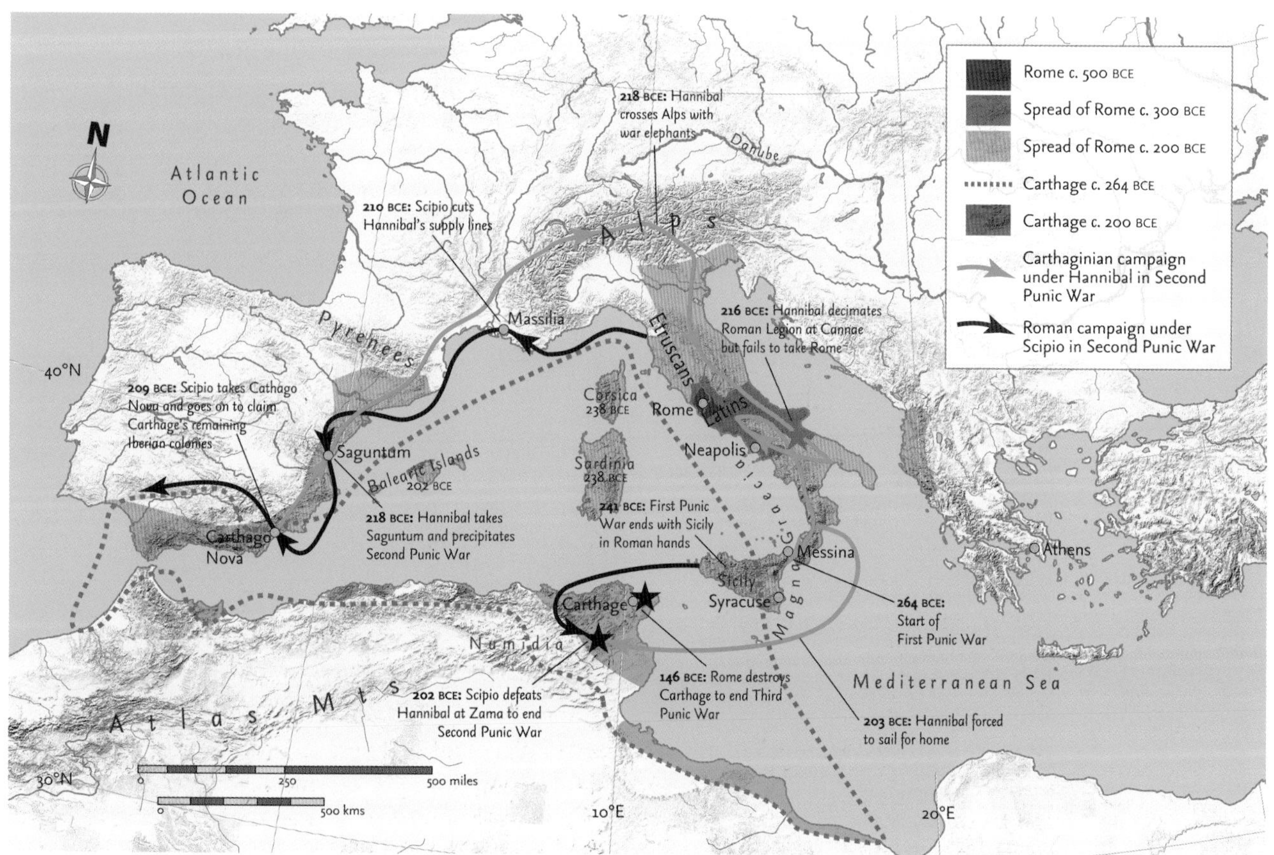

THE EARLY SPREAD OF THE ROMAN REPUBLIC FROM 509 BCE AND THE PUNIC WARS 264–146 BCE

War with Carthage brought Rome beyond the Italian peninsula. A first war (264–240 BCE) delivered Sicily, a second (218–202 BCE) parts of Spain, and a third (149–146 BCE) a foothold in North Africa.

Greater threats, however, lay at the heart of the establishment itself. The senate was where domestic and foreign policy was made. From the time of the Punic Wars it had become a vehicle for powerful families to vie with one another in the pursuit of imperial expansion for private gain. But personal rivalries caused the senate to splinter. Real power now shifted to the provincial generals.

The provinces were won for the republic by the army. War was no longer an occasional interruption but an inherent part of the republic's existence. This was too much for a conscript army of farmers. Hence, in 106 BCE, Gaius Marius assembled Rome's first paid troops to fight the Numidian king Jugurtha in North Africa. Generals now commanded a highly trained, permanent force, but with no military pension soldiers relied on a share of the spoils of conquest to ease their retirement. This created a bond of loyalty between soldiers and the general they looked to for these spoils.

The Roman legionary. As a self-equipped citizen, the backbone of the early republic. As a paid soldier, the extender of the empire and maker of emperors. These legionaries are from the time of Hadrian, when expansion ceased and their role became defensive.

In 49 BCE, the general in Gaul, Julius Caesar, crossed the Rubicon River, the northern border of the republic. He claimed to be acting to prevent Rome's decay, but by bringing his army into the republic he challenged the senate's authority and drew the other provincial generals into civil war. Four years later, Caesar had taken absolute control. The following year, he was assassinated by a group of senators fearful of a Rome dominated by one man's unchecked power, but it was too late to turn back the clock.

THE ROMAN PEACE

It fell to Caesar's adopted son Octavian to save Rome, after a second civil war in which he overcame Caesar's killers Brutus and Cassius, followed by his own brother-in-law and chief rival Mark Antony in 30 BCE.

Republicanism had made Rome, like Athens, dynamic but unstable. Once there were easy pickings being offered, too many had the right to fight over them. Octavian's solution was to separate republic and empire. He took personal control of the provinces, the armed forces, and the treasury, using provincial taxes to fund an army pension so soldiers would look to him for their retirement, not their generals. Within the republic, however, he agreed to be bound by the senate.

With the army his, this was in effect absolute rule clothed to keep republicans happy. Octavian knew just how to market himself. From 27 BCE, he became *Augustus* ("the Illustrious One," 27 BCE–14 CE) and constructed his own personality cult, commissioning countless portraits in suitably imperious pose. But he also became the democratic-sounding *Princeps* ("First Citizen"), and it was the senate who gave him both titles.

With the senate unable to affect foreign policy and the army's retirement taken care of, much of the incentive to conquer new territory was removed and expansion gradually slowed, coming to a halt entirely under Hadrian (117–138 CE). A new defensive strategy of building walls and policing borders was now adopted. The Roman Empire became a fortress.

Within this fortress, Rome embraced as many different cultures as the Persian Empire once had and, for the most part, took a similar policy toward them, requiring only public order and the payment of taxes. If this were challenged, there would be no compromise, as the Jews learned in 70 CE, when an uprising resulted in the sacking of Jerusalem and the dispersal of its people into Europe. Something of a common culture nevertheless emerged as roads, a common currency, and the use of Latin spread across the empire. In addition, jobs were opened to people from all parts. Trajan, who came from Spain, became the first of many non-Italian emperors in 98 CE.

This showed an understanding that to survive beyond a certain size, an empire must distribute benefits to its subject peoples. Even the empire's countless slaves received certain rights, including the chance to buy or be granted citizenship. A logical conclusion was reached in 212 CE, when the Emperor Caracalla extended Roman citizenship to the borders of the empire.

Following pages: Main map:

THE ROMAN EMPIRE AT ITS HEIGHT *around 120 CE*

The empire reached its greatest size under Trajan (98–117 CE), but risked becoming overextended. Hadrian (117–138 CE) gave up Mesopotamia, Assyria, and Armenia and turned from expanding to fortifying the empire with walls, border garrisons, and naval patrols.

Inset map:

THE REORGANIZATION AND DIVISION OF THE LATER EMPIRE *293–476 CE*

With tribes pressing on the Danube, Diocletian (284–305 CE) restructured the empire into 12 dioceses spread across four prefectures. In 395 CE the empire split and in 476 CE the western half fell.

N
Caledonia
142 CE: Antonine Wall begun
122 CE: Hadrian's Wall begun
North Sea
Baltic Sea
Hibernia
Eburacum
Deva
Britannia
Isca
Londinium
Dubrae
43 CE: Colonization of Britain begins under Claudius
9 CE: Germanic tribes under Arminius push Romans back to Rhine at Battle of Teutoburg Forest
ca. 83 CE: To close gap between Rhine and Danube, Limes Germanicus (series of frontier forts) begun
Vetera
12 BCE–9 CE
Germania
Colonia Agrippina
Bonna
Germania Inferior
51 BCE: Julius Caesar completes conquest of Gaul
Mogontiacum
Durocortorum
Belgica
Rhine
Germania Superior
Argentoratum
Danube
Augusta Vindelicorum
Vindobona
Carnuntum
Brigetio
Aquincum
Atlantic Ocean
Raetia
Noricum
Virunum
Aquitania
Octodurum
Burdigala
Lugdunum
Alpes Poeninae
Mediolanum (Milan)
Pannonia Superior
Legio (León)
Segusio
Ravenna
Narbonensis
Dalmatia
Narbo
Cemenelum
Pisae
Florenha
Salonae
Alpes Cottiae
Massilia
Forum Julii
Alpes Maritimae
Corsica
Tarraconensis
Adriatic Sea
Lusitania
Tarraco
Rome
Ostra
Italia
Emerita Augusta
Toletum
Sardinia et Corsica
Capua
Neapolis
Misenum
Tarentum
Sardinia
Baetica
Baleares
Tyrrhenian Sea
Corduba
Carales
Carthago Nova
Messina
214–148 BCE: Macedonia annexed in series of four wars
Tingis
Portus Magnus
Caesarea
Hippo Regius
Carthage
Sicilia
Syracuse
Mauretania Caesariensis
Mauretania Tingitana
Lambaesis
Numidia
Melita
Leptis Magna
Africa
Garamantes
Sahara Desert
10°E
Provinces ca. 150 CE
Provincial capital
Walled or fenced frontier
River frontier
Legion headquarters
Naval base
Roman territory ca. 200 BCE
Territory added by ca. 100 BCE
Added by death of Augustus 14 CE
Added by Hadrian 117–138 CE
Temporarily held territory

Picts
Scots
Jutes
Angles
Britannia
Frisians
Saxons
Thuringians
Lombards
Burgundians
Franks
Vandals
ca. 370 CE: Huns
Alans
Sarmatians
Ostrogoths
Atlantic Ocean
Gallia
Alemanni
Gepids
Caspian Sea
Visigoths
Viennensis
Italia
Pannonia
Black Sea
Thracia
Moesia
Byzantium (Constantinople)
Pontus
Rome
Hispania
Asia
Sasanian Empire
Africa
Mediterranean Sea
Berbers
395 CE: Division of Eastern and Western Empires
Oriens
Arabs
Red Sea
0 250 500 miles
0 500 kms
9 CE: Pannonia taken, enabling Danube to become continuous frontier
Sarmatia
Carpathian Mts
106 CE: Trajan pushes beyond Danube
Apulum
Troesmis
Bosporan Kingdom
63 BCE: Bosporan Kingdom becomes vassal state
Caspian Sea
Caucasus Mts
Black Sea
Durostorum
Oescus
Novae
Moesia Inferior
Trapezus
Artaxata
Bithynia Et Pontus
Satala
Thracia
Hadrianopolis
Armenia 114–117 CE
Byzantium
Nicomedia
Ancyra
Tigranocerta
Parthian Empire
Thessalonica
Cappadocia
Melitene
Caesarea
Samosata
Nisibus
Aegean Sea
Pergamum
Asia
Galatia
Assyria 116–117 CE
Mesopotamia 115–117 CE
Tarsus
Cyrrhus
Ephesus
Athens
Lycia
Cilicia
Antioch
Seleucia
Sparta
Syria
Dura Europos
Ctesiphon
Myra
Raphanaea
Palmyra
Tigris
Cyprus
Babylon
Paphus
Tripolis
Damascus
Syrian Desert
Creta
133 BCE: King of Pergamum offers Rome his kingdom
Euphrates
Bostra
Tyrus
115–117 CE: Trajan gains fleeting access to Persian Gulf
Caparcotna
Caesarea Maritima
Judaea
Jerusalem
Mediterranean Sea
Nicopolis
Alexandria
Arabia
Cyrenaica et Creta
Memphis
250
500 miles
500 kms
Aegyptus
Lake Moeris
30 BCE: Octavian defeats Mark Antony and claims Egypt
Red Sea
30°E
40°E

THE SLOW DISSOLVE

Caracalla's motive, however, was the need to widen the tax base to fund larger armies. In the east, Rome's familiar foe, Parthia, gave way to more aggressive Sasanian Persia in 226 CE. In the west, Goths crossed the Danube in the 250s, killing the emperor, and Franks crossed the Rhine. Rome found itself fighting a war on two fronts.

Silver bullion could pacify the western raiders, but this meant the silver content of the Roman *denarius* (the most common coin) had to be reduced. By 300 CE, it had lost 98 percent of its value a century earlier. Prices rose and worst affected were those on fixed incomes, namely soldiers and bureaucrats, the twin pillars of the empire. There was a move to collecting taxes in kind instead of in cash, but this made tax collectors so unpopular that no one wanted the job. As tax-collecting magistrates ran the towns

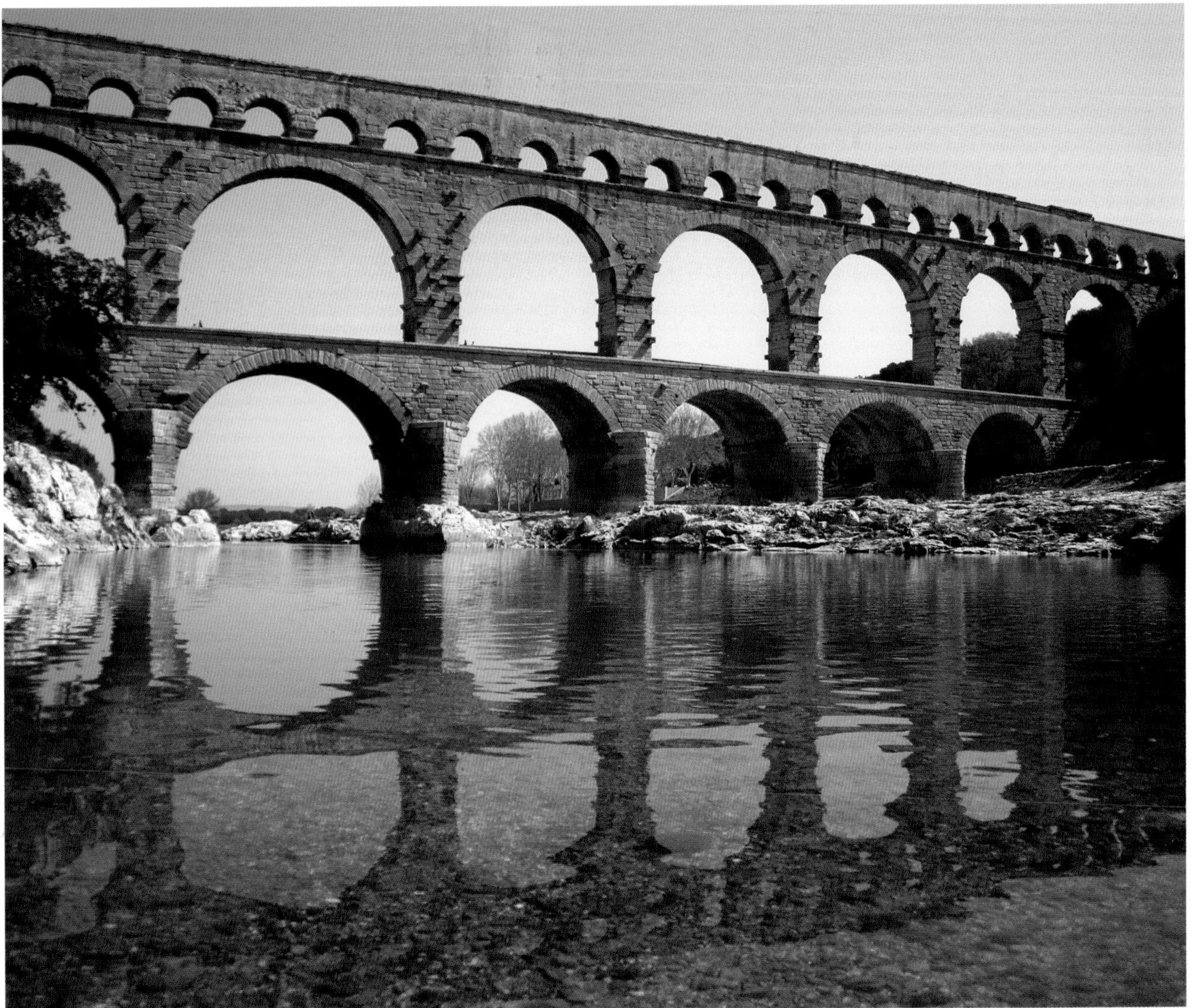

The Pont du Gard, part of a 30-mile (50-kilometer) aqueduct built in the 1st century CE to carry water to the city of Nimes in southern France. Blocks of stone weighing several tons were lifted into place and attached together without mortar. Engineering of this quality built the infrastructure for an empire.

through which Roman institutions spread, the result was urban decline and a loss of connection to Rome.

Stationed on the borders for generations, most soldiers were local men more concerned with protecting their own communities than Rome. Increasingly, their commanders came from the ranks, and regional sections of the army now fought to make their own commander emperor. Twenty-two emperors came and went in the 3rd century CE.

One of these was Diocletian (284–305 CE). He realized fundamental restructuring was needed to address both the new regionalism and disputes over succession. Diocletian chopped up the provinces so they could be more closely overseen and grouped these smaller units into a number of larger *dioceses* run by a *vicar*, a new representative of central government. The dioceses in turn he grouped into four *prefectures*, two in the east and two in the west. One of these Diocletian himself oversaw, the others he entrusted to a co-emperor and two junior emperors-in-waiting.

The *tetrarchy*, or "rule of four," was an attempt to stabilize the empire through bureaucracy, but one that nevertheless acknowledged the empire was slowly splitting into eastern and western halves. Constantine I (307–337 CE) reestablished single rule but built a second imperial capital in the east: Constantinople. The east now began to recover from the crisis of the previous century, due mainly to the persistence of trade. Demand for eastern luxuries remained high and trade routes were relatively safe from barbarian raiders. After the death of Theodosius I in 395 CE, the empire was officially divided.

The west was now left to succumb to creeping feudalism. Trade dwindled while improved farming techniques, spread by the empire, created self-sufficient communities able to function through barter. Such wealth as there was fell to local landowners, often former tax collectors or other servants of the empire. Smaller farmers found security in attaching themselves to these landowners as serfs.

The Goths across the border became familiar neighbors. Now, however, behind the Goths and the other European tribes, came fiercer and more alien Central Asian tribes. Goths were allowed in to help keep the Huns at bay but this was the thin end of the wedge. Attila the Hun stopped short of Rome in 452 CE, but it was only a matter of time before the last Roman emperor was toppled by a Germanic general in 476 CE.

Behind all this lay a disintegration of the ideals of the classical world. Diocletian had dropped the title Princeps and cast himself as a divine king. Constantine had made Christianity a state religion in 325 CE. The idea of Roman citizenship, once inseparable from the idea of civilization itself, had lost its power. But Rome remained as an example. The separation of domestic politics from imperial administration, the spread of empire through citizenship and institutions, experiments in direct and indirect rule, benefits for the provinces . . . Rome had left object lessons for all future empires to learn from.

And Rome remained as an idea. Europe at peace with itself, united by a common market and a set of shared ideals. For a thousand years and more, Europeans would dream of one day building a new Rome.

ALEXANDER

Alexander the Great was the first of a new kind of empire builder: the would-be liberator with a program for the makeover of society. The brevity of Alexander's whirlwind tour through the lands of the Persian Empire hardly qualifies him as an empire builder at all, but the cultural legacy he left behind lasted for centuries.

MACEDON

At the time of the Persian Wars, Macedon was a small kingdom on the edge of the Greek world, speaking a dialect southern Greeks found hard to understand. Good pasture for horses helped maintain a tribal, warrior society, closer to Homer's Greece than to city-states such as Athens. Macedon was a monarchy but its kings were elected, which gave them a potent combination of legitimacy and centralized power.

The defeat of Xerxes allowed Macedon to move into Persian-held Thrace, but it was hemmed in by Balkan tribes to the north, and Athens and then Thebes to the south. Its real growth began with Philip II (359–336 BCE), who modernized his kingdom using ideas he picked up while a prisoner in Thebes. He adapted Greek infantry to produce the Macedonian *phalanx*, a porcupine-like formation in which hoplite spears were replaced by *sarissas*, or pikes, more than twice as long. He organized mounted warriors into cavalry formations that would attack an enemy's flank while the phalanx held the line. He also made Macedon richer by working its mines harder, bringing in irrigation, and boosting trade.

Philip used his new power to expand north and south, creating an empire of two parts. The northward conquest of the Balkans he saw as a civilizing mission. Here he founded self-governing towns in which Macedonian settlers would help local people develop trade and agriculture for the surrounding area.

But Philip aspired to be accepted as truly Greek, so in the south he presented himself initially as a peacemaker between hostile city-states. Only when rejected by Athens and Thebes did he demonstrate his military might, at Chaeronea in 338 BCE, with his 18-year-old son Alexander leading the cavalry. Now he revived the old idea of forming a Greek league to free Ionia from the Persians, this time with Macedon at its helm. On the eve of his departure in 336 BCE, however, he was assassinated, and the league fell apart.

THE MARRIAGE OF EAST AND WEST

Philip's desire for Macedon to be the new Athens led him to hire Aristotle to educate his son. At the same time, Philip's wife Olympias claimed Achilles as an ancestor and

Following pages: main map:

THE CONQUESTS OF ALEXANDER *336–323 BCE*

Alexander set foot in Asia in 334 BCE and made the Persian Empire his with 10 years of campaigning. He founded Greek towns as he went, bringing India and Central Asia into contact with Europe.

Inset map:

THE HELLENISTIC WORLD IN *240 BCE*

Alexander's towns ensured that long after his death Greek civilization persisted as far east as Bactria, even though a unified empire did not. By 240 BCE, however, a new power was growing in Parthia.

her son grew up to see himself as a new Homeric hero: semidivine, invincible, destined for glory. Born to lead, Alexander III (336–323 BCE) was elected in Macedon to pick up Philip's mission.

Alexander's motives were mixed, however. There was glory to be had in fighting the Persians on the soil where Achilles had in legend fought the Trojans nine centuries earlier. But equally, Alexander admired Cyrus and, beyond liberating the Ionian Greeks, he felt a wider call to breathe new life into a once great empire fallen into decay.

In May 334 BCE, having pulled the Greeks back into line, Alexander crossed into Asia and made a symbolic visit to Troy. In June he brushed aside a slightly larger Persian force at the River Granicus. Sardis fell and by July Ionia had been conquered. But Alexander pressed on, installing garrisons along the coast since Persia still controlled the sea. At Issus in November 333 BCE he won his most meaningful victory yet, against a vast Persian army under Darius III (336–330 BCE), who fled the battlefield.

Issus opened the way south for Alexander to take the main Phoenician port of Tyre and remove Persia's naval threat. The pretext of rescuing Ionia was now fading. Alexander took Darius's family hostage in Damascus, demanding he be acknowledged as king of Asia, and had his divine status confirmed at the Oracle of Amun in Egypt.

In 331 BCE, Darius III lured Alexander to a final battle at Gaugamela in Assyria. He had chosen a flat plain to suit his chariots, but on September 20 an eclipse of the moon, symbol of Persia, foretold the eclipse of Persian power. On October 1, Alexander bore out the prophecy and Darius fled again.

Babylon and 50,000 talents of gold now became Alexander's, as did Persepolis, which he infamously set fire to, possibly while drunk. As inheritor of the Persian Empire,

Alexander and his horse Bucephalus fighting Darius III. Alexander replaced chariots with mounted cavalry and established the clean-shaven look for heroic figures. From a Roman mosaic at Pompeii ca. 100 BCE.

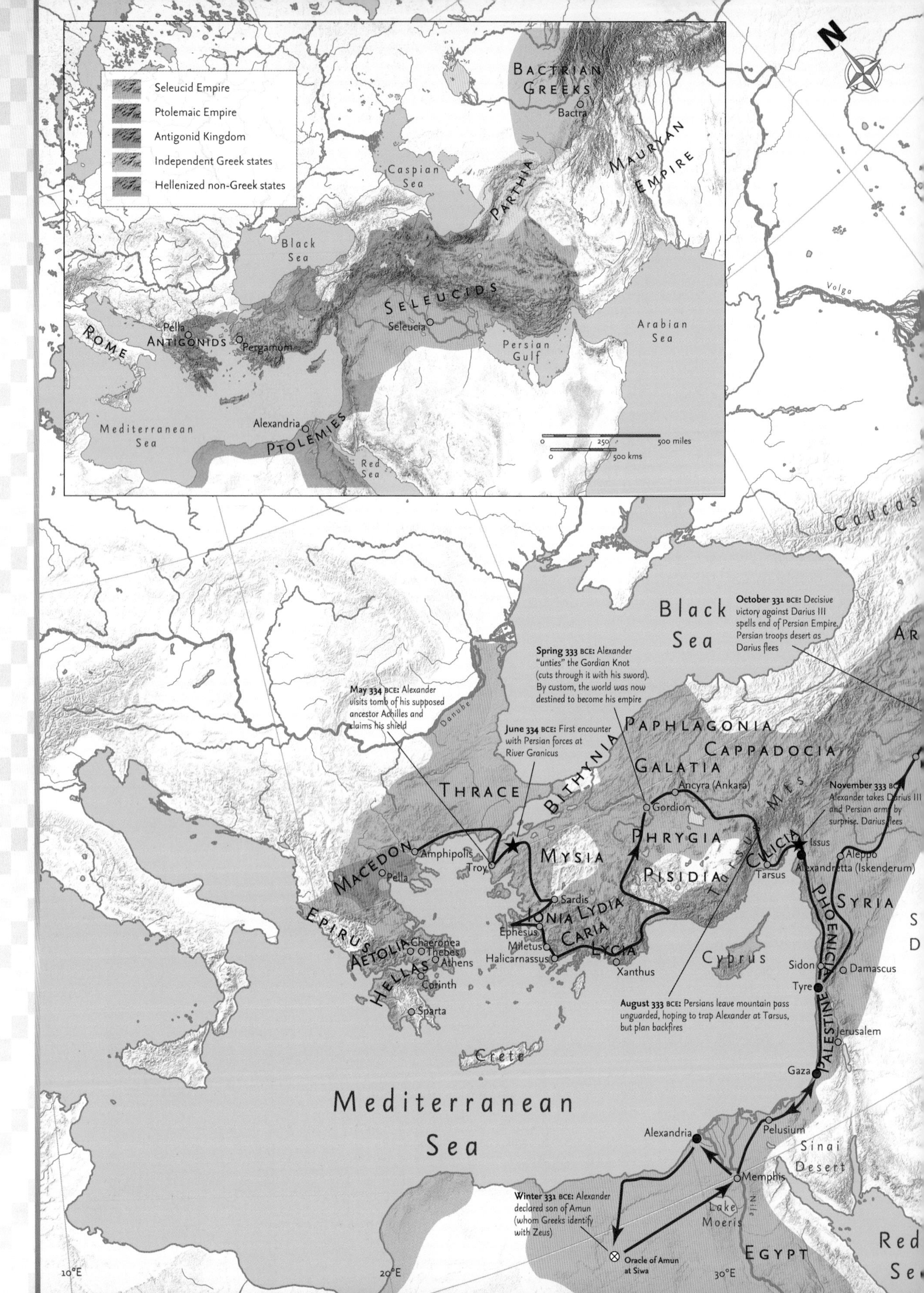

Seleucid Empire
Ptolemaic Empire
Antigonid Kingdom
Independent Greek states
Hellenized non-Greek states
Bactrian Greeks
Bactra
Mauryan Empire
Parthia
Caspian Sea
Black Sea
Seleucids
Seleucia
Arabian Sea
Persian Gulf
Pella
Antigonids
Pergamum
Rome
Mediterranean Sea
Alexandria
Ptolemies
Red Sea
0 250 500 miles
0 500 kms
Volga
Caucasus
Black Sea
October 331 BCE: Decisive victory against Darius III spells end of Persian Empire. Persian troops desert as Darius flees
Spring 333 BCE: Alexander "unties" the Gordian Knot (cuts through it with his sword). By custom, the world was now destined to become his empire
May 334 BCE: Alexander visits tomb of his supposed ancestor Achilles and claims his shield
June 334 BCE: First encounter with Persian forces at River Granicus
Danube
Paphlagonia
Cappadocia
Bithynia
Galatia
Ancyra (Ankara)
Thrace
Gordion
November 333 BCE: Alexander takes Darius III and Persian army by surprise. Darius flees
Taurus Mts
Phrygia
Mysia
Cilicia
Issus
Amphipolis
Troy
Macedon
Pella
Pisidia
Tarsus
Alexandretta (Iskenderum)
Aleppo
Sardis
Ionia
Lydia
Caria
Syria
Ephesus
Miletus
Halicarnassus
Lycia
Xanthus
Epirus
Aetolia
Chaeronea
Thebes
Athens
Hellas
Corinth
Sparta
Cyprus
Sidon
Damascus
Tyre
Phoenicia
August 333 BCE: Persians leave mountain pass unguarded, hoping to trap Alexander at Tarsus, but plan backfires
Palestine
Jerusalem
Crete
Gaza
Mediterranean Sea
Alexandria
Pelusium
Sinai Desert
Memphis
Winter 331 BCE: Alexander declared son of Amun (whom Greeks identify with Zeus)
Lake Moeris
Nile
Oracle of Amun at Siwa
Egypt
Red Sea
10°E
20°E
30°E

329 BCE: Alexander crosses Jaxartes to defeat Scythians
Jaxartes
Alexandria the Furthest (Cyropolis)
Spring 327 BCE: Revolt of Central Asian tribes ends with capture of mountain fort. Alexander marries Sogdian princess Roxana
Kyzyl Kum Desert
Aral Sea
SOGDIA
Sogdian Rock
Maracanda (Samarkand)
Alexandria on Oxus
Himalayas
80°E
30°N
June 326 BCE: Alexander's hardest-won battle, against King Porus. First time he sees elephants
Arigaeum
Taxila
Nautaca
Drapsaca
BACTRIA
Bucephala
Nicaea
Alexandria on Hyphasis
Khyber Pass
Tribactra (Bukhara)
Oxus
Alexandria Termita
Bactra
Alexandria in Caucasus (Kapisa)
Hindu Kush
GANDHARA
KINGDOM OF PORUS
Hyphasis
July 326 BCE: Army refuses to march further east
KHORESMIA
Kabul
329 BCE: Alexander tracks down Bessus, murderer of Darius
Alexandria (Ghazni)
September–November 326 BCE: Fleet built for return journey
Kara Kum Desert
Alexandria in Margiana (Merv)
May 326 BCE: Alexander's horse Bucephalus dies. City founded in his honor
Alexandria on Indus
September 330 BCE: Chasing Darius's killers east, Alexander takes southern detour to avoid mounted archers of Bessus, satrap of Bactria
Susia
Alexandria in Aria (Herat)
Caspian Sea
PARTHIA
Alexandria in Arachosia (Kandahar)
ARIA
Indus
Summer 330 BCE: Alexander catches up with Darius, to find him conveniently murdered by his own generals. Vowing to hunt down the killers gives Alexander chance to win Persian approval and excuse to conquer eastern part of empire
HYRCANIA
Zadracarta
Hecatompylos
Amol
SAGARTIA
Alexandria Prophthasia (Farah)
ARACHOSIA
Patala
Elburz
Caspian Gates
Salt Desert
Rhagae
Alexandria Rhambacia
GEDROSIA
70°E
CARMANIA
MEDIA
Ecbatana
Gabae (Esfahan)
Alexandria in Carmania (Gulashkird)
Zagros Mts
Arbela
February 324 BCE: Mass marriage of Macedonians and Persians. Alexander marries two Persian princesses
Pasargadae
20°N
Susa
Persian Gates
Persepolis
Harmozia
Arabian Sea
SUSIANA
Alexandria in Susiana
PERSIA
Spring 330 BCE: Alexander burns palace at Persepolis to ground
Babylon
BABYLONIA
11 June 323 BCE: Alexander dies after a heavy drinking session
Persian Gulf
Jan 330 BCE: At heavy cost, Alexander forces his way through mountain pass guarding Persepolis
Macedonian heartland
Alexander's Empire
Federated states
Alexander's route
Route of fleet under Nearchus
City founded or resettled by Alexander
Arabian Desert
Tropic of Cancer
0
250
500 miles
0
500 kms
40°E
50°E
60°E

however, he behaved with greater diplomacy when he found Darius, murdered by his own aides. In a style worthy of Cyrus, Alexander gave him a state funeral at Persepolis and promised to hunt down his killers.

Witnessing Alexander wooing the Persians, his Macedonian and Greek troops began to wonder what they were fighting for. He now disbanded the Greek league and recruited Iranian tribes to accompany him further east to Bactria, up to the Central Asian steppe and then down over the Hindu Kush into India. Here his beloved horse Bucephalus died and his army refused to march on to the Ganges during the monsoon, so Alexander turned back.

In India, only one-eighth of his army had been Macedonian. It had become multiethnic in the Persian style, and Alexander knew he would need Persian help to run his empire. To this end, he had in mind not so much cross-cultural cooperation as cross-cultural fusion: the breeding of a Greco-Persian nobility.

In 327 BCE, Alexander had married Roxana, a Sogdian princess, perhaps as part of his subjugation of the steppe tribes of the northeast, but also simply out of love. Returning to Susa in 324 BCE, however, he took Darius's daughter as a second wife and forced 80 of his Macedonian officers to marry Persian noblewomen given a Greek education since victory at Gaugamela. Later on he threw a multiethnic banquet for 9,000, in the interest of cultural harmony.

The Macedonians were alienated by Alexander's openness to unfamiliar customs and his increasingly despotic behavior. His attempt to get people to prostrate themselves before him, for example, seemed proof that he was becoming both more oriental and more intoxicated by his achievements. It was almost fitting that he should die, in 323 BCE, in Babylon, after a heavy drinking session to celebrate the start of a new mission to take Carthage, Sicily, and Italy.

A WIDER GREEK WORLD

The moment he died, Alexander's generals began to carve up his conquests, and 50 years later, three separate kingdoms existed under the families of Antigonus in Europe, Ptolemy in Egypt, and Seleucus in Asia.

An informal connection nevertheless remained. Alexander left behind around 70 towns, most bearing his name, in which he stationed garrisons to secure his supply lines. They were conceived as local administrative centers similar to Philip's new towns in the Balkans, running their own affairs while supplying recruits for an imperial army. Macedonian settlers were to set up Greek civic institutions and assimilate with the local population.

Alexander's plunder of treasuries across the Persian Empire freed up huge reserves of bullion from which he struck his own currency. This money began to circulate in the new towns, which soon lost any genuine independence as their wealth became apparent to kings and regional governors. These towns developed ties with each other through trade as well as through sports competitions, literary festivals, and so forth, often sponsored by rulers as compensation for their loss of political autonomy. Linked economically and culturally, they became a network transmitting ideas from Greece and receiving them from Mesopotamia, Egypt, and India.

The greatest of Alexander's cities stood at the mouth of the Nile, where Ptolemy I built a complex for secular learning containing a library, museum, and university. This Alexandria drew scholars from far and wide, becoming an intellectual capital larger, richer, more cosmopolitan by far than Athens ever was.

Outside the cities, however, lay another world. From here, Alexander's conquests looked like anything but the Persian Empire restored.

IRAN

While Alexander saw himself as a promoter of cultural integration, to many of those he conquered he was a marauder leaving alien rule in his wake. Over the centuries, East and West grew increasingly suspicious of each other as a movement to restore the former Persian Empire to its rightful owners took shape.

GREEKS IN IRAN

Under the Seleucids, the melting pot of Greeks and Persians Alexander had dreamed of never materialized. In Ptolemy's Egypt, Macedonian, Greek, and Egyptian gradually intermarried, but of Alexander's 80 forced marriages between his generals and Persian noblewomen, only Seleucus himself stayed married to his Persian wife, Apama. In the towns, Greco-Macedonian administrators became a class apart, and the spread of Greek learning and moneyed commerce remained confined to an urban network, outside of which Iranian tribes maintained their traditions and used barter to trade.

Restricted to an urban world, in particular to Seleucia on the Tigris, Seleucus and his successors found their far-flung possessions slipping from their grasp. Within a few years of Alexander's death, the Punjab had broken away. By the middle of the next century, Ptolemaic Egypt had invaded Syria, independent Greek states had set themselves up across Anatolia as well as in Bactria, and local tribes had reasserted themselves from Sogdia down as far as Parthia.

THE PARTHIANS

The Seleucids had retained the Persian provinces but around 247 BCE the governor of Parthia rebelled against a new Seleucid ruler. In the ensuing confusion, the Parni, a local Iranian tribe, took control and made Arsaces I (ca. 247–ca. 211 BCE) first of the Parthian kings. These kings paid tribute to the Seleucids until 141 BCE, when Mithridates I (ca. 171–ca. 138 BCE) took Seleucia itself.

While galloping away from the enemy, an archer turns to unleash a surprise arrow—the so-called Parthian Shot. This particular archer is a steppe nomad from around 500 BCE—known to the Persians as a Saka, to the Greeks as a Scythian—but the technique became known to the Romans through its use by the Parthians.

He began minting his own coins and conquered all lands to the east as far as Bactria. Shortly afterwards, a winter residence called Ctesiphon was built opposite Seleucia.

The Arsacids styled themselves on the Achaemenids, using Persian as the court language and calling themselves Shahanshah, though their rule was a far looser affair. Their power depended on the continued loyalty of 18 regional kings, each independent enough to mint his own currency. The Greco-Macedonian towns were largely left alone, so Western influence continued to irrigate urban life, but this began to change as the Parthians were drawn into a relationship with Rome, self-styled heir to Greek civilization.

Roman contact began from the time of Mithridates II (ca. 123–ca. 88 BCE), under whom Parthian rule reached its farthest spread. He established a western border on the Euphrates, but succession disputes following his death tempted Rome to prod. When it did so it found a weak Parthian center was more than compensated for by the solidarity of the regional kings and by their use of mounted archers able to turn in the saddle and fire—the so-called Parthian

THE PARTHIAN EMPIRE
247 BCE–226 CE

The Parni tribe, originally from east of the Caspian Sea, took control of Parthia in 247 BCE and the rest of the Seleucid Empire in 141 BCE. Endemic war with Rome followed.

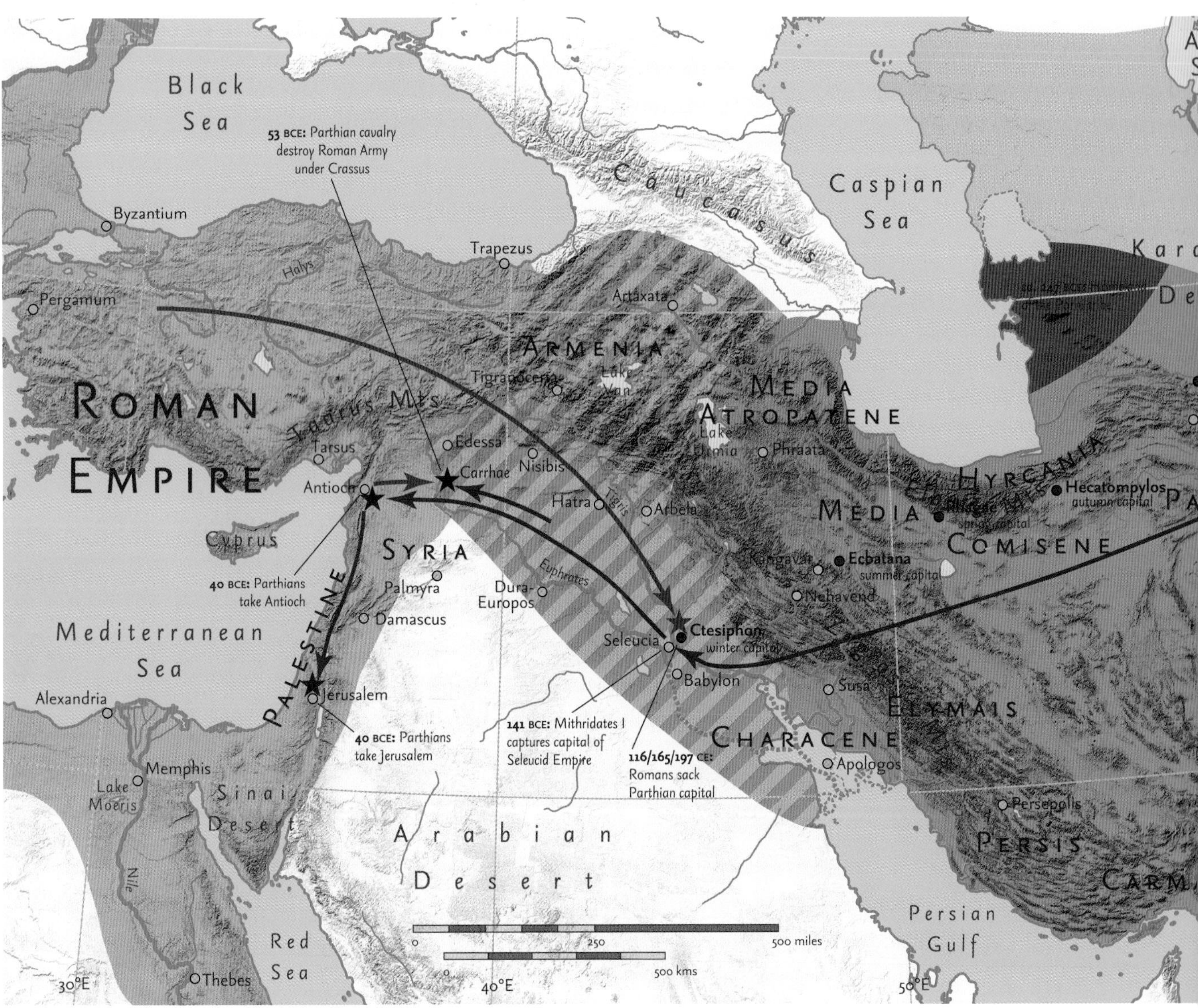

Shot. In 53 BCE, these archers delivered a shock defeat to a full-scale Roman invasion under Crassus.

But it was really in the next century that a new anti-Western climate developed. In 20 BCE the Parthians gave back the *aquila*, the eagle standard of the Roman legions, which they had taken from Crassus in battle. In return, Augustus gave the Parthian shahanshah an Italian concubine, Musa, who became his favorite wife and bore him a son. When he came of age, however, she poisoned the shahanshah, put her son on the throne, and married him.

From this time, rival Western and Iranian factions emerged. Around 8 CE, the Roman-backed Vonones I came to power, a man of effete manners who rode in a litter, did not care for hunting, and surrounded himself with a Greek court. Popular scorn toward Vonones encouraged Artabanus II (ca. 10–ca. 38 CE), a true horse-riding Parthian from east of the Caspian Sea, to wrest the throne from him. From now on the Greek towns declined as Iranian traditions were more consciously promoted.

What lay behind Roman interference was the fact the Parthians controlled the Silk Road to China. Rome was worried the rising demand for silk meant its gold reserves were draining into Parthian hands. But a decentralized structure gave the Parthians the ability to absorb attack. The city of Ctesiphon fell three times during the 2nd century CE without bringing the Parthians down, because they had other centers of power. However, the third time Ctesiphon was sacked, in 198 CE, Rome took so much bullion that even though they held on, the Parthians were bankrupt. By this time, their loose central control had allowed city-states such as Palmyra and Dura-Europos, as well as the Kushans further east, to take over much of the silk trade.

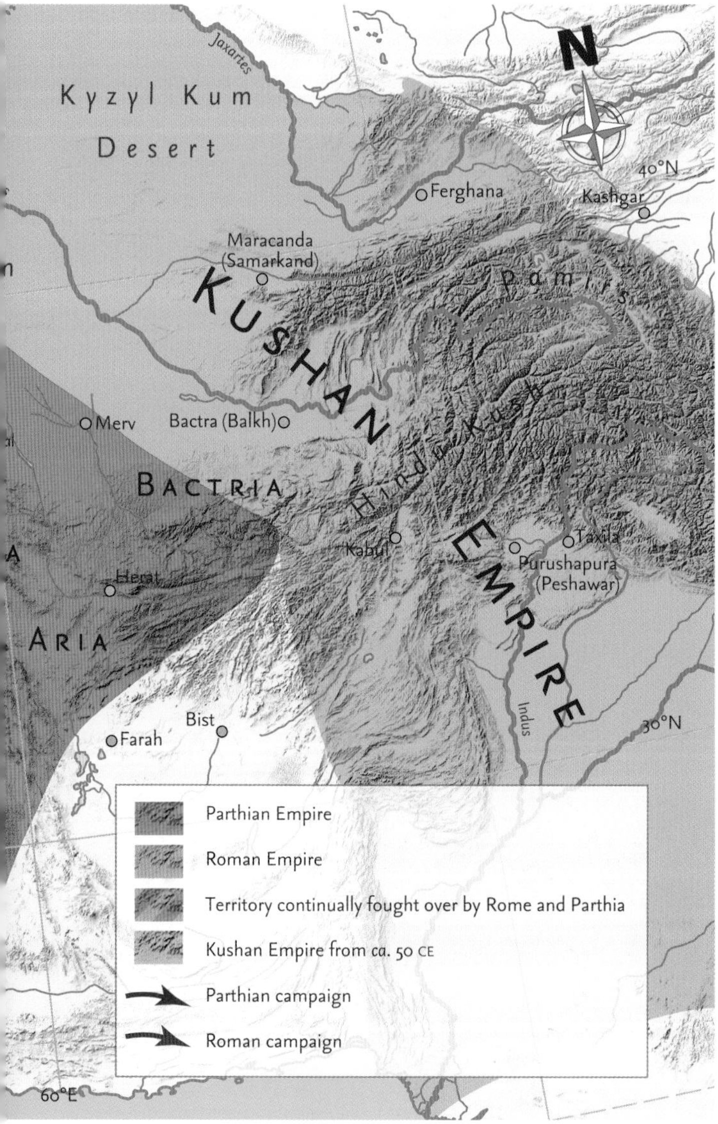

THE SASANIANS

Parthian decline allowed a Persian tribe first to stage a coup in Persia, then to take power in Ctesiphon in 226 CE under Ardashir I (226–240 CE). These were the Sasanians who claimed to be the true heirs of the Achaemenids, restoring rightful rule after 550 years. To this end, they were staunch promoters of a pan-Iranian identity based on Zoroastrianism. Zoroastrian priests officiated at Ardashir's coronation, served as judges, and collected taxes.

Under Ardashir's son, Shapur I (241–272 CE), the new Persian Empire expanded well beyond the limits of Parthian control, especially eastward, where it incorporated much Kushan territory. Official religion was now making unorthodox beliefs a threat to central control. The prophet Mani (ca. 216–ca. 276 CE), who preached a fusion of Zoroastrianism and Christianity, was put to death on the orders of Kartir, advisor and high priest, who strove to define Zoroastrianism with a rigor it never possessed in the days of Cyrus and Darius.

After Shapur's death, the empire began to fragment, but with Shapur II (309–379 CE) it was re-won and reached its greatest size. State support of religion now acquired a parallel in the Eastern Roman Empire. As both Zoroastrianism and Christianity claimed to be the one universal truth (unlike the merely local gods of Babylon or Greece), this fueled distrust of the West and purges of Christians began.

THE SASANIAN PERSIAN EMPIRE
226–637 CE

The Sasanians from Persia took control from the Parthians in 226 CE. They annexed Kushan lands in the east and expanded west and south. Conflict with Rome turned into religious war between state-supported Zoroastrianism and Christianity, before Islamic invaders brought final collapse.

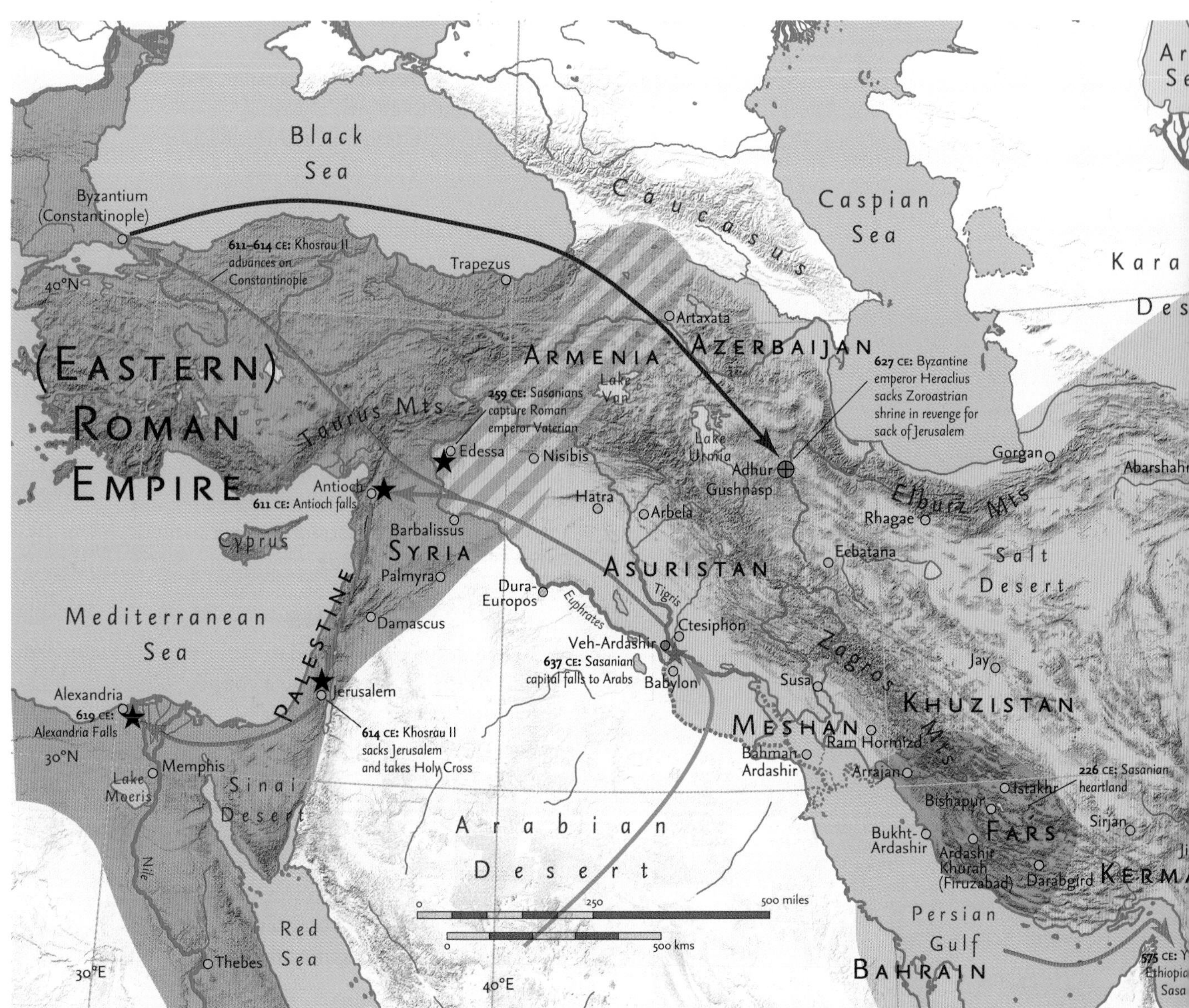

The centralized state the Sasanians aimed for brought them into a continual tug of war with the nobility, not helped by changes in warfare. In Parthian times, mounted archers had fought alongside armored cavalry carrying lances with which to charge Roman infantry. The Sasanians developed this style of warfare to the extent they came to depend on a class of feudal knights able to pay for the equipment from their estates. (Centuries of war with Rome brought this feudal model to Europe at a time when central control was weakening there, too.)

Khosrau I (531–579 CE) inherited a throne weakened both by a growth of noble power and by the teachings of Mazdak, a follower of Mani who preached essentially free love and equal distribution of property, thus managing to threaten the nobility as well as the religious establishment. Khosrau ordered a purge of Mazdak's followers and formalized Zoroastrianism to such a degree it began to lose its power to garner popular support. But he also broke the power of the feudal nobility by setting up a more efficient tax system able to fund a professional army.

This army allowed Khosrau II (590–628 CE) to wage a final round of wars against the Eastern Roman, or Byzantine, Empire in which he pushed up to the walls of Constantinople, sacked Jerusalem, and took the Holy Cross. The subsequent Byzantine campaign to take it back, during which Khosrau was assassinated, was, in a sense, the first crusade in all but name.

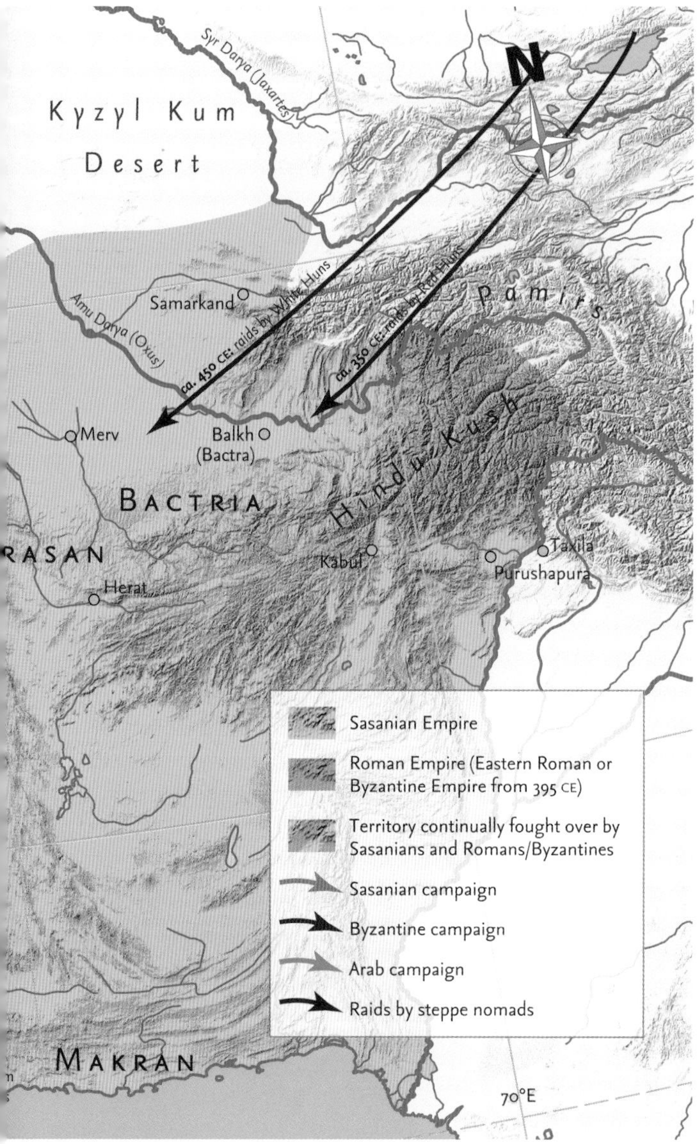

The opulence of Khosrau II's court came to epitomize Persian luxury, but by his time it was a façade the economy could not sustain. Perennial overtaxing to pay for incessant war with the Byzantine Empire had exhausted everyone. In 628 CE, both the Sasanians and the Byzantines received a letter from someone calling himself "Muhammad the Prophet of God," demanding that each acknowledge the "One True God." The strange letter was cast aside, but in its wake came armies fired by a new faith. By 651 CE the last Sasanian ruler lay dead.

The Muslim armies arrived like Alexander, with their own vision for the Persian Empire. Before long, however, they, like Alexander himself, would become changed by the empire they conquered, and others would follow suit. Through the centuries, Iran would prove able to absorb many invaders and rise anew.

Meanwhile, to the east, beyond the Hindu Kush, lay a land with even greater power to absorb and transform: India.

INDIA

Darius and Alexander both reached India but neither got farther than the northwest. India was too large, too different. Even for indigenous empire builders, a bewildering panoply of warring princes and overlapping religious and philosophical ideas stood in the way of single rule. At least two classical empires emerged from attempts to mold a unified India.

FROM THE INDUS TO THE GANGES

At the time of the earliest empires, the Indus Valley was home to an irrigation-based civilization, as in Sumer and Egypt. By 1700 BCE, its great cities lay deserted. Perhaps over-irrigation had destroyed them, perhaps invasion, but over the following few centuries tribes similar to those who spread across the Iranian plateau appeared in the Indus Valley.

Gradually these tribes spread down into the plain of the Ganges, bringing iron weapons with which they dominated the people they encountered. They also brought a religion evolved from their roving lifestyle. It involved animal sacrifice, worship of fire and water, a triad of gods headed by the heroic Indra, a sacred drink, and the chanting of sacred poems known as the *Vedas* (*veda*—"knowledge"). Bit by bit, the Vedas and local beliefs began to cross-fertilize.

These tribes set up numerous princely states within which society was divided into four *varnas* or classes, headed by the *brahmin*, a small class of scholars, priests, and lawmakers. By the time Darius arrived in the Punjab, constant warfare between these states was ravaging northern India. With instability came a questioning of traditional values and a rethinking of religious and ethical ideas. Spiritual teachers such as Gautama Buddha and Mahavira, the father of Jainism, drew followers around them.

These wars brought to the fore one state in particular that began to spread its political wings: Magadha on the lower Ganges. By the time Alexander arrived, Magadha was a centralized state collecting taxes to fund an army that enabled the ruling Nanda dynasty to control all of the Ganges plain. It was to depose the Nanda king from his throne at Pataliputra (Patna) that Alexander wanted to press farther into India.

THE MAURYAS

According to legend, Alexander was urged to help attack the Nanda by one Chandragupta Maurya, who ended up having to do the job himself. Whether they met or not, Alexander's retreat from the Punjab seems to have left a power vacuum that Chandragupta filled, either before or after ousting the Nanda around 321 BCE. With the resources of Magadha his, he stopped an attempt by Seleucus to retake the northwest in 305 BCE, and pushed south to the goldfields of the Deccan plateau. His empire was split into four provinces, each with a governor and a council of ministers answerable to him and a higher council in Pataliputra.

The architect of Chandragupta's empire was Chanakya, scholar at the university in Taxila, organizer of resistance to Alexander and author of the *Arthashastra*, a treatise on statecraft promoting stability at any cost. In it, Chanakya described how best to seize and retain power and plan the administration needed to support a strong state. A developed economy was fundamental. This depended on investment in public services such as roads and irrigation works, which in turn required a large bureaucracy.

Chandragupta possessed an army of over 600,000 run by a committee of 30 generals, each heading a subcommittee staffed by well-paid officers. With his army, Chandragupta enforced peace, allowing him to establish a single currency, watch the economy grow, trade textiles and spices with the Greek world, and reap the benefits in tax. Almost every human activity was taxed, which meant people were constantly monitored—from registration of births and deaths to the ominous-sounding "Subcommittee for the Care of Foreigners," which allocated accommodation to visitors and escorted them wherever they went.

Chandragupta's grandson, Ashoka (ca. 268–ca. 232 BCE) added just one new area to the empire, the lush and fertile kingdom of Kalinga on the east coast, but he achieved this only after a particularly bloody war in 261–260 BCE, during which perhaps 100,000 were killed. Seemingly overcome with remorse, he renounced violence and became a Buddhist.

Ashoka's Buddhism was not a purely personal matter; he rejected parts of the *Arthashastra* and tried to create a Buddhist state. He banned hunting for sport, protected certain animals, and abolished forced labor. He constructed canals and better roads, built hospitals, and funded research into medicinal herbs for human and animal medicine. Throughout his empire he inscribed first rocks, then pillars with an account of his conversion followed by an outline of his mission to spread Buddhist principles, with advice on how people should behave.

If Chandragupta's surveillance-orientated administration had displayed totalitarian overtones, the means by which Ashoka sought to bring enlightenment to his people did so even more. In addition to creating tiers of civil and military officials, Ashoka posted around his empire officers of *dharma*—officials responsible for the moral welfare of his people, charged with supervising their behavior.

There was more than an element of pragmatism about Ashoka's program. He conveniently renounced violence only after he had won Kalinga and needed to find a set of shared values to encourage people to identify with his rule. On the other hand, Ashoka sent Buddhist missionaries abroad—to Sri Lanka, Southeast Asia, and Greece—suggesting his evangelism was not simply self-serving.

In India, however, Ashoka's Buddhist empire did not long survive him. Central and local government soon became corrupt because there was no impartial procedure for appointing civil servants. The empire split, separating the Indus from the Ganges once more, and by 185 BCE a line of weak rulers had petered out.

NEW ARRIVALS FROM THE NORTHWEST

Ashoka's Buddhist India ranged well beyond the Khyber Pass, stemming the flow of invaders from the northwest for a while, but with its collapse the flow revived.

First to arrive were Greeks from Bactria, a breakaway kingdom split from the Seleucids. They reached as far as Pataliputra before establishing various independent kingdoms throughout the northwest. Menander I (ca. 155–130 BCE) was the most famous of these Bactrian

Ashoka erected stone pillars far and wide, inscribed with Buddhist edicts and crowned with lion capitals. This one from Sarnath, where the Buddha first taught, has become India's national symbol. An almost identical example exists in Thailand.

THE MAURYAN EMPIRE *321–185 BCE*

Alexander's retreat from the Indus Valley left Chandragupta Maurya (ca. 321–ca. 297 BCE) to take control. From a capital at Pataliputra, he also controlled the Ganges. His grandson Ashoka imposed Buddhism.

Greeks, ruling the Punjab as a convert to Buddhism. Here was something of the genuine cross-cultural marriage Alexander had sought. These kingdoms minted coins with Greek on one side and Pali on the other. But the Bactrian Greeks were only precursors to the Kushans.

Around 177 BCE, the Xiongnu, nomads from the eastern steppe, began pushing other tribes west into Central Asia. By the 1st century CE, a westward domino effect had brought the Kushans to power in Bactria, from where they followed the Greeks down into India. At its height, under Kanishka (ca. 127–ca. 147 CE), Kushan rule stretched from Samarkand on the Silk Road down to the mouth of the Indus and deep into the Ganges basin. Kanishka was able to reroute the silk trade from China down the Indus and on by sea to the West.

The Kushans promoted a fusion of Zoroastrianism and other beliefs, their coins displaying a range of gods from Greek and Roman through Hindu and Buddhist. Kushan Gandhara, in the Kabul valley, produced the first sculptures of the Buddha, carved in recognizably Greek style, and Kushan trade brought Buddhism to China.

After Kanishka, the Kushans began to lose their cross-cultural identity, becoming gradually more Indian. Pressure from a new Sasanian Persia around 240 CE led to the Kushan Empire breaking up, one part becoming a Sasanian province, the other dissolving into smaller states within India.

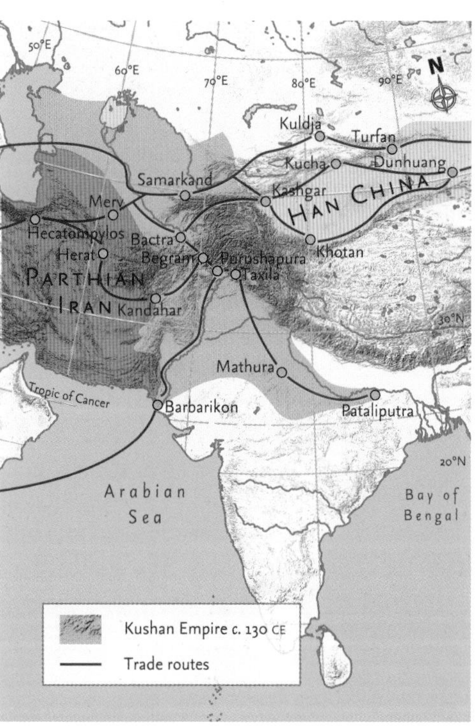

THE KUSHANS *ca. 50–ca. 300 CE*

The Kushans were originally Yuezhi nomads pushed west and south by Xiongnu control of the eastern steppe. They brought India and Iran in contact with China through the Silk Road.

THE GUPTAS

After 500 years of outside influence and regional rule, Ashoka's unified India stood out as an edifice of indigenous glory. The palace of the Mauryas was still standing in Pataliputra when a new Chandra Gupta I (ca. 320–ca. 335 CE) sought to make Magadha great once more. The neighboring Licchavi clan had sought to control Magadha since before Nanda times but Chandra Gupta bought them off by marriage and by putting the Licchavi name on the back of his coins.

From this base, his son Samudra Gupta (ca. 335–ca. 376 CE) created a new empire. The Kushans had brought horses down from the steppe and, in place of serried ranks of Mauryan infantry, Samudra Gupta's conquests were won by cavalry, together with longbowmen and elephants clad in leather armor.

Chandra Gupta II (ca. 376–ca. 415 CE) extended control westward by force and south into the Deccan by marrying into local ruling dynasties. The Gupta Empire now approached Mauryan rule in extent, but it was quite different in structure. Conquests near Magadha were, in effect, Gupta provinces, but they were run by local rulers, not by officials from Pataliputra. Farther afield, control was looser. Like Ashoka, Samudra Gupta conquered Kalinga, but he left the king in power in return for tribute. This was the pattern for outlying regions, some of whose rulers even had their own mini-empires tolerated by the Guptas.

This reflected a shift in political thought from the *Arthashastra*'s focus on the nature of power to ideas of justice as expressed in the *Mahabharata,* the great Hindu epic. To achieve "righteous conquest," a defeated ruler should be made to pay tribute but his territory should not be annexed and looted. Of course, these ideals relied on tribute being guaranteed either by an ever-present threat of force or by there being benefits to paying up. For a while, the Guptas were able to deliver both and create a golden age to surpass the Mauryas. The reign of Chandra Gupta II saw the rise of a leisure class expressing its refinement through chess, the *Kama Sutra*, and the birth of Indian scientific inquiry, which brought advances in medicine, astronomy, and mathematics.

The background to all this was a very stable social system based on *jati*, or caste—hereditary groups whose members must intermarry. An elaboration of the earlier and fewer varnas, the jati system achieved full complexity under the Guptas as part of a crystallizing Hindu cosmology. The planting of popular beliefs within Vedic concepts by the brahmins began to produce an all-embracing worldview. Assimilating rather than rejecting popular beliefs gave Hinduism a breadth of appeal Buddhism had lacked, and the Guptas made sure they were identified with this, granting land to Hindu temples and becoming patrons of a new style of Hindu sculpture very different from the Greek-influenced Buddhas of Gandhara.

The test for decentralized rule always comes with external pressure and, in the 5th century, this was provided by the White Huns, most likely unrelated to the Huns pressing on Rome around the same time. The Sasanians eventually managed to beat back the White Huns and so did Skanda Gupta (ca. 455–ca. 467 CE) in the 450s, but only by emptying the Gupta coffers and having to devalue the currency. Financial strain ushered in a predictable story of local kings ceasing to hand over tribute, and when the White Huns returned in the 490s, it took over 40 years to drive them away. By this time, the Guptas were shrinking back into Magadha, and by 600 CE they were spoken of no more.

The Guptas lacked the efficient bureaucracy of the Mauryas, but they lasted longer because they were more culturally attuned to the people they ruled. Ashoka knew the importance of shared values, but he attempted to impose them. He had also picked, in Buddhism, a value system with greater universal than local appeal. The Guptas, by contrast, were able to harness a genuine cultural groundswell, finding in Hinduism a much more localized system of thought linked to the history and everyday life of India. It allowed them to define India for all the Indias to come.

Even the Guptas, however, only partially and fleetingly succeeded in unifying the subcontinent. A more genuine unification had been achieved in China.

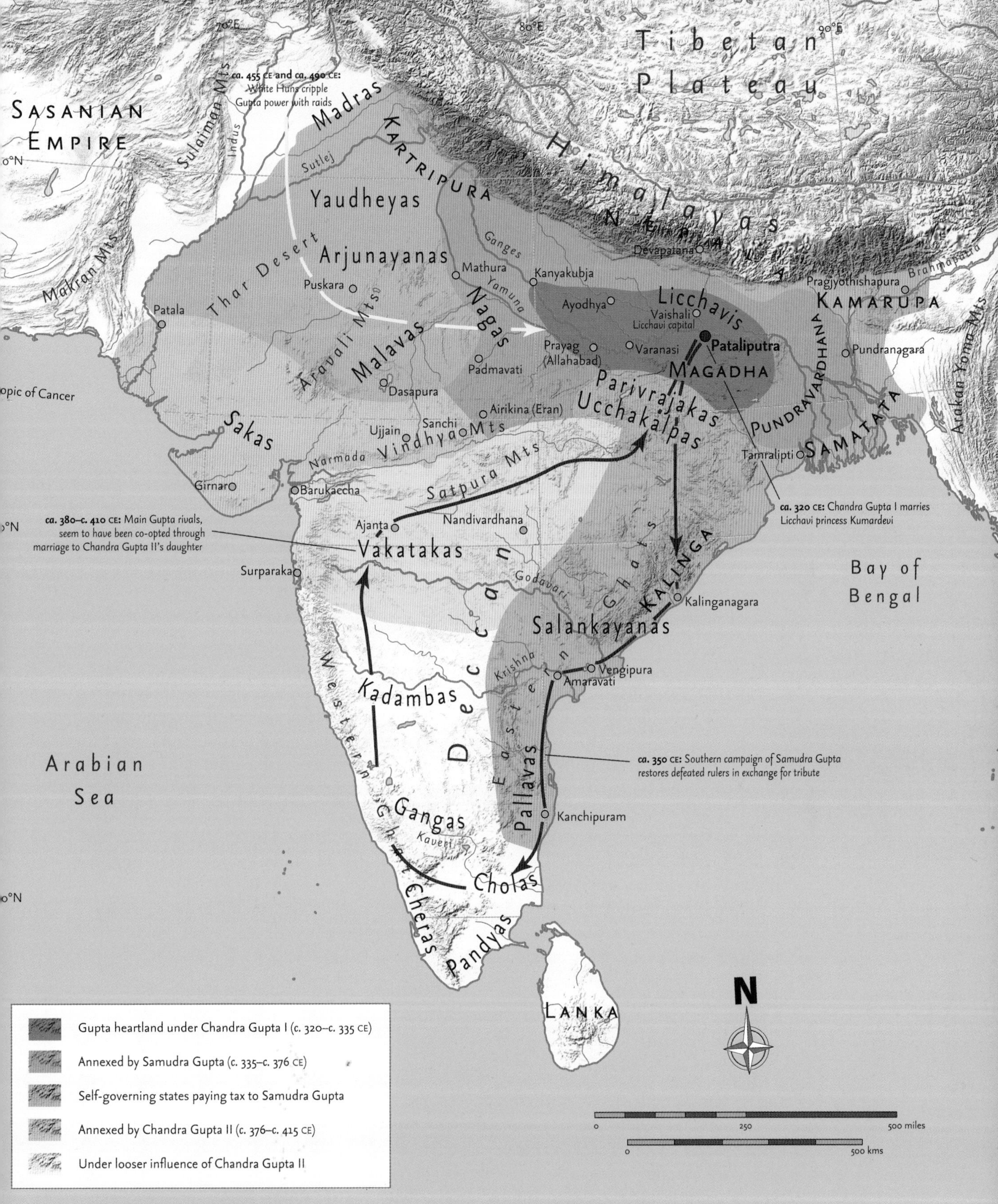

Tibetan Plateau
Himalayas
Sasanian Empire
Sulaiman Mts
Indus
Sutlej
Madras
Kartripura
Yaudheyas
Nepala
Makran Mts
Thar Desert
Arjunayanas
Ganges
Yamuna
Devapatana
Mathura
Kanyakubja
Puskara
Patala
Aravali Mts
Nagas
Malavas
Ayodhya
Licchavis
Vaishali
Licchavi capital
Pataliputra
Prayag (Allahabad)
Varanasi
Magadha
Padmavati
Dasapura
Parivrajakas
Ucchakalpas
Airikina (Eran)
Pragjyothishapura
Brahmaputra
Kamarupa
Pundravardhana
Pundranagara
Samatata
Arakan Yoma Mts
Tropic of Cancer
Sakas
Ujjain
Sanchi
Vindhya Mts
Narmada
Satpura Mts
Girnar
Barukaccha
Tamralipti
Ajanta
Nandivardhana
Vakatakas
Surparaka
Godavari
Kalinga
Kalinganagara
Bay of Bengal
Salankayanas
Krishna
Vengipura
Amaravati
Kadambas
Deccan
Western Ghats
Eastern Ghats
Pallavas
Kanchipuram
Arabian Sea
Gangas
Kaveri
Cholas
Cheras
Pandyas
Lanka
N
ca. 455 CE and ca. 490 CE: White Huns cripple Gupta power with raids
ca. 320 CE: Chandra Gupta I marries Licchavi princess Kumardevi
ca. 380–c. 410 CE: Main Gupta rivals, seem to have been co-opted through marriage to Chandra Gupta II's daughter
ca. 350 CE: Southern campaign of Samudra Gupta restores defeated rulers in exchange for tribute
Gupta heartland under Chandra Gupta I (c. 320–c. 335 CE)
Annexed by Samudra Gupta (c. 335–c. 376 CE)
Self-governing states paying tax to Samudra Gupta
Annexed by Chandra Gupta II (c. 376–c. 415 CE)
Under looser influence of Chandra Gupta II
0
250
500 miles
0
500 kms

INDIA UNDER THE GUPTAS *320–ca. 550 CE*

The Guptas reestablished Magadha as the homeland of an Indian empire, ruling from Pataliputra as the Mauryas had done.

CHINA

China, like India, was for a long time a battleground for countless feuding states, but eventually the whole area fell under a single empire that proved more enduring than the empires of India. In place of a common spirituality, its binding force was an administrative system based on ethical principles. In the north, however, China lay wide open to invaders; in keeping them at bay China's rulers faced the continual danger of having to share power with powerful families.

STABILITY AND INSTABILITY

Civilization in China began the same way as in Egypt, Sumer, and the Indus Valley: along the river—in this case the Huang He, or Yellow River. First millet was grown here, later rice. By the time of New Kingdom Egypt, the Yellow River valley was controlled by the Shang kings from a succession of capitals dotted around the middle course of the river. They ruled a society that produced bronze casting of great refinement and early experiments in writing. It was both connected to and set apart from future Chinas. Slave labor and human sacrifice ended with the Shang. At the same time, they practiced ancestor worship, and with respect for the dead came respect for tradition. This was a theme destined to resonate down the centuries.

The brutality of the Shang kings led to a coup around 1046 BCE by the Zhou. They saw their ability to seize power as proof the gods had transferred to them the "Mandate of Heaven"—the divine right to rule. In practice, Zhou power relied on a delicate balance of reciprocal responsibilities. The Zhou kings gave land to noble families in return for military service; the nobles gave land to peasants in return for a share of their produce.

In theory, the Zhou lasted until about 256 BCE, but after 771 BCE stable rule was lost. In that year, the Zhou capital was sacked and power dispersed among hundreds of noble clans who began to vie with each other, the strong taking over the estates of the weak during the so-called Spring and Autumn period. By 475 BCE, this had produced a handful of great estates whose rulers now fought it out during 250 years of war known as the Warring States period. Instability gave rise to the Hundred Schools of Thought—different theories on how best to order society.

Confucius (551–479 BCE) thought lasting peace could only come from a society based on mutual respect. He looked back with nostalgia at the early Zhou period, to him a model of a peaceful and harmonious society. Confucius saw Zhou stability as having been grounded in a respect for benefactors, symbolized by the practice of ancestor worship. Mencius (ca. 372–ca. 289 BCE) developed Confucius's ideas to argue that only rule worthy of the respect of the people was legitimate; control by force was an admission of defeat.

In opposition to Confucian thought stood the Legalists, who argued that legitimate rule is simply stable rule. Control by any means could be justified if it resulted in peace.

THE RISE OF THE QIN

One of the warring states belonged to the Qin (or "Ch'in"), a rough people from the west. Their power grew because they offered immigrants free accommodation and exemption from the army, then used them to develop the economy by digging canals and irrigation systems.

As the Qin had once been nobles under the Zhou, so they acquired a noble class of their own with the growth of their state, but their large-scale public works projects enabled the Qin to keep power centralized. The Qin labor force was composed of free peasants paying tax to the state, not serfs attached to noble estates as in the early days of the Zhou. Similarly, the administrators who ran the Qin planned economy were chosen on merit, not by birth, and rose insofar as they furthered Qin power. This produced Shang Yang, chief adviser from 350-338 BCE, whose Legalist policies helped the Qin exercise totalitarian control over their subjects. He held that a stable, efficient, productive state must make it worse to fall into the hands of the police than those of an enemy.

The Qin created an authoritarian state geared toward military buildup. State foundries churned out the iron farming tools on which economic growth depended as well as parts for weapons such as the new crossbow with its 650-foot (200-meter) range, a far more powerful weapon than anything Indian, Persian, or Roman. By the time the warring states had been whittled down to the two superpowers of Qin and Chu, each had a paid standing army of more than one million. The Qin army was more tightly organized, however, and the Qin economy had the resources to keep it supplied during the final war for supremacy.

By 221 BCE, the Qin had triumphed and Ying Zheng declared himself *Qin Shi Huangdi* ("First Qin Emperor," 221–210 BCE) of all those brought together under his rule—the first emperor of China. He faced two dangers: resistance from defeated rulers and raids from the Xiongnu, the steppe nomads to the north.

Li Si, Chief Advisor to Qin Shi Huangdi, broke the connection between noble families and their hereditary lands by deporting 120,000 to the Qin capital of Xianyang. He then organized the empire into 36 divisions, each run by a centrally appointed governor and a separate military commander. Mirroring yet isolated from empires further west, both were monitored by inspectors reporting back to central government and moved from region to region to prevent local power bases forming.

To deal with the Xiongnu, vast numbers were conscripted to build a continuous wall in the north. Earlier piecemeal walls were linked to create a 1,000-mile (1,600-kilometer) defense, a project infamous for its high death toll and consequent use as a form of punishment.

Qin unification brought uniformity. The economic infrastructure of China was built up with a common currency, common weights and measures, standard-length axles to run on standard-width roads, and a standard written language. Exchange of ideas, however, was seen not as a benefit to policy-making and government popularity but simply as potential subversion. Hence, criticism of the regime led first to book burning in 213 BCE, then to a purge of intellectuals the year after, with hundreds killed, two policies set to become hallmarks of totalitarion rule.

Book burning and forced labor meant it was not just dispossessed nobles who had a grievance against the Qin. Nobles began to rebel in the last year of the First Emperor's reign, but succession intrigues following his death in 210 BCE suggested the noble class would not be able to provide stable rule, and dissent became more widespread.

THE HAN SYNTHESIS

The man who this wave of popular revolt brought to power in 206 BCE was the peasant-born Liu Bang, who became Gaozu, the first Han emperor (206–195 BCE). Gaozu aimed at inclusion. He had little time for the highborn, but he was conscious of the need not to alienate sections of society. His first act was to declare an amnesty for all sides involved in what had been a civil war.

Han China started as a compromise between central government and noble power. Gaozu gave land to his supporters and restored many noble estates. There was a dual system of administration for the provinces, some run by Gaozu's officials, others by feudal lords, although both were overseen by government inspectors.

Concessions also had to be made to the Xiongnu, now too strong to hold beyond the wall. In 200 BCE, they captured Gaozu, after which the Han government paid them yearly sums to stay away.

But gradually the Han grew stronger. In 154 BCE, rebelling landowners unwittingly ushered in a decline in their own power. The law was changed to give all sons equal inheritance rights with the result that estates began to dwindle as they were shared out among several heirs. Eventually, by around 100 BCE, Emperor Wudi ("Warrior Ruler," 141–87 BCE) was able to end the power-sharing compromise of Gaozu. But central control did not bring a return to Qin-style rule.

By Wudi's time, the fall of the Qin was being compared to the fall of the Shang; both had lost the Mandate of Heaven through their despotism. In contrast, Gaozu had opened administrative jobs to all, regardless of their politics. He could not read and had nothing in common with intellectuals, but he realized the value to government of a healthy exchange of ideas. His rule marked the beginning of Confucian influence on government.

Wudi's ending of power-sharing meant more jobs for civil servants, but like Gaozu he wanted innovative thinkers, not mere yes-men. His desire to recruit the most able led to him setting the first civil-service examinations in 130 BCE, followed by founding an imperial university in 124 BCE.

The civil-service exams began to require years of study to pass, which meant most candidates were the sons of landowners able to support them while they studied. Once employed, however, civil servants were not allowed to serve or own land in their home province, or to work in the same department as a relative. The key relationship in Han society now ceased to be between ruler and nobles; as the civil service became the way to get on, literacy became the big divide, and the successful came to identify more and more closely with the state.

THE SILK ROAD

Wudi was an exception among Han emperors for expanding beyond the area conquered by the Qin. He was forced to fight the Xiongnu once annual payments no longer satisfied them, but troops were hard to supply far out on the steppe. So, in 138 BCE, Wudi sent an envoy, Zhang Qian, to find the Yuezhi, enemies of the Xiongnu driven west about 40 years earlier.

The Yuezhi, now living on the Oxus River, were no longer interested in fighting the Xiongnu, but on the way to visit them Zhang Qian found beautiful horses in the Kushan-controlled Ferghana valley, larger and faster than the Mongolian ponies of the Xiongnu. Wudi began to import these horses in exchange for Chinese silk, which eventually found its way to Rome. Thus the Silk Road was born and China became aware of other civilizations.

The Xiongnu threat also drew Wudi into Korea. Here, there was a growing iron industry able to supply weapons to the Xiongnu, plus a ruler sympathetic to rebel elements within China. To the south, a potentially contagious uprising of nobles in independent Nam Viet provoked Wudi to annex it. Beyond what were essentially reactive measures, however, the Han did not seek new territory.

After two centuries in power, economic problems and Xiongnu resurgence led to the Han losing authority and a usurper, Wang Mang (9–23 CE), seizing power. His attempt to radically restructure the economy produced famine and incited the nobles to bring back Han rule for a further two centuries, but this time central government could not break noble power and had to make deals with the Xiongnu. Nearer tribes were allowed to settle the borderlands, providing a buffer to more distant tribes. Then, in 150 CE, the Xiongnu took the Western Regions, laying the ground for a final collapse.

Within their palace, the Han emperors trusted none so much as the eunuchs with whom they surrounded themselves. Although they could not have children and thus give rise to rival families, the eunuchs' closeness to the emperor increasingly made them the real power behind the throne, distrusted and resented by most of the court. The assassination of a general in 189 CE provoked a massacre of the eunuchs and a de facto coup by General Cao Cao, who ruled in all but name until the last Han emperor abdicated in 220.

The Qin built an empire of conquest to which they gave the name "China" and which they controlled with Legalist severity, but it was the Han who genuinely unified China by creating institutions that embodied Confucian ideals of mutual responsibility. From Han times, the Chinese came to see themselves as guardians of a genteel way of life thrown into sharp relief by barbarians beyond their wall.

The two greatest empires of the classical world, Rome and China, knew of each other but never made direct contact. Each had reached the limit of their expansion and turned inward to focus on the society they had created. Between them, they had defined the East and the West.

A ceramic model of a watchtower from the end of the Han period. Pressure from the Xiongnu forced the Han to share power with feudal landowners—increasingly so in later years. Watchtowers guarded landed estates as well as the great northern wall.

Following pages: main map:

HAN CHINA *206 BCE–220 CE*

The Han were brought to power on a wave of protest against the harshness of Qin rule. They consolidated the south and pushed west, seeking allies to help fight the Xiongnu.

Inset map:

CHINA UNIFIED UNDER THE QIN *221–206 BCE*

From 475 BCE, there was constant war, dominated at first by the Han, Wei, Qi, and Chu. By 300 BCE, the rising Qin state had claimed the northwest and, by 221 BCE, had subdued all other warring states.

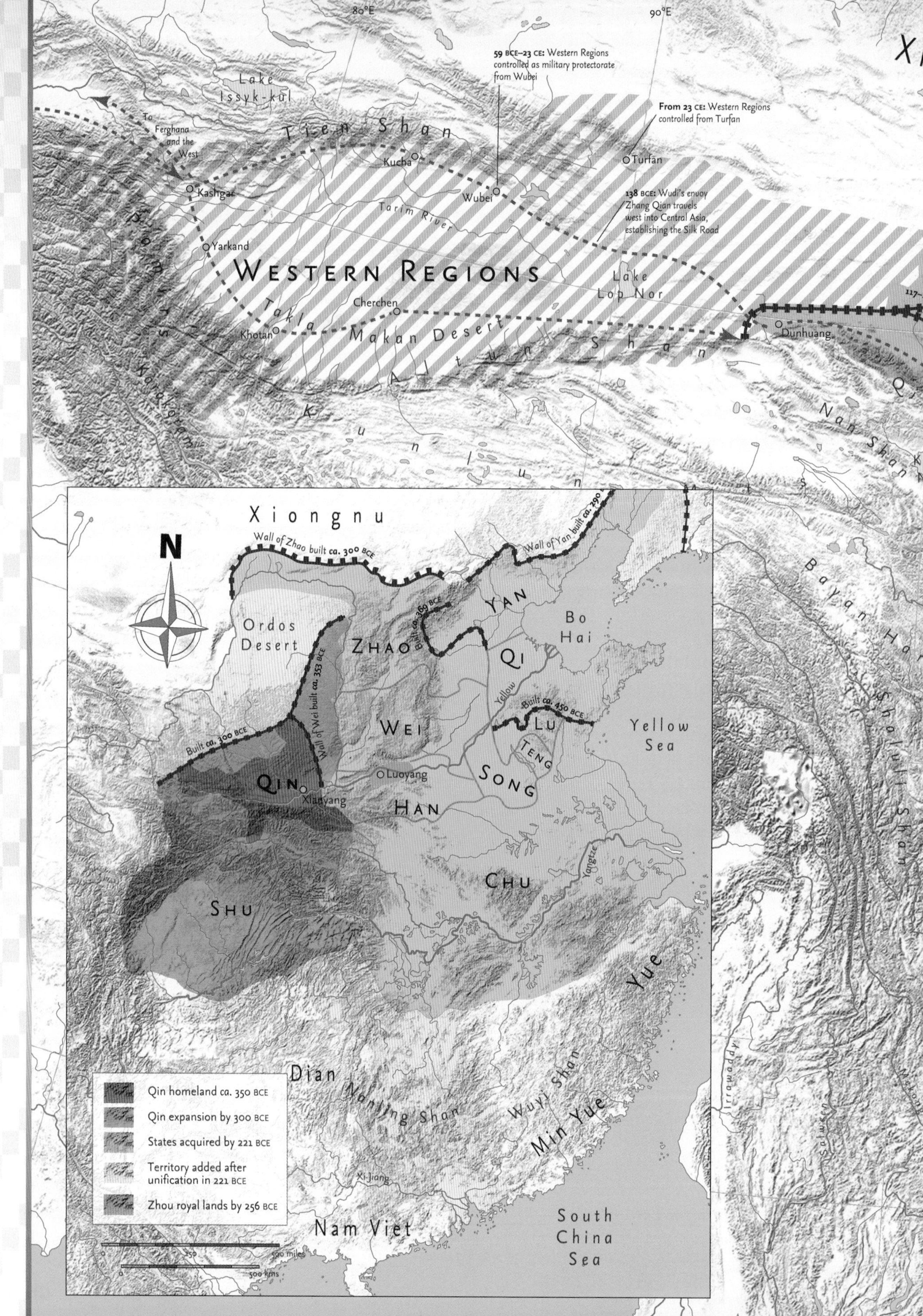

80°E
90°E
59 BCE–23 CE: Western Regions controlled as military protectorate from Wubei
From 23 CE: Western Regions controlled from Turfan
138 BCE: Wudi's envoy Zhang Qian travels west into Central Asia, establishing the Silk Road
Lake Issyk-kul
Tien Shan
To Ferghana and the West
Kucha
Turfan
Kashgar
Wubei
Tarim River
Yarkand
Western Regions
Lake Lop Nor
Cherchen
Khotan
Takla Makan Desert
Altun Shan
Dunhuang
Kunlun Shan
Nan Shan
Bayan Har Shan
Shaluli Shan
Xiongnu
Wall of Zhao built ca. 300 BCE
Wall of Yan built ca. 290
Built ca. 369 BCE
Wall of Wei built ca. 353 BCE
Built ca. 300 BCE
Built ca. 450 BCE
Ordos Desert
Zhao
Yan
Bo Hai
Qi
Yellow
Wei
Lu
Teng
Yellow Sea
Qin
Xianyang
Luoyang
Song
Han
Chu
Yangtze
Shu
Yue
Dian
Nanling Shan
Wuyi Shan
Min Yue
Xi Jiang
Nam Viet
South China Sea
Irrawaddy
Salween
Mekong
Qin homeland ca. 350 BCE
Qin expansion by 300 BCE
States acquired by 221 BCE
Territory added after unification in 221 BCE
Zhou royal lands by 256 BCE
250
500 miles
500 kms

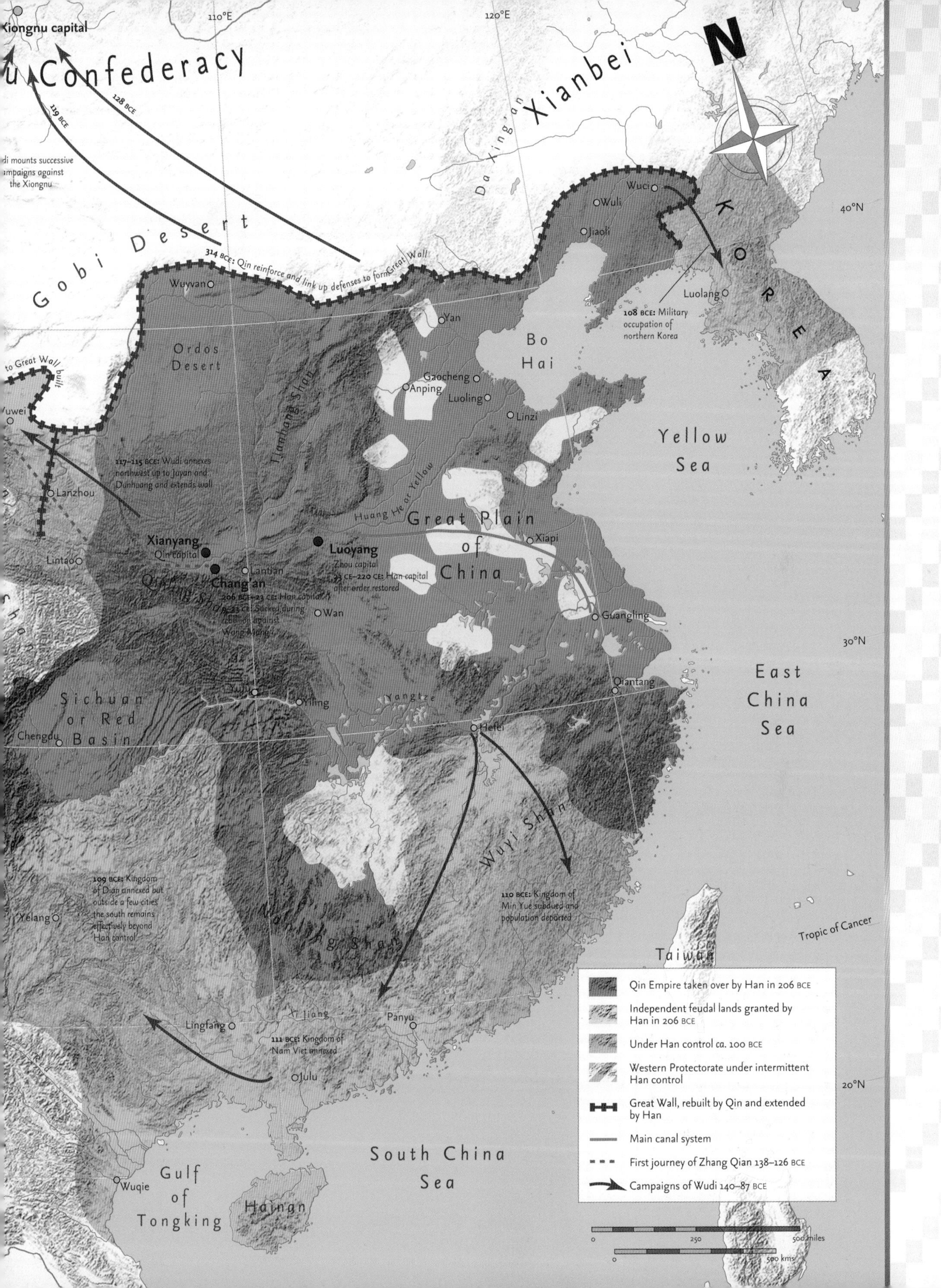

Xiongnu capital
Confederacy
Xianbei
N
110°E
120°E
128 BCE
119 BCE
Wudi mounts successive campaigns against the Xiongnu
Gobi Desert
314 BCE: Qin reinforce and link up defenses to form Great Wall
Da Xing'an
Wuci
Wuli
Jiaoli
KOREA
40°N
Luolang
108 BCE: Military occupation of northern Korea
Wuyvan
Yan
Ordos Desert
Bo Hai
to Great Wall built
Wuwei
Gaocheng
Anping
Luoling
Linzi
Taihang Shan
Yellow Sea
117–115 BCE: Wudi annexes northwest up to Juyan and Dunhuang and extends wall
Lanzhou
Huang He or Yellow
Great Plain of China
Xiapi
Xianyang
Qin capital
Luoyang
Zhou capital
23 CE–220 CE: Han capital after order restored
Lintao
Lantian
Chang'an
206 BCE–23 CE: Han capital
9–23 CE: Sacked during rebellion against Wang Mang
Wan
Guangling
30°N
Qiantang
East China Sea
Sichuan or Red Basin
Yuju
Yiling
Yangtze
Chengdu
Hefei
Wuyi Shan
109 BCE: Kingdom of Dian annexed but outside a few cities the south remains effectively beyond Han control
Yelang
110 BCE: Kingdom of Min Yue subdued and population deported
Tropic of Cancer
Taiwan
Lingfang
Xi Jiang
Panyu
111 BCE: Kingdom of Nam Viet annexed
Julu
20°N
South China Sea
Wuqie
Gulf of Tongking
Hainan
Qin Empire taken over by Han in 206 BCE
Independent feudal lands granted by Han in 206 BCE
Under Han control ca. 100 BCE
Western Protectorate under intermittent Han control
Great Wall, rebuilt by Qin and extended by Han
Main canal system
First journey of Zhang Qian 138–126 BCE
Campaigns of Wudi 140–87 BCE
0
250
500 miles
500 kms

3 EMPIRES OF FAITH

The Byzantine Empire / The Holy Roman Empire / The Abbasid Caliphate

All the classical empires found ways to supplement control by force with a measure of consent delivered by shared beliefs. As the classical world crumbled and people looked for something to hold on to, however, religious ideas promising salvation exerted a stronger pull than political ideas such as citizenship. In Europe, the Roman emperors looked to Christianity for support as they sought to preserve the empire from a new eastern capital at Constantinople.

In the West, all that was left of Rome after 476 CE was the church. Throughout western Europe, Christianity slowly spread and began to form something of a common culture to overlay regional differences. A church able to direct the conscience of European society could have its pick of powerful states to help build a new Rome. That was the idea. Whether such a union could be achieved was another matter.

Neither eastern nor western attempt to revive the Roman Empire confined itself to the empire's former extent. Christianity was an evangelical faith and both its branches reached farther afield, bringing with them forms of imperial influence as converts were won. They also brought religious intolerance and holy war, especially as they collided with another faith claiming universal truth.

While Christianity took centuries to spread through Europe, Islam exploded across thousands of miles in decades. Like Western Christianity, this was a religious movement without the protection of a state, but Islam was able to solve the problem of how to bring the two together because it was a political faith from the outset. The Qur'an contained a combined religious, ethical, and political program, which meant Islam created its own state wherever it went.

The Emperor Justinian I presents a higher authority, the infant Jesus and his mother, with a model of the Hagia Sophia, the cathedral he built for Constantinople, capital of the Eastern Roman Empire. From Hagia Sophia's southwestern entrance, 944 CE.

ΜΡ
ΘΥ

THE BYZANTINE EMPIRE

Rome's most enduring legacy was Christianity, a religion able to grow and take shape within the empire before spreading its wings far beyond. At Constantinople, the second Rome, employing Christianity to serve the state allowed the empire to persist another thousand years.

THE SECOND ROME

Jesus was born at a pivotal moment in the history of Rome. Augustus was in power and two centuries of imperial stability had begun. During this time, political and economic integration spread a common way of life across the empire, underpinned by the concept of citizenship. In the 3rd century CE, however, the Roman peace began to crumble and with it the secular values on which it was based.

Under Diocletian, a new pyramid-like administration was topped by an emperor who presented himself as both secular and spiritual guardian of his people. The emperor as Princeps, or "First Citizen," gave way to one modeled on the divine kings of the East. That Christians refused to worship an emperor styled as a savior exposed them to persecution, but concern to safeguard classical civilization was fast becoming concern to hold the empire together with any legitimizing force that would work. After Diocletian, Christianity became popular enough for persecution to be counterproductive and with Constantine I, this popularity was harnessed to serve the empire.

In 312 CE, while fighting to restore the empire after Diocletian's tetrarchy had collapsed, Constantine had a vision and ordered his soldiers to paint a Christian symbol on their shields. The following year he and his co-emperor lifted the ban on Christianity. Once he re-established single rule in 324 CE, Constantine strove to establish a unified church, calling the Council of Nicaea in 325 CE, at which 300 bishops under his patronage met to produce an orthodox line on the nature of Christ. By 380 CE, Christianity as defined by the Nicene Creed, which held Christ to be equal to God the Father, had become an official state-backed religion.

This new Christian Rome was strongest in the east where in 330 CE, Constantine had founded a second capital, Constantinople, on the site of the old Greek city of Byzantium. It turned its face toward the other early centers of the church at Antioch, Jerusalem, and Alexandria and, by 395 CE, had become the capital of a separate Eastern Roman Empire, within which Greek began to replace Latin.

A dream of reunifying the empire persisted, however. After Rome fell in 476 CE, a unified empire remained a habit of thought as much for Odoacer, first barbarian king of Italy, and his successor Theodoric the Ostrogoth, as for the Emperor Justinian I (527–565 CE) in Constantinople, who was proud of having Latin as his mother tongue. Justinian was also fortunate to have as a general Belisarius, who retook most of the western Mediterranean in 540 CE.

But the achievement of Belisarius was illusory. His battle to retake Italy destroyed far more of its classical heritage than the Goths and Vandals ever had and simply weakened the country, making it easier for the Lombards to invade from the north in 568 CE.

More lasting was the style of Justinian's rule, which set a trend for future emperors to follow. To buy time for Belisarius he entered into labyrinthine diplomatic negotiations between barbarian tribes, client states around the Black Sea, and Sasanian Persia. Inside the empire, after a ruthless crackdown in 532 CE, he displayed a mania for regulation, particularly in religious matters. He made the Nicene Creed of 325 CE, together with the rulings of later ecumenical councils, state law and pursued nonconformists as heretics. All other faiths or philosophical schools he either suppressed or controlled, from the Jews to the Academy at Athens.

Justinian's attempt to impose religious conformity alienated churches throughout the Middle East and in Rome. As such, Belisarius's reconquest of Italy could never have lasted and after Justinian, preserving the empire ceased to mean reunifying it.

A NEW IDENTITY

The next two centuries saw the Eastern Roman Empire shrinking back to a heartland around Constantinople and redefining itself as an entity better known as the Byzantine Empire. This process began with Heraclius (610–641 CE) making Greek the official language and waging Europe's first holy war. In 614 CE, the Sasanians invaded Jerusalem and took the Holy Cross. In reply, Heraclius destroyed the Zoroastrian fire temple at Adhur Gushnasp before breaking the Sasanians at Nineveh in 627 CE and reclaiming the Cross.

Within 10 years, however, Heraclius had lost Jerusalem and the rest of Palestine and Syria to the dramatic appearance of Arabs charged by a new Islamic faith. By the 670s CE, an Arab fleet was attacking Constantinople itself and the empire was putting everything it had into its defense.

By sea, the Arabs were held back by Greek fire, a secret napalm-like liquid that burned on water. It was so feared that simply holding up the flamethrower that dispensed it was often enough to provoke a hasty retreat.

By land, the Arabs were held back by the *themes*, regions of Anatolia entrusted to the Byzantine armies as they retreated after losing the Levant. Each soldier received a plot of land to settle, farm, and protect. As the centuries passed, the original five themes were reorganized and split up into many more administrative districts. The distinction between

Greek fire, the flammable liquid that protected Constantinople against Arab naval attacks from the 670s CE. The secret of its recipe was closely guarded, but probably included petroleum collected from wells around the Black Sea. From the Madrid Skylitzes, *12th century.*

military commanders and provincial governors disappeared as a frontier society was created with echoes of Rome's early citizen army.

But there was also pressure from the north. The Central Asian tribal confederation with which Attila the Hun terrorized much of Europe in the 440s had included Bulgars as crack troops, many of whom settled and mixed with Slav tribes above the Danube. Bulgars also settled between the Black and Caspian Seas, but as the Khazars, another Central Asian people, began to take over this area they pushed these Bulgars west and south. As Arab ships attacked Constantinople, Bulgars and Slavs were crossing the Danube into the empire.

This encouraged links to be forged with the Khazars. They had helped Heraclius against the Persians, fought Arabs and Bulgars, and now allied with the empire through marriage. Nonetheless, as the Byzantine Empire shrank it became less cosmopolitan and more conformist.

In Justinian's time, a tradition of painting icons for teaching and to focus worship had been well established, but the advancing tide of Islam struck many as proof of God's displeasure at a form of idolatry and, in 730 CE, Leo III issued a ban. By the time the ban was lifted in 843 CE, a century of iconoclastic purges had further alienated the Western Church. Rome had now given up on Constantinople and, in 800 CE, crowned a new emperor of its own. As if that were not enough, 811 CE, the Bulgars had massacred Byzantine forces at Pliska and made it the capital of a new Bulgar state.

A NEW EMPIRE

With Arab power waning, however, the empire was able to look north and begin a new cultural and territorial expansion. In 862 CE, two missionary brothers, Cyril and Methodius, were invited to the Slav state of Great Moravia, eastern neighbor to the Franks, who were defenders of Rome. Rastislav, ruler of Great Moravia, had fought off attacks by the Franks and wanted to counter the influence of Roman Catholic priests by establishing an independent Slavonic Church.

At this time, the various Slav peoples had no writing. Cyril and Methodius developed an alphabet based on Greek letters with which to translate parts of the Bible into what became known as Old Church Slavonic. Great Moravia did not last, but Slavonic students continued refining their alphabet into Cyrillic, which they took to Bulgaria in the 880s CE, and eventually to Kiev.

By the time Bulgaria received the Cyrillic alphabet, it had already become the first convert to Eastern Orthodox Christianity. Sandwiched between Constantinople and Rome, Boris I had invited Roman Catholic priests to convert his people in 863 CE, when the Byzantines invaded and forced him to accept the Eastern Church instead. This incited a revolt in 865 CE which Boris crushed, setting a precedent for Slav states to be converted from the top down.

Opposite page: main map:

THE MATURE BYZANTINE EMPIRE *ca. 860–1204 CE*

From the 860s CE an eastern empire no longer concerned with the west turned north to reclaim the Balkans and send missionaries farther afield. Byzantine power peaked under Basil II (976–1025 CE), but afterward Turks, Normans, and Crusaders ushered in decline.

Inset map:

THE FLEETING RECONQUEST OF THE WEST UNDER JUSTINIAN I *527–565 CE*

In a last backward glance at Roman glory, Justinian's general Belisarius retook key parts of the west. Soon after Justinian's death, however, the Lombards invaded Italy and these gains were lost.

Byzantine Empire on accession of Basil I in 867 CE
Byzantine Empire on death of Basil II in 1025
Kievan Rus ca. 1025
Republic of Venice ca. 1025
Themes of Anatolia ca. 867 CE, intended to prevent Arab invasions
Byzantine campaign
Mission to spread influence of Orthodox Church
Campaigns against Byzantine Empire
30°E
40°E
N
Novgorod
11th century: After baptism of Kiev, similar forced baptisms follow in Novgorod and other Rus cities
Vladimir
1299: Becomes center for Rus Church
Moscow
1325: Becomes head of Rus Church. Does not gain independence from Constantinople until 1448
After Mongol sack of Kiev (1240), head of Rus Church relocates to northeast
Rus
Germanic States
Great Moravia (833–907 CE)
860s CE: Cyril and Methodius translate Bible into Old Church Slavonic, paving way for conversion of Slavonic peoples
Mikulčice
Nitra
Bratislava
Dnieper
Kiev
867–988 CE: Initial introduction of Orthodox Christianity slow to penetrate beyond an elite
988 CE: Vladimir orders the people of Kiev to be baptized in the River Dnieper
Don
50°N
Volga
Alps
Carpathians
9th century CE: Ally with empire against Bulgars, Magyars and Rus
c. 1000: Broken by Rus
Pechenegs
867 CE: Prince Mutimir accepts Orthodox Christianity for the Serbs
971 CE: Serb lands annexed
Hungary
894 CE: Magyars ally with empire against Bulgars
867 CE
Venice
Ravenna
Croats
Sirmium
862 CE: Cyril and Methodius
Danube
Sea of Asov
Khazars
Adriatic Sea
1017: Normans enter southern Italy
Singidunum (Belgrade)
Spalatum
988 CE: Vladimir of Kiev baptised
Kherson
Theodosia
8th century CE: Ally with empire against Arabs and Bulgars
ca. 900 CE: Adopt Judaism as state religion
965–969 CE: Broken by Rus
Serbs
Nicopolis
863 CE: Boris I accepts Orthodox Christianity for the Bulgars
Rome
Ragusa
Gradina
867 CE
Serdica (Sofia)
Pliska
Varna
Black Sea
Bulgars
863 CE
1204: Fourth Crusade sacks Constantinople at request of Venice
Caucasus
Naples
Amalfi
Bari
Dyrrhachium
Ochrida
Philippopolis
Adrianople
Sinope
Constantinople
Kleidion 1014
Paphlagonia
Armenia
Trebizond
rrhenian Sea
1025: Comes under Rome
1071: Captured by Normans
1081: Captured by Normans
Thessaloniki
Optimaton
Bukellarion
Armeniakon
Chaldia
Abydus
Nicaea
Koloneia
Theodosiopolis
40°N
Aegean Sea
Ancyra
Charsianon
Manzikert
Sicily
Syracuse
Nicopolis
Ionian Sea
Opsikion
Cappadocia
Sebastea
Patras
Athens
Corinth
Smyrna
Sardis
Anatolikon
Ephesus
Philadelphia
Caesarea
Thrakesion
Iconium
alta
Mistra
1014: Basil II defeats Samuel of Bulgaria, blinding 99 percent of prisoners. Bulgars are crushed and Basil annexes Bulgar state in 1018
Kibyrrhaioton
Attalia
Seleucia
Tarsus
1071: Seljuk Turks push into Anatolia following victory at Manzikert
961 CE: Retaken from Muslims
Antioch
Mediterranean Sea
Crete
Candia
Cyprus
Nicosia
Abbasid Caliphate
964 CE: Retaken from Muslims
969 CE: Retaken from Abbasids
1084: Falls to Seljuks
Tigris
Euphrates
0
250
500 miles
500 kms
Atlantic Ocean
Franks
Lombards
N
Ravenna
Danube
Black Sea
Pyrenees
Visigoths
Rome
Constantinople
Sasanians
Antioch
Berbers
Mediterranean Sea
Alexandria
Arabs
Nile
Red Sea
Red Sea
Eastern Roman Empire at fall of Western Empire in 476 CE
Reconquests on eve of Lombard invasion of Italy in 568 CE
Campaigns of Emperor Justinian's general Belisarius 533–540 CE

The Bulgarians, however, remained a thorn in the empire's side, pushing it to ally with a new power in the northeast. This was Rus, precursor to Russia, centered around Kiev on the Dnieper. Viking raiders appearing in the 860s CE had mingled with local Slavs and settled here to control trade between the Black Sea and the Baltic. They were richer and stronger than the Khazars had been and potentially more useful.

Basil II (976–1025 CE) turned to Vladimir, Grand Prince of Rus, for help when he faced an attempted coup after a botched campaign against Samuel of Bulgaria. Basil gave Vladimir his sister Anna's hand in return for 6,000 mercenaries to suppress the revolt—and into the bargain Vladimir adopted Eastern Orthodox Christianity.

In fact, Vladimir had already decided he needed a state religion to bind his people together and had sent emissaries out to sample what was being offered in Rome, Baghdad, and Constantinople. The Byzantines impressed him most. The splendor of the Byzantine court and the Orthodox Church seemed part and parcel of each other. Both exuded tradition, order, and sophisticated complexity. Both were suffused with a sumptuousness of theatrical display that clothed the emperor in an aura of otherworldliness. The empire he presided over and the god he represented far surpassed the competition in awe-inspiring majesty. So Vladimir chose Eastern Orthodox Christianity for himself and for the people of Kiev, through a mass baptism in the Dnieper in 988 CE. Nominally independent, Vladimir's church was, in practice, controlled by the Patriarch of Constantinople.

With Rus on his side, Basil could concentrate on revenge against Samuel. Thirty years of gradual progress reached a turning point at the battle of Kleidion in 1014, with the capture of 15,000 Bulgarian prisoners. Of each 100, Basil blinded 99, leaving one to lead the rest home. When Samuel saw his blinded troops returning, he died of shock. After this, Bulgaria caved in and Basil was ever after known as *Bulgaroktonos*—"the Bulgar Slayer."

THE RISE OF VENICE

The reign of Basil saw the climax of Byzantine power and influence, but soon afterward new threats appeared from both east and west.

In 1054, 700 years of Christian discord culminated with the patriarch in Constantinople and the pope in Rome excommunicating each other following disagreement over the Trinity. In 1071, however, the Seljuk Turks broke through at Manzikert, gateway to Anatolia, and were soon camped on the Bosporus opposite Constantinople. Fearing a Muslim invasion, the emperor was forced to ask the pope for help.

The pope launched a propaganda campaign throughout the Christian west, resulting in the First Crusade, but with no love lost between the two churches, the Crusaders kicked out Jerusalem's Greek patriarch when they took the Holy City in 1099. Here were tensions waiting to be exploited by the business-minded, maritime city-state of Venice.

The Seljuks had arrived just as a last wave of raiders was sweeping through western Europe. These were the Normans, Vikings settled in northern France, who began taking Byzantine lands in southern Italy and Sicily. Venice helped repel the Normans in return for trading concessions within the empire and sank the profits into expanding its fleet.

In 1204, Venice lent ships to ferry a Fourth Crusade to the Holy Land—on condition the Crusaders took Constantinople first. The city was ransacked and set on fire. Most of the cash was pocketed by the Crusaders, the bronze horses from the Hippodrome were taken to St. Mark's in Venice, and the Venetians ruled in Constantinople for half a century. After they left, in 1261, the empire never recovered, and Constantinople's eventual capture by the Ottoman Turks in 1453 was a formality.

Under the Ottomans, however, life in Constantinople continued much the same. The Hagia Sophia cathedral became a mosque but Byzantine institutions and a Byzantine style of rule largely remained. Farther afield, this style lived on in Russia, where tsar and Orthodox Church formed a partnership modeled on the Byzantine Empire. It even left its mark on the autocratic yet bureaucratic Soviet Union.

The Hagia Sophia ("Holy Wisdom"), built by Justinian I between 532 and 537 CE, was the largest church in the world for a millennium and pioneered the use of the dome in religious architecture. More than any palace, it symbolized Constantinople's power and its continuity, living on as a mosque after 1453 and acquiring minarets.

THE HOLY ROMAN EMPIRE

In the east, the structure of the Roman Empire persisted and could simply reinvent itself in Christian form. In the west, it fell apart and would have to be pieced together using mostly new parts. This was a tall order made taller by the ambitions of kings and by a church that cast itself in opposition to the secular world. Even so, there was a moment when the outline of a Christian empire in western Europe came into view.

THE CHURCH

In 410 CE, Rome was sacked by Alaric the Visigoth, an event that shocked and bewildered the Mediterranean world and provoked Augustine of Hippo, a theologian from northwest Africa, to write his *City of God* in explanation. Christians in the west were less influenced by the secular bent of Greek thought than in the east, and Augustine saw the church as an ark built to ferry people from the "Earthly City" of this world to the "City of God" beyond. A state that failed to protect this ark, attending only to the wants of the Earthly City, would lose God's favor and fall, which was what had happened to Rome.

Here was the idea that the church's role was that of a spiritual organization set apart from the secular world, not the legitimizing organ of the state it had become in Constantinople. If they came together, the state should be the servant of the church. Having lost its state for good after 476 CE, however, the Western Church had to stand on two legs of its own: monasteries and the pope.

The earliest monks had been hermits living in the Egyptian desert but, in 529 CE, St. Benedict founded a monastery on Monte Cassino, between Rome and Naples, where monks were to be sociable and industrious, able to give charity, not ask for it. This form of socially involved monasticism allowed Roman Catholicism to seep into the fabric of western European society.

Meanwhile, the bishop of Rome found himself holding the remnants of Rome's imperial authority. Belisarius's reconquest of the west for Constantinople delivered the Duchy of Rome into papal hands and unwittingly reinforced the pope's authority, as Justinian's representative at Ravenna was seen as a foreign imposition.

Gregory I (590–604 CE) was the first pope who had himself been a monk. As the Lombards took over more of Italy, cutting Rome off from Ravenna, he lost touch with the east and turned north, sending Augustine of Canterbury, a fellow Benedictine, to convert the Anglo-Saxons and cultivate relations with a power that might one day better protect Rome: the Franks.

THE STATE

In 481 CE, Clovis I became king of the Western Franks, kicked out the Roman governor of Gaul, and expanded his territory down to the Loire. He now became king of the Eastern Franks, too, gaining control of the lower Rhine. In 496 CE, he married a Roman Catholic princess from Burgundy and subsequently converted to her faith (apparently on the battlefield), which lent his campaigns a religious flavor. When he took the rest of

Gaul from the Visigoths and the Burgundians, the emperor in Constantinople named him consul.

The Roman Empire was still seen as the only model of civilization and barbarian leaders eagerly sought the legitimacy it could provide, but this depended on religion. The Ostrogoths, then ruling Italy from Ravenna, were also Christian, but they were Arians, holding Christ to be subordinate to God the Father. It was to condemn Arianism, widespread at the time, that the Nicene Creed had been formulated in 325 CE, so neither Rome nor Constantinople could do business with them. Clovis's kingdom lacked anything like Roman administrative know-how to hold it together and began to fragment after his death in 511 CE. Nonetheless, Clovis's conversion to Roman Catholicism had bound the Franks to Rome.

Clovis's successors found power passing to the mayors of their palaces east and west of the Rhine until in 714 CE, Charles Martel, one such mayor, began to revive Clovis's kingdom. By this time a new infidel had arisen for Christian Europe to define itself against, and near Tours in 734 CE, he halted the Muslim advance into western Europe. He also backed the Benedictine missionary Boniface in his efforts to bring Christianity to the Saxons and other Germanic peoples.

Meanwhile, iconoclastic purges had been discrediting Constantinople in the eyes of Rome, and then, in 751 CE, the Lombards finally took Ravenna, which had held out as a shrinking Byzantine enclave till now. Seeing his opportunity, Pope Stephen II produced *The Donation of Constantine*, a forged document supposedly written by Constantine, giving the pope jurisdiction over the Western Roman Empire in return for baptizing him and curing him of leprosy. In 754 CE, Stephen crossed the Alps to give his blessing to Pepin, Charles Martel's son, as rightful protector of the church. He showed him the document and invited him to Italy. In 756 CE, Pepin defeated the Lombards, handing over Ravenna to Rome and creating a belt of papal states from coast to coast.

The conquests of Charles Martel and Pepin culminated in those of Pepin's son Charlemagne. He pushed east to the lower Danube, north to Denmark, and south to Spain, creating *marches*, or buffer zones, on his borders. He crushed and forcibly converted the troublesome Saxons, broke Lombard power once and for all in northern Italy, and guaranteed the security of the papal states.

St. Peter bestows spiritual authority on Pope Leo III and secular authority on Charlemagne, seemingly in equal measure. In practice, Leo was desperate to assert his authority over Charlemagne, whom he knew held greater power. From the Lateran Palace, Rome, ca. 800 CE.

CHARLEMAGNE

On Christmas Day, 800 CE, Pope Leo III (796–816 CE) crowned Charlemagne Emperor of the Romans, quickly slapping the crown on his head before Charlemagne did it himself, to clarify who was in charge. Charlemagne was furious because he hardly needed Leo. He had riches plundered from the Avars, Saxons, and other subjugated peoples, a centralized administration, and his own vision for a Christian empire.

THE EMPIRE OF CHARLEMAGNE *by 814 CE*

After the fall of Rome in 476 CE, the Franks became the new power in the north, soon adopting Roman Catholic Christianity. In 734 CE, Charles Martel halted the Arab advance near Tours and, in 754 CE, the pope sought protection from Charles Martel's son Pepin against the Lombards. In 800 CE, Pepin's son Charlemagne was crowned emperor of a new Christian Rome.

The lands he ruled were organized into around 600 counties, run by centrally appointed counts. Counties in the marches received a special type of "march count," or *marquis*, who was allowed to mobilize forces against border raids without waiting for Charlemagne's go-ahead. The *missi dominici*, pairs of inspectors, one secular, one ecclesiastical, made annual tours of the counties and reported back to Charlemagne at Aachen.

But Charlemagne was only too conscious of an existing Christian empire in Europe, one that laid claim to be the true heir to the Roman Empire. He needed to distinguish his own empire from Constantinople and cast it as more legitimate. So through the conduit of the numerous monasteries that dotted his realm, he began to cultivate a common Catholic culture indebted to classical Rome.

He borrowed from Roman architecture in the design of churches and palaces such as his main palace at Aachen. Mindful of the Byzantine ban on icon painting currently in force, he promoted representational Christian art through frescoes, the first Christian sculpture, and above all the production of illuminated manuscripts containing realistic depictions of Bible stories.

This touched Charlemagne's foremost concern: education. Low rates of literacy plus a fragmentation of Latin into regional dialects in the centuries following the fall of Rome created problems both for the spread of church teaching and the administration of an empire. Medieval Latin needed to be standardized into a common language for western Europe.

So to Aachen Charlemagne brought scholars from across western Europe. He funded the copying of all surviving Latin texts and the development of monasteries as centers of learning. The driving intellectual force behind Charlemagne's program was Alcuin of York, adviser at Charlemagne's court, then abbot at the monastery of Tours, which he made the foremost training ground for the clergy. Abbey schools such as Tours were not oases of contemplation but engines disseminating Christian learning to the reaches of the empire, and with this came a newly uniform Latin as *lingua franca* for Europe's educated classes, together with a new and quicker way of writing it down using lowercase letters—the way the words are printed in this book.

Charlemagne himself practiced his handwriting in a notebook kept under his pillow, but he began learning to read and write too late in life to make much progress. What he did achieve was a first revival of classical learning and a moment to look back on when a shared culture spanned much of western Europe.

THE GERMAN PRINCES AND THE POPE

Despite Charlemagne, however, Franks east and west of the Rhine had been diverging for centuries, Germanic dialects persisting on the eastern side, fusions of these dialects and Latin evolving into French across the river. As the 9th century CE wore on, the empire split and two distinct peoples emerged.

In 919 CE, the Eastern Franks chose Henry Fowler, Duke of Saxony, to be their king and to organize their defense against Magyar raiders from the Hungarian plains. Henry was succeeded by his son Otto I (936–972 CE), who was helped in 938 CE by the discovery in Saxony of Europe's main source of silver for the next 200 years. In 955 CE, Otto finished off the Magyars and went on to rebuild the eastern part of Charlemagne's empire, including safeguarding the papal states.

In 962 CE, he was crowned emperor by Pope John XII in Charlemagne's palace at Aachen. Unlike Charlemagne, Otto politely accepted the pope's favor as his position was less assured than Charlemagne's had been. The Germans traditionally elected their king, but Otto had inherited his title and as a result had already faced a noble revolt early in his reign. He could use the church to give him leverage over the German dukes.

By now, the network of churches and monasteries spanning western Europe wielded great economic power, as well as cultural influence. The church's lands had steadily grown as people, especially those without heirs, were encouraged to show penitence by bequeathing property. Otto added to this by handing over lands taken from rebellious dukes and taking back control of churches built on noble land. As he himself appointed bishops, abbots, and estate managers, church lands and the taxes they raised became an arm of his imperial government.

Together, emperor and church could keep the nobles in their place, but only if the pope cooperated. Twice, Otto had to remove a difficult pope and install his own man to keep things running smoothly. This tension between emperor and pope would prevent the Holy Roman Empire from ever becoming the coherent commonwealth of Charlemagne, to which it aspired.

In January 1077 CE, Henry IV, having been excommunicated and stripped of his right to rule by Pope Gregory VII, asks Matilda, Countess of Tuscany, to intercede on his behalf at the fortress of Canossa in northern Italy, where she has given Gregory refuge. The pope's power is confirmed.

THE POWER OF THE POPE

Church reformers became increasingly unhappy at being used to serve the interests of secular power, and in 1059 they set up a college of cardinals to elect popes without secular interference.

Pope Gregory VII (1073–1085) took things further. He made celibacy compulsory for the clergy, distancing them from society and bringing them under closer control from Rome. He also cracked down on *simony*, the buying and selling of jobs in the church. Most important, he restricted the right to appoint clergy to the pope.

This last restriction meant the emperor stood to lose control of up to half the lands in his empire. The inevitable fight between emperor and pope came to a head in January 1076 when Henry IV (1056–1105) tried to depose Gregory, who then excommunicated him, removing his right to rule the empire. In fact, this was a bluff Gregory was unsure would work, but the following January Henry stood barefoot in the snow for three days outside Gregory's window begging him to reconsider.

This was proof the pope now held the conscience of western Europe in his hands and over the next century he demonstrated this through the Crusades. But his power relied on moral authority and could easily be lost.

THE HOLY ROMAN EMPIRE OF THE GERMANS *from 962 CE*

After Eastern and Western Franks divided, the empire was refounded east of the Rhine by Otto of Saxony, who crushed Magyar invaders and was crowned emperor by the pope in 962 CE. Centuries of unease between pope and emperor followed, however, weakening both.

The pope kept control of the emperor and other kings with two powerful threats: excommunication, and the imposition of an interdict, whereby priests could not perform mass, marry people, or bury the dead. These were threats liable to hurt ordinary people, already becoming alienated from a celibate and ever wealthier clergy. Grassroots religious movements began to spring up and when the pope clamped down on them, he only lost more popular support.

By the reign of Frederick II (1220–1250), the idea of a Christian empire had been seriously damaged. Frederick had little interest in either church or empire. He inherited Sicily from his mother and spent his life there enjoying a cultivated lifestyle his German lands could not offer, due largely to Arab influence—Frederick spoke Arabic plus five other languages. A Sixth Crusade he promised the Pope turned into a bloodless negotiation for the return of Jerusalem. Excommunicated several times, Frederick responded by denouncing the papacy and inviting Europe's rulers to plunder its wealth for its own moral good.

Would-be papal protectors began to vie with one another. Popes switching between French and German strongmen led to a papal kidnapping in 1303, followed by the French moving the papacy to Avignon and, after 1378, by two popes, one at Avignon, one at Rome. After 1417 there was once more a single pope at Rome, but he was no longer the voice of Western Christendom, able to sanction legitimate rule from Rome to the North Sea. He had lost his authority and without that the power of the empire was illusory. The wealthy towns of northern Italy broke away and the emperor's hold over the German princes became little more than a façade.

In the centuries that followed, the title of Holy Roman Emperor would fall to the Habsburgs, Europe's most powerful family. But they would draw their power from outside the Holy Roman Empire, from lands held across Europe and beyond. As titular defenders of the church, they would feel obliged to play a leading part in the religious wars that tore Europe apart for a century following the Reformation, which itself began from one of the German principalities. But any substance to the idea that this represented reasserting control over an empire had long since vanished.

The Holy Roman Empire lumbered on in name only, until Napoleon finally dissolved it in 1806. Charlemagne had had his moment, but the egos of emperors and popes were too strong for each other. In the west, the marriage of secular and spiritual never succeeded as it did in Constantinople—and in Baghdad.

THE ABBASID CALIPHATE

The expansion of Islam was uniquely sudden. After Constantinople had joined religion to an existing state, Rome tried to attach a state to an existing religious establishment, with less success. Meanwhile, the Arabs had simply sidestepped the need to fit secular to spiritual by developing a faith that was in itself political.

ARABS AND MUHAMMAD

By the time the Sasanians and Byzantines were exhausting each other in war, the marginal tribes to the south had long been known as Arabs. A shared language, Arabic, defined these tribes as Arabs, but they were not a unified people. There were farmers in Yemen, trading communities along the Red Sea, and fiercely partisan nomads in the central desert, each with their own gods.

Lacking the institutions of settled communities, the Bedouin desert tribes were held together by ties of honor and family. They were also the purest speakers of Arabic and brought poetry to a zenith in the 6th and 7th centuries CE. The poets, however, used their art to eulogize their own tribe and denigrate others, so Arabic, the potential unifier, only served to sharpen tribal rivalry.

Zoroastrian, Jewish, and Christian monotheistic ideas filtered through to the Arabs from the desert caravans and the Red Sea, especially to wealthy market towns such as Mecca. Among the merchants of Mecca, new religious ideas combined with a growing belief that war between the Persian and Byzantine superpowers was about to bring the known world to an end.

One such merchant was Muhammad. After the age of 40, around 610 CE, he began to have visions in which the Archangel Gabriel spoke to him. At first he only told his wife, but around 613 CE he began publicizing his revelations, speaking in short bursts of highly poetic prose dictated to him by God. His followers wrote down his words to form the *Qur'an*, or "recitation."

Muhammad's message was simple. There was one God, Allah, who stood behind all others. He was the same compassionate, all-powerful God that Christians, for example, had obscured with embellishments such as the Trinity. All he asked was that people set aside their other cults and submit to him (*Islam*—"submission"). They need only pray, kneeling in the direction of Jerusalem, like Jews and Orthodox Christians.

This was not warmly received in Mecca, where there was money to be made from the cult of the Black Stone of the Ka'bah, which Muhammad's own clan controlled. The oasis of Medina, northeast of Mecca, was more receptive. Here, tribal conflict led to Muhammad being invited as a peacemaker in 622 CE.

In Medina, Muhammad's message took on a political focus. He combined his teachings with Bedouin concepts of honor and brotherhood to create a new tribe of all *Muslims* ("those who submit") that anyone could join. It drew members of weaker tribes, then others, and observed laws based on Muhammad's religious revelations (the beginnings of *Shari'ah*), which sought to overcome tribal blood-feuding.

With his new Muslim tribe, Muhammad stormed Mecca in 630 CE, showing magnanimity to the defeated Meccans, almost all of whom now joined him. He cleared the Ka'bah of the many idols that surrounded it and made it a pilgrimage site for Muslims. From here he took his movement throughout Arabia.

AN ARAB EMPIRE

Muhammad created a wider Arab community built on a handful of devotional practices: prayer, fasting, pilgrimage, and giving to charity. Its simplicity was universal but its structure was still tribal. When he died in 632 CE, there was the inevitable withering of a movement built on personal charisma, but a devoted core saw the chance to reassert a pan-Arab tribal identity against outsiders.

Abu Bakr (632–634 CE), Muhammad's father-in-law and *Caliph* ("successor"), began by reunifying the Arabs through forced conversion. He then started to move beyond Arabia, but died soon after, leaving the task to Umar (634–644 CE). Under Umar, Islam exploded across the Middle East, Iran, and North Africa at the expense of the far more advanced Sasanian and Byzantine empires. They were exhausted and the Arabs were fired up, but the Arabs also met little resistance from local people.

The Muslim armies were not out to convert. They sought booty plus a tax payable by all non-Muslims. Locals regarded them as just this year's raiders, often more lenient than their present overlords. They kept their heads down and waited for them to leave. But the Arabs neither left nor integrated. Umar built garrison towns for his soldiers and forbade them to settle on the land, source of the taxes that supported them. So they became a separate urban class.

Inequalities in soldiers' pay led to a leadership battle after the death of Umar's successor Uthman in 656 CE. Muhammad's cousin and son-in-law Ali became caliph, his supporters saying he should have been Muhammad's successor from the start. This gave rise to Shi'ah Islam, stressing divinely appointed leadership in contrast to mainstream Sunni Islam.

In 661 CE, however, the Sunnis regained power with the Umayyad dynasty, under which Islam began to spread beyond the Arabs. In Egypt, Arab soldiers took up with local women and farther along North Africa, Berber prisoners converted and joined the Muslim armies. The Berbers were desert people like the Bedouin: hard to subdue but sharing a natural affinity—which the prospect of booty enhanced.

The tribal militarism of early Islam was beginning to outlive its usefulness, however. As Muslim communities formed, so merchants, bureaucrats, and *ulema* (interpreters of Shari'ah law) became just as important as soldiers. Abd al-Malik (685–705 CE) minted a Muslim currency and established Arabic as an administrative language for all job seekers to learn (outside Iran). A series of conquests won by Muslim armies was becoming an empire. Looking at Constantinople, al-Malik and his son al-Walid I (705–715 CE) realized an empire needed something more than a holy book to take pride in: it needed architecture. So they began to build mosques.

Following pages: main map:

THE ABBASID CALIPHATE AT ITS GREATEST EXTENT *ca. 850 CE*

Arab armies moved north to claim the Sasanian Empire soon after Muhammad's death. By 750 CE, the Umayyad Caliphate stretched from Central Asia to the Atlantic, but lacked unity and provoked rebellion. The Abbasids added little territory but created an inclusive Islamic empire.

Inset map:

THE LATER CALIPHATE TO 1258

A breakdown of central authority in the 10th century led to a series of military tribes working alongside Abbasid administrators to preserve the caliphate. Most notable was a partnership with the Seljuk Turks.

By the 740s CE, the Umayyad Caliphate stretched from Spain to Central Asia, but its original, tight identity had been lost. Revenue had declined both as people converted to Islam and became tax-exempt and as Arabs settled outside the cities. Accordingly, tax was levied on land itself rather than on non-Muslims, but this meant Arabs were no longer a people apart. New social divisions were forming and feeding into old tribal rivalries. The stage was set for a takeover.

AN ISLAMIC EMPIRE

As descendants of Muhammad's uncle, al-Abbas, the Abbasids claimed to have greater legitimacy to rule than the Umayyads. They also capitalized on changing times, siding with Shi'ah opposition to Sunni Umayyad rule as well as with two other disaffected groups from Khorasan, the eastern portion of the old Persian Empire: indigenous converts and non-Bedouin Arab settlers. After revolts in Khorasan, the Abbasids took power in 750 CE, some of the Umayyads fleeing to set up a breakaway state in Spain.

The Abbasids now abandoned their Shi'ah supporters but not their wider constituency. Under the Abbasids, the caliphate matured as a potentially universal empire drawing on Islam and Arabic rather than Arab tribalism headed by the Bedouin.

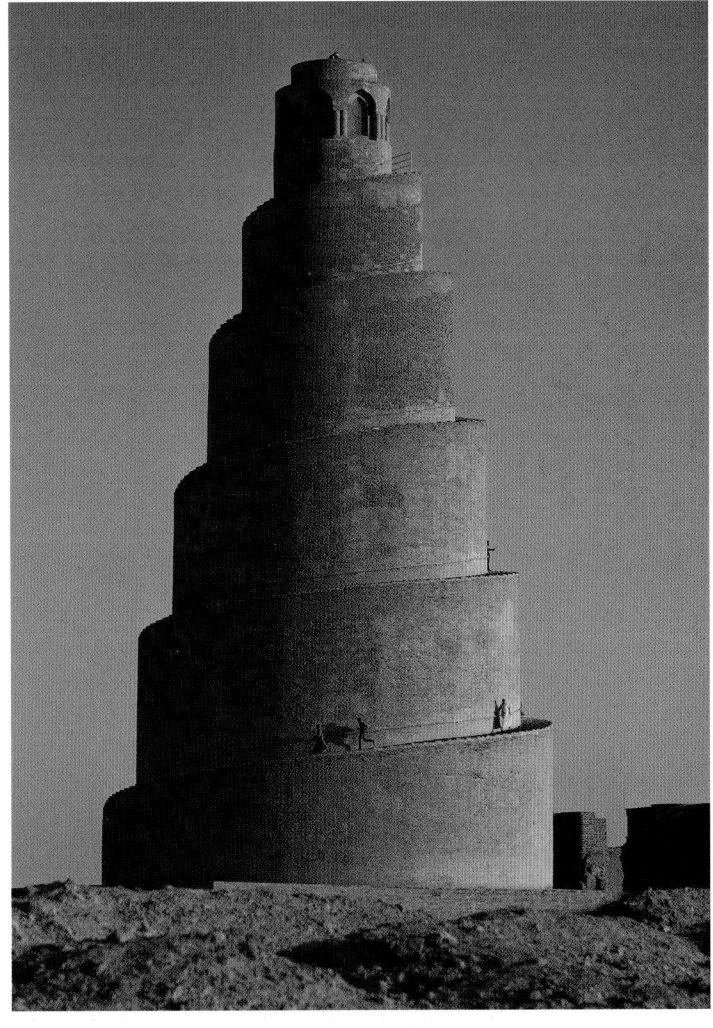

The Great Mosque at Samarra, built between 848 and 851 CE after the caliphs had temporarily relocated from Baghdad. For a long time the world's largest mosque, its design reflected a fascination with mathematics and engineering encouraged by the Abbasids.

The Abbasids moved the capital east from Damascus to Baghdad and built a circular city, with roads radiating out to all points of the caliphate. With the move east came a more formal Persian-style court. Tiers of officials now stood between the caliph and his people. A *vizier* ("advisor") functioned as head of government, with the caliph removed to a more ceremonial role as head of state—a family of Persian nobles, the Barmakids, held the post of vizier for generations. A harem developed and, in time, became a powerful female court standing alongside the male court—twin hierarchies brought together in the person of the caliph.

In 751 CE, the spread of Islam met the spread of Tang China at a battle in Central Asia at which Chinese papermakers were captured by the Abbasids. Within the caliphate, paper quickly replaced more expensive papyrus and parchment, creating a publishing industry in which writers and booksellers could make money. Poets such as Abu Nuwas would go to Basra, the great market on the edge of the desert, to learn their craft. Here the Bedouin came to trade. They were still the guardians of Arabic and knew all the pre-Islamic poetry together

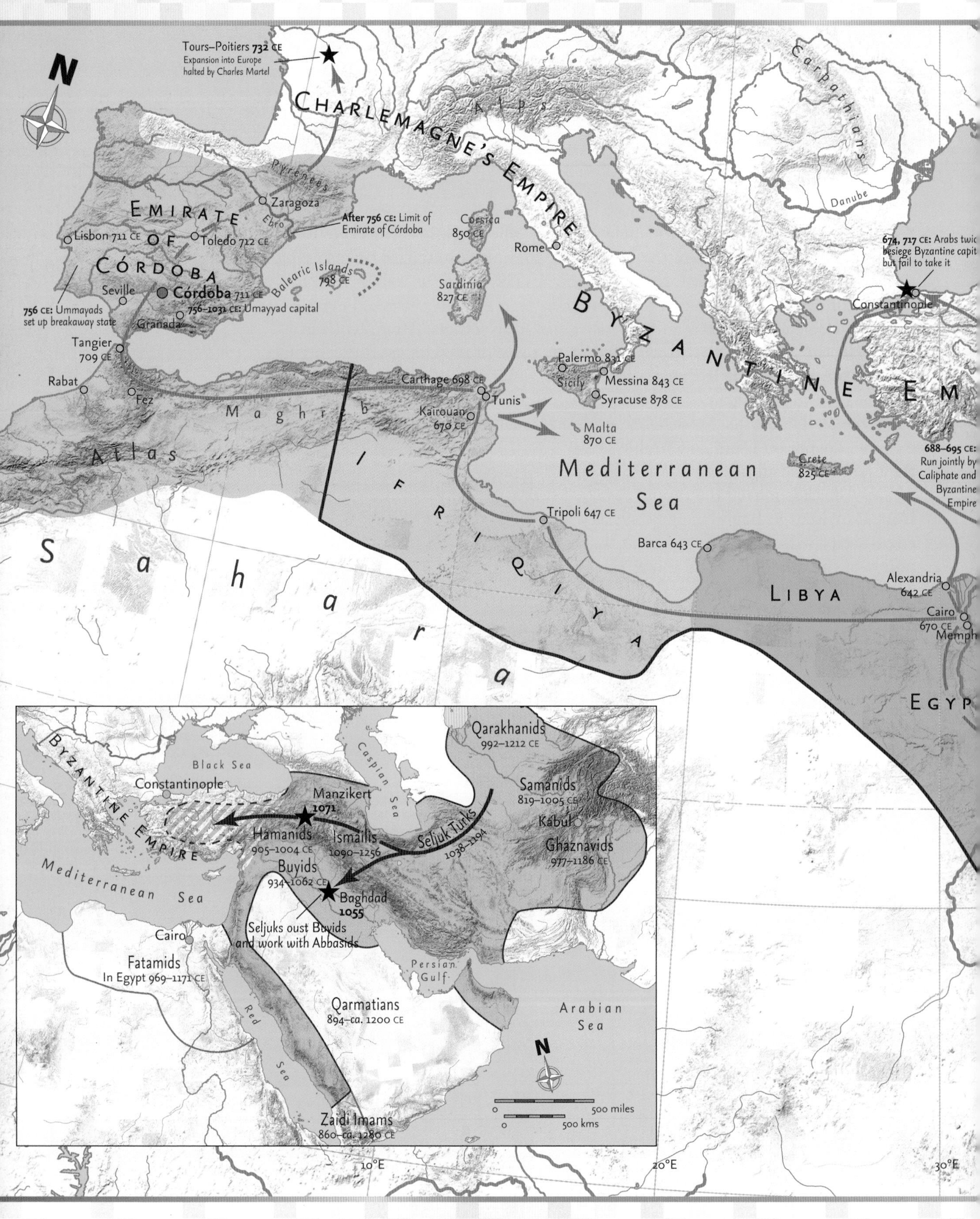

N
Tours–Poitiers 732 CE
Expansion into Europe halted by Charles Martel
Charlemagne's Empire
Alps
Carpathians
Danube
Pyrenees
Zaragoza
Ebro
After 756 CE: Limit of Emirate of Córdoba
Emirate of Córdoba
Lisbon 711 CE
Toledo 712 CE
Corsica 850 CE
Rome
674, 717 CE: Arabs twic besiege Byzantine capit but fail to take it
Balearic Islands 798 CE
Seville
Córdoba 711 CE
756–1031 CE: Umayyad capital
756 CE: Ummayads set up breakaway state
Granada
Sardinia 827 CE
Byzantine Em
Constantinople
Tangier 709 CE
Rabat
Fez
Maghreb
Atlas
Carthage 698 CE
Tunis
Kairouan 670 CE
Palermo 831 CE
Sicily
Messina 843 CE
Syracuse 878 CE
Malta 870 CE
688–695 CE: Run jointly by Caliphate and Byzantine Empire
Crete 825 CE
Mediterranean Sea
Ifriqiya
Tripoli 647 CE
Barca 643 CE
Sahara
Alexandria 642 CE
Libya
Cairo 670 CE
Memph
Egyp
Byzantine Empire
Black Sea
Constantinople
Caspian Sea
Qarakhanids 992–1212 CE
Samanids 819–1005 CE
Manzikert 1071
Kabul
Hamanids 905–1004 CE
Ismailis 1090–1256
Seljuk Turks 1038–1194
Ghaznavids 977–1186 CE
Buyids 934–1062 CE
Baghdad 1055
Mediterranean Sea
Seljuks oust Buyids and work with Abbasids
Cairo
Fatamids In Egypt 969–1171 CE
Persian Gulf
Qarmatians 894–ca. 1200 CE
Arabian Sea
Red Sea
N
500 miles
500 kms
Zaidi Imams 860–ca. 1280 CE
10°E
20°E
30°E

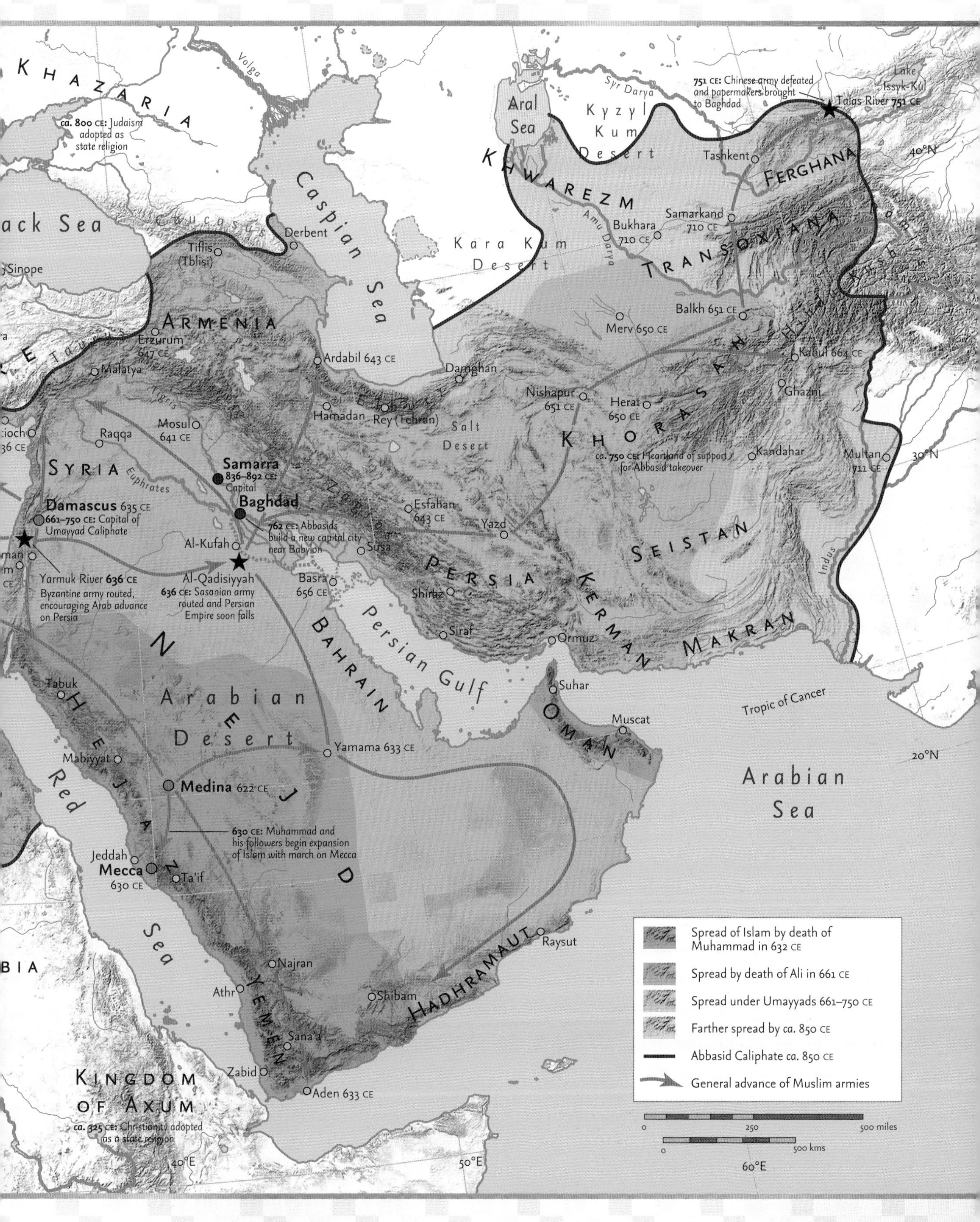

KHAZARIA
ca. 800 CE: Judaism adopted as state religion
Volga
Aral Sea
Syr Darya
Kyzyl Kum Desert
751 CE: Chinese army defeated and papermakers brought to Baghdad
Lake Issyk-Kul
Talas River 751 CE
Tashkent
FERGHANA
KHWAREZM
Caspian Sea
Black Sea
Caucasus
Derbent
Tiflis (Tblisi)
Sinope
Amu Darya
Bukhara 710 CE
Samarkand 710 CE
TRANSOXIANA
Kara Kum Desert
ARMENIA
Erzurum 647 CE
Taurus
Malatya
Ardabil 643 CE
Damghan
Balkh 651 CE
Merv 650 CE
Kabul 664 CE
Ghazni
Nishapur 651 CE
Herat 650 CE
KHORASAN
Hamadan
Rey (Tehran)
Salt Desert
Tigris
Mosul 641 CE
Raqqa
SYRIA
Euphrates
Samarra
836–892 CE: Capital
Baghdad
762 CE: Abbasids build a new capital city near Babylon
Damascus 635 CE
661–750 CE: Capital of Umayyad Caliphate
ca. 750 CE: Heartland of support for Abbasid takeover
Kandahar
Multan 711 CE
Zagros
Esfahan 643 CE
Yazd
Susa
Al-Kufah
Al-Qadisiyyah
636 CE: Sasanian army routed and Persian Empire soon falls
Yarmuk River 636 CE
Byzantine army routed, encouraging Arab advance on Persia
SEISTAN
Indus
PERSIA
KERMAN
Basra 656 CE
Shiraz
Siraf
Ormuz
MAKRAN
Persian Gulf
BAHRAIN
NEJD
Arabian Desert
Suhar
OMAN
Muscat
Tropic of Cancer
Tabuk
HEJAZ
Yamama 633 CE
Mabiyyat
Medina 622 CE
630 CE: Muhammad and his followers begin expansion of Islam with march on Mecca
Jeddah
Mecca 630 CE
Ta'if
Red Sea
Arabian Sea
Raysut
HADHRAMAUT
Najran
Athr
Shibam
YEMEN
Sana'a
Zabid
Aden 633 CE
KINGDOM OF AXUM
ca. 325 CE: Christianity adopted as a state religion
40°N
30°N
20°N
40°E
50°E
60°E
Spread of Islam by death of Muhammad in 632 CE
Spread by death of Ali in 661 CE
Spread under Umayyads 661–750 CE
Farther spread by ca. 850 CE
Abbasid Caliphate ca. 850 CE
General advance of Muslim armies
0 250 500 miles
0 500 kms

with obscure words and idioms. Paper and the growth of literacy brought this richness of language to a newly receptive multicultural society.

Paper also fed the growth of scientific and philosophical learning by kick-starting a large manuscript-copying program. Jewish scholars translated Aristotle into Arabic, as well as countless other Greek texts on mathematics, astronomy, mechanics, and medicine. Indian mathematicians brought a new decimal counting system—the system we use today. The Abbasids collected all this and built on it. Combining Greek geometry and Indian arithmetic, they produced algebra. Mechanical innovation produced pumps, water clocks, and automata. The first medically staffed hospitals were built in Baghdad.

A golden age of Abbasid culture peaked under Harun al-Rashid (786–809 CE), contemporary of Charlemagne, with whom he corresponded, and caliph of *One Thousand and One Nights*—a weaving of Indian and Persian stories into legends surrounding real people such as al-Rashid, Abu Nuwas (his favorite poet), and Ja'far ibn Yayha (his Barmakid vizier), all given expression through Arabic.

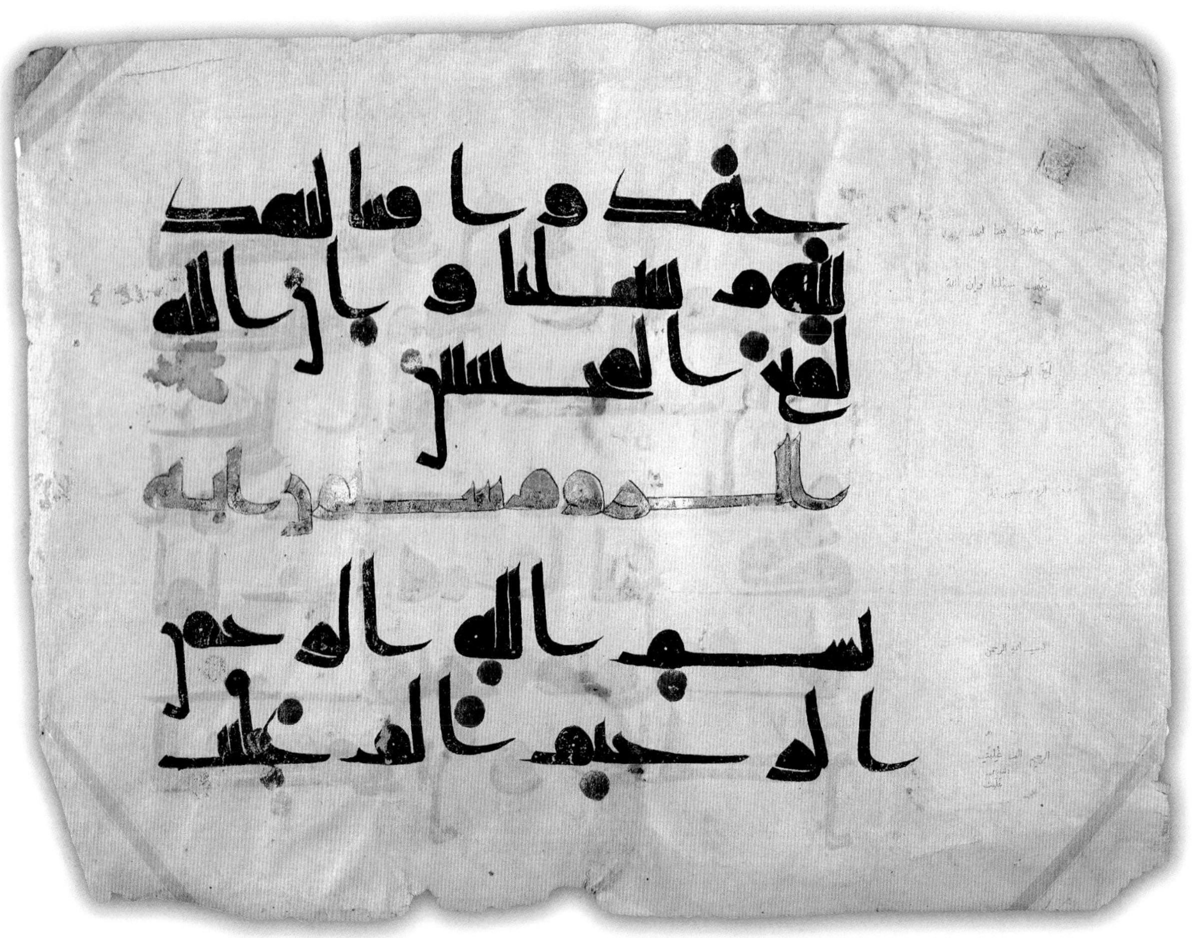

A page from a 9th-century CE Qur'an written in Kufic script, the lettering first used to record Muhammad's words. Arabic's connection with Islam plus a ban on representational images made Arabic calligraphy an art form worthy to copy out the Qur'an as well as to decorate buildings and carpets.

THE LAW AND THE SWORD

When Harun al-Rashid died, his sons, the pro-Arab al-Amin and the pro-Persian al-Mamum, fought for the caliphate. Al-Mamun (813–833 CE) won and continued making Baghdad a cosmopolitan capital of learning. But civil war had devastated the city and the postwar caliphs were obsessed with security, so they tried to recruit soldiers from outside the caliphate, unconnected to internal factions. To begin with, Turk prisoners of war were chosen to form the caliph's personal bodyguard. These were the *ghilman*. But in the 860s CE they murdered four caliphs.

So the *mamluk* system was brought in, whereby Turks and Circassians were taken as children and brought up to be Muslim soldiers loyal to the caliph. After riots in Baghdad against the ghilman, however, the caliphs had moved to a specially built administrative center at Samarra. Here, in relative isolation, they gradually became hostage to their mamluks and their grip on the caliphate loosened.

The caliphs' waning power allowed a succession of revolutionary movements to gain ground, the most dangerous being the Ismailis, a radical Shi'ah sect. They destabilized the caliphate to such an extent that by the 940s CE the western half had all but gone and central control over Mesopotamia and Iran was breaking up.

In response, the Buyids, warlords from the Caspian, arrived in Baghdad in 945 CE to restore order in the name of the caliph. In 1055, they were ousted by the Seljuks, Muslim Turks from the northeast, who took over the role of the caliph's protector and also ruled in his name.

This was not simply a story of power lost to newcomers. The mamluks, the Buyids, and the Seljuks were all seduced by Islam and accepted the need for Abbasid administrators. The caliphate became a partnership between the "men of the law" and the "men of the sword," each needing the other.

The Abbasid Caliphate carried on in this fashion until 1258 when Baghdad was razed by the Mongols and the last caliph was rolled up in a carpet (to avoid spilling his royal blood) and trampled to death. But like Rome and so many other empires, the caliphate lived on as an idea—the idea of an Islamic empire able to transcend regional identities through appeal to a simple set of beliefs.

What had made the Abbasid Caliphate a model to aspire to, however, was not simplicity, but complexity and fusion. Its hallmark was inclusiveness and receptivity to all manner of ideas. By the time the Mongols arrived, many of these ideas had begun to filter into Europe, preparing the ground for Europe's own intellectual flowering.

4 EMPIRES OF THE HORSE

The Mongols / Chinese Empires / Muslim India / The Ottoman Empire

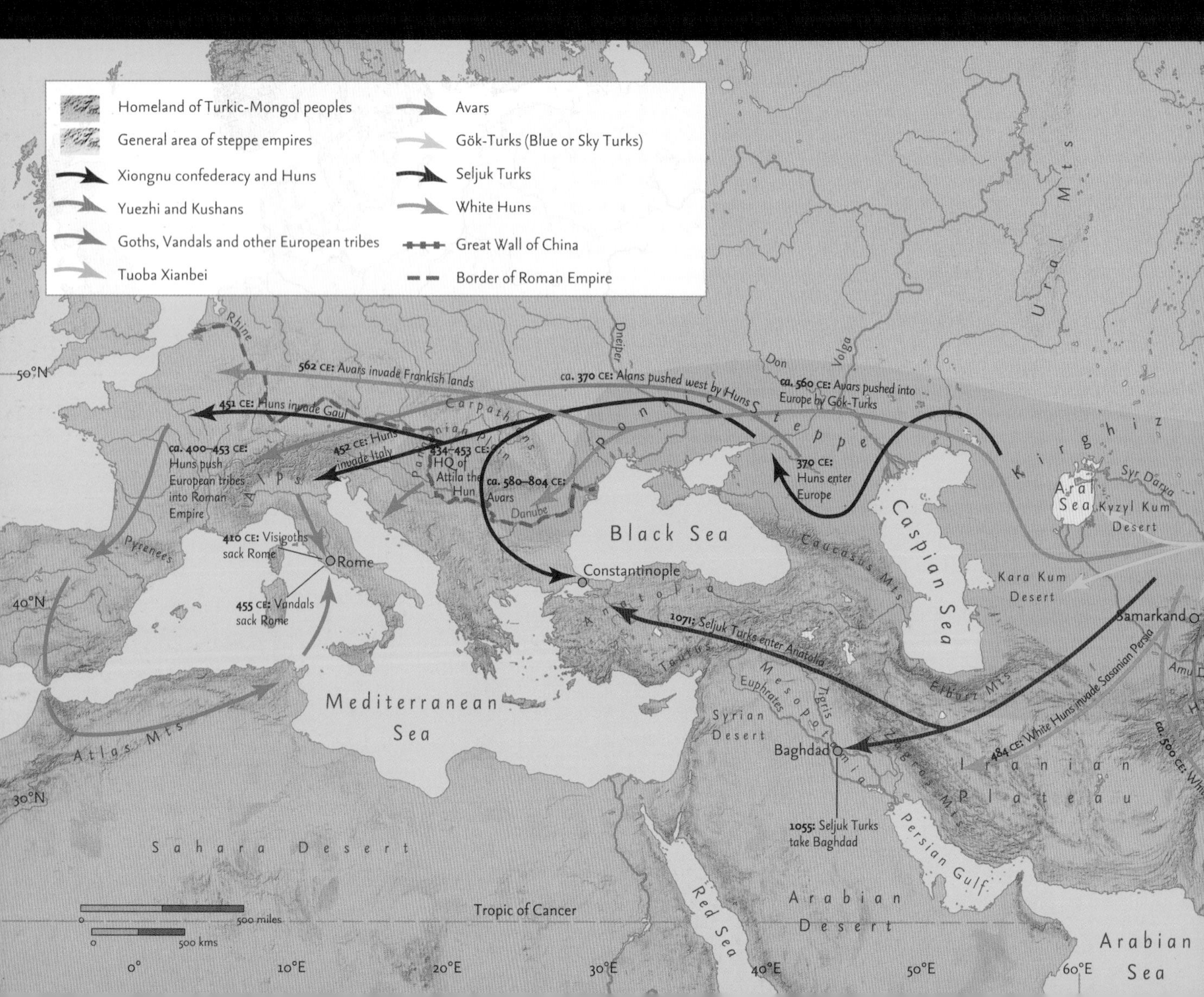

Homeland of Turkic-Mongol peoples
General area of steppe empires
Xiongnu confederacy and Huns
Yuezhi and Kushans
Goths, Vandals and other European tribes
Tuoba Xianbei
Avars
Gök-Turks (Blue or Sky Turks)
Seljuk Turks
White Huns
Great Wall of China
Border of Roman Empire
562 CE: Avars invade Frankish lands
ca. 370 CE: Alans pushed west by Huns
ca. 560 CE: Avars pushed into Europe by Gök-Turks
451 CE: Huns invade Gaul
452 CE: Huns invade Italy
434–453 CE: HQ of Attila the Hun
ca. 400–453 CE: Huns push European tribes into Roman Empire
ca. 580–804 CE: Avars
370 CE: Huns enter Europe
410 CE: Visigoths sack Rome
455 CE: Vandals sack Rome
1071: Seljuk Turks enter Anatolia
484 CE: White Huns invade Sasanian Persia
1055: Seljuk Turks take Baghdad
Rome
Constantinople
Baghdad
Samarkand
Black Sea
Caspian Sea
Aral Sea
Mediterranean Sea
Red Sea
Persian Gulf
Arabian Sea
Arabian Desert
Syrian Desert
Sahara Desert
Kyzyl Kum Desert
Kara Kum Desert
Iranian Plateau
Pontic Steppe
Kirghiz Steppe
Ural Mts
Caucasus Mts
Elburz Mts
Zagros Mts
Taurus
Atlas Mts
Alps
Pyrenees
Carpathians
Pannonian plain
Anatolia
Mesopotamia
Rhine
Dnieper
Don
Volga
Danube
Euphrates
Tigris
Syr Darya
Amu Darya
Tropic of Cancer
50°N
40°N
30°N
0°
10°E
20°E
30°E
40°E
50°E
60°E
500 miles
500 kms

The early city-states of Eurasia all emerged from settled farming societies. Farming requires careful planning to produce a food surplus able to support the soldiers, administrators, and other professionals upon which states depend.

For millennia, the great fear was that all this effort might be swept away at any moment by famine or by riders from the vast Eurasian steppe. Warring farming states could murder, burn, and enslave, but nomads might destroy a whole way of life. There was nothing to stop them from wiping out what they neither needed nor understood.

Lacking boundaries, the steppe riders were a dynamic force. They kept moving to find new pastures for their herds so they were constantly bumping into each other and skirmishing over the best grasslands. Fighting and raiding sat at the heart of their lifestyle, which the horse spread over thousands of miles.

The horse made light work of invading Eurasia's agricultural civilizations but building empires was another matter. The steppe riders faced the usual tribal problem of creating a larger community. They also faced the dilemma of what to do with the societies they conquered. If they destroyed they gained little. If they bent themselves to an alien way of life they stood to lose their identity.

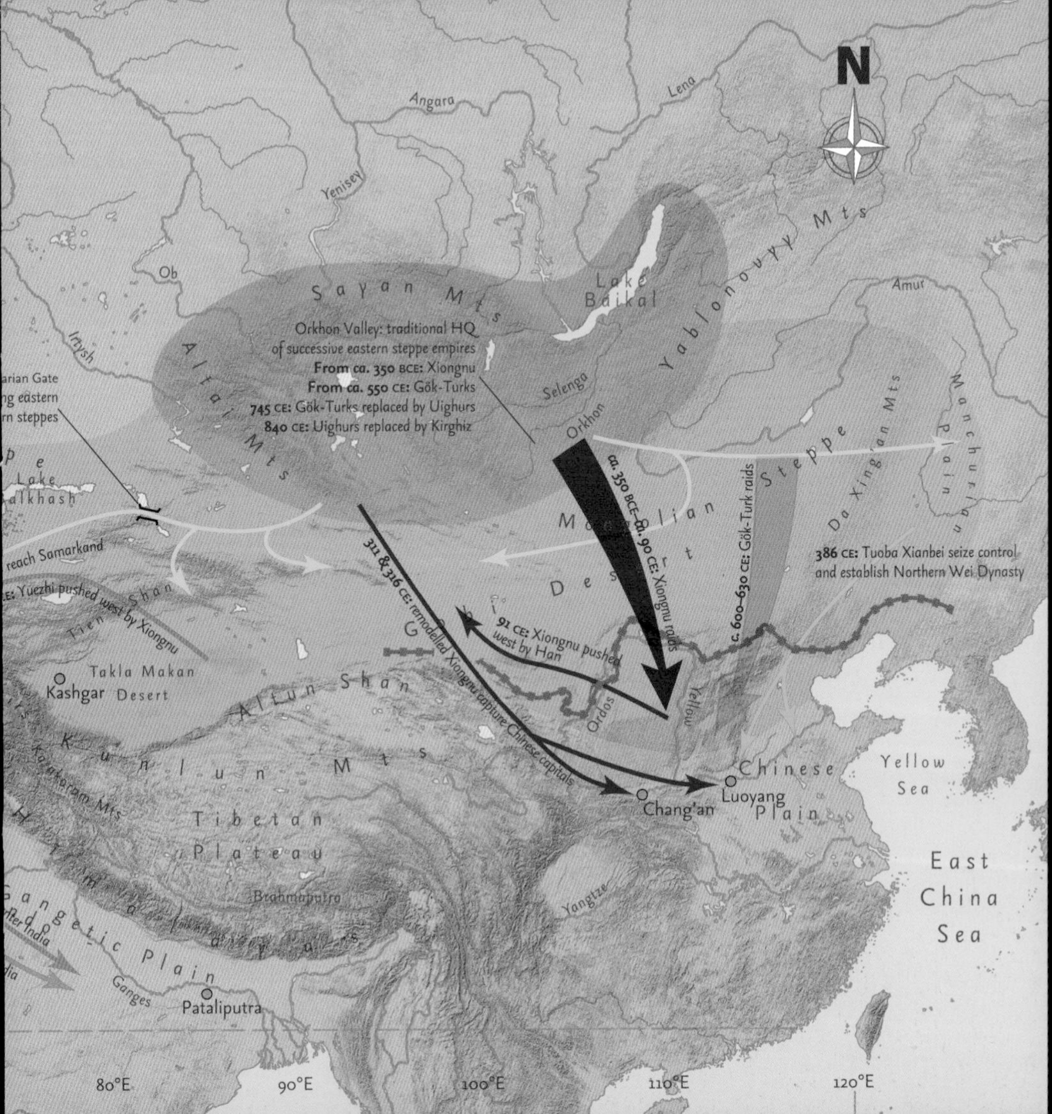

THE EURASIAN STEPPE FROM THE CLASSICAL AGE TO THE COMING OF THE MONGOLS.

Rome, Han China, Gupta India, and Sasanian Persia all suffered attacks by the Xiongnu, Huns, and White Huns, with only Persia managing to survive. Afterwards, the Gök-Turks and others rose and then splintered, while Islam reached the steppe to produce militant Muslim tribes such as the Seljuks.

THE MONGOLS

The Mongols were the last of the great raiders of the Eurasian steppe, successors to the Sakas (or Scythians), the Xiongnu, the Huns, and the various Turkic confederations of the medieval world. After the Mongols, the power of the horse began to give way to gunpowder, but while they lasted the Mongols managed to overcome the tribalism that had dogged previous steppe empires and link the regions of Eurasia as never before.

TEMÜJIN

Around the time of the Crusades, the area to the south of Lake Baikal in Siberia was home to the Mongols, one of five nomadic tribes played off against each other by the Jin Dynasty of northern China. The main enemies of the Mongols were the Tatars and the Merkits. The two other tribes were the Kereits and the Naimans.

In 1162, a son, Temüjin, was born to the leader of the Mongols. When Temüjin was eight or nine his father was poisoned by the Tatars, leaving mother and children to fend for themselves on the steppe. The experience bred in Temüjin a thirst for restitution.

While his father lived, a girl named Börte had been promised to Temüjin as a wife. Temüjin's mother was a Merkit whom his father had kidnapped, so when Börte came of age, the Merkits kidnapped her in return. But Temüjin did not give chase. He waited.

On the steppe, special friendships were sealed by exchange of blood, creating a bond of trust often stronger than family. Temüjin asked for help from his father's blood brother Toghril, leader of the Kereits, and from Jamukha, his own Mongol blood brother, whose family had abandoned him as a child. Toghril and Jamukha each drummed up a force of 10,000 men. Temüjin himself assembled a smaller band—mostly shepherds who were not part of any tribe.

Together they defeated the Merkits, freed their slaves, and won Börte back. Normally, booty would have been taken by the most powerful warriors, but Temüjin shared it out among all, including shepherds and freed slaves. These outsiders from the tribal system now became loyal to him.

But now Temüjin's egalitarian outfit began to tempt Jamukha's followers to defect, driving a wedge between the two that ended in war. Jamukha prevailed but would not press his victory by killing his blood brother. So defections continued.

Presently, Jin China took notice of Temüjin. The Jin had helped the Tatars maintain order on the steppe but subsequently watched with disquiet as Tatar power grew. So in 1196, they backed Temüjin and Toghril to stamp out the Tatar threat.

With the Merkits and Tatars gone, Temüjin became a danger to Toghril himself, who now joined Jamukha and drove Temüjin out of the area. During a three-day feast, however, Temüjin returned to ambush Toghril and the Kereits while they were drunk. Toghril fled and his tribe joined Temüjin.

This left only the Naiman, whom Temüjin drove over a cliff in 1204 after building extra campfires and putting dummies on horseback to suggest a far greater force than he truly possessed.

The following year he captured Jamukha and asked him to join him. But Jamukha could not live with the shame of defeat. He appealed as a blood brother to be accorded the dignity of being killed and Temüjin could not refuse.

The only person on the eastern steppe still above Temüjin was Teb Tengri, the shaman. At a *kurultai*, or assembly, in 1206, he declared Temüjin *Genghis Khan* ("Fierce/Supreme Ruler"), by order of the sky-god Tengri. But when Teb Tengri beat Temüjin's son in public, Temüjin killed him and appointed his own shaman. Now his power was absolute.

Over the next decade, Genghis Khan took control of all the Eurasian steppe and invaded Jin China. China was a traditional target for steppe raiders; it had good pastures on its northern borders and, as an agricultural society, it had food stores and other accumulated wealth—plus experts in explosives and siege warfare.

At some point, though, it seems Genghis Khan moved beyond the idea of sporadic raiding to that of universal conquest. Invading northern China began a long struggle to take the rest of East Asia. Avenging the execution of his ambassadors in Central Asia in 1218 brought Mongol horsemen into the West. By the time he died, in 1227, Genghis Khan's rule reached from the Caspian to the Pacific.

Chinese porcelain in a Persian painting suggests the reach of Genghis Khan's power, though he holds court in a simple yurt, a tent made of felt and in this case colorful carpets. Outside hang white yak tails signifying an interlude of peace (black tails meant war). From Rashid al-Din's Compendium of Chronicles *ca. 1300.*

GENGHIS KHAN'S SYSTEM

Temüjin faced the same task of overcoming tribal allegiances as Muhammad, but where Muhammad preached spiritual submission, Temüjin promoted the personal loyalty of blood brothers, a loyalty able to transcend family and tribe. He cast himself as blood brother to all his followers and made this tangible by sharing out booty and promoting people on merit. In return, he required total and unquestioning discipline.

To this end, he structured his army in decimal units across which tribes were split up. Where Muhammad had Shari'ah, Temüjin had his *yassa*, a law code laying out this and other principles designed to produce stability, such as freedom of religion and the election of successors by kurultai.

Military discipline was, to an extent, natural on the steppe, where the hunt required riders to form a circle often hundreds of miles across and slowly close in, letting no animal escape and resisting the kill until the leader took his pick. This amounted to military training for all male members of society, stressing discipline, coordination, and communication.

Efficient communication across the steppe was provided by the *yam* system. Steppe custom obliged people to give food to a passing horse and messenger. Temüjin developed this into a network of postal stations supplying food, shelter, and fresh horses, with riders displaying a metal tag to show they were his couriers. Merchants could also use the system, at first for free. Later it became a postal service.

The yam system was fundamental to the web of spies that prepared the ground for successful Mongol campaigns, transmitting both information and disinformation, such as forged letters sent to sow discord and destabilize enemy rulers. This was one of numerous tricks the Mongols used. They would drag branches behind their horses, creating the dust storm of a much larger force, and they would abandon heavy booty, allowing others going the same way to carry it off before ambushing them and taking it back when they reached their destination.

They also used psychological warfare, massacring the entire population of a resisting city so word would spread and prevent resistance elsewhere. Where this happened, the only people to escape were craftsmen, often sent to specialist silk-weaving or metalworking villages in Mongolia, and sometimes religious leaders. Where there was no resistance, the ruler was deposed, a local chosen to collect tribute, and the people left to their own devices.

Genghis Khan's bloodthirsty reputation came from his merciless campaign against the Khwarezm shah after two parties of Mongol envoys were killed in 1218. After three days of deliberation, Temüjin decided he could not afford to let this pass. The issue was not bloodlust per se but the need to maintain authority.

THE MONGOL PEACE

On Genghis Khan's death, his lands were divided among his four sons with Ögedei elected as *khagan* ("ruler of rulers") in 1229. Ögedei finally took Jin China in 1234 with help from the southern Song Dynasty, before turning on them. He built roads across the empire and began replacing a collection of yurts in the Orkhon Valley his father had called Karakorum with a walled city complete with palace, temples, mosques, and a church.

In 1237, Ögedei launched an invasion of Europe under the command of his nephew Batu. This began with a lightning winter gallop up frozen Russian rivers. Kiev and many other cities were wiped out before spring came and the rivers thawed. Then, in 1241, a pincer movement prepared by Mongol spies crushed a pan-European force in Poland and Hungary.

The rest of Europe was only saved by Ögedei's death and Batu's withdrawal to attend the kurultai to elect his successor. A standoff between Batu and the other members led to a decade-long war, during which Batu's conquests began to form the independent Khanate of the Golden Horde.

Eventually, Temüjin's grandson Möngke was elected khagan in 1251 and charged his brother Hülegü with completing the conquest of Iran and the Middle East. Hülegü founded the Il-Khanate to cover this region, took Baghdad in 1258, and pressed on to the Mediterranean. In 1259, however, Möngke died, Hülegü withdrew for the kurultai and, the year after, Egypt, now ruled by a dynasty of mamluks, gave the Mongols their first taste of defeat in Palestine.

Despite the kurultai, another succession war broke out, this time between Arigbökh in Karakorum and Temüjin's grandson Kublai in China. The Golden Horde and the Il-Khanate took sides and the Chagatai Khanate in Central Asia became a pawn in the quarrel. In 1264, Kublai was recognized as khagan, but now there were four khanates, or kingdoms, each going its own way. Kublai, for example, relied heavily on the Chinese civil service and, in the process, became more Chinese himself, especially after finally conquering the Song south in 1279.

Nonetheless, the khanates represented regional differences, not a reversion to tribalism, and in this lay Temüjin's achievement. They continued to form an economic commonwealth, guaranteeing communication across Eurasia and making the Silk Road safe for 100 years.

By the mid-14th century, however, the Mongol peace had become fragile. The Il-Khanate fragmented in 1336, and in 1368 the Mongols were kicked out of China. The Golden Horde broke up into a number of smaller khanates—although it took the Russians centuries to remove these, the last hanging on in the Crimea until 1783.

TIMUR THE LAME

Some 150 years after Genghis Khan, the embers of his empire flared up for a final moment under his descendant Timur the Lame (he had a bad hip). In the 1360s, Timur was a tribal leader fighting alongside the Chagatai khan to save his khanate. Culturally, he was a Muslim from Turko-Persian Khorasan, not a steppe nomad, and he lacked Temüjin's instinct to stay above religious and cultural divides. In 1369, however, he gained control of Samarkand and began trying to recreate Temüjin's empire.

From the 1380s Timur began reclaiming the Il-Khanate and also taking over the Golden Horde under his right-hand man Tokhtamysh—before having to fight Tokhtamysh himself after he turned renegade.

In 1398, he devastated Delhi, a mainly Hindu city run by Muslim sultans. Perhaps 100,000 Hindus were beheaded and Delhi's vast wealth was taken to allow craftsmen and architects captured in various campaigns to transform Samarkand into a city of Persianate splendor.

Beyond Samarkand, however, Timur built very little. He was greatly feared, perhaps more so than Genghis Khan himself, but he had no political vision. The

Following pages: main map:

THE MONGOL CONQUESTS *1206–1294*

By the time Genghis Khan died in 1227, he controlled almost all the Eurasian steppe and had invaded northern China and Iran. His sons and grandsons built on his conquests, even mounting a seaborne invasion of Java. Expansion ceased with the death of Kublai Khan in 1294.

Inset map:

THE FOUR MONGOL KHANATES *1279–1368*

Temüjin split his empire between his four sons, with one in overall charge. Gradually, four distinct realms crystallized, especially after Kublai's conquest of China in 1279, though communication remained open between them.

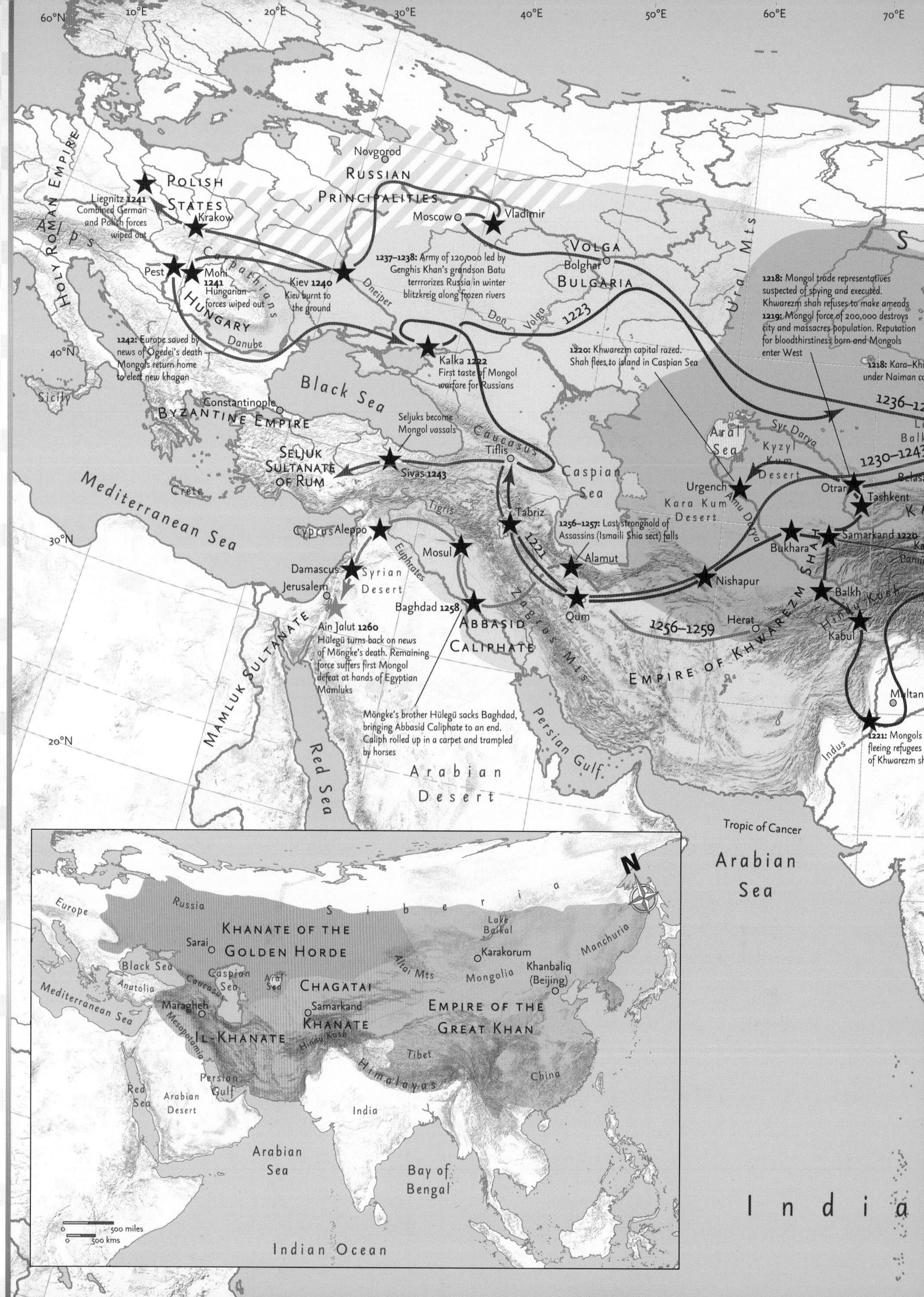

HOLY ROMAN EMPIRE
POLISH STATES
Liegnitz 1241 Combined German and Polish forces wiped out
Krakow
Alps
Pest
Mohi 1241 Hungarian forces wiped out
Carpathians
HUNGARY
Danube
1242: Europe saved by news of Ögedei's death. Mongols return home to elect new khagan
Sicily
Novgorod
RUSSIAN PRINCIPALITIES
Moscow
Vladimir
Kiev 1240 Kiev burnt to the ground
Dnieper
1237–1238: Army of 120,000 led by Genghis Khan's grandson Batu terrrorizes Russia in winter blitzkrieg along frozen rivers
VOLGA BULGARIA
Bolghar
Don
Volga
1223
Kalka 1222 First taste of Mongol warfare for Russians
Black Sea
Constantinople
BYZANTINE EMPIRE
Seljuks become Mongol vassals
SELJUK SULTANATE OF RUM
Sivas 1243
Crete
Mediterranean Sea
Caucasus
Tiflis
Caspian Sea
Tabriz
1221
Tigris
Cyprus
Aleppo
Mosul
Euphrates
Damascus
Syrian Desert
Jerusalem
Ain Jalut 1260 Hülegü turns back on news of Möngke's death. Remaining force suffers first Mongol defeat at hands of Egyptian Mamluks
Baghdad 1258
ABBASID CALIPHATE
MAMLUK SULTANATE
Möngke's brother Hülegü sacks Baghdad, bringing Abbasid Caliphate to an end. Caliph rolled up in a carpet and trampled by horses
Zagros Mts
Persian Gulf
Red Sea
Arabian Desert
Alamut
1256–1257: Last stronghold of Assassins (Ismaili Shia sect) falls
Qum
Nishapur
1256–1259
Herat
Ural Mts
1220: Khwarezm capital razed. Shah flees to island in Caspian Sea
Aral Sea
Kyzyl Kum Desert
Kara Kum Desert
Amu Darya
Syr Darya
Urgench
Otrar
Tashkent
Bukhara
Samarkand 1220
Balkh
Kabul
Hindu Kush
EMPIRE OF KHWAREZM SHAH
1218: Mongol trade representatives suspected of spying and executed. Khwarezm shah refuses to make amends
1219: Mongol force of 200,000 destroys city and massacres population. Reputation for bloodthirstiness born and Mongols enter West
1218: Kara-Khita under Naiman con
1236–12
1230–1243
Multan
Indus
1221: Mongols sh fleeing refugees le of Khwarezm sha
Tropic of Cancer
Arabian Sea
India
60°N
40°N
30°N
20°N
10°E
20°E
30°E
40°E
50°E
60°E
70°E
Europe
Russia
Siberia
KHANATE OF THE GOLDEN HORDE
Sarai
Lake Baikal
Karakorum
Manchuria
Black Sea
Caspian Sea
Aral Sea
Caucasus
Anatolia
Mediterranean Sea
CHAGATAI KHANATE
Samarkand
Altai Mts
Mongolia
Khanbaliq (Beijing)
Maragheh
Mesopotamia
IL-KHANATE
Hindu Kush
EMPIRE OF THE GREAT KHAN
Tibet
Himalayas
China
Persian Gulf
Red Sea
Arabian Desert
India
Arabian Sea
Bay of Bengal
Indian Ocean
500 miles
500 kms
N

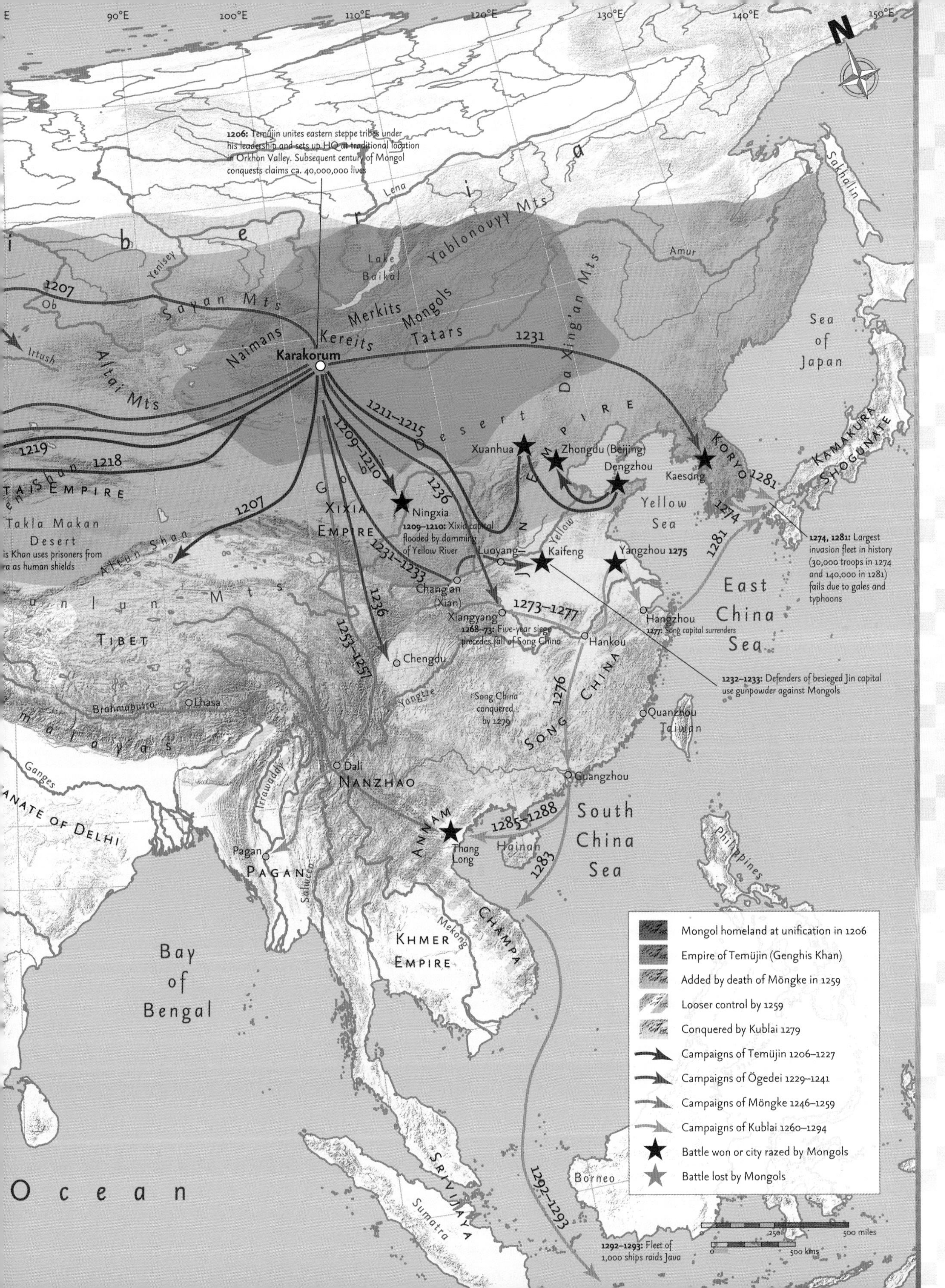
90°E
100°E
110°E
120°E
130°E
140°E
150°E
N
1206: Temüjin unites eastern steppe tribes under his leadership and sets up HQ at traditional location in Orkhon Valley. Subsequent century of Mongol conquests claims ca. 40,000,000 lives
Lena
Yablonovyy Mts
Sakhalin
Lake Baikal
Amur
Yenisey
Ob
Sayan Mts
Merkits
Mongols
Tatars
Naimans
Kereits
Karakorum
Irtush
Altai Mts
Da Xing'an Mts
Sea of Japan
1207
1231
1211–1215
1209–1210
1219
1218
1207
1236
1231–1233
1236
1253–1257
Xuanhua
Zhongdu (Beijing)
Dengzhou
Kaesong
Koryo
Kamakura Shogunate
1281
1274
1281
Yellow Sea
Ningxia
1209–1210: Xixia capital flooded by damming of Yellow River
Xixia Empire
Takla Makan Desert
is Khan uses prisoners from ra as human shields
Altun Shan
Kunlun Mts
Luoyang
Kaifeng
Yangzhou 1275
Chang'an (Xian)
Xiangyang
1273–1277
1268–73: Five-year siege precedes fall of Song China
Hankou
Hangzhou
1277: Song capital surrenders
1274, 1281: Largest invasion fleet in history (30,000 troops in 1274 and 140,000 in 1281) fails due to gales and typhoons
East China Sea
Tibet
Chengdu
Lhasa
Brahmaputra
Yangtze
Song China conquered by 1279
1276
Song China
1232–1233: Defenders of besieged Jin capital use gunpowder against Mongols
Quanzhou
Taiwan
Ganges
Dali
Nanzhao
Guangzhou
Irrawaddy
anate of Delhi
1285–1288
South China Sea
Annam
Thang Long
Hainan
1283
Pagan
Pagan
Salween
Philippines
Mekong
Champa
Khmer Empire
Bay of Bengal
Mongol homeland at unification in 1206
Empire of Temüjin (Genghis Khan)
Added by death of Möngke in 1259
Looser control by 1259
Conquered by Kublai 1279
Campaigns of Temüjin 1206–1227
Campaigns of Ögedei 1229–1241
Campaigns of Möngke 1246–1259
Campaigns of Kublai 1260–1294
Battle won or city razed by Mongols
Battle lost by Mongols
Ocean
Srivijaya
Sumatra
1292–1293
Borneo
1292–1293: Fleet of 1,000 ships raids Java
250
500 miles
500 kms

result was a series of wasteful campaigns followed by the continual need for reconquest. His invasions of the Golden Horde simply wrecked the economy. In Delhi, he replaced the sultan with his own man but put no imperial infrastructure in place. From Khorasan to Anatolia he carried out around 1,400 raids but all he constructed were pyramids built from thousands of skulls.

In 1405, Timur died of plague, en route to retake China from the Ming. Instead of rebuilding the empire, Timur's raiding left Central Asia weakened and succumbing to tribalism once more. Power now shifted back from the center to the edges of the Eurasian landmass: to China, India, and the Middle East.

But in these regions lay empires themselves shaped by the steppe.

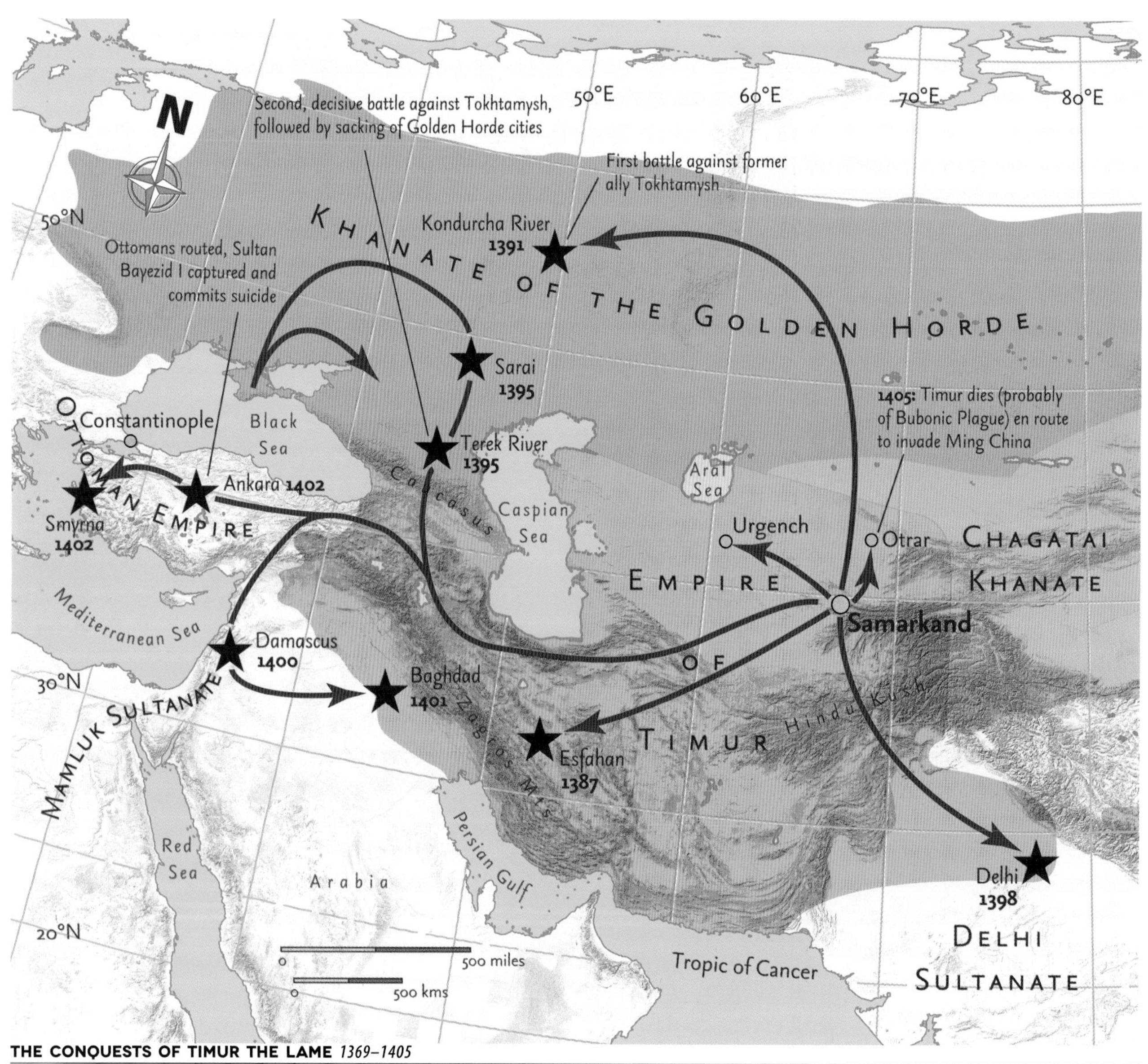

THE CONQUESTS OF TIMUR THE LAME *1369–1405*

The year after the Ming threw the Mongols out of China, Timur took power in Samarkand and embarked on a mission to reunify the Mongol Empire.

CHINESE EMPIRES

Han China was a society defined by the steppe. It was the strength of the Xiongnu at any one time that allowed the Han emperors to keep central control or else forced them to share power with their nobles. But this did not end with the Han. The casting of China's identity in opposition to horse-riding tribes from the steppe became a recurring theme. At the same time, several Chinese dynasties themselves arose from these tribes, each of which both brought something to China and was changed by it.

THE SUI AND THE TANG

The decline and fall of the Han Empire brought similar demographic changes to the collapse of the Western Roman Empire. The steppe tribes the Han had tried to keep out began to settle the good pastures near the Yellow River. By the 4th century CE their jostling pushed many to leave for a lush, mountainous China of wet rice farming and river transport south of the Yangtze. From 420 CE, there were two Chinas: dynasties of Han Chinese in the south with their boats and steppe dynasties in the north with their horses.

As China's traditional heartland, however, the Yellow River valley retained many Han Chinese and shaped its new rulers in the same way as the legacy of Rome shaped the Franks. During the 5th and 6th centuries, lifestyle and intermarriage made steppe tribes like the Tuoba Xianbei (the Northern Wei Dynasty) increasingly Chinese.

Toward the end of this period, an official named Yang Jian gained control in the north, then built a fleet of riverboats and took the south, too, reuniting China as Emperor Wendi of Sui in 589 CE. The Sui Dynasty followed tradition and stationed its army on the northern border to keep further newcomers at bay. To feed the army, the Sui linked the two Chinas, building what is still the world's longest canal to move rice and tea north. The taxes and labor needed to build this canal, however, led in 618 CE to a peasant rebellion, another recurring theme in Chinese history.

By 626 CE, the Tang, another northern dynasty related to the Sui by marriage, had restored order. They went on to build an empire to rival the Han, venturing even farther into the west than they had, initially to check the Gök-Turks, a new power on the steppe.

But the Tang were more outward-looking than the Han and contained the Turks partly

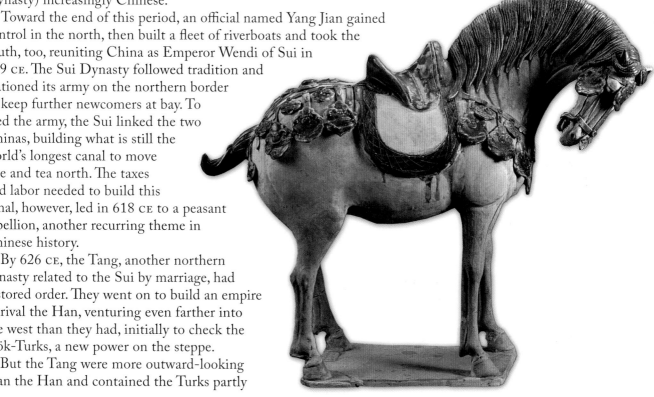

The Tang were a northern dynasty, only one stage removed from their enemies on the steppe. Horses and the contact with peoples across Central Asia they made possible sat at the heart of Tang culture and ceramic representations of foreign merchants, camels, and in particular horses themselves came to typify their art.

through intermarriage. Their idea of China was less defined by the Great Wall and, once in the west, they pursued wider imperial ambitions, spreading across Central Asia, receiving tribute from Tibet, Nepal, and Kashmir and being stopped only by encountering the Abbasid Caliphate in 751 CE. At the end of the Silk Road, which they reopened in 639 CE, Chang'an, the world's largest city, soaked up technology, fashions, and ideas from India and the West. Here, mosques, churches, synagogues, and Zoroastrian temples sat alongside Daoist and Buddhist places of worship.

The growth of Buddhism became part of a growing interest in Indian culture stimulated by Tang imperialism. Buddhist temples received tax breaks and became rich landowners, using their wealth to issue loans, sponsor public works, and promote education. In 868 CE, *The Buddhist Diamond Sutra* became the world's first printed book.

By this time, however, the Tang were in decline and had seized the assets of Buddhist temples in a bid to hang on. The largely free hand the Tang gave the generals who ran their military protectorates had produced a coup in 755 CE. With help from Uighur tribes in the west it was eventually quashed, but the cost was 35 million lives. The Tang never properly subdued their generals, Islam claimed Central Asia, and by 907 CE, China had fragmented once more.

THE SONG

In 960 CE, most of China came under the rule of the Song Dynasty. The Song were not horse people and struggled to gain control of the north, so they co-opted the help of the Jurchen, a tribe from the Manchurian steppe. The Jurchen took the north, setting up the Jin Dynasty, but then turned on their former allies and, in 1126, took the Song capital at Kaifeng on the Yellow River.

The Song moved south to a new capital at Hangzhou in the Yangtze delta and began to defend themselves, building warships and using gunpowder to hold the Jin back. This type of warfare gave rise to a culture of technological innovation, which the Song soon applied to building up their agricultural economy, expanding irrigation networks and developing new, fast-growing strains of rice.

The resulting population explosion shifted China's center of gravity south and stimulated the growth of a market economy based on paper money, which the Tang had introduced. The circulation of money funded improvements in industry such as new water- and wind-powered machinery, which delivered huge increases in iron and textile production.

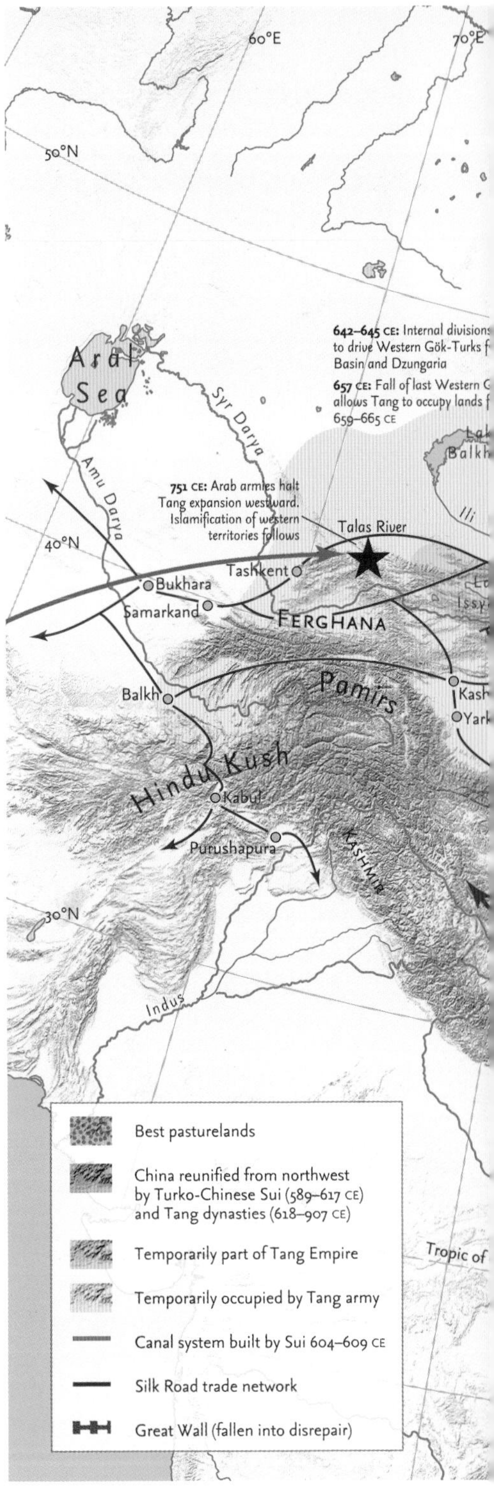

386 CE: The Tuoba clan, a branch of the Xianbei confederation from Manchuria, are one of several steppe tribes to invade northern China and become gradually assimilated (as the Northern Wei Dynasty 386–535 CE)
550s–744 CE: Headquarters for Gök-Turks
745–840 CE: Headquarters for Uighurs
630 CE: Tang defeat Eastern Gök-Turks and try to control eastern steppe
682 CE: Gök-Turks rise again but collapse 744 CE
745–840 CE: Uighurs dominate eastern steppe before being destroyed by Yenisey Kirghiz
645–769 CE: Under Tang control
645–763 CE: Under Tang control
763–843 CE: Under Tibet
668–76 CE: Under Tang control
ca. 650–840 CE: Unified Tibetan Kingdom expands, eating into Tang-controlled territory in west
DZUNGARIA
TIBET
CHINA
SILLA
ANNAM
Gobi Desert
Qilian Shan
Qinling Shan
Nanling Shan
Yellow Sea
East China Sea
South China Sea
Hainan
Chang'an
Luoyang
Kaifeng
Yangzhou
Changzhou
Hangzhou
Taiyuan
Jizhou
Weizhou
Xiangzhou
Cangzhou
Lanzhou
Ganzhou
Dunhuang
Hami
Turfan
Kucha
Kuldja
Chengdu
Yungzhou
Guangzhou
Annanduhufu
Lhasa
Lake Baikal
Kirghiz
Selenga
Orkhon
Amur
Yenisey
Ob
Yellow River
Yangtze
Xi Jiang
Red
Mekong
Salween
Irrawaddy
Ganges
Brahmaputra
80°E
90°E
100°E
110°E
120°E
130°E
140°
N
0
250
500 miles
500 kms

THE TANG EMPIRE *618–907 CE*

After the Sui reunified China in 589 CE, the Tang took over and began to expand. They reestablished Chinese rule in Central Asia and reached India before being checked by Arab armies at the Talas River in 751 CE. Soon after, they withdrew from the west.

The Southern Song inhabited a landscape of mountains and rivers unsuited to horses. Cut off from the steppe, their art turned away from horses, travel, and trade to meditate on nature. Scholar by a Waterfall, *by Ma Yuan (ca. 1160–ca. 1225).*

This was an economic revolution that fed into foreign trade, now conducted by sea instead of overland. Despite this, Song China remained inward-looking, concerned with security and stability and with promoting traditional Confucian and Daoist values, which seemed to serve these concerns. Tang pottery, with its horses and merchants in foreign dress, gave way to contemplative paintings of southern Chinese landscapes and it was under the Song that the Confucian civil service reached its mature form.

THE YUAN

The Song created a China of unprecedented wealth and sophistication, so when the Mongols took the traditional northern heartland from the Jin, they saw the real prize lay farther south. This was a prize they could not just carry off as they galloped through. It took half a century to win and required Kublai to copy the Sui and build a navy. The south finally fell in 1279, but for it to be of any use to him Kublai would have to adapt further.

In conquering northern and southern China, Kublai had brought together two complex agricultural economies. Linking them and encouraging production for export was a network of waterways plus a market economy involving paper money and the use of credit. Coordinating all this, as well as managing defense, was an enormous bureaucracy staffed by thousands of experts. If he wanted to get his hands on China's riches, Kublai could not impose a way of life learned out on the steppe; he had no choice but to mold himself to the Chinese system.

Kublai left all of China's structures in place and, even before the south was won, began to assimilate himself culturally. His rule became known as the Yuan Dynasty, and, as khagan, he moved the Mongol capital to Daidu (Beijing) in 1272, provoking outrage in Karakorum. Many Mongols felt humiliated and deeply offended by Kublai's increasing sinicization. They had conquered most of the known world only to find they were not good enough for the Chinese. It was a classic example of a developed subject society molding a less developed conquering power to its own design.

But the Mongols also left their own mark on China. Having preserved the Song economy, they exposed it to fresh contact with the West through reopening the Silk Road. Foreign trade rose to new levels and there was a revival of cultural interchange reminiscent of Tang days. With the navy they had built the Mongols tried to expand into Southeast Asia and Japan. Here they had fleeting success at best, but Yuan China was, nevertheless, a China once again facing outward.

THE MING

Despite Kublai's assimilation, however, the Yuan never became as Chinese as the Sui and the Tang. Theirs had been a sudden invasion, not a century or two of gradual naturalization. They had also kept themselves apart for fear of losing their identity, forbidding intermarriage, preventing the Chinese from learning the Mongol language, and appointing non-Chinese officials where possible, such as the Venetian traveller Marco Polo.

Although daily life changed little for much of the south, the Yuan Dynasty was always seen as a foreign yoke. When this was supplemented by floods, droughts, and epidemic disease, the result was rebellion spearheaded by the Buddhist-inspired White Lotus Society and Red Turban Movement. In 1358, a peasant rebel, Zhu Yuanzhang, seized Beijing and set up the Ming Dynasty.

The Ming were much like the Song. Both were Han Chinese and eager to protect traditional Han society from northern intruders. Yuanzhang, as Emperor Hongwu, was inspired by a utopian vision of self-sufficient farmers freed from the need to sell their wares and thus from involvement with the corrupting forces of money, towns, and contact with the outside world. He focused on rebuilding China's agricultural base, which had been strong under the Song.

Just as in Song times, the result was not less trade but more, as farmers found they had a surplus to sell. In the early 15th century, the Grand Canal was restored, increasing the exchange of goods. A century later, the Portuguese arrived at Guangzhou and South American silver began to flow into the Ming economy.

The mindset of the Ming emperors, however, was fixed by the age-old defensiveness toward the steppe. In the early 1400s, the Ming admiral Zheng He made voyages as far as Africa, driven by trade, imperialism, and plain curiosity. Control of the seas and the discovery of the New World might have fallen to the Chinese rather than the Europeans had a new emperor not canceled spending on exploration and diverted money into rebuilding the Great Wall into the form it has today.

THE QING

The enlarged wall kept the Mongols out but, by the 1640s, an ossified Ming government was struggling to keep internal order in the face of failed harvests and a shortage of silver caused by the eclipse of the Spanish and Portuguese empires. Meanwhile, descendants of the Jin had rebuilt Jurchen power in Manchuria and set up a Chinese-style administration there. Much of the Ming army saw their only hope in siding with this new Manchu state. As peasant rebels advanced on Beijing in 1644, the last Ming emperor hanged himself, and a gate in the Great Wall was opened to let the Manchu riders through.

They set up the Qing Dynasty. Even before they took Beijing, the Qing ordered everyone to wear their hair in a pigtail, in accordance with Manchu custom, making it easy to spot resisters to their rule. After a decade of massacres, the pigtail had been accepted everywhere and Manchu order established. But the Qing knew the only way to run China was to preserve the Confucian bureaucracy they had themselves copied in Manchuria. They were generally in awe of Chinese culture and restored Beijing in Ming style after its destruction during their takeover.

The Qing were nevertheless a naturally expansive steppe dynasty, very different from the Ming. Once installed in Beijing they continued to move outward, chasing off the Mongols once and for all as well as overrunning Tibet, driving back Russia, and taking Taiwan. In the 18th century, Korea, Indo-China, and Burma also fell under their sway, and by the 19th century the Qing presided over by far the largest Chinese empire the world had seen.

By this time, however, maintaining their empire was slowly neutering the Qing as a military force. In the early days they had drawn their strength from the eight Banners, military orders across which tribal warriors had been separated out, so as to replace allegiance to the tribe with loyalty to the state. Originally much feared, Bannermen had been garrisoned around the empire as a visible presence of Qing domination, but this meant they drew a regular salary, saw no action, and gradually grew soft.

When coastal trade with European powers began destabilizing the economy, provoking rebellions from the mid-19th century on, the Qing could no longer restore order as they had done in the 1640s. The army had changed but so had the Qing emperors. Despite their origins on the wide-open northern plains, after two centuries within the Great Wall they had become as tradition-bound and inward-looking as the Ming.

In part, however, the Qing simply faced the wrong way. Since the Han, China had been defined by its relationship to the steppe, bringer of invaders to resist, bringer of new dynasties to rejuvenate Chinese society. The largest of all China's empires was also the last of Eurasia's great steppe empires, pursuing overland links with Central Asia when the future lay with the sea.

By this time a similar story was unfolding in India.

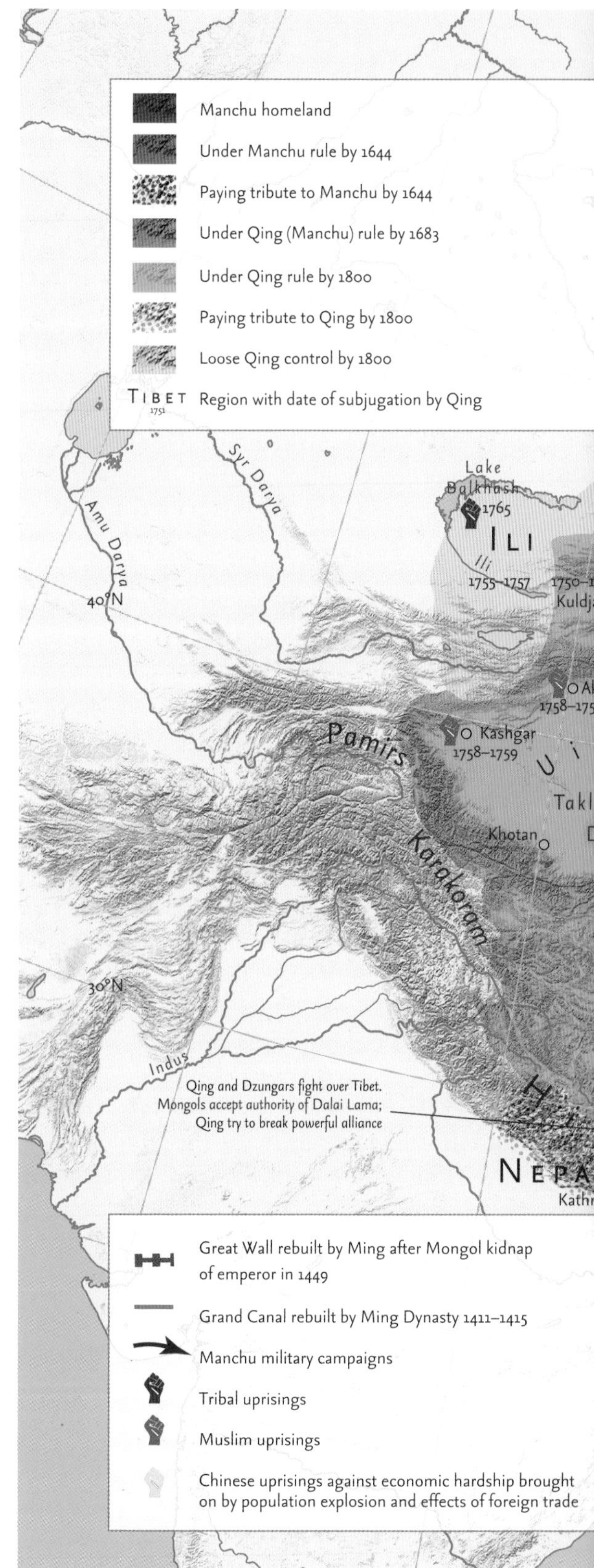

THE MANCHU OR QING EMPIRE *1644–1911*

The Manchu were invited in from their Chinese-style state in Manchuria to restore order in Ming China. By the 1680s their rule was secure and over the next century they built the largest Chinese empire of them all.

MUSLIM INDIA

Like China, the empires of India displayed a tension between north and south. Maritime trade came to the south of India and, at times, powerful states arose from here. Yet it was generally the north, with its two great rivers, that dominated and to which new influences had always come over the Khyber Pass. Islam came this way, as did Timur, followed by the Mughals.

ISLAM COMES TO INDIA

By 751 CE, Arab armies had brought Islam to the Central Asian steppe and by early the next century, the area from eastern Iran up to Samarkand was ruled by the Samanids, a dynasty of Persian Muslims loyal to the Abbasids. The Samanids aped the Abbasid practice of converting captured Turks for use as palace guards. Through the Samanids, these Turks were introduced to a Persian form of Islamic culture, to which they brought their own steppe warrior traditions.

As with the Abbasids, the Samanids fell increasingly into the grip of their mamluks or slave guards, who vied with each other for power until one family won out to become *sultans* ("powers") in their own right, ruling from Ghazni. Under Mahmud (997–1030 CE), the Ghaznavids crossed the Hindu Kush, annexing the Punjab and raiding progressively eastward into the Ganges plain as the wealth of India's temples became clear.

There had been a small Muslim colony in Sindh since Umayyad days, but Mahmud's raids brought a new Turko-Persian Islamic influence to northwest India. After being sacked, Lahore was rebuilt, resettled, and eventually made into a center of learning using booty taken from farther east. Most of this booty, however, went to make Ghazni a far greater city and cultural center than Lahore. Under Mahmud's patronage, Ghazni became the crucible of Islamic Persian literature and hence of the modern Persian language, a blend of pre-Islamic Persian and Arabic.

After Mahmud's death, the Seljuks took over Iran, and Lahore began to replace Ghazni as the seat of Ghaznavid power. A century later, a dynasty from neighboring Ghur displaced the Ghaznavids. They seized control of Ghazni in 1160 and Lahore in 1186–1187. The Ghurid sultan Muhammad continued east to sack Delhi in 1193 in a style reminiscent of Mahmud, except this time the raiders had come to stay.

Both the Ghaznavids and the Ghurids recruited slave soldiers, as the Abbasids and Samanids had done. Muhammad of Ghur had no sons and passed his conquests to his slave general Qutb ud-Din Aybak, who became the first sultan of Delhi in 1206. Four years later, Aybak was killed playing polo, a Persian sport originally used for training cavalry, but he had begun centuries of Muslim rule from Delhi.

The Delhi sultans spread a loose influence over almost all of northern India, as well as farther south for a short while in the early 14th century. Under their rule, many Hindu states were left alone as long as they paid tax as non-Muslims, making the sultanate a patchwork of states with habitual tendency to fragment.

Then, in 1398, Delhi was laid waste by Timur on the pretext that its sultans were not promoting Islam fervently enough. The sultanate was effectively finished, but its final collapse came only with the arrival of Timur's descendant: Babur.

THE WANDERINGS OF BABUR

Babur was born in 1483 in the Ferghana Valley, whose legendary horses the Han emperor Wudi had imported 1,500 years earlier. Descended from Timur through his father and Genghis Khan through his mother, Babur had something to live up to. At the age of 12, he succeeded his father as ruler of Ferghana and at 14 captured Samarkand, a few days' ride southwest, but a noble uprising and the desertion of his army soon left him with neither. Homeless, Babur was now a ruler in search of a kingdom (not unusual on the steppe), with 200–300 men and their families to look after.

GHAZNAVIDS, GHURIDS, AND THE DELHI SULTANATE
1206–1526

Mahmud of Ghazni sacked Lahore ca. 1025 and rebuilt it as an Islamic city before it fell to Muhammad of Ghur in 1186–1187. In 1206, he set up a dynasty of mamluks at Delhi, but administration was loose and the sultanate never recovered after Timur sacked Delhi in 1398.

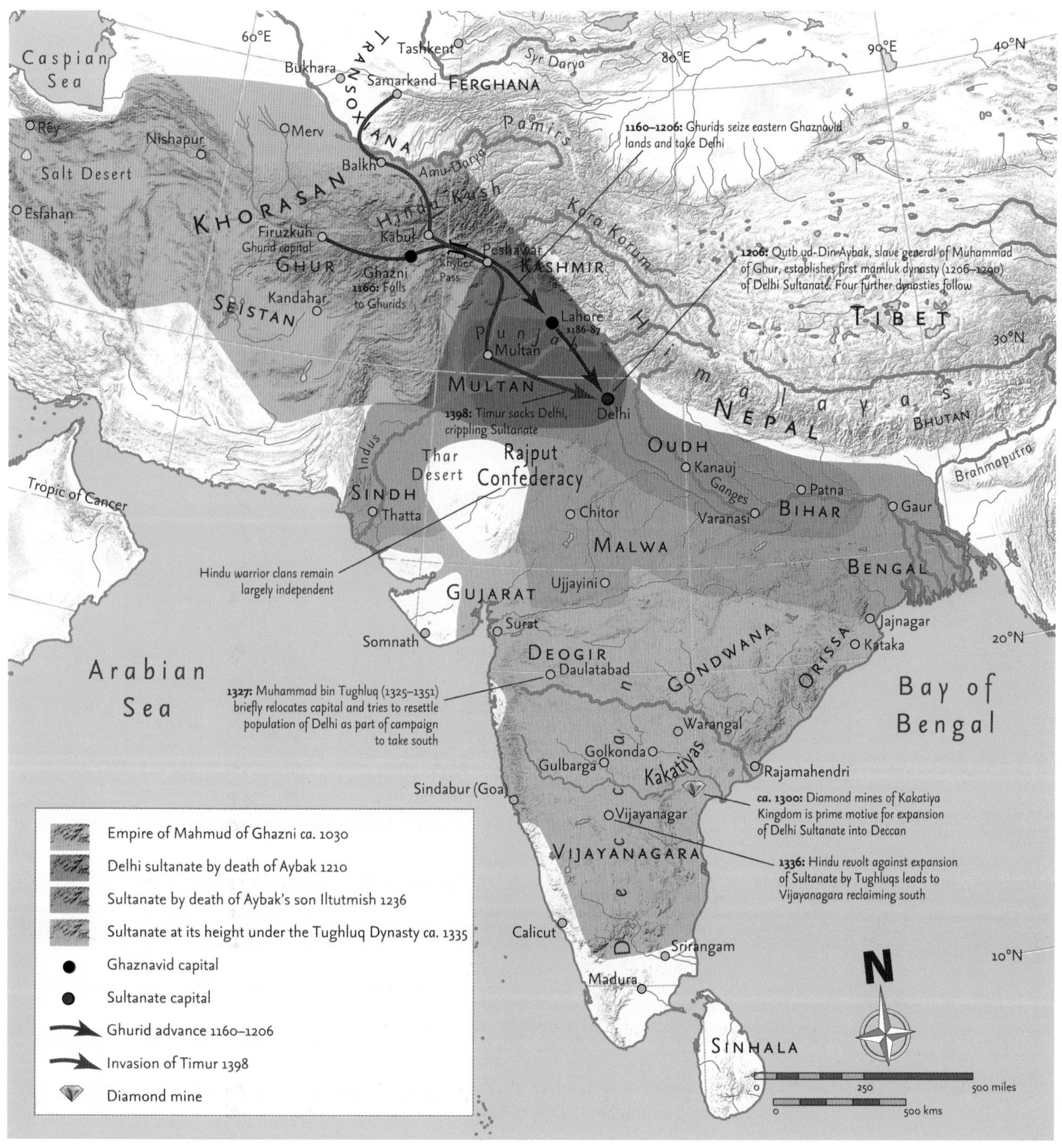

At 17, he retook Samarkand, but lost it a year later to the Uzbeks under Muhammad Shaybani, another descendant of Genghis Khan who saw the relatives of Timur as usurpers. Babur was lucky to escape with his mother and a small band of followers. After hiding out in the mountains, he turned south and began to assemble a new force, many of whose members were neither Mongols nor Turks but Iranian peoples such as Tajiks and Pashtuns. At 21, he took Kabul and was back in the game. Now he was able to form an alliance with Isma'il I of

MUGHAL INDIA *1526–1707*

Dispossessed in Central Asia, Babur took Kabul in 1504 and Delhi in 1526, setting up Mongol rule, but it was his grandson Akbar who built an empire. Later expansion south brought rebellion and decline in the 18th century.

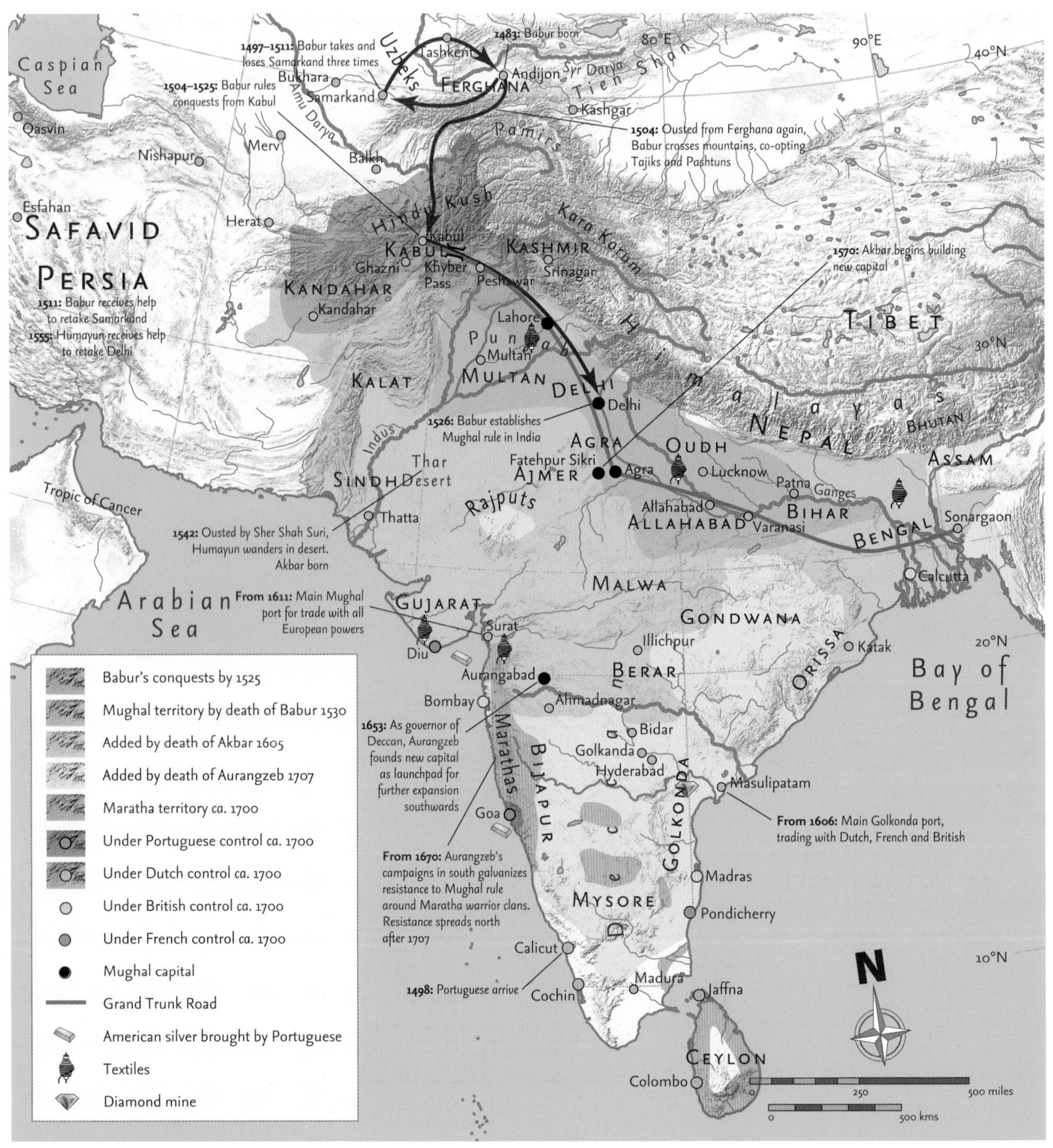

Persia, first shah of the Safavid dynasty, founded in 1501. With Persian backing he returned to reclaim Samarkand in 1511.

Babur was Mongol by descent, but, like Timur and Mahmud of Ghazni, he was culturally a Turko-Persian Muslim. He spoke Persian alongside his Chagatai mother tongue, itself a mixture of Turkic, Persian, and Arabic elements. His education had bred in him a love of poetry, music, miniature painting, architecture, and gardening—all part of Persian courtly life. So it was natural he should seek Persian support.

The new Safavid Persia, however, was a Shi'ah state surrounded by Sunnis. To keep the Safavids happy, Babur wore Shi'ah clothes when taking Samarkand, and the offense this caused led to the Shaybani Uzbeks being able to retake the city once more. This time, Babur gave up on Central Asia for good, made Kabul his spiritual home, and looked to the lands across the Khyber Pass. Timur had, at least in theory, established Timurid rule at Delhi, but it had not lasted. It was up to Babur to put this right.

Crossing into the Punjab, Babur won over the Janjua Rajputs, a powerful warrior clan hostile to Delhi, by helping them against local enemies. Together they advanced east. Babur had brought just 12,000 men with him to fight an army of 100,000, but his men were disciplined. He had mounted archers from the steppe, he had firearms from the Ottomans—unknown in India—and, as he approached Delhi, people joined his ranks. In 1526, he took Delhi and Agra and set up *Mughal* (Persian for "Mongol") rule in India.

Babur recorded his adventures in his colorful autobiography the *Baburnama*. Besides detailing his campaigns, he wrote about the people of different regions and their various customs, as well as of the wildlife and plants he encountered on his travels. A part of Babur's heart remained on the high plains and mountain passes to the north and west; he created gardens throughout his lands but those he loved most were in Kabul, where he asked to be buried.

THE EMPIRE OF AKBAR

In 1530, Babur left his son Humayun ("Lucky") with an insecure administration and a fight for succession. Humayun was not the man to deal with this. His interest was astrology, not war, and he was quick to forgive his three treacherous brothers who plotted against him. In the end he was driven out by Sher Shah Suri, a Pashtun who had served with his father.

Humayun wandered in the Sindh desert, was refused help by his brothers in Kabul, and ended up in Persia. Here he shed his softness toward his brothers, acquired better military judgment, and received help to reclaim the throne. He brought a recharged Persian influence back to India, replacing Chagatai with Persian at court and enlisting two of the most famous Safavid painters to found a Mughal school of painting. Despite his name, however, only a year after his return Humayun tripped on the stairs, arms laden with books, and tumbled to his death.

The man who really created Mughal India was Humayun's son, born while Humayun and his wife Hamida were exiles in the desert. Akbar (1556–1605) came to power at 13 and had his grandfather's force of character. He loved horseback riding, hunting, and archery and became a vigorous warlord who consolidated and extended his father's only recently retaken empire. Akbar was a strong and visible leader, moving between Delhi, Agra, and Lahore to keep an eye on his subjects. He was also a diplomat, abolishing a tax on non-Muslims, marrying the daughters of defeated Hindu princes and allowing local rulers to retain their own courts free from Shari'ah law. These measures went some way to smoothing over his brutal military conquests.

Akbar took things further, however. He saw himself as the spiritual father of his subjects but was conscientious about not imposing Islam. Instead he brought religious leaders from various faiths together to look for common ground and developed his own fusion religion, *Din-i-Ilahi* ("Divine Faith"). It won all of 19 converts but nonetheless established the principle of divine kingship.

The tax on non-Muslims was replaced by a complex property tax (indebted to Sher Shah Shuri), requiring a fastidious and equally complex bureaucracy to run. Tax bills were calculated by surveying the land in question, estimating yields of viable crops for that area, and consulting an index of market prices—a system the British later adopted. The revenue collected was sorted into 12 different treasuries by currency: one for jewels, one for gold, and so on.

Akbar's tax rate was high (33–50 percent) but he had achieved peace and his economy was booming. He gave tax breaks for breaking in new land, which had a domino effect on textile production, and invested directly in silk-weaving.

He was also born at the right time. As Mughal rule took hold inland, a string of Portuguese trading ports was springing up along the coast. Mughal India produced 60 percent of the world's cotton textiles, which the Portuguese were only too happy to buy with silver from South America.

MUGHAL SPLENDOR AND DECLINE

Much of Akbar's riches went to create a court style that overwhelmed the Portuguese and others with its splendor, particularly when they visited Fatehpur Sikri, a new city of carved red sandstone he built near Agra that expressed in architectural terms his desire to fuse Islamic and Hindu traditions. Akbar possessed a rare degree of cultural receptiveness, and at Fatehpur Sikri he set painters and scholars to work on a factory-scale program of cultural production. Unlike Babur and Humayan, Akbar could not read, but this did not stand in the way of a love of books—particularly if those books were illustrated. He commissioned Persian translations of Sanskrit texts, and sponsored a new school of miniature painting, used chiefly to illustrate books. Together, Persian painters brought by Humayun and Indian painters patronized by the Rajput princes, with whom Akbar had formed marriage alliances, combined their skills to develop a recognizably Mughal style of painting.

Mughal expansion and assimilation continued under Akbar's son, Jahangir, born to a Hindu princess, and under his grandson Shah Jahan (1628–1658), in whose reign Mughal style reached its apogee. When Shah Jahan's favorite wife Mumtaz Mahal died in childbirth, he built a mausoleum for her, the Taj Mahal, modeled on the Persianate tomb of Timur in Samarkand, in which Timurid and Indian elements combined to produce a synthesis. Shah Jahan also commissioned the jewel-studded Peacock Throne, set with the Koh-i-noor, the world's largest diamond, passed from the Delhi sultans to Babur and destined for the crown jewels in London. All the world's diamonds came from India at this time.

Opposite page: Akbar tames the Savage Elephant, Hawa'i, outside the Red Fort at Agra, *from the* Akbarnama *of Abul Fazl, ca. 1590, commissioned by Akbar as his biography and record of his empire.*

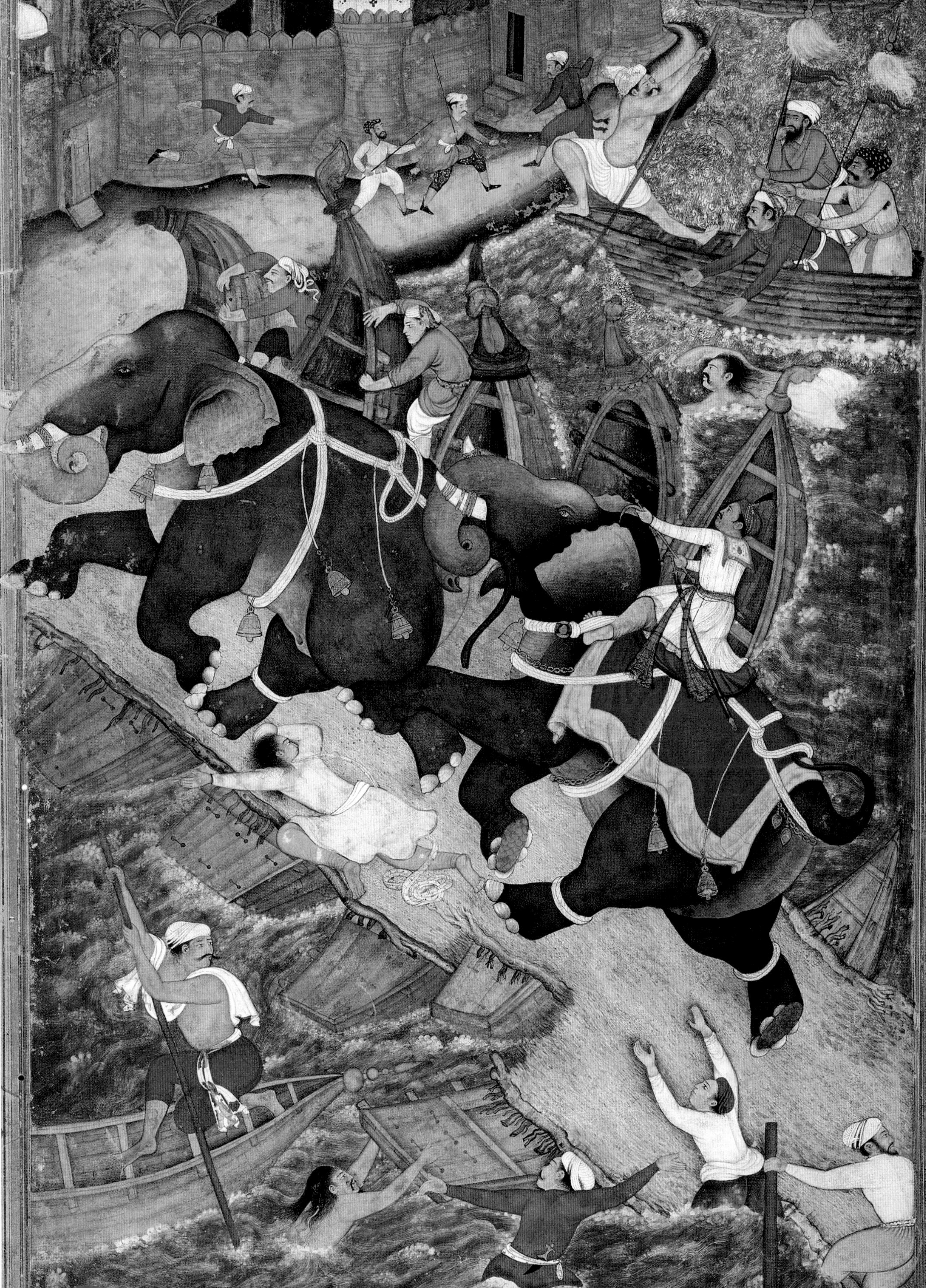

The Mughal succession, however, was always fought over. Shah Jahan's son Aurangzeb (1658–1707) killed three brothers and imprisoned his father to get the throne. The story is he placed the Koh-i-noor by the window of Shah Jahan's cell so that in its facets he could just make out the refracted image of the Taj Mahal.

Aurangzeb was a religious zealot whose indifference toward the complex administration needed to keep control over the subcontinent precipitated Mughal decline. He reinstated the tax on non-Muslims and tried to take the far south, provoking the Hindu Maratha Confederacy to rebel. Support for the Marathas spread north, revealing the extent to which Mughal rule, for all Akbar's religious tolerance and Shah Jahan's architectural harmonizing, was still seen as imperial oppression. After Aurangzeb, the Mughals increasingly lost control; rich states such as Bengal became effectively independent and local rivalries allowed the British to get a foothold.

But something would remain to outlast the British. Neither the Delhi Sultans nor the Mughals ever properly penetrated the south, and, despite artistic expressions of cultural fusion, neither genuinely consolidated their grip on the people they ruled. After Aurangzeb's death, an independent Islamic state grew up at Mysore in the far south, whose ruler Tipu Sultan would cause the British problems, but this was an exception. For the most part, Muslim India was an India more at home in the north, one that overlay a Hindu India that had been maturing since the time of the Guptas. The tension this produced would simmer for another two centuries while the British held sway, ready to boil over the moment they left in 1947. The result would be bloodshed and a subcontinent partitioned along religious lines.

Meanwhile, on the eve of the British takeover, the mistake of the Mughals was to overlook the importance of the sea. India was vast, it possessed immense wealth, and to the north lay the steppe, home of the horse and gateway to the riches of China and the West. For thousands of years the horse had meant trade, communications, and mastery in war. The Mughals had themselves come riding down from the steppe to take possession of huge territories and populations. It was only natural that they should fail to see that the times were changing and the future lay with a handful of European trading settlements on the coast.

But in the Mediterranean, there was one steppe tribe who had exchanged the horse for the ship.

THE OTTOMAN EMPIRE

The rise, expansion, and metamorphosis of the Turks is an epic story on a par with that of the Arabs. Like the Arabs, the Turks were tribal nomads who created settled, sophisticated societies. Their journey was a far longer one, however, and the greatest of their empires was more solid and longer lasting than the Arab caliphates.

FROM THE STEPPE TO THE MEDITERRANEAN

Among the peoples roaming the vast Eurasian steppe were the Turks. They originated perhaps in the Ordos Desert where the Yellow River takes its great bend, before evolving into various tribes sucked into shifting confederations such as the Xiongnu. The Turks faced the nomads' standard problem of how to get beyond the tribe. To begin with they looked to strong leaders.

In 546 CE, Turkic tribes under the Ashina clan were working as blacksmiths in the Altai mountains for a confederation called the Rouran. That year, Bumin, leader of the Ashina, helped put down a rebellion, expecting the hand of a Rouran princess as reward. Finding himself refused, he threw off the Rouran in 552 CE, with help from the Northern Wei in China—and married a Wei princess instead.

Bumin united the Turks as the Gök-Turks ("Blue/Sky Turks"). Under his son Mukan (553–572 CE), they wiped out the Rouran, beheading 5,000, and gained control of the entire steppe. Soon after, however, they split into two. One half ruled the eastern steppe from the Orkhon Valley until broken up by Tang China in the 620s CE. A western half helped both the Sasanians repel the White Huns and the Byzantines fight the Sasanians, but soon splintered into Khazars, Bulgars, and other tribes.

The Gök-Turks rose again from the 680s, before the Uighurs, themselves a Turkic tribe, took over the steppe in the 740s. Now, however, the new galvanizing force of Islam was arriving in Central Asia. First Uighurs and other Turks were captured by the Abbasids and Samanids for use as slave soldiers. Then whole tribes began to convert.

Among the first of these were the Seljuk Turks who swept down through the waning Abbasid Caliphate in the 11th century, bringing with them a Turko-Persian brand of Islam similar to that which the Ghaznavids, Ghurids, and Timurids brought to India. The Seljuks, having taken most of Anatolia from the Byzantines after 1071, called their newly-won kingdom Rum (Rome), as they saw the Byzantines as Romans.

To secure their borders against attempts at reconquest by Byzantines and Crusaders alike, the Seljuks of Rum enlisted *ghazis*—warrior tribes, themselves mostly Turkic, united in the cause of protecting Islam. They were organized as military–religious orders similar to the Crusaders. The Seljuks provided money and weapons and the ghazis fought. In the process, the border zones they defended became settled principalities known as *beyliks*. Islam had given the ghazis common cause; now they were putting an end to centuries of nomadism once and for all.

In the end, the ghazis could not stop the Mongols in 1243 and, by the end of the century, the Sultanate of Rum was finished. During this time, however, western beyliks, such as that of Osman I (1299–1324), had become refuges for Seljuks and ghazis fleeing the Mongols. Now the beylik of Osman (known to the English as Ottoman) became an independent state and, with a growing population, began to take over neighboring beyliks.

Osman's son Orhan (1324–1360) gave the fledgling Ottoman state a proper capital by taking the Byzantine city of Bursa in 1326. Byzantine pretender John VI Kantakouzenos asked Orhan to help him seize power and, once emperor, gave him his daughter's hand and allowed him across into Thrace. Orhan quickly resettled Byzantine estates and his son Murad I (1360–1389) established a new European capital at Adrianople.

But the European estates were given to highborn warriors who, as rich landowners, began to threaten Ottoman power. So the *devsirme* system was developed whereby Christian boys were taken from the Balkans, converted to Islam, and trained to be loyal to the sultan, first as crack troops and later as government officials. They were known as *janissaries* and were basically Ottoman mamluks. They began as slave soldiers but, later on, a need for larger forces plus their growing prestige attracted volunteers. The basis of this prestige was the first great victory of the janissaries at Constantinople.

A NEW CONSTANTINOPLE AND A NEW CALIPHATE

By 1394, Constantinople was all that was left of the Byzantine Empire and a six-year siege began. The city's walls held, however, and in 1402 Timur ravaged Anatolia and captured Bayezid I (1389–1402). It was 50 years before the Ottomans recovered and Constantinople finally fell to Mehmed II (1444–1446 and 1451–1481).

Mehmed entered Constantinople with care, conscious of the prize he had won. He respected its cultural and administrative traditions, but this created a problem because Byzantine administration was closely linked to the Orthodox Church.

Mehmed's solution was to establish Greek Christians as a *millet*: a self-governing religious community with its own law courts and tax system—an idea first suggested by Osman himself. The Ottomans established millets for several religious groups, including Jews, who found a haven from persecution in Christian Europe, and made Constantinople and Thessaloniki great Jewish cities.

Islam had enabled the Turks to transcend tribalism, but it was the millet system that became the basis for running the multicultural empire the Ottomans found themselves landed with. As such, the Islamic community itself also functioned as a millet. This potential nightmare of different administrative structures was actually something similar to Augustus's separation of republic and empire at Rome. The Ottomans were separating community politics from the administration of their empire. As with the senate under Augustus, the true independence of the millets was something of a fiction since atop parallel hierarchies lay a tier of officials answerable only to the sultan. On a day-to-day level, though, the millet system produced tolerance, consent, and stability.

From Constantinople, the Ottomans looked north and west to the lands of the old empire. Serb-led Balkan resistance had been crushed at Kosovo in 1389 but centuries of further resistance to stop the Ottomans from inching north followed. In 1462, Vlad the Impaler of Wallachia, better known as Dracula, drove Mehmed II back by impaling over 40,000 Turks on wooden stakes.

In 1501, however, Persia was reunited under the Safavids, a Shi'ah dynasty that backed uprisings on the borders of the Ottoman Empire. This drew the attention of Selim I (1512–1520) away from Europe, and, in 1514, he drove the Safavids back at Chaldiran. They moved east to a new Persian capital at Esfahan, and Selim secured the Levant, the Mamluk Sultanate of Egypt, Mecca, and Medina. His son Suleyman I ("the Magnificent," 1520–1566) took Baghdad and gained access to the Persian Gulf.

Having inherited the Byzantine Empire, acquiring Mecca, Medina, and Baghdad made the Ottomans heirs also to the Abbasid Caliphate. The Ottoman Empire now claimed to be the home of all Muslims.

SULEYMAN'S EMPIRE

With the taking of Constantinople, the Ottoman Turks became rulers of a maritime empire that reached its height under Suleyman. It relied on naval dominance and this was largely the work of one man: Khizr Reis, "Barbarossa," most feared of the Barbary Corsairs.

Khizr and his three brothers were sailors from Lesbos. Their father was a Turk, their mother a Greek Christian. After run-ins with the Knights of St. John on Rhodes, during which one brother was killed, they became Ottoman privateers—state-sponsored pirates—and moved west across the Mediterranean, raiding from Italy to Spain. Here,

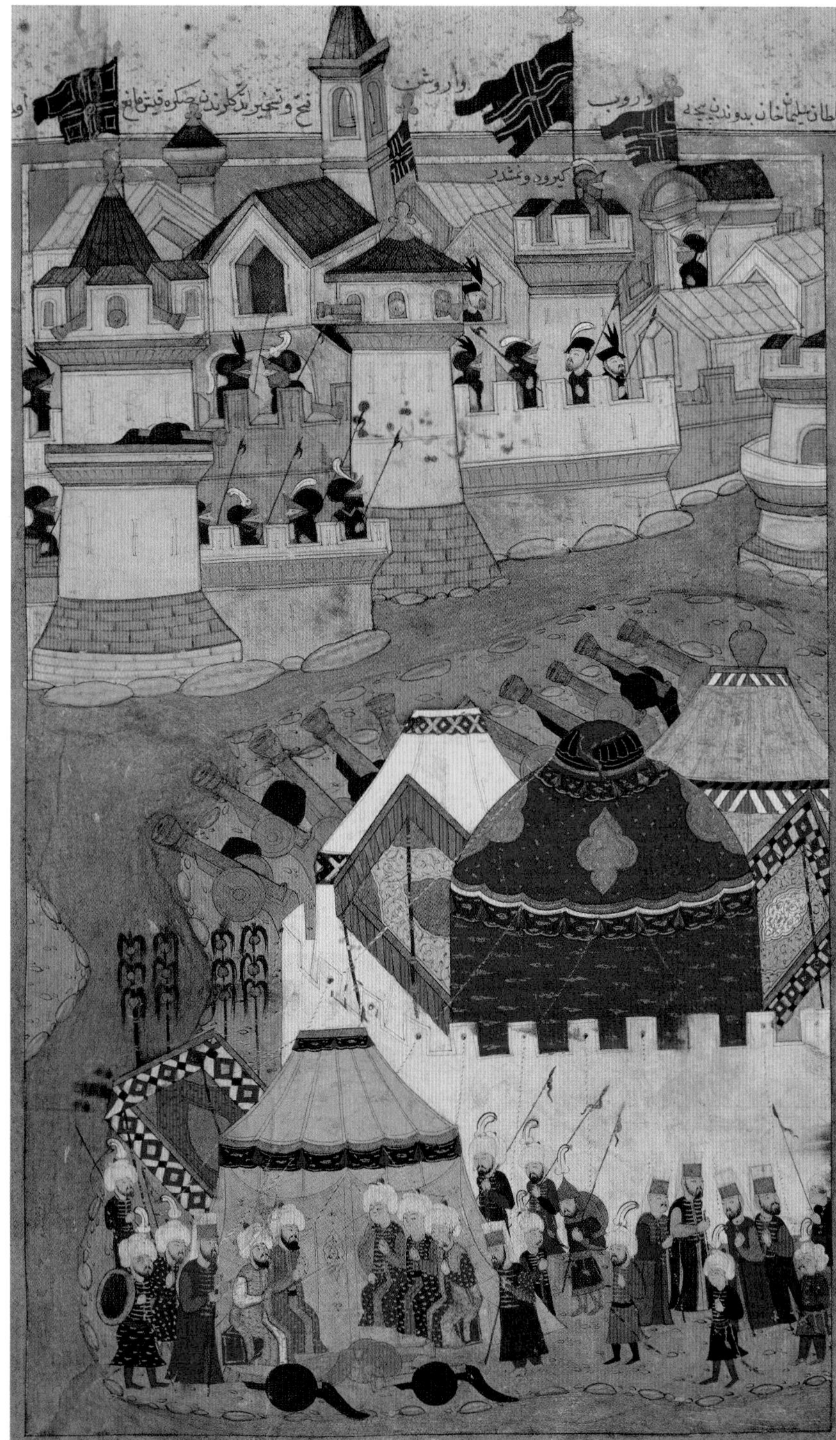

Suleyman the Magnificent and his janissaries with their plumed hats lay siege to Habsburg Vienna in 1529, employing cannon as they had done at Constantinople in 1453. Unlike Constantinople, however, Vienna resisted, and the Ottoman advance into Europe was halted. The failure of another siege in 1683 marked the beginning of a gradual Ottoman retreat from Europe. From the Hunername, *1588.*

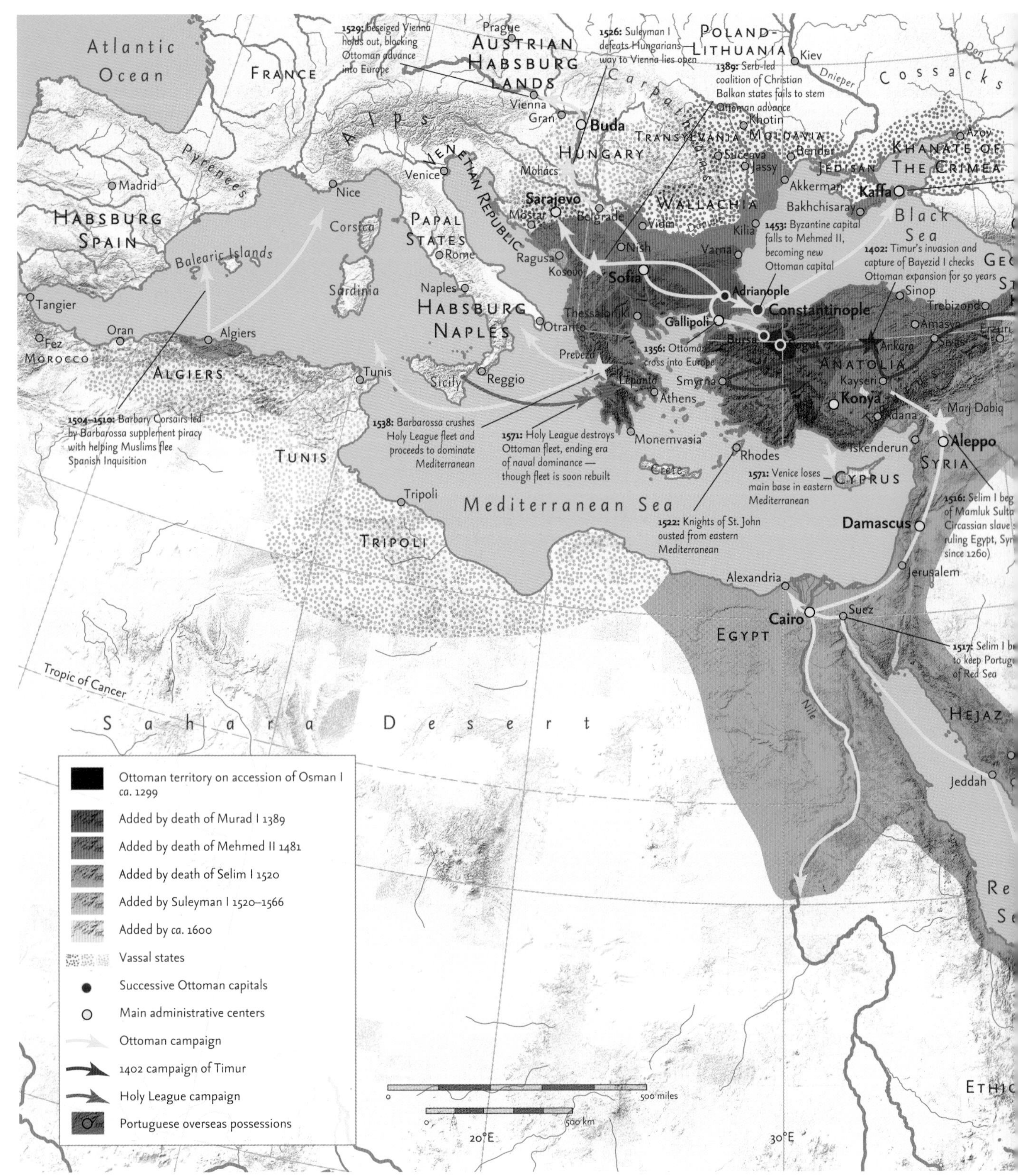
Atlantic Ocean
France
Prague
Austrian Habsburg Lands
1529: beseiged Vienna holds out, blocking Ottoman advance into Europe
1526: Suleyman I defeats Hungarians—way to Vienna lies open
Poland-Lithuania
Kiev
Dnieper
Cossacks
Don
1389: Serb-led coalition of Christian Balkan states fails to stem Ottoman advance
Carpathians
Vienna
Gran
Buda
Alps
Hungary
Transylvania
Moldavia
Khotin
Suceava
Jassy
Bender
Jedisan
Khanate of the Crimea
Azov
Pyrenees
Madrid
Nice
Venice
Venetian Republic
Mohacs
Sarajevo
Mostar
Belgrade
Wallachia
Akkerman
Kaffa
Bakhchisaray
Vidin
Kilia
Habsburg Spain
Corsica
Papal States
Rome
Nish
Varna
1453: Byzantine capital falls to Mehmed II, becoming new Ottoman capital
Black Sea
1402: Timur's invasion and capture of Bayezid I checks Ottoman expansion for 50 years
Balearic Islands
Ragusa
Kosovo
Sofia
Adrianople
Sinop
Trebizond
Sardinia
Naples
Tangier
Habsburg Naples
Thessalonik
Gallipoli
Constantinople
Amasya
Oran
Algiers
Otranto
Bursa
Sögut
Ankara
Sivas
Fez
Morocco
Prevesa
1356: Ottomans cross into Europe
Anatolia
Algiers
Tunis
Sicily
Reggio
Lepanto
Smyrna
Kayseri
Athens
Konya
Adana
Marj Dabiq
1504–1510: Barbary Corsairs led by Barbarossa supplement piracy with helping Muslims flee Spanish Inquisition
1538: Barbarossa crushes Holy League fleet and proceeds to dominate Mediterranean
1571: Holy League destroys Ottoman fleet, ending era of naval dominance—though fleet is soon rebuilt
Monemvasia
Iskenderun
Aleppo
Tunis
Rhodes
Syria
Crete
1571: Venice loses main base in eastern Mediterranean
Cyprus
Tripoli
Mediterranean Sea
1522: Knights of St. John ousted from eastern Mediterranean
Damascus
Tripoli
Jerusalem
Alexandria
Cairo
Suez
Egypt
Tropic of Cancer
Sahara Desert
Nile
Hejaz
Jeddah
Ottoman territory on accession of Osman I ca. 1299
Added by death of Murad I 1389
Added by death of Mehmed II 1481
Added by death of Selim I 1520
Added by Suleyman I 1520–1566
Added by ca. 1600
Vassal states
Successive Ottoman capitals
Main administrative centers
Ottoman campaign
1402 campaign of Timur
Holy League campaign
Portuguese overseas possessions
0
500 miles
0
500 km
20°E
30°E

Muslims and Jews were suffering under Habsburg rule, and they helped many escape through North Africa via their main pirate base of Algiers on the Barbary Coast, which they took in 1516.

Faced with a hostile Spain, the brothers gave Algiers to Selim I in return for assistance. Selim made the eldest, Baba Oruç ("Barbarossa" to Western ears), Ottoman governor of Algiers, but when he was killed by the Spanish, Khizr inherited his position and his nickname. Once Barbarossa had the whole of the western Mediterranean sewn up, Suleyman brought him back east to attack Habsburg Naples and take Greek islands still under Venetian control. In 1538, the pope assembled a league of Christian forces, but Barbarossa defeated them south of Corfu. The Mediterranean had become an Ottoman lake, and the Habsburgs tried in vain to bribe Barbarossa to work for them.

The empire now stretched from the Persian Gulf almost to the Atlantic and brought in huge revenues, mainly from commission-based tax collection in the east. Suleyman supplemented this with a modernization program based on a new secular law code. Shari'ah he could not change, but he distilled prior rulings on civil matters such as crime, property ownership, and taxation into a set of principles called the *kanuns*. Working from the kanuns, Suleyman effectively abolished serfdom, replaced much capital and corporal punishment with fines, and expanded the education system, giving it a more secular emphasis.

STAGNATION

Suleyman was famously besotted with Hurrem, a Ukrainian concubine. When his principal wife Gulbahar beat her up, Suleyman banished Gulbahar and her son Mustafa, made Hurrem his wife, and had four sons by her. Mustafa, however, was still groomed for office and promised to be a more than able successor to his father. So the scheming began, rumors

THE OTTOMAN EMPIRE AT ITS HEIGHT *around 1580*

From 1299, the Ottomans spread through Anatolia and the Balkans, encircling Constantinople before taking it in 1453. A century later they had expanded in all directions, fighting the Safavids in Persia and the Habsburgs both in central Europe and across the Mediterranean.

were circulated, Mustafa was strangled by eunuchs while his father peered around the curtain, and Hurrem's son became sultan.

Strangling was the standard means of determining succession (in 1595, Mehmed III had all 19 of his brothers strangled to secure the throne). But the strangling of Mustafa ushered in a long slide into stagnation, during which the sultan's power ebbed away. Harem intrigue aside, this was partly a function of the empire's success. While it expanded, it drew its impetus from dynamic leaders, as earlier Turkic empires on the steppe had done. But once the empire reached its greatest extent, leadership from the front became less important than bureaucracy.

At the same time, external pressures were mounting. The Ottoman rise had taken advantage of Byzantine and Seljuk decline, and of Safavid Persia and Mamluk Egypt standing alone. At Lepanto in 1571 and Vienna in 1683, however, European forces stood together and drove the Ottomans back. Between these dates the Safavids had their own golden age and joined with the Habsburgs, forcing the empire to fight on two fronts.

In addition, Europeans were spreading farther afield, partly in reponse to Ottoman control of Eastern trade. The Portuguese, seeking a new route to Asia, had arrived in the Persian Gulf in the early 16th century. When Persia began to disintegrate in the 18th century, the British and the Russians were already there, and the Ottoman Empire found itself encircled by more advanced European powers.

Structural solidity, once its great strength, now hindered the empire's ability to respond to a changing scene. Ottoman society was ordered by religion into different millets and by profession into different guilds that fixed prices and standards and protected their members. It was a stable system but one that had blocked the introduction of the printing press for 50 years.

The janissaries became part of the problem, too. They took salaries without doing any work, they took over noble estates, and they held their ruler ransom as the mamluks had done. In 1826 they were done away with, but by this time, it was too late. Russia had broken Ottoman control of the Black Sea and national independence movements were beginning to eat away at the empire. In the end, the Turks themselves would replace it with a nation-state in 1922.

The Ottoman Empire became known as "the sick man of Europe" for its failure to adapt to a changed world, but this very intransigence meant it took centuries for it to finally breathe its last. The Turks built an empire able to endure for 600 years. In the process, they left the steppe behind, took over what was left of the second Rome, built ships, and became part of the story of Europe.

But the Mediterranean was Europe's past. Its future lay on the Atlantic, where new ocean-going ships would bring it into contact with hitherto undiscovered worlds.

Opposite page: The Ottoman Turks left the steppe for a largely maritime empire in the Mediterranean, but retained links to their former way of life. Polo, first developed in Persia, was a game played from Constantinople and Cairo to Beijing by societies all sharing something of a common equestrian culture. Safavid Persian miniature, 16th century.

EMPIRES OF ISOLATION

The Empire of Mali / The Aztec Empire / The Inca Empire

The early history of empire is the story of the great civilizations of Eurasia; an account of development within Eurasia's four traditional zones of settlement and their linking by trade, religion, and riders from the steppe. During this time, however, empires were growing and decaying in long-established zones of civilization partly or totally isolated from Eurasia's story.

Sub-Saharan Africa remained a "dark continent" to the rest of the world right up to the end of the 19th century. There were few natural harbors and few rivers that reached any distance inland before rapids and waterfalls made them unnavigable. The Sahara itself kept overland travel from the Mediterranean the preserve of desert nomads and their camel caravans. As such, West Africa's gold reserves, the richest in the world, stayed in the hands of African emperors even after European ships began plying the coast in search of slaves to work plantations across the sea.

The civilizations of Central and South America were completely cut off from Eurasian developments until Europeans arrived around 1500. They lacked iron and steel and, without draft animals, did not even use the wheel, except for toys. They were also all but cut off from each other by dense jungle separating the Andes from the highlands of Mexico. Within different environments and traditions, the Aztecs and the Incas built up very different sorts of empire, each of which astonished the Spanish with its riches.

The interlinking of Eurasia's zones gave them a rough technological equality not shared by those beyond. In Africa and the Americas, isolation produced splendor but also a technology gap and unfamiliarity with both Eurasian customs and diseases, all of which brought catastrophe when contact finally came.

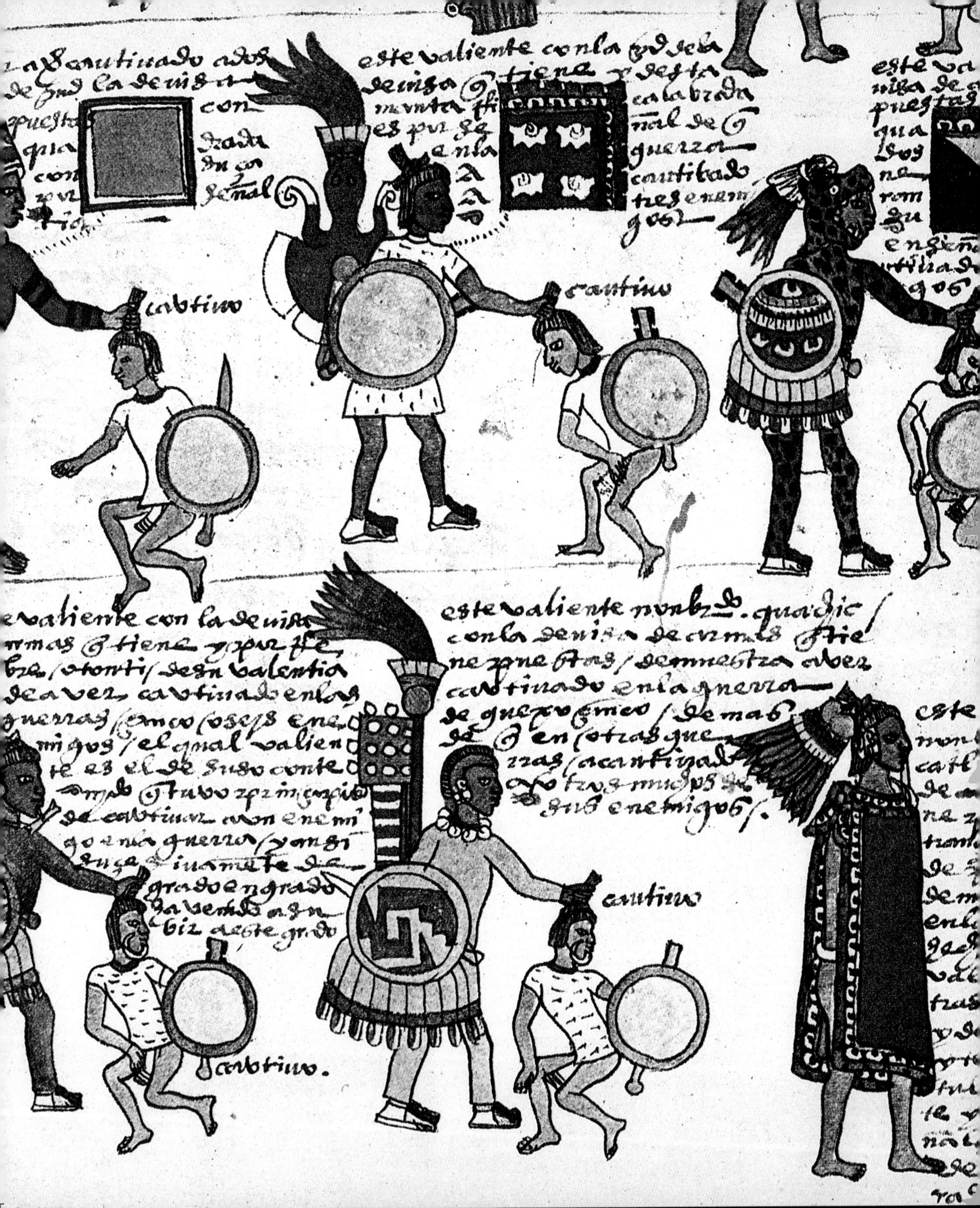

Aztec warriors ensure promotion for
From the Codex Mendoza, ca. 1540.

THE EMPIRE OF MALI

In Sumer's time, the middle reaches of the River Niger were home to a civilization slowly becoming cut off from the outside world. To the south was jungle, to the north a spreading desert. But the desert contained something needed by the people of the grasslands in between: salt.

THE SAHARAN GOLD ROAD

By classical times, the Mediterranean world knew West Africa possessed gold of rare purity but did not know its source. There were stories of Carthaginian traders leaving their wares on the beach, withdrawing, then returning to find them replaced with gold left by Tuareg Berbers from the desert.

By around 300 CE, the camel, brought to Egypt by the Persians, had spread to the western Sahara. Camels could travel twice as fast as steers (bullocks), which meant getting from oasis to oasis more safely. They could also carry twice the load and, by Justinian's time, large quantities of the Roman *solidus* were being minted from West African gold. The Tuareg now led thousand-strong camel caravans and controlled the desert salt mines at Taghaza, 20 days from the nearest town. Here they worked sub-Saharan slaves, bringing them food and water for the salt they mined. Now stories circulated of the Tuareg journeying south with slabs of salt a man's bodyweight, leaving them on the ground and returning to find them replaced with gold.

An air of mystery shrouded the gold trade, not least because the Tuareg traded their salt on the edge of the desert with a merchant clan called the Wangara. Only the Wangara knew the whereabouts of the goldfields in the Bambuk Mountains to the south, and they kept it that way. Salt and gold brought to the desert's edge made the area rich and made the *ghana* ("king") of Kumbi Saleh a powerful man. By the 10th century, neighboring tribes were paying him tribute, and an Empire of Ghana reached up to the caravan terminuses of Oualata in the northeast and Aoudaghost in the northwest.

In 1055, Aoudaghost was seized by the Almoravids, Sanhaja Berbers who ran caravans to Morocco near the west coast. Their leader, Yahya ibn Ibrahim, had returned from Mecca in 1040 to create an empire that stretched into Spain, based on the gold trade and a strict interpretation of Islam.

In 1076, the Almoravids invaded Kumbi Saleh, bringing Islam into the heart of Ghana. By 1088, they were gone but Islam stayed to take root among merchants, for whom Arabic was a useful *lingua franca*. Ghana now had two sets of ministers: animist to oversee agriculture, Islamic to oversee trade.

From this time on, however, Ghana's power began to wane as the desert crept farther south. In 1180, the Sosso, who paid tribute to Ghana, overthrew their masters and in 1203 their despotic leader Sumanguru established Sosso rule in Kumbi Saleh.

Opposite page: Mansa Musa sits on his throne near "Tenbuch" (Timbuktu) inspecting his gold, for which a Tuareg Berber has crossed the Sahara on his camel. To the north, the Atlas Mountains form a wall separating the desert from the Mediterranean. From the Catalan Atlas, *1375.*

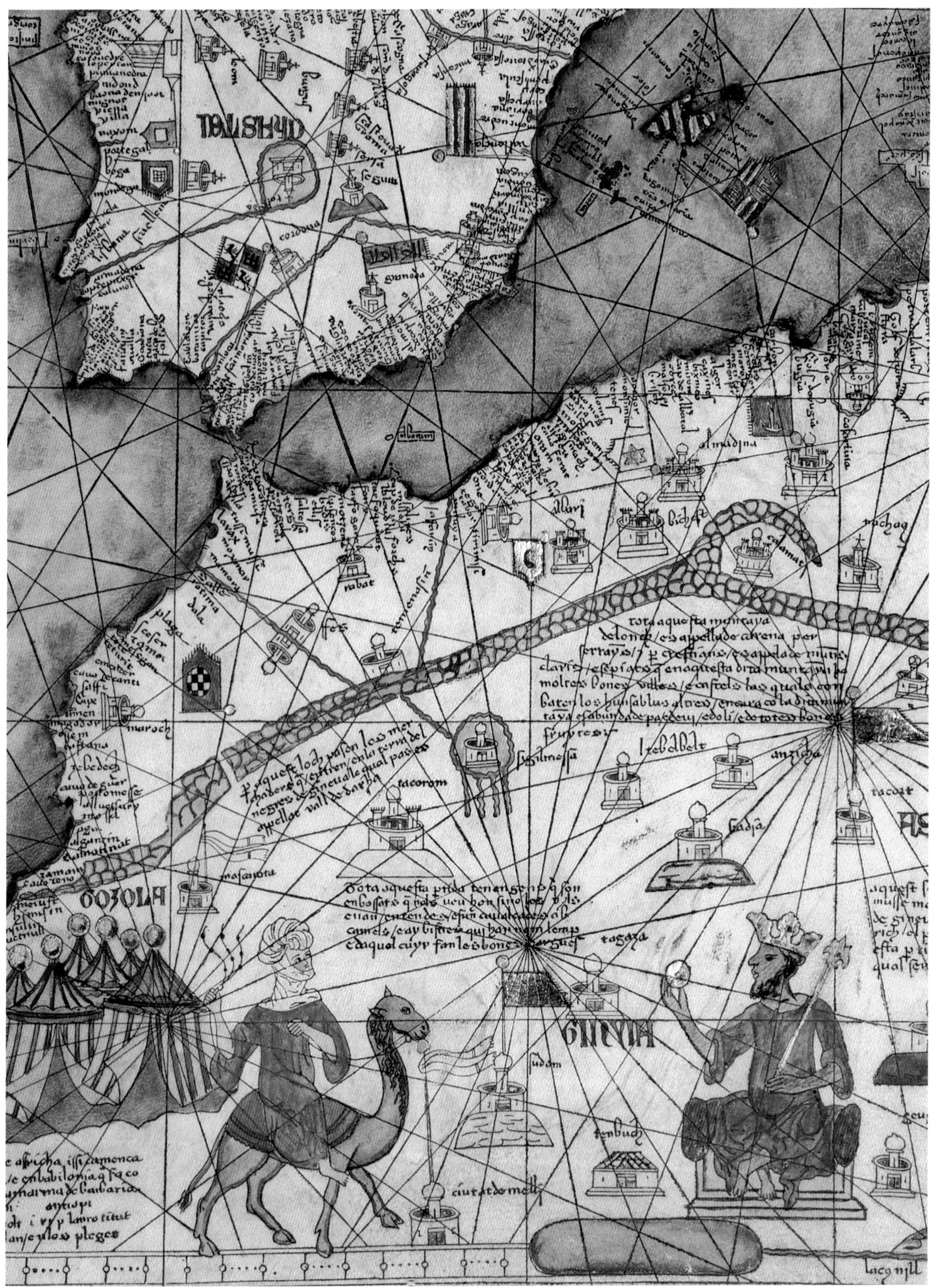
rabat
fes
tacorom
tagaza
sudam
tenbuch

THE RISE OF MALI

Also former tribute-payers to Ghana were the Mandenka, the people of Manden, a collection of small city-states to the south. One of these was Niani on the upper Niger. Here, around 1217, a prince called Sundjata was born. According to legend, the boy was born lame. Sundjata was exiled with his mother and sisters but after Sumanguru attacked Manden and Sundjata's ruling brother fled Niani, the Mandenka sought his help. Around 1235, he led an uprising, first to repel the Sosso, then to take their lands.

Sundjata (ca. 1235–ca. 1255) arranged the Mandenka and other allied tribes into the *Manden Kurufa* ("Manden Federation"), with a capital at Niani and himself as *mansa* ("king of kings"). An oral constitution, the *Kurukan Fuga* ("Division of the World"), established a code of law, an assembly, administrative tasks for different clans, and a standard currency.

The heartland of Mali, as the Manden Kurufa became known, was more fertile than Ghana, allowing Sundjata to step up cultivation of beans and rice and bring in cotton farming. It was also nearer the Bambuk Mountains, contained more gold mines at Bure, and lay on the river, which greatly increased trade.

Sundjata and his son Mansa Ouali built Mali up and expanded southwest to the goldfields of Bambuk and nearby Galam, north to Aoudaghost, and east to Gao, but Ouali's brother and successor, Mansa Khalifa, provoked a rebellion by shooting arrows at people just for fun. Power passed to court officials, and, by 1285, a freed royal slave named Sakura had seized power. Sakura reinforced central control, replacing self-equipped mounted warriors sporting chainmail, swords, and lances with a tax-funded slave infantry equipped with spears and poisoned arrows.

By the time of Mansa Musa (ca. 1312–ca. 1337), the federated tribal regions were reorganized as provinces of the Empire of Mali, with governors appointed by the mansa collecting tribute in the form of gold dust supplied by three goldfields. Mali was producing most of the world's gold and shortages in Europe and the Middle East maintained its value.

In 1324, Mansa Musa made his *hajj* (pilgrimage to Mecca) with a caravan of 60,000 people. He was attended by 12,000 slaves in colorful silks and 80–100 camels carried over 220 pounds (100 kilograms) of gold dust each. On his way through Cairo, inflation soared as the value of gold fell through the floor. On his way back he found himself short and had to borrow all he could at extortionate interest. Cairo's economy stabilized, but as soon as Mansa Musa got home he cleared his debt in a single payment, ruining his moneylenders as the gold price plummeted again.

Mansa Musa annexed Timbuktu, where the Niger comes closest to the Sahara, and this became the main transit point for salt, gold, and culture. A building program to beautify Mali's cities made Timbuktu grandest of them all. Here an Islamic education program for the wealthy gave rise to Sankore University. With 400,000–700,000 manuscripts, it housed the largest African library since Alexandria.

Opposite page: main map:

THE EMPIRE OF MALI *by 1325*

Sundjata of Niani took over Ghana's gold trade beginning in 1235 and set up a tribal federation. More goldfields were added and rule became more centralized until Mansa Musa replaced the federation with an imperial administration.

Inset map:

EMPIRES OF TRANS-SAHARAN TRADE

The empires of Ghana, Mali, and Songhay succeeded one another, with the Almoravids bringing Islam to western Africa toward the end of the Ghana period.

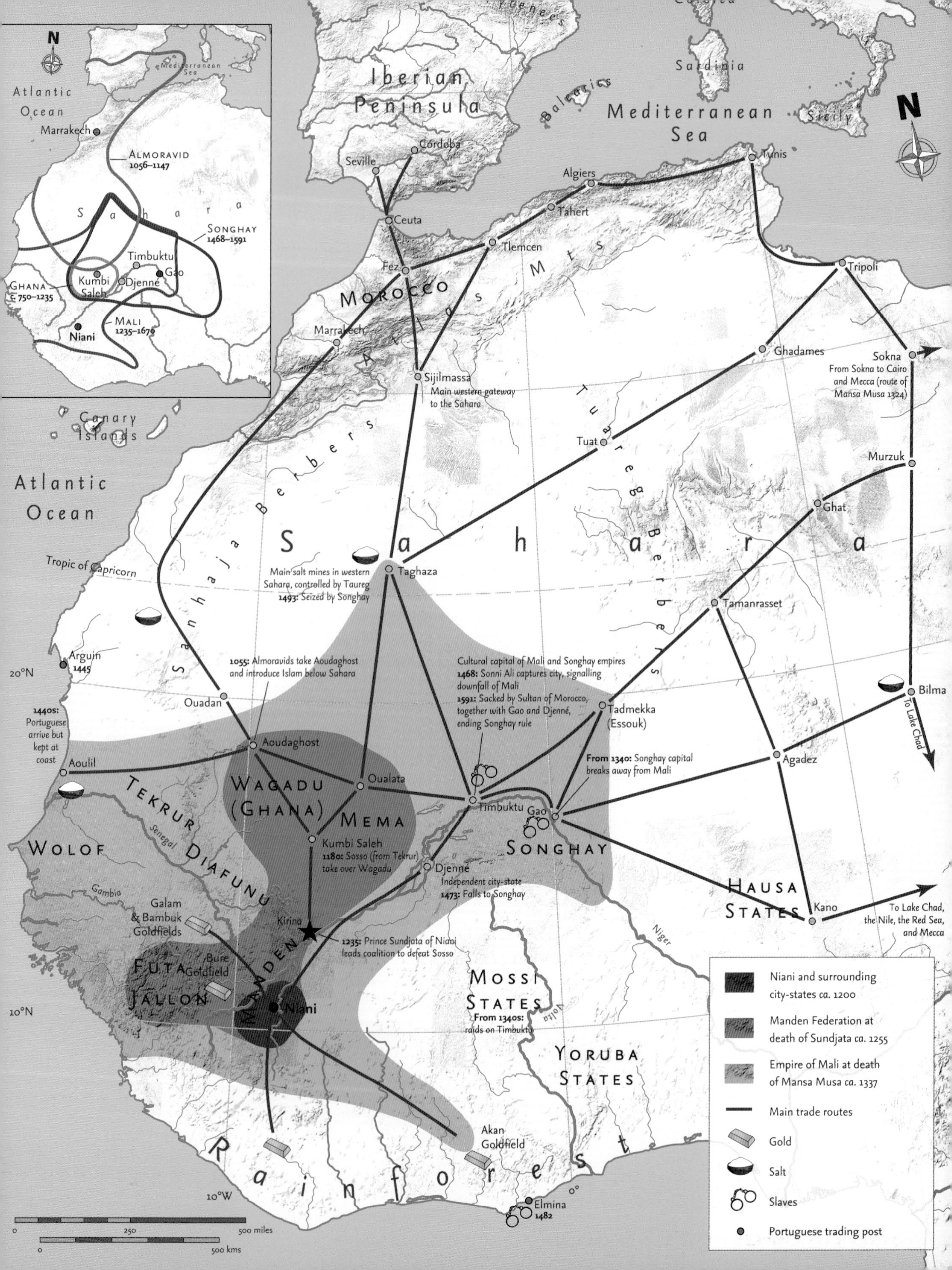

N
Mediterranean Sea
Atlantic Ocean
Marrakech
Almoravid 1056–1147
Sahara
Songhay 1468–1591
Timbuktu
Gao
Kumbi Saleh
Djenné
Ghana c. 750–1235
Mali 1235–1670
Niani
Iberian Peninsula
Sardinia
Balearics
Mediterranean Sea
Sicily
Córdoba
Seville
Ceuta
Algiers
Tunis
Tahert
Tlemcen
Fez
Morocco
Atlas Mts
Tripoli
Marrakech
Sijilmassa
Main western gateway to the Sahara
Ghadames
Sokna
From Sokna to Cairo and Mecca (route of Mansa Musa 1324)
Canary Islands
Sanhaja Berbers
Tuareg Berbers
Tuat
Murzuk
Atlantic Ocean
Ghat
Sahara
Tropic of Capricorn
Taghaza
Main salt mines in western Sahara, controlled by Taureg
1493: Seized by Songhay
Tamanrasset
Arguin 1445
20°N
1055: Almoravids take Aoudaghost and introduce Islam below Sahara
Cultural capital of Mali and Songhay empires
1468: Sonni Ali captures city, signalling downfall of Mali
1591: Sacked by Sultan of Morocco, together with Gao and Djenné, ending Songhay rule
Bilma
To Lake Chad
Ouadan
Tadmekka (Essouk)
1440s: Portuguese arrive but kept at coast
Aoudaghost
Aoulil
From 1340: Songhay capital breaks away from Mali
Agadez
Wagadu (Ghana)
Oualata
Tekrur
Mema
Timbuktu
Gao
Senegal
Kumbi Saleh
1180: Sosso (from Tekrur) take over Wagadu
Wolof
Diafunu
Songhay
Djenné
Independent city-state
1473: Falls to Songhay
Gambia
Hausa States
Galam & Bambuk Goldfields
Kano
To Lake Chad, the Nile, the Red Sea, and Mecca
Kirina
1235: Prince Sundjata of Niani leads coalition to defeat Sosso
Niger
Futa Jallon
Bure Goldfield
Manden
Mossi States
10°N
Niani
From 1340s: raids on Timbuktu
Volta
Yoruba States
Akan Goldfield
Rainforest
10°W
0°
Elmina 1482
0 250 500 miles
0 500 kms
Niani and surrounding city-states ca. 1200
Manden Federation at death of Sundjata ca. 1255
Empire of Mali at death of Mansa Musa ca. 1337
Main trade routes
Gold
Salt
Slaves
Portuguese trading post

SONGHAY

Mansa Musa, famous for his largesse, and his brother Mansa Suleyman (ca. 1341–1360), notorious for his meanness, were both strong leaders, but after Suleyman's death, civil war broke out and order was only restored by a court official fronted by a puppet mansa. By 1400, Bure was producing less gold and Mali's power was fading.

Already in 1340, the Songhay from Gao had broken away. They controlled the canoes that carried Mali's trade along the Niger. Under Sonni Ali (1464–1492), they took Timbuktu in 1468 and, in 1473, the great city of Djenné, which Mali could never capture because it was built on an island in the river. Being farther away, Songhay could not gain as tight a grip on the goldfields as Mali, but there were big slave markets in both Gao and Timbuktu. Under the Songhay, therefore, slaves replaced gold as the main commodity traded across the Sahara.

Askia Muhammad I (1493–1538) was as much a successor to Mansa Musa as to Sonni Ali. He was a centralizer, replacing the tribal basis of Songhay administration with a bureaucracy based on Islamic law. He also presented himself culturally as the preserver of Mali's empire, promoting Islamic scholarship as Mansa Musa had done and presiding over Timbuktu's golden age.

However, the Songhay Empire, which reached to Cameroon at its height, was run by a tiny Islamic urban elite, just 3 percent of the population, and was beset by increasing revolts. In addition, it made enemies in the north by taking the Taghaza salt mines in 1493 and, in 1591, firearms enabled Morocco to destroy Songhay and cart Timbuktu's scholars off to Marrakech. In Niani, meanwhile, Mali's mansas hung on in name until 1670, when the city was razed by Djenné.

By this time, gold had long been moving south to European traders on the coast and in 1663, the English began minting the *guinea* (a corruption of either "Ghana" or "Djenné"). But European colonies in the Americas meant demand for West Africa's gold was giving way to demand for slaves, so that here on the coast, as across the Sahara, the gold trade dwindled. The transatlantic slave trade had arrived, yet the Europeans themselves were kept at bay. Dense jungle and unnavigable rivers kept inland areas removed from the effects of European imperialism until well into the 19th century. By then, centuries of isolation from Europe's technological advancement made its sudden appearance all the more devastating.

Just such a clash of civilizations had already brought down two great empires across the Atlantic.

THE AZTEC EMPIRE

The Aztecs were the heirs to over 2,000 years of civilization in Mesoamerica. Long before their arrival, human sacrifice and a cyclical idea of time had become widespread and the Valley of Mexico established as the heartland of successive empires. The Aztecs built on these traditions to create an empire that fed on a continual state of war.

THE DEPARTURE OF QUETZALCÓATL

The groundwork for Mesoamerican society was laid by the Olmecs, a farming people on the Caribbean coast most productive around 900–400 BCE. The Olmecs built pyramids, devised an alphabet, and produced a calendar.

The Maya, who spread across the Guatemalan highlands and the jungle of Yucatán beginning around 250 CE, developed these elements—particularly the calendar. They also began a tradition of sacrificing human blood so as to give back some of the life force the gods had themselves given humans. The Maya viewed time as a series of cycles, from the daily cycle to a longest cycle of 144,000 days. Renewing these cycles of life sometimes entailed human sacrifice.

Meanwhile, an imperial tradition was emerging in the highlands of the Valley of Mexico. Here an obsidian quarry made possible the rise of Teotihuacán, a city-state at its height between 300 and 750 CE. Teotihuacán contained 400 obsidian workshops churning out blades, 60 percent of which were exported as far abroad as Guatemala. It was an ordered metropolis of 100,000–200,000 people, able to exert economic and perhaps military control over the Maya at Tikal.

Teotihuacán's several temple complexes included a central pyramid adorned with friezes of rain gods and feathered serpents. Its downfall following frequent droughts was accompanied by the rise of Xochicalco, a smaller city also centered around the temple of a feathered serpent. Xochicalco's ruler wore a feathered headdress and ruled in the name

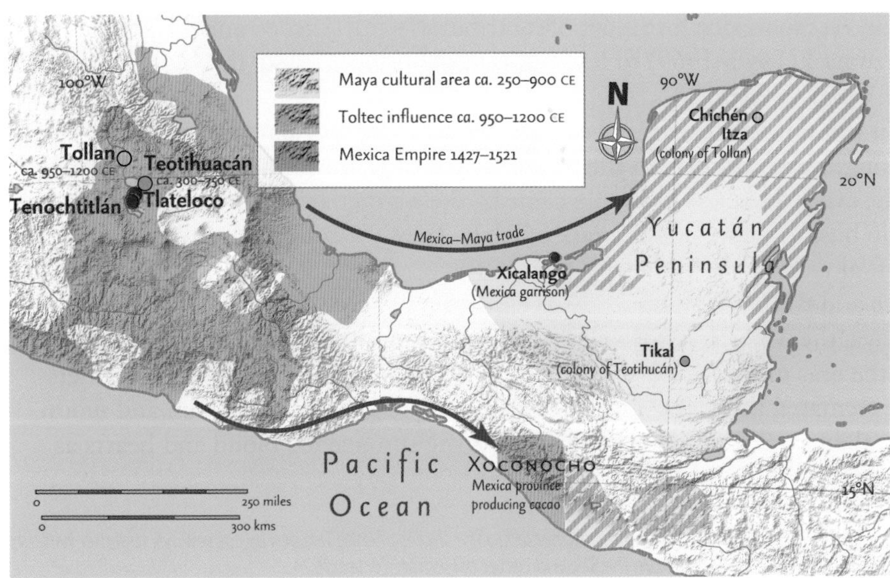

CENTURIES OF WIDER IMPERIAL INFLUENCE FROM HIGHLAND MEXICO

Teotihuacán, the Toltecs, and the Mexica all sought to dominate relations with the Maya of the Yucatán Peninsula and the Guatemalan Highlands.

of *Quetzalcóatl—cóatl* ("snake") and *quetzal*, the sacred bird whose long green tail feathers were used to make the headdress.

Around 950–1200 CE, another city near the obsidian quarry became dominant. This was Tollan, city of the Toltecs. Its rise followed the arrival of immigrants escaping desertification in the northwest, led by Topiltzin (ca. 923–ca. 947 CE).

We are told that Topiltzin became a popular ruler in Tollan in part by restricting sacrifice to bloodletting, by which small amounts of blood could be offered up by piercing fleshy parts of the body without endangering life. Like Xochicalco, Tollan had its temple to Quetzalcóatl, and Topiltzin wore the feathered headdress. Like Teotihuacán, the Toltecs spread their tentacles east, colonizing Chichén Itzá and building a temple to Quetzalcóatl there, too.

Later generations confused man and god to the extent that Tollan's founder passed into legend as Topiltzin Quetzalcóatl. Topiltzin had left Tollan for the Gulf Coast and this became the basis for stories of the god Quetzalcóatl journeying to the east. In one version, his nemesis Tezcatlipoca kicked him out of Tollan for ending human sacrifice. Bloodletting had long been a means to ensure individual well-being, but it provided a meager diet for the gods if they were to guarantee the health of a whole society. The time would once again come when only the engine of the blood system itself would do.

THE RISE OF TENOCHTITLÁN

In the 13th century, new immigrants from the northwest appeared in the Valley of Mexico, saying their ancestors had left a place called Aztlán (hence "Aztecs") a century earlier. These were the Mexica. Around 1300, they came under the protection of the Culhua, heirs to the Toltecs, before ending up in the salt marshes of Lake Texcoco.

Here, in 1325, they founded an island city named Tenochtitlán. They built dikes, causeways, and aqueducts and sowed crops on *chinampas*, high-yielding island beds of scooped-up mud.

The first *tlatoani* ("ruler") of Tenochtitlán came from the Culhua royal family, who traced their line back to Topiltzin. The Mexica used their Culhua lineage to claim legitimate rule, but Topiltzin's exodus to the coast created a problem. The solution was to elaborate on earlier stories and have Quetzalcóatl sail away, leaving the Mexica to run things until his return.

They now turned to two neighboring powers: Texcoco and the stronger Azcapotzalco. After a civil war, Azcapotzalco lost most of its tributaries to Texcoco and Tenochtitlán, leaving Moctezuma I (1440–1469) to lead an imperial triple alliance that soon expanded far beyond the Valley of Mexico.

Tenochtitlán was a highly organized city funded by taxes that paid for public works and army training. Revenue came in the first instance from the chinampas and from control of trade; every day, 60,000 people came to the market at Tenochtitlán's twin city Tlatelolco to do business overseen by state officials. Then there was tribute. Provinces were largely left alone as long as they paid up, but tribute included supplying victims for human sacrifice and the army stood ready to enforce payment.

Like the Maya, the Mexica saw time as a series of cycles of renewal. Underpinning them all were the eras of five successive suns. The age of the fifth sun had begun when two gods were cremated in great ovens at Teotihuacán, producing a new sun and moon. The other gods then sacrificed themselves because the sun needed blood and hearts as

The island city of Tenochtitlán, crisscrossed by canals and connected to the shores of Lake Texcoco by causeways, together with an aqueduct bringing spring water from the west. From the Second Letter *of Hernán Cortés, 1524.*

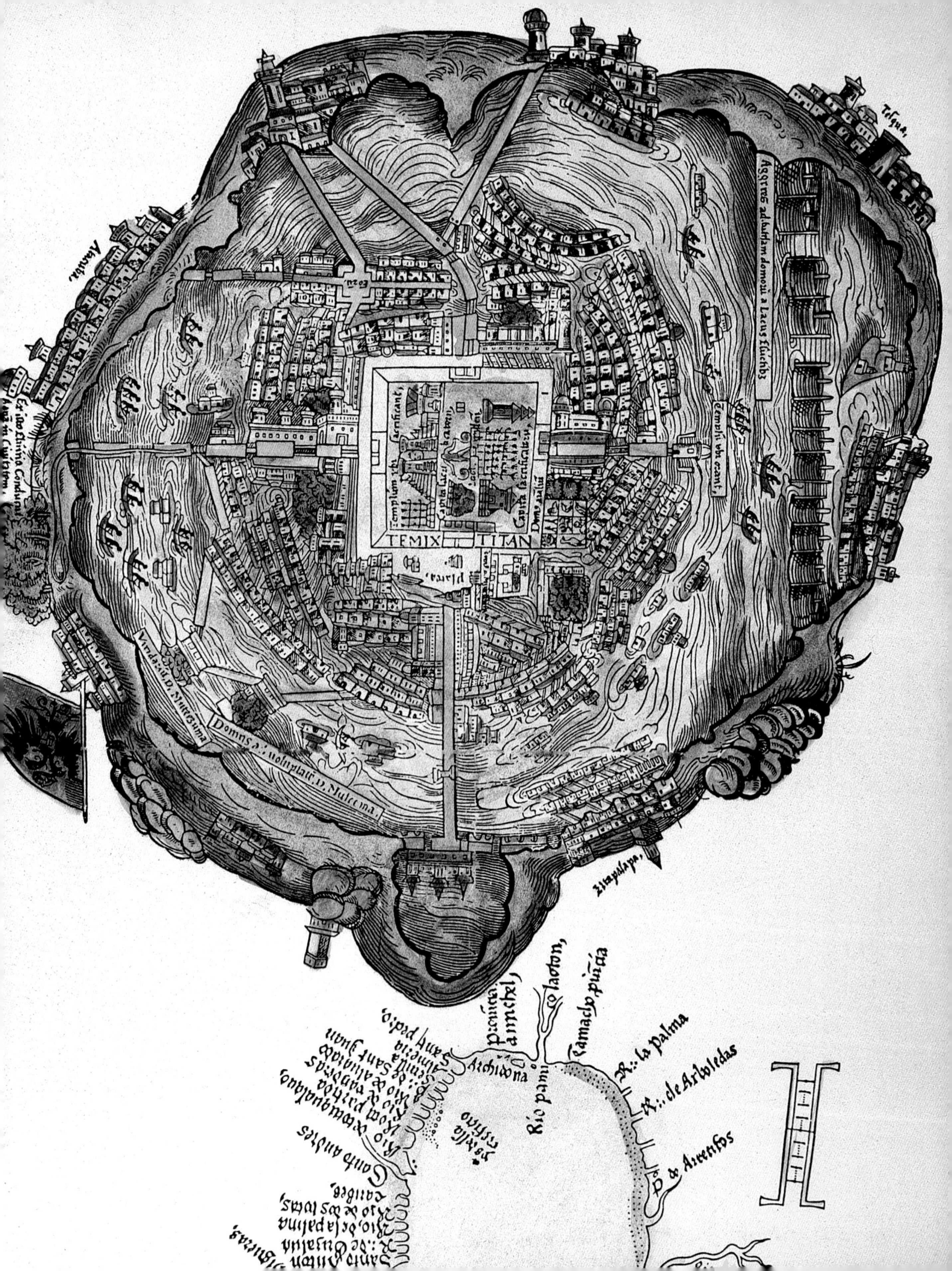

TEMIX TITAN
Tesqua,
R.: la palma
R.: de Arboledas
Rio pamo
Archidona

fuel. Within this there were shorter cycles. To make the transition from one cycle to the next, the sun and other nature gods needed further feeding. Tezcatlipoca, banisher of Quetzalcóatl, had created war so victims could be captured for sacrifice.

Tezcatlipoca required a yearly victim. Huitzilopochtli, sun god and Mexica patron, also needed victims yearly, as well as at the end of every 52 years—on top of which, the dedication of his new temple in 1487 demanded about 20,000. Victims were held down while a priest cut them open and tore out their beating hearts.

Human sacrifice escalated in the face of a growing sense of imminent disaster. This may have been driven by population pressure in an empire of 25 million, but there was nevertheless a structural demand for instability. A soldier had

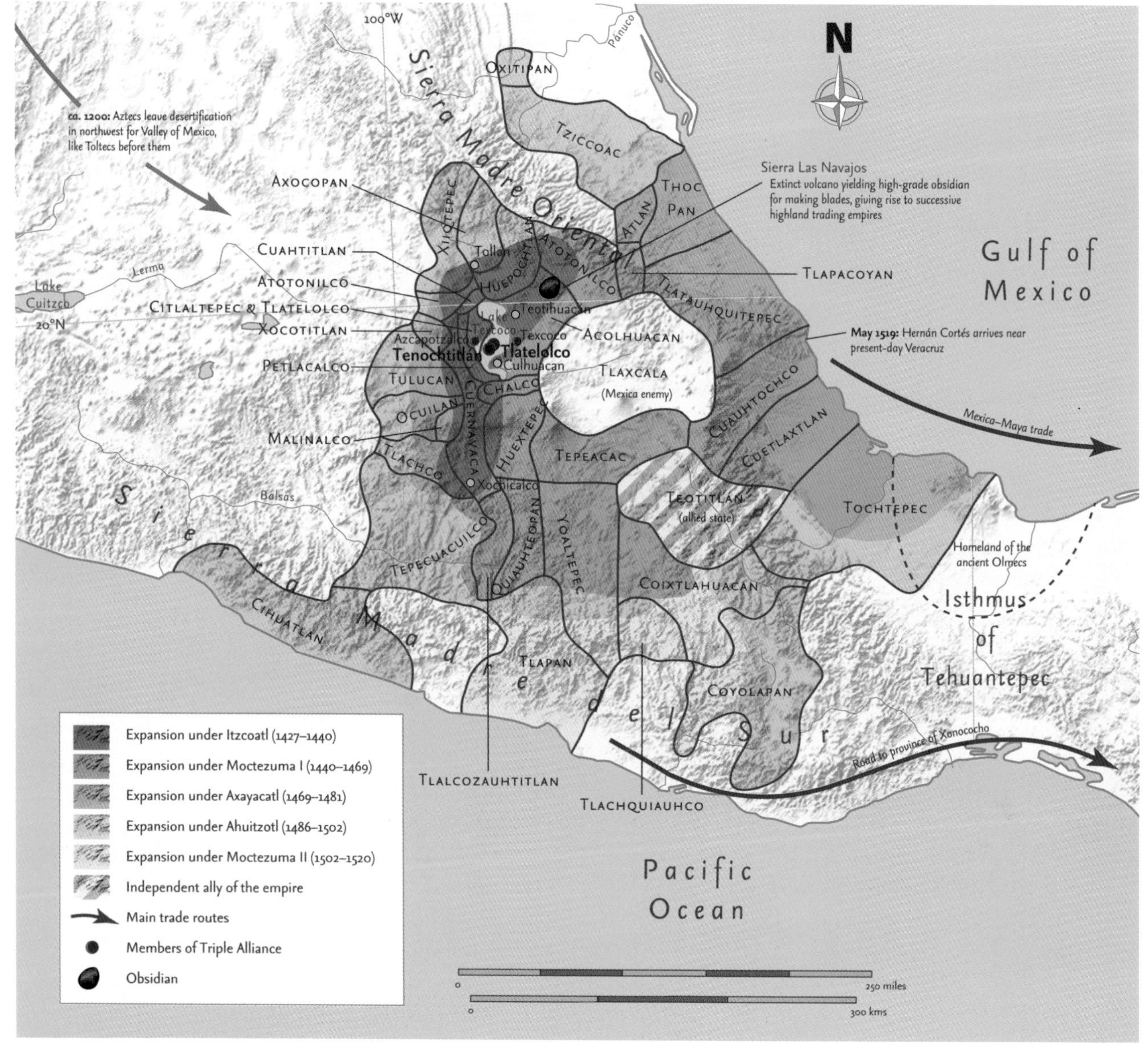

THE EMPIRE OF THE CULHUA MEXICA, BETTER KNOWN AS THE AZTECS, *1427–1521*

The Mexica founded Tenochtitlán in 1325, but remained under Azcapotzalco until a rebellion in 1426 delivered most of its provinces to Tenochtitlán and Texcoco. The Mexica then expanded as leaders of an imperial triple alliance.

to capture at least one victim for sacrifice to be eligible for promotion, so when provincial rulers failed to hand over their quota, the army was only too willing to step in. This system created no incentive to court the consent of subject peoples.

THE RETURN OF QUETZALCÓATL

By the reign of Moctezuma II (1502–1520), Tenochtitlán was at the height of both its power and its unease. Moctezuma was a priest from the temple of Huitzilopochtli, chosen as a prudent move regarding appeasement of the gods. Things began well, with 5,000 sacrificed at his coronation, but Moctezuma was soon claiming to be the equal of the gods. A series of bad harvests, a purge of nobles, and a rise in tribute to adorn the court was capped in 1510 by a comet foretelling the return of Quetzalcóatl and the consequent end of the Mexica regency.

In spring 1519, at the start of a new 52-year cycle, Hernán Cortés arrived on the coast near where Topiltzin Quetzalcóatl had supposedly left. The subject peoples of the Mexica, farmed as victims for human sacrifice, saw their chance to break free and escorted Cortés to Tenochtitlán. On the way, Moctezuma's envoys brought Cortés the feathered headdress and, in November, Moctezuma invited Cortés into the city. Apparently he told Cortés he did not take him for a god, but he was nonetheless cautious.

This was the beginning of months of mounting tension during which Moctezuma became a prisoner in his palace, caught between the Spanish and his own nobles, in whose eyes he had lost credibility by allowing a foreign power to occupy his city. When the Spanish became jumpy and massacred participants at a religious festival, this provoked a full-scale Mexica uprising. Moctezuma was killed and Cortés, with a third of his men, only just managed a nighttime escape across the causeway in the driving rain.

Cortés returned at the head of 200,000 provincial rebels eager to see the end of the Mexica. They laid siege to Tenochtitlán, now trying to recover from both civil unrest and an epidemic of smallpox brought by the Spanish. The lakeside cities were taken, Tenochtitlán's aqueducts were cut off, and a fleet was built with which to invade the island. After three months, the city was entered and up to 240,000 people killed. Unfortunately for the Mexica's liberated subjects, the fall of Tenochtitlán merely delivered them into the hands of the Spanish.

When the Spanish came they found themselves with a number of advantages. They brought with them horses, steel, and smallpox. They were lucky enough to fit into a story that gave the Mexica only temporary rule. And, most decisively, they found a subject population looking for an opportunity to rebel. To an extent the Mexica were simply unlucky in having their legimitizing narrative work against them. But in alienating the provinces so completely, their religious practices sowed the seeds of the empire's downfall, and to take no reforming measures was a mistake of administrative judgment. Any empire that feeds off of unchecked exploitation will be inherently unstable.

Meanwhile, far to the south, a more carefully administered empire had been developing.

THE INCA EMPIRE

The Incas, like the Aztecs, were the last and greatest inheritors of traditions stretching back thousands of years. Unlike the Aztecs, however, the Incas were interested in consent. Instead of extracting tribute from a collection of states always ready to rebel, they aimed to produce a stable, unitary state that controlled the lives of its subjects as much as possible.

BEFORE THE INCA

By the time of the Inca, civilization on the western fringe of South America was 4,000 years old. Here highland plateaus of varying altitudes rising behind coastal plains of varying degrees of fertility created a range of environments.

The best highland plateaus lay around Lake Titicaca. As different plants grew at different altitudes so cooperation between communities arose, with the llama carrying produce up and down the mountainsides. The best coastal plains lay farther north, where fishing villages and farming communities digging irrigation networks emerged. Before the Inca, there had been two attempts to bring together these very different kinds of society.

First came the Chavín. Sometime before 1200 BCE, they began building a temple complex in the mountains whose influence spread ever wider over the following millennium. After about 200 BCE, the draw of Chavín de Huántar lessened and more regionally distinct cultures appeared, but around 600 CE, two highland cities, Tiahuanaco, by the shores of Lake Titicaca, and Huari, further north, began to pull the Andes together for a second time.

Tiahuanaco seems to have been primarily a religious center, presided over by a weeping god with echoes of a deity from Chavín de Huántar. Huari was a militaristic city-state with the organization to carry out large-scale terracing and road-building programs. Their combined powers looked forward to a unified Andean realm, but once again this did not last.

Around 1200, the whole of the coastal region to the north fell under the control of the Chimú who developed a classic, centrally managed state based on irrigation agriculture that became the economic powerhouse of the Andes.

The stage was now set for the Inca.

THE INCA CONQUESTS

While the Chimú were at their height, the Inca were a small highland kingdom with a capital at Cuzco and troublesome neighbors. In 1438, after the Inca had themselves been flexing their muscles, the Chanca to the northwest invaded Cuzco just as the Inca were deciding who should succeed to the throne. The old king and his chosen heir retreated, leaving a younger son, Pachacuti Inca Yupanqui (1438–1471), to defend Cuzco. To secure his hometown, Pachacuti now fought off the Chanca, siding with the nearby Quechua against them, at the same time as fighting his father and brother for the title of *Sapa Inca* ("Only Ruler").

The process of safeguarding Cuzco and securing his rule involved Pachacuti killing another brother when he exceeded orders to control the Chanca and headed north to take Chimú-friendly Cajamarca. In place of a brother and potential rival, Pachacuti relied on his sons. Two of them he sent south to annex the Lake Titicaca region. A third, Topa Inca Yupanqui, he sent north to deal with the Chanca and the Chimú.

After subduing the Chanca, Topa Inca marched to Quito in the far north in an effort to outflank the Chimú, main threat to the Inca but also the main prize they coveted. Chan Chan, the great Chimú capital on the coast, was heavily defended by a fortress to the south, from which direction an Inca attack was expected. But coming down from Quito, Topa Inca was able to take Chan Chan by surprise and win an easy victory. The wealth of the Chimú now fell to him, together with the secrets of their administration.

Meanwhile, Pachacuti was developing structures to consolidate his gains. The immediate concern was to break up regional loyalties and improve agricultural productivity, both of which threatened to make Inca rule unsustainable. To this end, he introduced *mitma*, a policy of resettling sections of recently captured populations within longer-established Inca provinces and replacing them with *mitmaqkona*, colonists charged to instill loyalty and demonstrate new farming practices.

Regional rulers were co-opted into a growing imperial administration, roads and

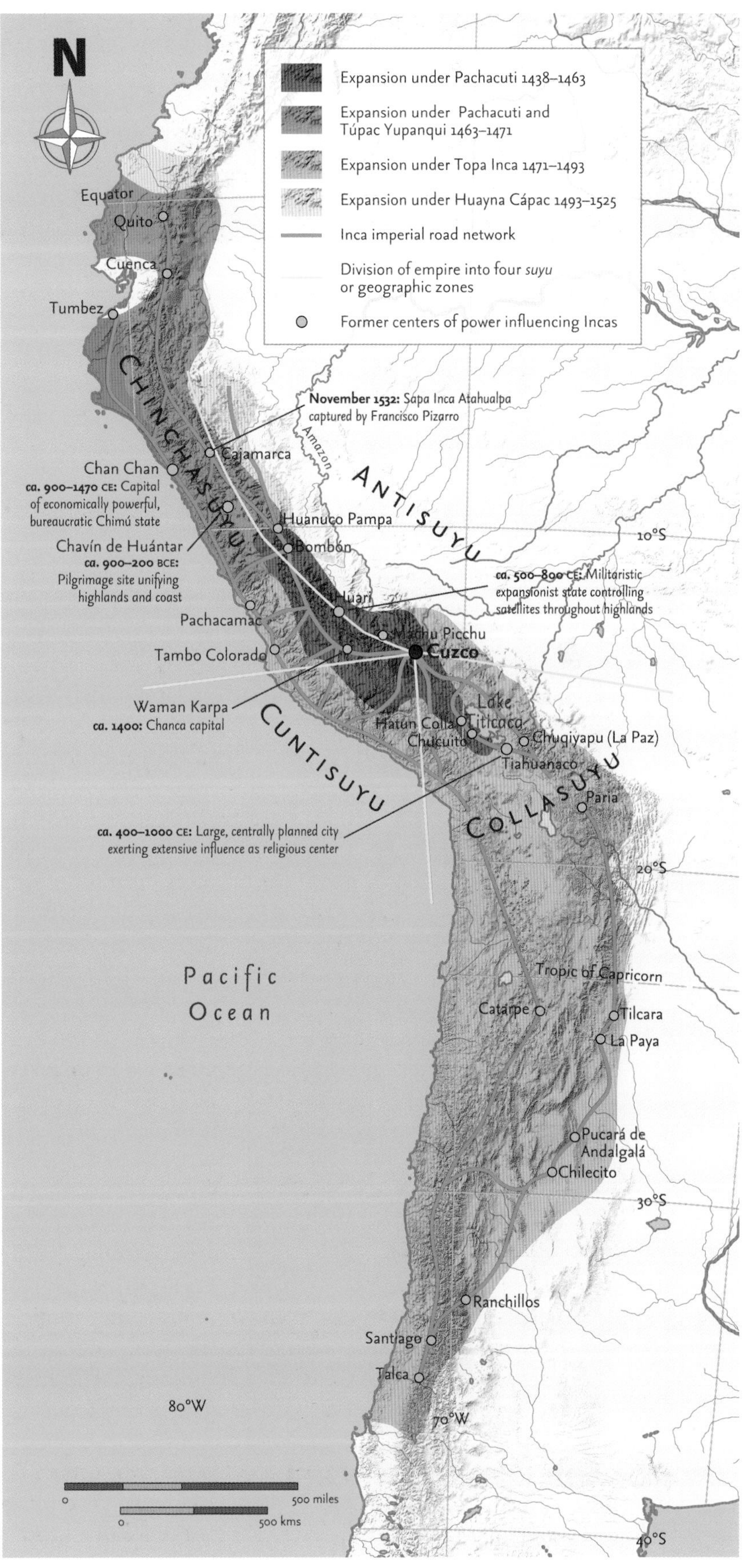

THE INCA EMPIRE *1438–1532*

From defending Cuzco against invaders in 1438, Pachacuti went on to create an empire. In 1463, he left his son, Topa Inca, to continue extending the empire while he concentrated on organizing the administration of a single state stretching the length of the Andes.

roadside food stores were built to make communications and movement of troops more efficient, and the language of the Quechua was adopted as a lingua franca. The Inca began to prepare new conquests by sending spies to glean information, followed by a messenger explaining to the local ruler the economic benefits of submission. It was often not necessary to send in the army.

At the heart of the empire, Pachacuti established a custom preventing a new ruler from inheriting his predecessor's wealth, which went instead to his other offspring and to maintain a cult surrounding his mummified remains. It promoted political harmony, but it also meant that each new sapa Inca had to make his own fortune.

Accordingly, after Pachacuti abdicated in 1471, Topa Inca embarked on an epic campaign to extend Inca rule south of Lake Titicaca. From Quito to what is now Santiago, he carved out an empire the length of Alexander's, without horses and over far more challenging terrain.

By the time Topa Inca's son Huayna Capac acceded in 1493, the size of the empire made further expansion difficult. But by this time a wealth-producing machine had been built.

An Inca official delivers a report to Topa Inca using a quipu, *an abacus-like arrangement of knotted strings used to keep accounts and also to record historical events. From the* First New Chronicle and Good Government *of Waman Poma, a Quechua nobleman who wrote to the king of Spain protesting against Spanish rule (1600-1615).*

TAHUANTINSUYU

The Inca machine was fueled by the taxpayer, who contributed labor in various ways. There were state farms to work on. Then there was *mita*, or public works service: terraces and irrigation channels to dig; bridges, tunnels, and 15,500 miles (25,000 kilometers) of roads to construct; stores, temples, and offices to build. There was also army service. In return, the government fed, clothed, and housed taxpayers while they worked for the state. It gave out food in times of need and trained officials to run the whole system.

The taxpayer belonged to an *ayllu*, an extended family providing for itself by farming its own plot of land. If the harvest failed, the state would make up the difference. The ayllu formed the base of an organizational pyramid managed at each level by officials. Ayllu were grouped into *saya* ("districts"), which in turn were grouped into *waman* ("provinces"), which made up the four *suyu* or geographic zones of *Tahuantinsuyu*, the "Land of Four Quarters," as the empire was called. Central government at Cuzco was staffed by members of 10 or 11 clans related to the sapa Inca. To preserve the royal bloodline, the sapa Inca's main wife was his sister.

The nobles and their *yanakonas* ("serfs") were tax exempt, as were state officials, professional craftsmen, and other specialists such as litter-bearers and the *chasqui* messengers. The chasqui were relay runners, chewing coca leaves to keep going and often carrying a *quipu*, a recording device using knotted string, in their knapsacks. The *mitmaqkona*, or colonists, were another tax-exempt group.

In addition, the Inca promoted a state religion. The Inca ruling class worshipped Viracocha the creator-god, but ordinary people felt closer to the sun-god Inti, whose warmth ripened their crops. So Inca power expressed itself in the sapa Inca becoming Inti's son and temples being erected in all the new territories where Inti took his place heading the local gods.

But this was destined to have unexpected consequences.

TEARS OF THE GODS

The Inca did not use money. Tax was paid in labor, produce was exchanged by barter, and there were no merchants traveling on their roads, which were reserved for the army and state officials. But there was no shortage of gold.

Gold was valued by the Inca, not because it symbolized wealth but because it linked them to the gods. Gold was tears wept by Inti in his concern for the world, and the Andes were full of it. Hence, gold lined the walls of the Temple of the Sun at Cuzco, the mummies of the sapa Incas it housed dripped with gold jewelry, and gold maize and llamas stood in its garden.

But in Europe, gold meant something quite different.

In 1525, Huayna Capac died of a unknown illness that was beginning to infect the land, as did his heir. This was either smallpox or measles, spread through the jungle from Spanish adventurers looking for gold on the Caribbean and Atlantic coasts.

A succession dispute between the half brothers Huáscar and Atahualpa now erupted and spiraled into a seven-year civil war. Then, in 1532, just as Atahualpa was savoring victory, Francisco Pizarro appeared at Cajamarca with 168 Spanish soldiers.

The Incas had never seen horses, steel swords, or guns before, never mind men with white skin, but Atahualpa, with all the Andes under his thumb, misread the danger. Huáscar was still alive and, seeing the Spanish as a potential ally, he gave Pizarro an audience. Pizarro promptly kidnapped him and demanded a roomful of gold and two of silver in ransom. When it was paid, Pizarro had him killed and replaced with a puppet ruler. Over the next few years, the Inca roads, which the Spanish found to be the equal of anything built by the Romans, allowed Pizarro and smallpox to claim the empire while its puppet ruler fled into the mountains to establish a remote Inca rump state that held out until 1572.

Tahuantinsuyu was more work in progress than finished achievement. The empire was still young, its different ethnic groups unused to being closely monitored, and some collaborated with the Spanish. They soon came to regret doing so. The Spanish melted down fine Inca craftsmanship into gold bullion, then replaced their complex infrastructure with a primitive economy based on mining silver for export, using a labor system copied from Inca state farms.

For the Spanish there was nothing else to learn from the Inca—beyond the cultivation of the potato, the tomato, and a handful of other plants a growing Europe would come to depend on as it proceeded to take over the world.

THE FIRST GLOBAL EMPIRES

The Empires of Spain and Portugal / The Dutch / Britain and France in America

In 1453, Constantinople fell to the Ottoman Turks, Venice was in decline, and Christian Europe was a gaggle of small, squabbling states just emerging from the shadow of the Black Death. Fifty years later, a new continent had been discovered and European ships were creating a new kind of empire.

Up to this time, most empires had covered a continuous stretch of land. There had been maritime empires in the Mediterranean and also in Southeast Asia, but not on this scale. European colonies in the New World or in the East were thousands of miles away and many times the size of the states that governed them. Managing such far-flung empires was a new challenge.

It was partly a question of money. To squeeze profit from the silver mines of Peru or the nutmeg trees of the East Indies, ships had to be built, voyages that could take two years had to be financed, and things had to keep going smoothly at home.

In the background lay old rivalries transposed to a new global stage. Jealous powers vied for the same trade and, with ships moving plants, animals, and people around the world, what happened in one place affected another. There could be no more empires of isolation. Now wars were fought across the oceans to settle disputes in Europe, and vice versa.

In the midst of all this sat the task of controlling those who settled and made their fortunes in the remote colonies. Sooner or later, these people would challenge the authority of kings and queens beyond the horizon. Rulers already faced a similar problem governing lands scattered throughout Europe. Both at home and abroad, the first murmurings of national independence could be heard.

THE EUROPEAN CONTEXT TO THE EARLY COLONIAL EMPIRES

In 1500, Europe was not yet a continent divided into nation-states. Great dynasties such as the Habsburgs, the Bourbons, and the Tudors owned accumulated lands and sought more, both in Europe and overseas. The Habsburgs, who were also hereditary Holy Roman emperors, ruled so many lands they struggled to keep control—especially of the Dutch.

N
Ruled by Spanish branch of Habsburg family beginning in 1558, with date of acquisition
Ruled by Austrian branch of Habsburg family beginning in 1558, with date of acquisition
Economically dependent on Spain
Portugal
Dutch Republic 1581–1795
French lands with dates of acquisition
British Isles
Scotland
Great Britain
From 1707
Ireland
1155 to England
Wales
1536 to England
England
Baltic Sea
1581: Northern provinces break away as Dutch Republic
1508: Holy Roman emperor becomes hereditary Habsburg title
Holy Roman Empire
Rhine
Silesia
1526
Bohemia
1526
Moravia
1526
Hungary
1526
Austria
1282
Styria
Tyrol
1363
Carinthia
1335
Carniola
Danube
1679 to France
50°N
Atlantic Ocean
Brittany
1491
Anjou
1481
Burgundy
1477
1477
Bourbon
1527
France
(Bourbon from 1589)
Alps
1580: Portugal annexed by Spanish Habsburgs
1640: Independence reestablished
Navarre
1512
Pyrenees
Provence
1481
Genoa
Corsica
Sardinia
Balearic Islands
40°N
Mediterranean Sea
1492 to Castile
0
250
500 miles
0
500 kms
0°
10°E

THE EMPIRES OF SPAIN AND PORTUGAL

The European Age began with mariners of the Atlantic seaboard taking a leap into the unknown. Maritime exploration brought a clash of cultures astonishing to the explorers, devastating to the discovered. In the process, a global economy was created, which the Spanish Habsburgs tried to contain within a global empire.

THE PORTUGUESE EAST

The 14th century was a difficult one for Europe. The Crusades had brought Eastern luxuries and economic growth, but now came harvest failure, famine, and, in 1347, bubonic plague, which claimed over a third of Europe's population. Output dropped, prices rose, demand slumped, and recession lasted for almost 100 years while, in the east, Ottoman power grew.

Nevertheless, Christian Europe had acquired a new confidence since the Crusades. Cathedral spires now scraped the sky as testaments to European enterprise and technological expertise. In the far west, the Crusades continued in the form of the *Reconquista*, a war to sweep Islam from the Iberian peninsula. Since 1248, the Moors had been confined to Granada and, in retaliation, Moroccan pirates habitually raided the Portuguese coast for Christian slaves. Then, in 1415, Henry, Prince of Portugal, drove an invasion of the main pirate base at Ceuta.

In Henry the Navigator, religion merged with economics and a taste for the exotic. Pirates aside, he wanted to find the source of the Moors' African gold and was lured by the legend of Prester John, supposed ruler of a Christian kingdom beyond Muslim lands. In 1420, he began funding expeditions down the African coast in strong but small and maneuverable ships known as *caravels*.

At first, Henry's program seemed an eccentric indulgence. It yielded Madeira and the Azores, but they seemed of little worth. The Canaries had been claimed for the Spanish kingdom of Castile by Jean de Bethencourt in 1402 and nearby was Cape Bojador, where changing winds had long prevented further exploration. By sailing out to sea on a 15th attempt, however, Henry's caravels journeyed beyond this point and on past the Sahara. By 1444, West African slaves were on sale in Lisbon, and, in 1452, the Portuguese *cruzado* ("crusader") was minted from African gold. Henry's enterprise had paid off.

Explorers continued south until Bartolomeu Dias rounded the Cape of Good Hope in 1487. Ptolemy of Alexandria's map of the world, accepted since the 2nd century, showed the Indian Ocean as a landlocked sea, but Dias disproved this just as merchants were looking for a new route to the East bypassing the Ottomans. Then, in 1497, Vasco da Gama sailed for India, returning in 1499 with pepper and cinnamon.

Da Gama had not been gently received at Calicut, however. The Indian Ocean had its own merchants who would have to be elbowed out. Now caravels were joined by much bigger carracks, able to carry large cargoes and take the recoil from heavy guns. Asian ships, held together by rope and wooden pegs, were no match.

The Portuguese arrive at Nagasaki in a carrack. A high forecastle from which to shoot and several cannon to deliver broadsides helped force open trade. A 16th-century Japanese namban *("foreigner") screen.*

The Portuguese now moved from curiosity and exploration to building a trading empire. In 1503–1504, Afonso de Albuquerque built a fort near Calicut at Cochin, the first of a series he envisaged closing off the Indian Ocean. After operations along the east African coast and the Persian Gulf, he took Goa in 1510 and Malacca (Melaka) in 1511.

The Malacca Strait controlled eastern access to the Indian Ocean and opened the door to China and Japan. From Malacca in 1513, Albuquerque sent an expedition to Canton (Guangzhou). By the 1530s, the Portuguese were trading in Macau and, by the 1540s, they had reached Nagasaki.

THE SPANISH WEST

The Portuguese took a century to reach the East by sailing around Africa. No one dared to simply sail west instead. Ptolemy's map showed Eurasia spanning half the earth and his contemporary, Eratosthenes, had fairly accurately calculated the earth's size. That left an ocean no ship could carry enough food and water to cross. Genoese navigator Christopher Columbus, however, used a smaller estimate of the earth's size and a bigger estimate of the size of Eurasia, a miscalculation that seemed to bring China much closer.

It sounded risky but, by 1492, Ferdinand of Aragon and Isabella of Castile were ready to gamble. They had united the Spanish and finally brought the Reconquista to an end by conquering Granada. Now they needed to pay for the war and check the imperial ambitions of Portugal. So they gave Columbus three ships. After five weeks at sea, he hit the Bahamas in a lifesaving stroke of luck. His real achievement, figuring out how to use the trade winds to get back again, opened the way for colonization.

Colonization began on the island Columbus named La Española (Hispaniola), where the settlement of Santo Domingo soon became the center of operations in the New World. To begin with, there was unregulated murder and enslavement of the indigenous Taíno. Early in the new century, the Spanish government tried to control the situation by issuing settlers with *encomiendas*, licences entrusting a certain number of natives to their care. Encomiendas obliged settlers to "civilize" the Taíno by teaching them Spanish and introducing them to Catholicism; in return, they could use their labor, but the native population was not to be enslaved.

Then, from the mainland, came reports of gold and silver. In 1519, Hernán Cortés, Secretary to the Governor of Cuba, disobeyed orders and led a private expedition that ended in him founding Mexico City on the ruins of Tenochtitlán. A decade later, Cortés's second cousin, Francisco Pizarro,

The New World as it appeared in Sebastian Munster's Cosmographia, *a best-selling illustrated atlas published in 40 editions from 1544. Cathay (China) is labeled fairly near North America, though by this time Magellan had sailed across the Pacific and discovered just how far it really was.*

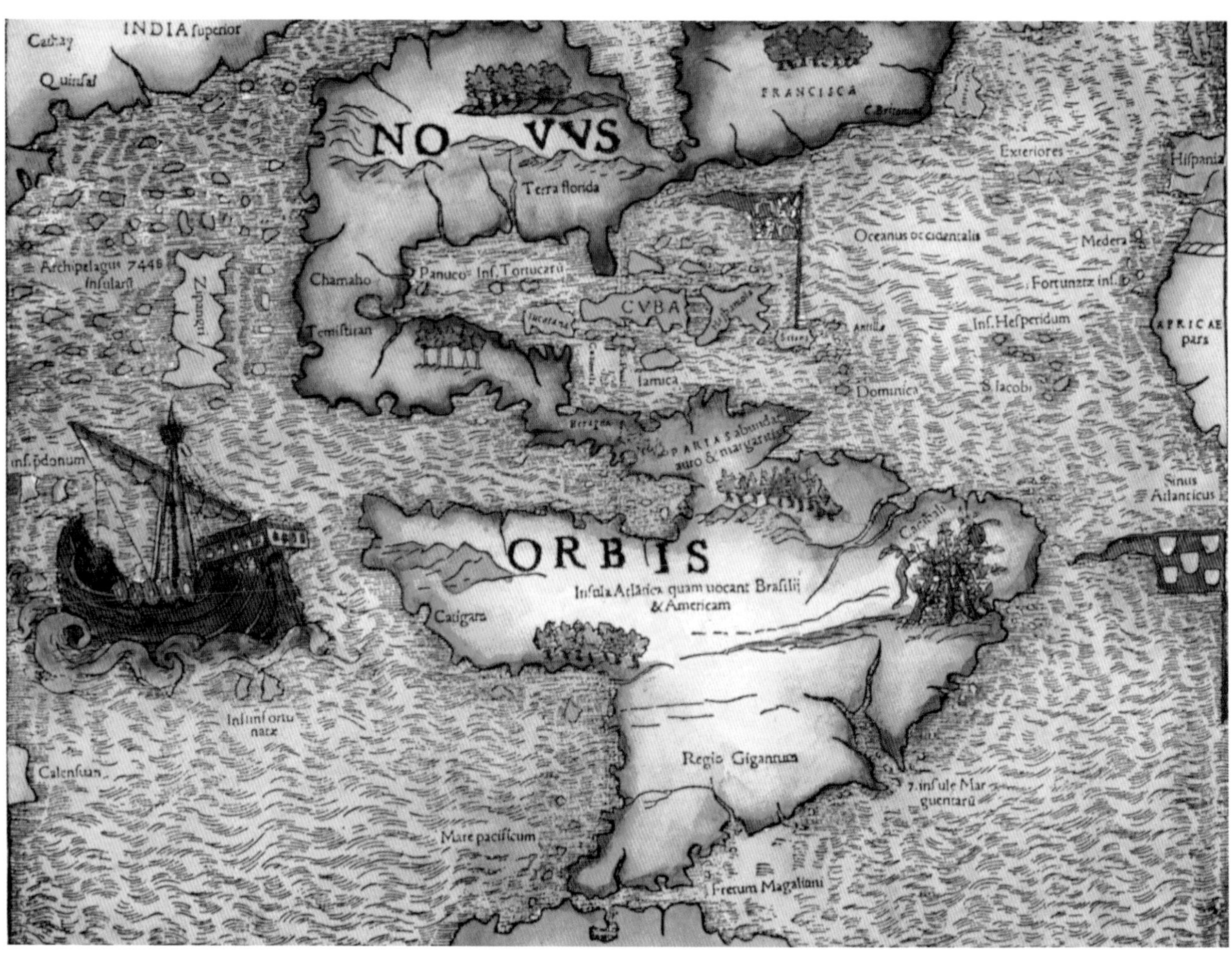

received state backing to take Tahuantinsuyu from the Incas. In neither case were the *conquistadors* ("conquerors") interested in taking over the running of a great empire, but sought only short-term plunder. Before long it became unclear whether they were acting for Spain or for themselves.

In the 1520s, silver was discovered north of Mexico City at Guanajuato. The encomienda system now provided the Spanish with miners who were soon concentrated into *reducciones*, settlements with a church and priest, where the population could be both educated and exploited as a work force more easily. In practice, it was hard to see much difference between the encomienda system and slavery. All land was owned by the Spanish crown, but control of labor was the real source of power, and this lay in the hands of the conquistadors. As such, the Viceroyalty of Peru became a de facto private kingdom for Pizarro and his brothers.

In 1542, reforms were brought in after lobbying by Bartolomé de Las Casas, a Catholic priest concerned for the native peoples. Under the New Laws they could not be forced to work, they had to be paid, and they could not be sent down the mines. In addition, encomendias could not be passed on, threatening the future of family fiefdoms. This provoked revolt in Peru with Gonzalo Pizarro claiming independence from Spain. His power was such that the government backed down and brought in weaker laws in 1552. In the meantime, much richer silver deposits were discovered at Zacatecas in Mexico and especially at Potosí in the Andes, and mining continued.

GLOBAL EXCHANGE

In 1494, the Treaty of Tordesillas drew a line through the Atlantic, later sanctioned by the pope, giving everything east to Portugal and the New World in the west to Spain. In 1500, however, Pedro Álvares Cabral discovered that part of Brazil lay east of this line and claimed it for Portugal. Then, in 1521, having sailed west around South America and across the Pacific, Ferdinand Magellan claimed the Philippines for Spain. In 1529, the Treaty of Saragossa drew a second line to separate spheres in the East Indies.

Between them, Spain and Portugal had encircled the world and lines on a map to apportion shares of it did little more than express Europe's new swaggering sense of entitlement. Soon a global movement of people and all manner of goods was underway. In the East, Portuguese carriers made more money from illicit trade between Asian ports than from official journeys back to Lisbon, and a black market developed. In the West, plantation agriculture and the loss of a native labor force to smallpox brought new crops and new people.

The key crop was sugarcane and the plantation system had been moving west since the Crusades. Before then, Europeans had used honey as a sweetener, but the Crusaders discovered sugarcane from the East Indies being grown in Palestine and saw a business opportunity. Extracting the sugar was labor-intensive but this was the only limit to production, and crusading knights began to set up plantations on islands in the Mediterranean. Unlike feudal estates, sugar plantations were commercial enterprises streamlined for maximum productivity, using slave labor to keep costs down. After 1453, the Ottomans controlled the Black Sea slave markets, but by this time the Portuguese had found a new labor source in Africa.

Portuguese plantations on São Tomé were the first to use mostly West African slaves, but these slaves escaped to the mountains and began raiding. Across the Atlantic, however, Africans had nowhere to run. So far from home, their spirits were broken and they were easier to control. By the 1550s, therefore, the Portuguese were setting up sugar

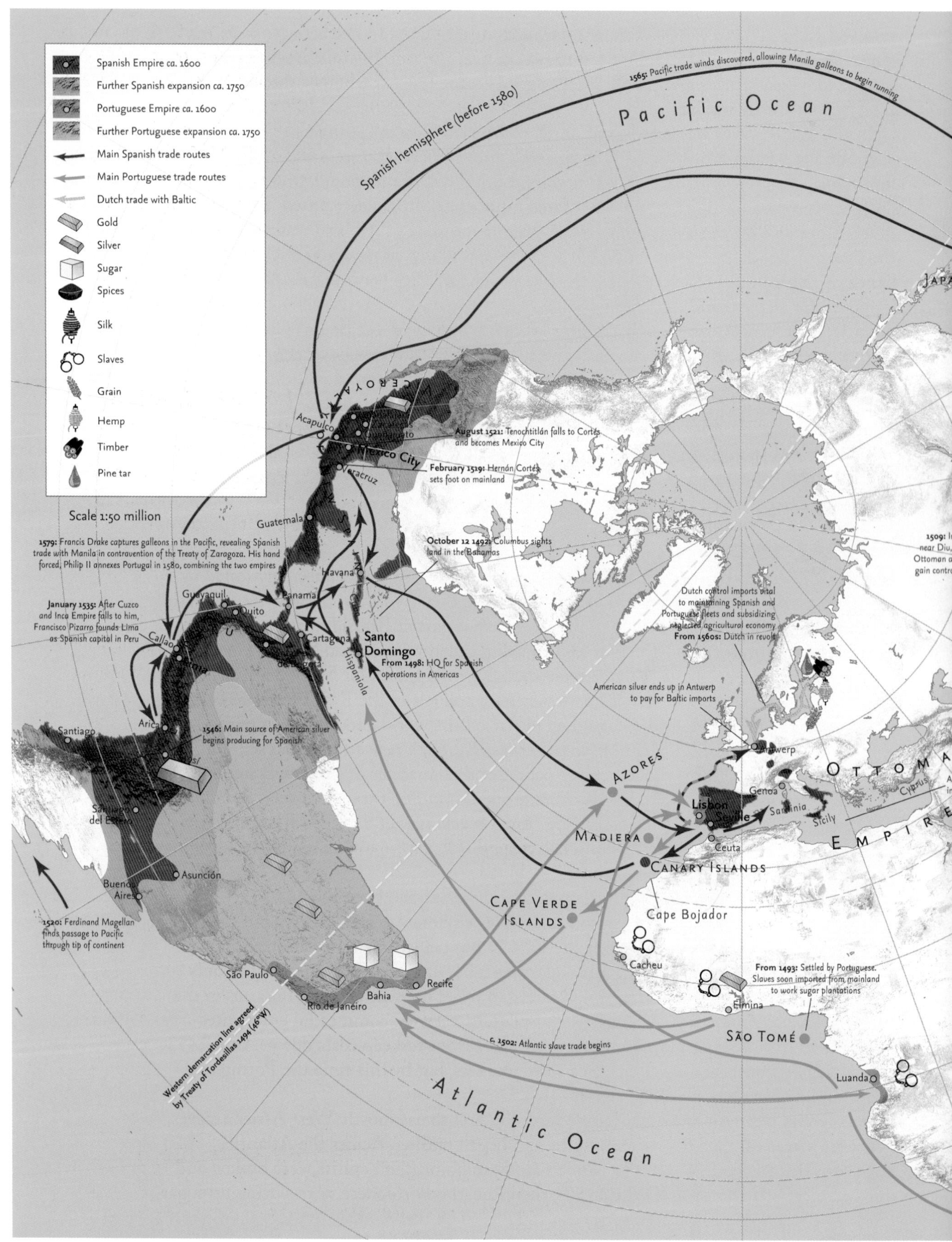
Spanish Empire ca. 1600
Further Spanish expansion ca. 1750
Portuguese Empire ca. 1600
Further Portuguese expansion ca. 1750
Main Spanish trade routes
Main Portuguese trade routes
Dutch trade with Baltic
Gold
Silver
Sugar
Spices
Silk
Slaves
Grain
Hemp
Timber
Pine tar
Scale 1:50 million
1565: Pacific trade winds discovered, allowing Manila galleons to begin running
Pacific Ocean
Spanish hemisphere (before 1580)
Acapulco
Mexico City
Veracruz
August 1521: Tenochtitlán falls to Cortés and becomes Mexico City
February 1519: Hernán Cortés sets foot on mainland
Guatemala
1579: Francis Drake captures galleons in the Pacific, revealing Spanish trade with Manila in contravention of the Treaty of Zaragoza. His hand forced, Philip II annexes Portugal in 1580, combining the two empires
October 12 1492: Columbus sights land in the Bahamas
Havana
Panama
Guayaquil
Quito
January 1535: After Cuzco and Inca Empire falls to him, Francisco Pizarro founds Lima as Spanish capital in Peru
Callao
Cartagena
Santo Domingo
From 1498: HQ for Spanish operations in Americas
Hispaniola
Arica
Santiago
1546: Main source of American silver begins producing for Spanish
Santiago del Estero
Asunción
Buenos Aires
1520: Ferdinand Magellan finds passage to Pacific through tip of continent
São Paulo
Rio de Janeiro
Bahia
Recife
Western demarcation line agreed by Treaty of Tordesillas 1494 (46°W)
Atlantic Ocean
c. 1502: Atlantic slave trade begins
Azores
Madiera
Canary Islands
Cape Verde Islands
Cape Bojador
Cacheu
Elmina
São Tomé
From 1493: Settled by Portuguese. Slaves soon imported from mainland to work sugar plantations
Luanda
Lisbon
Seville
Ceuta
Genoa
Sardinia
Sicily
Cyprus
Antwerp
American silver ends up in Antwerp to pay for Baltic imports
Dutch control imports vital to maintaining Spanish and Portuguese fleets and subsidizing neglected agricultural economy
From 1560s: Dutch in revolt
Ottoman Empire

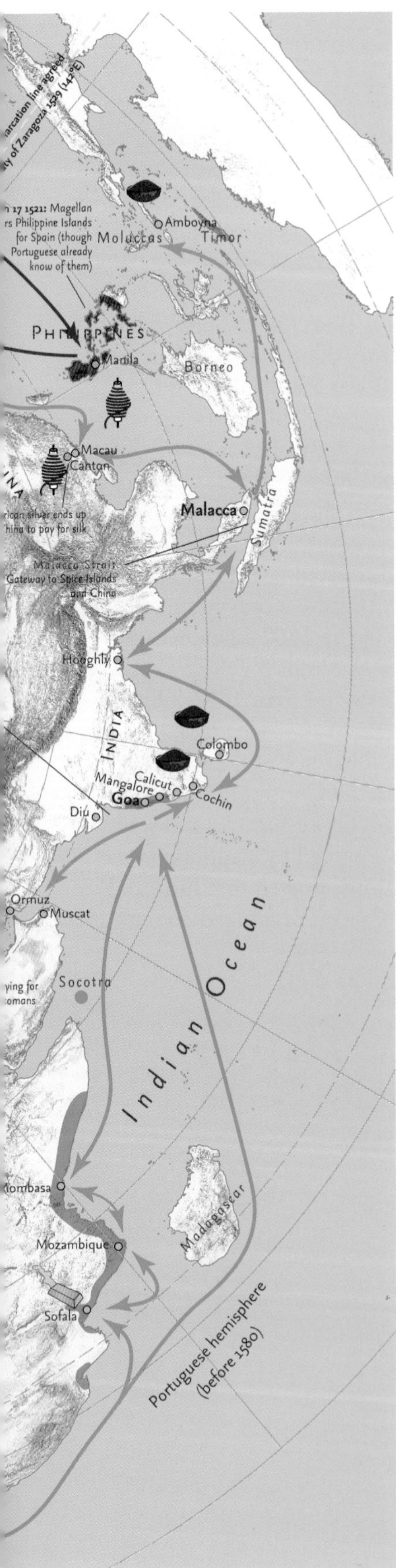

plantations in Brazil. After six years of working flat out, a slave was finished, but the planter's investment had been tripled. It made more financial sense to buy a new slave than improve working conditions.

The development of mines and plantations focused attention on the Americas but in the 1560s Spain began settling the Philippines. Huge Spanish galleons, the biggest ships so far built, sailed from Acapulco to Manila to exchange American silver for silk and porcelain from China, cotton from India, and spices from the Moluccas.

In 1580, Philip II of Spain (1556–1598) took over the Portuguese Crown and the first global empire was created, moving products, people, and money between Africa, America, Asia, and Europe.

THE FAILURE OF GLOBAL EMPIRE

The year Cortés set foot in Mexico and Magellan set sail to circumnavigate the globe, Charles, head of the Habsburg dynasty, became Holy Roman emperor. He already possessed lands throughout Europe, including Spain and the Netherlands, and as the Emperor Charles V (1519–1556) found himself fighting expensive wars across the Continent, mostly against Suleyman the Magnificent.

During his reign, silver began arriving from America but Charles had to spend it on Baltic timber, tar, and hemp for shipbuilding. A switch from arable farming to less intensive wool production in Spain meant importing wheat, also from the Baltic. So Charles had to borrow from the Fuggers, Europe's top bankers, whose wealth came from silver mines in Germany. They saw lending to the Habsburgs as an investment, but as more American silver arrived it drove down the value of their own mines, created general inflation, and got spent on new wars. In 1557, Charles's son Philip II (1556–1598), who inherited Spain and the Netherlands, faced the first of several bankruptcies, bringing the Fuggers down and branding himself a bad risk.

To raise money, Charles had begun standardizing the various tax laws of his European lands. He met resistance, particularly in the Netherlands, where Baltic trade was handled, but the fact that Charles was a

SPAIN AND PORTUGAL ENCIRCLE THE WORLD *ca. 1500–ca. 1600*

In 1492, Columbus discovered a new continent in the west for Spain and by 1498 the Portuguese had found a route to the east around Africa. The world became divided into Spanish and Portuguese spheres until Philip II of Spain annexed Portugal in 1580, creating a single global empire.

Flemish speaker born in Ghent helped. His son Philip was more a Spaniard, more an autocrat, and met greater hostility.

Into this situation came religion. Since German theologian Martin Luther had challenged papal authority in 1517, independent Protestant churches had spread throughout the Holy Roman Empire and beyond. The Holy Roman emperor was Philip's uncle and the Habsburgs were Europe's foremost defenders of the Catholic Church. Philip's attempt to crack down on religious dissent in the 1560s only further alienated Flemish and Dutch Protestants, sparking off 80 years of bitter religious war.

Most American silver was now ending up in China. Piracy in the Caribbean was rife and Philip's takeover of Portugal in 1580 turned Dutch eyes toward the Portuguese East Indies. The Spanish Armada of 1588 was Philip's attempt to suppress Dutch and English shipping by invading England, but this failed when a storm blew his fleet off course, and so began a shift in control of the seas. By 1648, the Holy Roman Empire had to recognize new Protestant states within its borders and Spain had to accept the independence of the Dutch, who now controlled the East Indies.

As early as the 1540s, settlers in the Americas had resisted laws imposed from Spain. Subsequently *criollos*, those of unmixed blood, became a rich colonial class, albeit without political power. As plantations spread in the 1600s they became the owners of big *haciendas*, or estates, but high office was kept for the Spanish-born. In the early 19th century, following the American and French Revolutions, the criollos finally threw the Spanish out.

Three hundred years earlier, Spain and Portugal had made Europe rich. The fabulous wealth they brought home spread across the Continent, fueling a century-long boom. But coping with distant colonies cost a fortune and was beyond the communications technology of the time. Plagued by crippling wars, Spain's domestic economy was neglected and profits flowed to China and Holland. Despite their gunships, the Portuguese were never organized enough to sew up the East quite as Albuquerque had planned.

The Dutch would have to show them how it should be done.

THE DUTCH

The empires of religion, glory, and plunder that Spain and Portugal built foundered on economic mismanagement. But they brought wealth to Europe and this benefited the Dutch, a people with few natural resources, dependent on trade and finding ways to make their money work. With financial planning, the Dutch took over Portugal's erratically run trading empire and created a dependable shipping line.

AMSTERDAM

In 1282, a terrifying flood created the Zuiderzee, a large inlet that opened Amsterdam to the North Sea, producing a port well-placed to trade with the Baltic. Below the nearby Rhine, textile towns such as Bruges were already drawing Genoese merchants and bankers. By 1500, Bruges had silted up, leaving neighboring Antwerp as northern Europe's commercial and financial hub.

The Low Countries, or "Netherlands," passed between powerful families, ending up in the lap of the Habsburgs in 1477. Under Charles V, Antwerp became, in effect, the center of an overseas empire. First pepper and cinnamon from Lisbon, then American silver from Seville arrived here to pay for materials from the Baltic.

In 1576, however, after resisting Philip II's legal, fiscal, and religious policies, Antwerp was sacked by Spanish troops. Merchants and bankers fled north to Amsterdam, taking their skills and their silver with them. Here the Dutch were prepared to open their dikes rather than submit to Spain, and Amsterdam became a cosmopolitan business community, attracting Jews, Huguenots, and others fleeing religious intolerance.

Spain tried to squeeze Amsterdam by moving pepper shipments to Hamburg in 1591 but the Dutch were already planning to import their own spices, emboldened by the failure of the Spanish Armada in 1588. While secretary to the Archbishop of Goa in the 1580s, Jan Huyghen van Linschoten had copied top secret Portuguese maps showing an entrance to the East Indies between Sumatra and Java, which avoided Portugal's stranglehold on the Malacca Strait. In 1595, Cornelis de Houtman assembled four ships and set sail for the Sunda Strait. In 1597, he returned with a third of his crew and a few peppercorns.

Subsequent expeditions highlighted problems the Portuguese and Spanish had not solved. These two-year journeys were expensive and tied money up for a long time. Individual moneylenders could not reliably fund them. They were also high risk: ships might not return, or several might return at once, producing a glut that drove prices down.

So in 1602, the Dutch formed a joint-stock company to attract the high levels of long-term investment required. A large group of people, mostly uninvolved in running the company, each invested a sum of money that could not be withdrawn; this represented not a temporary loan but a permanent share of the company. Each year, company profits were split between an amount for reinvestment and an amount to be divided among shareholders. In order to make investing in the company a more attractive proposition, a stock exchange was created in Amsterdam where shares could be bought and sold again at any time. The value of shares rose and fell with the fortunes of the company. Risk was limited by government charter, which gave monopoly rights to control supply and thereby protect prices. It also gave the company the right to use military force, make alliances, set up courts, and mint currency.

The *Verenigde Oostindische Companie (VOC)*, or Dutch East India Company, funded a production line of *fluytships*, smaller and lighter-armed than Portuguese carracks, but able to carry more for their size and cheap enough to outperform the opposition by force of sheer numbers. With a consistency Portugal never attained, the VOC began a systematic takeover of the East Indies, beginning in 1605 with Amboyna.

EMPIRES OF SHAREHOLDERS

Amboyna lay in the Moluccas, or Spice Islands. With Ternate and Tidore, it supplied the world's cloves and was near the tiny Banda Islands, the only source of nutmeg. In 1621, the people of the Banda Islands were driven out or killed so VOC Governor General Jan Pieterszoon Coen could set up slave-run nutmeg plantations. In 1623, the VOC tried and beheaded employees of the much smaller English East India Company, recently arrived on Amboyna, and England quietly left the Moluccas to the Dutch.

By this time, Coen had established a centrally placed headquarters for the VOC on Java by burning both locals and the English out of Jakarta, renamed Batavia. He had big plans for Dutch settlement in the East but had to limit himself to the string of trading forts and spice plantations the VOC Board was willing to invest in—a theme to be repeated elsewhere.

The VOC took over Malacca in 1641, Colombo, center for cinnamon, in 1658, and, from there, the pepper ports of southern India. Everything was geared toward controlling supply. Native nutmeg plantations were burnt to keep prices high and pepper was slightly oversupplied to keep its price just low enough to dissuade English competition. All produce was collected at Batavia, then shipped onward.

Further east, the VOC traded with China from a base on Formosa (Taiwan) and with Japan from Dejima, a specially built island in the harbor of Nagasaki from where it monopolized European trade with Japan from 1641 to 1857.

In 1621, the *Geoctroyeerde Westindische Compagnie (GWIC)*, or Dutch West India Company, was formed.

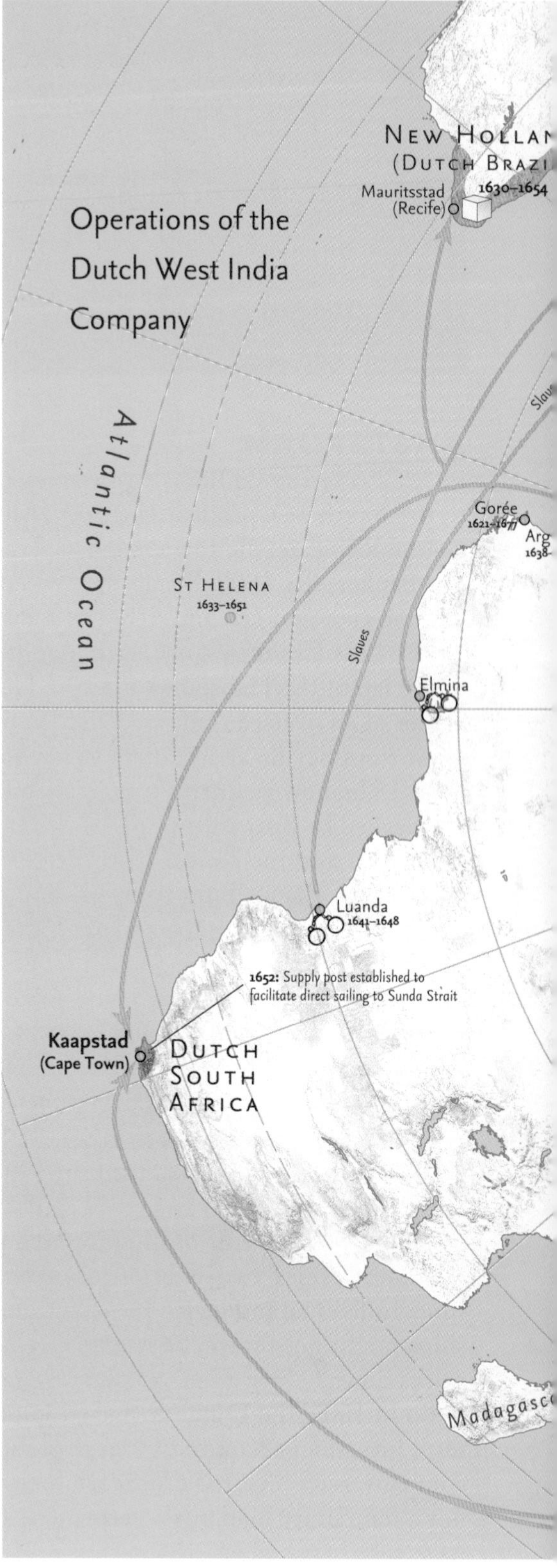

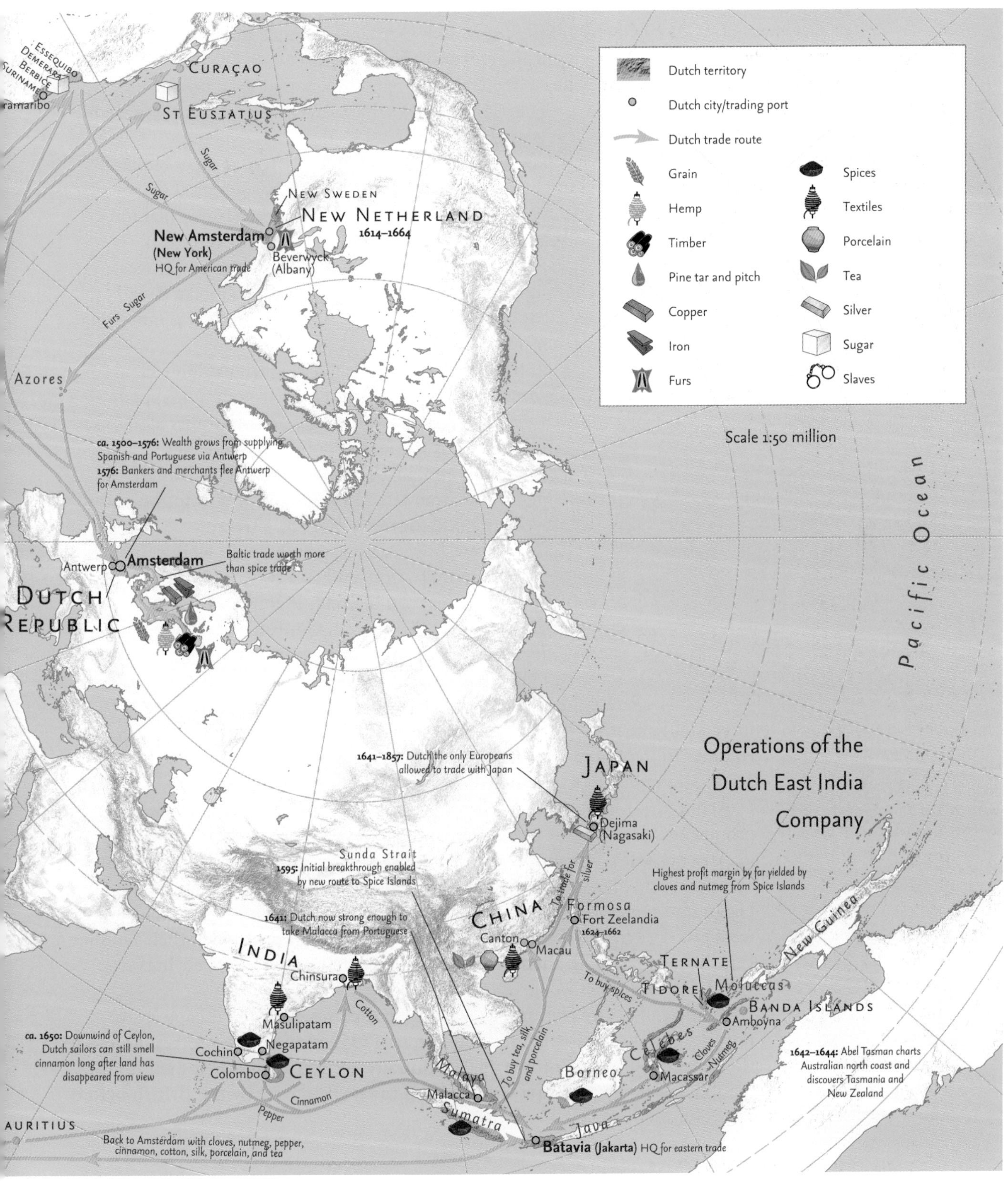

THE HOLDINGS OF THE DUTCH EAST AND WEST INDIA COMPANIES *ca. 1650*

In the 1590s, the Dutch found an entrance to the East Indies avoiding the Portuguese stronghold of Malacca and soon wrested control of the spice trade. Meanwhile, they set up trading posts in the New World—all supported by Dutch control of Baltic trade.

In the early 17th century, the Dutch pioneered modern finance, creating the world's first stock exchange in 1602. In 1636–1637 a craze for tulip bulbs created a futures market and the first speculative bubble. Before it burst, 12 acres of land were offered for a single Semper Augustus bulb.

Working for it were Caribbean pirates such as Piet Heyn, who captured 16 Spanish ships in 1628, producing a 50 percent dividend for shareholders that year. From the Portuguese, the GWIC took slave ports in West Africa and sugar plantations in Brazil.

Johan Maurits van Nassau, Governor of New Holland (Dutch Brazil) beginning in 1637, saw potential for immigration. He promoted road building, town planning, and local assemblies, but Amsterdam wanted only a business empire and would not back his project. It was a shortsightedness that allowed Portugal to retake Brazil and its sugar plantations in 1654. A similar story was unfolding farther north.

In 1609, the VOC contracted English explorer Henry Hudson to find a route to the East through unmapped North America. He failed but instead found furs along the river that bears his name. The colony of New Netherland was established and, in 1626, Governor Peter Minuit "bought" Manhattan Island for 60 guilders from the locals—a purchase they saw more as a treaty.

Tension grew, however, between Minuit, who wanted to encourage immigration, and a GWIC board interested only in trading forts. So in 1647, Pieter Stuyvesant, a good company man, was brought in. Contrary to plan, numbers now began rising (especially after the loss of New Holland), towns grew, and the colony flourished. But the GWIC was reluctant to spend on defense, which alienated settlers facing increasingly hostile tribes. It also underestimated the threat from English colonies to the north and south, and when four English ships turned up in 1664, Stuyvesant had to hand over New Netherland without a fight.

Across the Atlantic, inflexible company policy cost the Dutch their most promising settler colony of all. The Cape of Good Hope at the southern tip of Africa was the last supply post for VOC ships sailing directly to the Sunda Strait. In 1652, Jan van Riebeeck built a fort here, planted vegetables, and began trading with the local Khoekhoe for cattle. In 1657, VOC employees were given slaves from the East Indies and allowed to settle with their families. But the company told them what to grow, took a large cut of their harvests, and controlled trade.

By the end of the century, settlers began moving inland to escape VOC restrictions. The company followed but, by 1795, receiving no protection for their taxes and having grown apart culturally, settlers set up their own frontier republics, leaving the Cape Colony itself to be taken over by the British before much longer.

THE BALTIC

Just as the Spanish Empire benefited the Dutch, so the Dutch benefited the Swedish. Since the 1420s, Denmark had made money by charging a toll to pass through the narrow sound between Denmark and the Swedish mainland. After 1500, Dutch ships appeared in ever greater numbers and, consequently, received a discount. They brought a growing demand for Swedish iron, copper, and timber needed for shipbuilding and Sweden's rise began.

The first step was taken in 1523, when Gustavus Vasa took Sweden out of a Danish-controlled Scandinavian union. During the next century, Sweden fought Denmark–Norway for access to the North Sea, began to colonize the Baltic, and became a Protestant country.

Gustavus Adolphus (1611–1632) saw Sweden as a northern bulwark against the Counter-Reformation. He perfected a new, disciplined yet flexible fighting force that influenced Napoleon. Cannon were lighter, infantry units more mobile, and musketeers were trained to fire at three times normal speed. Crucially, infantry, cavalry, and artillery were cross-trained so they could fill in anywhere they were needed, with no pecking order between them. As the Dutch Revolt against Spain and the religious wars sparked off by the Reformation entered their final phase between 1618 and 1648, Sweden emerged as a major player. Gustavus Adolphus crushed the imperial Habsburg forces at Breitenfeld in 1631 and invaded as far south as Bavaria.

Six years after Swedish help against the Habsburgs, Peter Minuit, having fallen out with the short-sighted GWIC, helped set up New Sweden, a colony of around 600 settlers who built America's first log cabins along the Delaware River at the southern end of New Netherland. But this was land already claimed by New Netherland, and, in 1655, Pieter Stuyvesant took over New Sweden (though it remained largely autonomous).

By this time, the Baltic power the Dutch had spawned was becoming a potential threat to their interests, the more they depended on imported grain and shipbuilding materials. When, in 1658, Charles X marched through Denmark and across its frozen waters to take control of the Sound Tolls, the Dutch could not allow this and sent their fleet to the aid of Copenhagen.

Before the end of the century, however, the Dutch were cut out by Scandinavian ships directly supplying the rising powers of England and France. Then, in 1700, Peter the Great began pushing back the Swedes to create a Russian presence in the Baltic.

TIGHTER MARGINS

By now, the golden age of the Dutch was over. China had closed its doors to them in the 1660s and Japan set trade limits in the 1680s. When interruption of the pepper supply led to the English, Danes, and French all entering the market starting in the 1670s, the VOC began to question how much they should spend to protect their monopoly.

SWEDISH POWER AT ITS HEIGHT *in 1658*

Dutch trade made Sweden rich and powerful, enabling it to eat up the Baltic, fight Denmark for access to the North Sea, and defeat the Habsburgs in 1631.

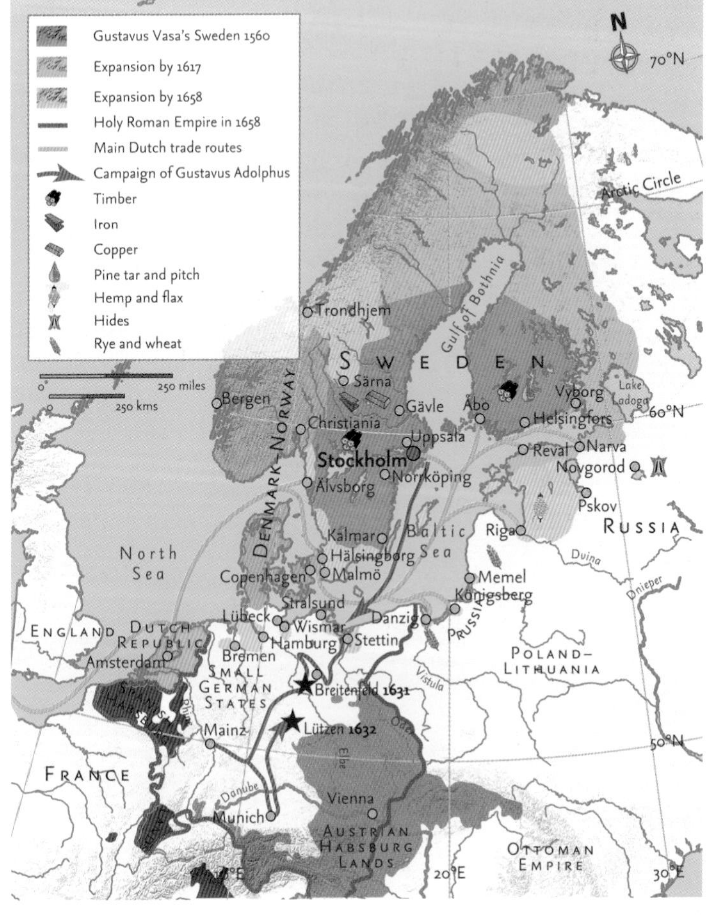

In the early 18th century, having smuggled seedlings from the Yemeni port of Mocha, the VOC began importing coffee from plantations on Java. Coffee, tea, sugar, and textiles seemed to be where the future lay. But these were high-volume, low-margin commodities compared to the spices the Dutch were used to. Nutmeg and cloves had sold in Europe for 300 times their cost. A readjustment was called for, but it was slow to appear.

Sugar from the East Indies cost more to ship than sugar from the Caribbean. Dutch tea brought to Batavia before forwarding was competing with English tea shipped directly from China. Profits began to fall, but dividends remained much as they had been. In the short term, shareholders back in Holland were happy, but for all that the Dutch had pioneered the transformation of glory and plunder into a sound business proposition, this was not sound business practice. It pointed to a change in the quality of management and behind that, to a social change that signaled the passing of an age. The entrepreneurs of the early 1600s had used the money they made from the spice trade to buy property back home and their children grew up thinking more in terms of rental income and home furnishings than commerce. They were a new generation with different interests.

In the end, the Dutch shared a vulnerability with the Portuguese: theirs was a maritime empire destined to fall to a stronger navy. In the Fourth Anglo–Dutch War, during the American War of Independence, the VOC lost half its fleet to the British and, in 1796, the government was forced to take over the company. By 1800 it had been dissolved. After Britain took Ceylon and the Cape Colony in the Napoleonic Wars, the Dutch state gave up wider imperial ambitions to concentrate on rebuilding its economy by expanding plantations in the East Indies and Suriname.

In the 1640s, Abel Tasman had charted parts of the coastlines of both Australia and New Zealand for the VOC, but these discoveries were left for the English to follow up on because they yielded no obvious opportunities for trade. The VOC was a commercial proposition; where Spain and Portugal had sent missionaries, it sent businessmen. It delivered a consistent return to its shareholders but overlooked the long-term potential of settling a continent such as Australia, just as the GWIC had overlooked America.

As it turned out, the settlement of North America was a prize worth fighting much harder for than the spice islands of the East Indies.

BRITAIN AND FRANCE IN AMERICA

North America was slow to be exploited by Europeans in the New World. It contained no dazzling civilizations to match the Aztecs and the Incas, no great silver mines to draw plunder. Yet this was to be the richest prize of all. The fight for it between France and Britain led to the first global war and the first successful colonial rebellion.

PIRATES IN THE CARIBBEAN

Henry VIII (1509–1547) built the biggest warships of his time but his first wife was Catherine of Aragon, daughter of Ferdinand and Isabella and aunt of Charles V, so his warships were not used against Spain. In 1554, Catherine's daughter, Mary I, married Charles's son, the future Philip II of Spain. Silver was now flowing into Spain from America but Mary saw neither silver nor her husband, who cared nothing for her. Still, she could hardly raid her husband's empire.

When Mary's Protestant half sister Elizabeth I, daughter of Anne Boleyn, came to the throne in 1558, things changed. Elizabeth had only a small navy but she had pirates. In 1579, Francis Drake captured a Manila galleon off Peru and helped himself to 26 tons of silver. Elizabeth received half—most of her income for that year.

In 1588, Elizabeth's pirates, plus her support for the Dutch Revolt against Spain, pushed Philip to invade England. The defeat of his Armada gave birth to England's pride as a maritime power, but a properly funded navy lay in the future. For now, piracy and privateering held sway.

Jamaica was a favorite target for pirates from Elizabeth's time on. It was formally seized from Spain in 1655, but remained a pirate base until the end of the century. In the 1620s, the west of Hispaniola was also lost to pirates, in this case French, before becoming the French colony of Saint-Domingue in 1697.

In both cases, piracy gave way to plantations on the model of those on St. Kitts, where English and French planters had arrived in the 1620s, massacred the locals, and carved up the island between them. They imported slaves to grow first tobacco, then sugar, and reproduced this pattern as they captured other islands. Jamaica and Saint-Domingue became the biggest and most productive of such colonies. By the time of the French Revolution in 1789, Saint-Domingue supplied 40 percent of Europe's sugar and 60 percent of its coffee.

The scale of English and French plantations in the Caribbean stimulated an upsurge in the transatlantic slave trade, which did 80 percent of its business after 1700.

EXPLORERS AND SETTLERS

Columbus's voyages both drew pirates to the Caribbean and prompted a search for a route to the East further north, where sailing nearer the pole would shorten the distance. In 1497, another Italian explorer, Giovanni Caboto (John Cabot), discovered Newfoundland for England and, in 1524, a third, Giovanni da Verrazzano, charted the North American east coast for France. Instead of a northwest passage, they found cod, and French and English fishermen were soon spending the summer season in North America.

By the 1530s, Jacques Cartier was exploring the St. Lawrence, seeking the Kingdom of Saguenay, a land of furs and gold spoken of by the Algonquin tribe. He tried to found Québec City in 1541 but permanent settlement had to wait until Samuel de Champlain arrived in 1608. De Champlain's beaver-skin trading post survived by supplying guns to the Algonquin and Huron to use against the Iroquois. Land was claimed for the French crown and, in 1627, Cardinal Richelieu (1624–1642) parceled out lots along the banks of the St. Lawrence to *seigneurs*, landlords whose tenants worked subdivisions of their land.

Meanwhile, in the 1580s, Walter Raleigh and a few friends had tried to found an English colony in Virginia, but it was small, Spain interrupted supplies, and it failed. After peace with Spain, James I (1603–1625) granted royal charters to explore North America for whatever treasures it might yield, and in 1607, the Virginia Company sent a group of hopefuls to found Jamestown, Virginia. Expecting to trade and become rich rather than plant crops, this colony starved and almost failed, too.

In 1611, however, John Rolfe, a member of a rescue party sent from England (and future husband of local princess Pocahontas), began planting tobacco in Jamestown and created a demand for labor. In England, peasants had been expelled from the land to make way for sheep and there was widespread unemployment. Starting in 1618, 50 acres (20 hectares) in Virginia were given to anyone able to afford the journey across. This led to the wealthy paying the passage of the poor in return for a set number of years of unpaid work, and gaining land in the process. After the 1660s, a rising standard of living at home made this deal less attractive to England's poor, and African slaves were imported instead.

Farther up the coast, it was too cold and the soil too poor for tobacco. But the winter brought migrating Newfoundland cod and, in the summer, vegetables could be grown on soil fertilized with fishmeal. The increasingly conservative and reactionary Church of England under Charles I (1625–1649) drove radical Protestant groups to make a new life here. In 1620, a small, ill-organized party arrived aboard the *Mayflower* at Cape Cod and managed to survive with the help of a local tribe. The 1630s brought a decade of far

After founding Québec in 1608, Samuel de Champlain secured his position by playing local tribes against each other. In 1609 he helped the Algonquin defeat the Iroquois on the banks of what is now Lake Champlain. From Champlain's Voyages*, 1613.*

more organized mass emigration by well-educated, high-minded Puritans with a program for a new society. They transplanted communities wholesale and made New England the economic and political engine of North America.

De Champlain, however, had reached the Great Lakes and, in 1660s, French exploration revived. In the 1680s, René-Robert Cavelier de La Salle journeyed all the way from Niagara down the Mississippi to the Gulf of Mexico, naming this region Louisiana, after his king.

FRANCE LOSES AMERICA

The rise of England's navy really began in the 1650s under Oliver Cromwell. From the Dutch, Cromwell took the principle that the navy should protect merchant shipping so taxes from trade could fund it. Once this was established, improvements to ships and guns were made, signaling was standardized, and press-gangs began delivering recruits. England now edged out the Dutch.

Meanwhile, Louis XIV (1660–1715) was building a French army. Louis seduced his nobles with Europe's most lavish court while appointing advisors from outside the nobility. This enabled him to centralize power and collect more taxes to make France's army the strongest in Europe. When his grandson inherited the Spanish throne in 1700, the rest of Europe feared the Bourbon family becoming the new Habsburgs and a war was fought (the War of the Spanish Succession, 1701–1714) to prevent France and Spain from uniting to control Europe and monopolize the New World.

But France did not need Spain's help to vie with Britain for global mastery. France had Saint-Domingue, worth more than Britain's 13 North American colonies combined. France had Québec, holding its own against the Hudson's Bay Company, chartered in 1670 by Charles II (1660–1685) to take over the fur trade. France had slave ports in Africa and pepper ports in India.

In North America, however, the British outnumbered the French 30 times and rising, and France's control of the Mississippi meant this expanding population was encircled. From the 1740s on, Virginians and Pennsylvanians began looking for new lands to the west, but in the 1750s the French built a chain of forts to keep them back. In 1754, fighting broke out in America. By 1756, there was a world war—the Seven Years' War (1756–1763).

Banking on its army, France planned to accept losses overseas while making gains in Europe, then to trade European gains to get its colonies back. But by now Frederick the Great had built a Prussian army to outclass the French, and Britain, whose kings had been German since 1714, was his ally. The war in Europe centered on Prussia and Austria, France's new ally, fighting over Silesia. Britain planned to use the navy to supply Prussia while blockading France and attacking its colonies, a strategy that worked better than France's plan.

In Europe, Austria lost Silesia. In India, France lost its main trading port of Pondicherry. In the Caribbean, Britain took Guadeloupe and Martinique, enclosing the Caribbean before invading Cuba, which sucked Spain and Portugal into the war. The deciding moves, though, were made in the north after James Wolfe took Québec for the Brittish in 1759. The year after, Montréal fell and, in 1762, the French surrendered on Newfoundland.

Main map:

BRITAIN AND FRANCE IN THE NEW WORLD *before 1763*

Europeans colonized the Caribbean in similar style, but in North America the English settled the coast, while the French explored inland from the St. Lawrence.

Inset map:

NEW TENSIONS IN BRITISH NORTH AMERICA *1763–1775*

Winning land west of the Appalachians from France, Britain fenced most of it off as an Indian Reserve and taxed its 13 colonies to pay for an army presence.

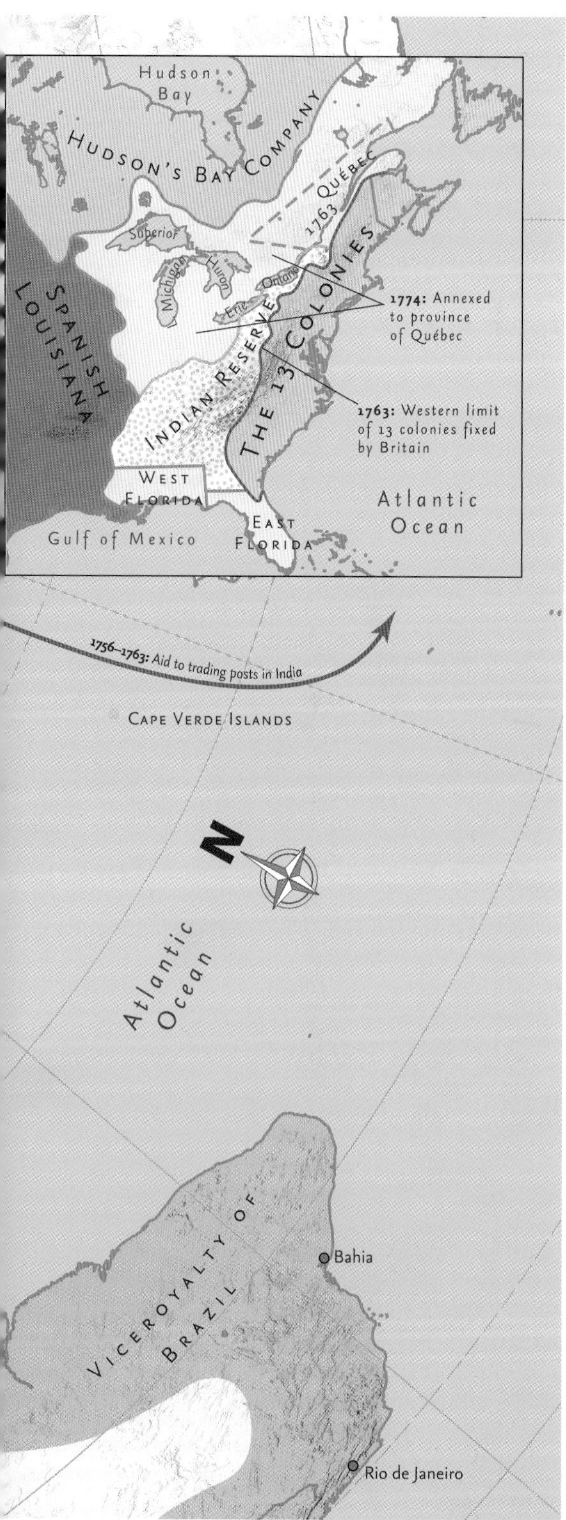

Under the Treaty of Paris (1763), France got back its sugar colonies of Guadeloupe and Martinique but gave up Louisiana, which was split down the Mississippi, between Britain in the east and Spain in the west.

BRITAIN LOSES AMERICA

Britain's gains now had to be paid for, and the interests of French settlers, Native Americans, and its own 13 colonies balanced. In 1763, George III (1760–1820) made the area between the Appalachians and the Mississippi an Indian Reserve, which incensed those who had just finished fighting the French for access to this region. In 1774, equal rights were given to French Catholics in Québec, seigneurial privileges were retained, restricting resettlement, and part of the Indian Reserve was annexed for Québec. To cap it all, the 13 colonies had to pay for this themselves.

New England traded salt-cured cod for Caribbean molasses with which to make rum. In 1733, duty had been charged on French molasses to keep trade channeled to Jamaica, though this merely encouraged smuggling. In 1764, the duty was halved, but this time it was actively enforced; Britain now needed to raise money more than manipulate trade. The following year brought the Stamp Act, a much-resented tax on newspapers, legal documents, and most other printed material.

The 13 colonies had little in common. Each had its own history, its own traditions, and a governor binding it to the mother country, not to its neighbors. But there was one thing they shared: each had developed a representative assembly. When the Stamp Act was passed without consulting the assemblies, it drew the colonies together in common cause for the first time and in 1766 it was repealed. After this, several new taxes were introduced and withdrawn one by one—all except a 3 percent duty on tea.

In 1721, Britain had forced its colonies, by law, to buy only British tea. This meant inflated prices, and by the 1770s a healthy smuggling racket in cheaper Dutch tea was operating. So Britain waived a 25 percent duty paid by the East India Company in London. Even with 3 percent due in America, British tea was now cheaper than Dutch. Despite this, it was the last straw for the colonies.

Many well-to-do American smugglers were ruined by legally cheap tea. Beyond this, the principle of having any tax imposed from Westminster, never mind its economic effect, had come to symbolize for the assemblies a political relationship both unfair and inconsistent. In Britain, laws were passed by Members of Parliament (MPs) the British electorate had chosen as representatives. But the 13 colonies had no MPs at Westminster. How then could laws passed there apply to them?

This argument incited a war of independence in which various grievances were aired. It was, primarily, an uprising of penniless merchants and rich slave-owning planters with their eye on land to the west. At the same time, in the southern colonies, small backwoods farmers fought the big planters, whose power they resented as much as the big planters resented the British. In similar spirit, many African slaves fought alongside the British—20,000 leaving with them after independence. Spanish, Dutch, and French all weighed in to check the new dominant European power and tipped the balance in favor of the colonies.

American independence brought starvation to Caribbean slaves cut off from salt cod and wheat from New England. In 1787, therefore, HMS Bounty sailed to Tahiti for breadfruit plants to grow as a new Caribbean food (mutiny necessitated a second voyage). The global economy pioneered by Spain and Portugal had come to stay.

The loss of the 13 colonies demonstrated something else discovered by Spain back in the 1540s: the danger of alienating a colonial elite. Those who really suffered from imperialism were never a threat, but the Virginian planters and Puritan businessmen of British North America had economic power and the same sense of entitlement as the empire builders of Seville, Amsterdam, and London. Now they took their freedom from Britain and went on to build a proud republic fired with a belief in its own destiny.

And across the ocean, this new republic was noted in France.

The British blockade Boston in 1768, sending troops ashore to enforce taxes and search for smugglers. In 1773, protestors dumped British tea in Boston Harbor and in 1775, the American Revolution began nearby. Paul Revere, 1768.

7 EMPIRES AND NATIONS

Napoleon / Russia / The Austrian Habsburgs

The tensions that hurt Europe's early colonial empires had their counterpart within Europe itself. In 1789, inspired in part by the revolt of the American colonies, France began its own revolt against unrepresentative rule and, in 1792, created a French republic. The subjects of a ruling dynasty were now the citizens of a nation-state.

This new state quickly created an empire around itself. From the start, the French Revolution faced the enmity of Europe's other ruling dynasties. It had to respond or wither, and the ensuing wars gave Napoleon a pathway to power. Napoleon both saved and compromised the revolution. Moreover, through war, he brought it to the rest of Europe.

As much in opposition to French occupation as in sympathy with French ideals, national independence movements sprouted across the Continent. The age of the nation-state had arrived, with first Greece and later Italy, Germany, and others finding their modern form.

In central and eastern Europe, however, two ancient multiethnic empires continued to grow. Russia and Austria–Hungary were both collections of lands acquired over the centuries by just the kind of archaic dynasties the rise of nationalism was sweeping aside elsewhere. The rulers of Russia had become so divorced from their subjects they did not even speak Russian, let alone any of the hundreds of other indigenous languages spoken within the Russian Empire.

Until 1806, the Austrian Habsburgs still claimed the title "Holy Roman Emperor." After Napoleon and the subsequent wars of Italian and German unification, the Habsburgs tried to preserve their empire by sharing power with its largest ethnic minority, the Hungarians. But the Austro-Hungarian Empire reached into the Balkans. Here, imperial rivalry between the Habsburgs, the Russians, and the Ottomans sharpened the desire of the Balkan peoples for independence, and dragged Europe into a war to bring down the old order once and for all.

The French Revolution proclaimed modernity, scientifc and technological as well as political and administrative. In this 1789 engraving, the newfangled electric current generated by the Declaration of the Rights of Man *jolts from their thrones Joseph II of Austria, Catherine the Great of Russia, and the Pope, among other imperial has-beens.*

NAPOLEON

Napoleon, like Alexander, was a bringer of new ideas and a pursuer of well-worn imperial ambition in equal measure. His march through Europe lasted little longer than Alexander's whirlwind tour of Asia, and the empire he built broke up even more quickly after his fall. But he left behind him the experience of living in a modern nation-state, and in doing so opened the door to the future.

THE END OF THE OLD ORDER

The American Revolution was an uprising against imperial rule from Europe, but was itself shaped by the European intellectual movement known as the Enlightenment.

For a thousand years after the fall of Rome, the kings of Europe effectively shared power with the church and the great landowning families of their realms. The lives of ordinary people through these centuries were regional in character, and dominated by the local priest and lord of the manor.

Things began to change around 1500, with increased trade and silver from the New World. Kings became richer and the machinery of state began to grow, edging out the feudal nobility from politics. During the 17th century, many rulers styled themselves as leaders of modern, centralized administrations wielding absolute power. This accompanied the birth of modern science and reflected a new rationalistic attitude to the ordering of society that reached full flower in the 18th century. Rulers like Frederick the Great of Prussia and Catherine the Great of Russia now saw themselves as "enlightened absolutists," and invited thinkers such as Voltaire and Diderot to develop progressive policies for them.

But the ideas of the Enlightenment contained a threat to unchecked power. Theories of natural rights and representative government had been put forward by the English philosopher John Locke in the 1680s, and his ideas were built on by later French thinkers such as Montesquieu, whose concept of separation of powers formed the basis of the American Constitution, and Rousseau, whose Social Contract of 1762 was banned for its incitement to overturn the established order.

In addition, the church and the old feudal aristocracy, though largely sidelined from political life, still possessed enormous wealth, calling into question the true extent of state power.

By this time, both Britain and France had been hurt financially by war over America. Britain had been modernizing its economy, but in France the population had mushroomed while agricultural production stagnated and food prices rose. Hence in 1789, after two years of bad harvests, Louis XVI (1774-1793) tried to raise money from the church and the nobility, those who held most of the country's wealth but paid hardly any tax. In doing so, he was forced to call the Estates-General, France's general assembly, for the first time in 175 years.

Proceedings were soon hijacked by the "third estate," the 95 percent who were neither nobility nor clergy, and who were under-represented in the

Estates-General. They set up a new body they called the National Assembly and demanded a constitutional monarchy together with a bill of rights and abolition of noble and church privileges. When Louis tried to break up the Assembly, his troops joined rioters in the streets and helped them storm the Bastille—royal arsenal and symbol of the king's power.

The National Assembly now laid out its principles in the Declaration of the Rights of Man and the Citizen, and followed this in 1791 with a constitution that transferred power from the king to an elected parliament.

The revolution might have ended there with a constitutional monarchy on the British model, but several pressures pushed it further. Louis, chosen as figurehead of the new arrangement, became instead the focus of opposition to it. The peasantry was uneasy with much that was new, especially changes affecting the church. And neighboring powers saw in the revolution both a potential threat and a France now made temptingly vulnerable.

Things came to a head in 1792, when fears of an Austro-Prussian attempt to restore absolute rule prompted a preemptive strike into the Austrian Netherlands. Thanks to Marie Antoinette smuggling French plans to Austria, it failed. Then Prussia invaded.

Now an emergency war government took over, executed the king, and declared a republic. Aid was promised to any rebellion abroad and war was declared on Britain, Holland, and Spain. But this brought only further military setbacks plus a British blockade of grain imports.

Faced with war, runaway inflation, and a starving urban population, Maximilien de Robespierre, head of the Committee of Public Safety, capped the price of grain, forced loans from the rich, and brought in conscription. Resistance from farmers to fixed grain prices led to requisitioning, accusations of betraying the revolution, and killings, which spiraled into a year of purges known as the Terror.

In 1794–1795, a conscript army of 750,000 effectively annexed the Rhineland and the Low Countries and forced peace with Prussia and Spain. Now the Directory, a more moderate annually elected government, took over. It tried to steer a middle course between monarchists and republicans, but it was weak and feared counter-revolution. By 1799, there seemed to be a simple choice: return to radical chaos or impose military control. The Directory chose the latter and invited Napoleon Bonaparte (1799-1815) to stage a coup.

THE NEW ORDER

Napoleon, a 30-year-old lawyer's son from Corsica, had risen through the ranks of the revolutionary army to conquer northern Italy in 1796-1797. On the battlefield he was agile and persuasive, employing light, maneuverable cannon and troops organized into independent divisions, which gave him speed, flexibility, and decisive force. Off the battlefield he was equally imaginative and bold, negotiating his own peace deal with Austria after victory in Italy, before setting up a state modeled on republican France.

The French Republic had introduced a centralized administration beyond the dreams of Europe's absolute monarchs and once invited to take power, Napoleon began consolidating and extending this. In 1800, a new constitution established a Roman-style system with consuls and a senate, but as First Consul, Napoleon

NAPOLEON'S EUROPE *1796–1815*

Napoleon established himself with his first Italian campaign of 1796–1797 and after his expedition to Egypt, took power. Subduing Austria and Prussia brought land east of the Rhine, but enforcing an embargo on British trade meant invading both Spain and Russia. Fighting a war on two fronts was too much even for Napoleon.

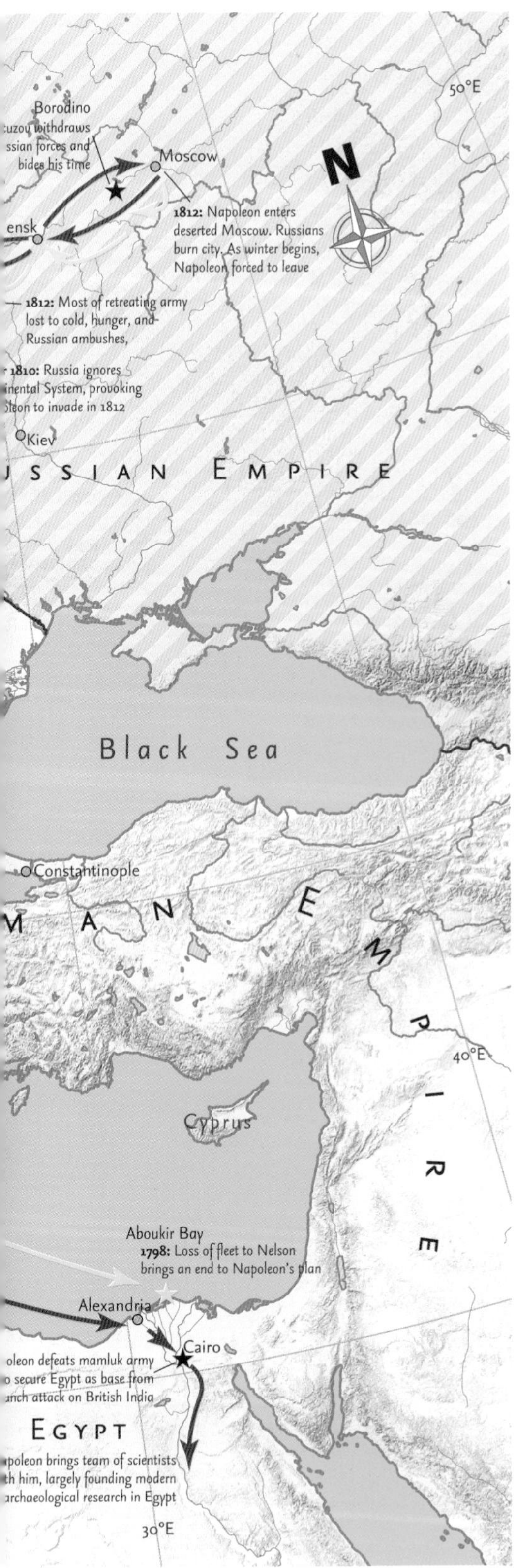

Borodino
Moscow
50°E
N
1812: Napoleon enters deserted Moscow. Russians burn city. As winter begins, Napoleon forced to leave
1812: Most of retreating army lost to cold, hunger, and Russian ambushes,
1810: Russia ignores
Kiev
Black Sea
Constantinople
40°E
Cyprus
Aboukir Bay
1798: Loss of fleet to Nelson brings an end to Napoleon's plan
Alexandria
Cairo
Egypt
30°E

could appoint both central government and provincial officials, as well as the senate itself, from 1802 on. The government's size increased several-fold, a national bank was created, and a national education program set up to train army officers and civil servants. Then, in 1804, Napoleon made himself emperor.

Representative government had been undermined, but Napoleon was seen as savior of the revolution rather than its betrayer because he used his position to uphold the majority of its other ideals. His legal code, the Code Napoléon, reaffirmed equality before the law, abolition of feudal privileges, and confiscation of church property together with state control of the clergy. It confirmed France as a secular republic. To make this a reality, he created the Gendarmerie, a police force drawn from the army that scoured the country, gradually stamping out counter-revolutionary activity and general lawlessness.

Maintaining order enabled Napoleon to rise above the factionalism that had plagued previous revolutionary governments. His administration was mostly staffed by existing officials, and both nobles who had fled France and radicals deported after the Terror were welcomed back. Naturally, some benefited more than others from Napoleon's policies. Confiscated lands were sold in large lots only the wealthy could afford. This meant returning nobles and the rising professionals who had the education to take advantage of careers now open to all. Together, they became the notables, a new landowning class. With trade still depressed, land remained a good investment, not least because landowners were now able to add the value of abolished tithes to their rents.

Nonetheless, with an efficient administrative machine behind him, Napoleon was able to export his system to the powers that had threatened France since the revolution. Between 1800–1807, with a series of astonishing victories against Austria, Prussia, and Russia, he abolished the Holy Roman Empire and built an empire of his own, bringing French republican institutions to conquered states as he had done in northern Italy. These were conquests maintained by force, but to many former subjects of tradition-bound German principalities, breaking the power of church and nobility came as liberation.

Britain, however, remained a threat. Accordingly, Napoleon now embarked on a second round of conquests designed to squeeze the British economy. But in taking on the old imperial rival, he overreached himself.

THE OLD ENEMY

Rivalry with Britain had not ended with defeat in the Seven Years' War. France had fought against the British in the American War of Independence and retained colonies in the Caribbean. During the 1790s, Britain's blockade plus a slave rebellion on Saint-Domingue inspired by the French Revolution cut overseas trade by almost two-thirds. So Napoleon took action against the British early on.

In 1798, he invaded Egypt with an eye on the Red Sea route to India. He wanted to make contact with Tipu Sultan, the "Tiger of Mysore," who

In January 1805, after a familiar pattern of Anglo–French war had reemerged, Napoleon suggested an imperial carve-up with British prime minister William Pitt in the interests of peace. He was turned down. James Gillray, 1805.

dreamed of annihilating the British. He also saw India as a source of cotton and as a market for French exports. Unfortunately, Admiral Nelson followed him to the Nile, destroying his fleet, and the year after, Tipu was killed by the British East India Company.

So in 1800, Napoleon turned west and pressed Spain to give back its part of Louisiana. He planned to revive French New Orleans as a sugar depot and, hence, charged his brother-in-law Leclerc to retake Saint-Domingue and reintroduce slavery. But this idea also failed. In 1803, debts forced Napoleon to sell Louisiana to the United States, and the following year he had to recognize Saint-Domingue as the newly independent state of Haiti.

From then on, Napoleon concentrated on Europe. The Louisiana Purchase had been handled by Barings Bank in London, but this did not stop him putting the $9 million he cleared towards the Continental System, a new scheme to lock the British out of European trade. How much this would really have hurt Britain's economy remains unclear because it never fully materialized. The Continent did not want to stop trading with Britain, and Napoleon had to enforce his embargo.

To begin with, this meant securing the North Sea coast from Holland to Denmark, as well as invading central Italy. These conquests, however, brought Napoleon a strength of resistance he had not hitherto encountered, ensuring neither French institutions nor the Continental System took hold in these parts. In Italy removing the pope earned Napoleon deep resentment and all along the North Sea coast the Royal Navy sponsored an industrial-scale smuggling racket.

Elsewhere the story was similar. In 1808, he was forced to invade Spain, a country the size of France itself, and become embroiled in a five-year guerilla war exacerbated by the British counterattacking from Portugal. He put his brother Joseph on the Spanish throne, but here, too, fierce resistance prevented the establishment of a French-style administration. Meanwhile, Sweden could not be made to comply with the Continental System and from 1810 Russia reopened trade with Britain.

This was the occasion for Napoleon's great error of judgment. In 1812, he took 600,000 men east to force Russia back into line. This was three times Russia's forces, but Napoleon did not organize sufficient supply lines for such a long journey. His armies were used to living off what they found locally, but the Russian peasants burnt their crops and disappeared into the vastness of the land as the French advanced.

Napoleon reached Moscow to find a city deserted and in flames. As he waited for the tsar to show up, winter approached and his men grew cold, exhausted, and hungry. Eventually, they were forced to leave, only to be continually ambushed by the Russians on the way home. Just 30,000 made it back.

And now, having pulled so many troops from the west to fight in the east, the French were finally driven out of Spain.

After this, Napoleon was weak and his enemies united. In spring 1814, Paris was taken and he was banished to the Mediterranean island of Elba. A year later, he escaped to make a triumphant comeback but met final defeat at Waterloo in June 1815. This time he was deported to St. Helena in the South Atlantic, where he died in 1821.

THE NATION

While Napoleon was on Elba, Europe's ruling families had met in Vienna under Austrian Minister of State Prince Metternich to decide what to do with his empire. In essence, they turned back the clock. Bourbon kings reclaimed the French throne and across Europe rulers deposed by Napoleon were restored.

The memory of republicanism, however, was not so easy to erase. France and the lands Napoleon won by 1807 had experienced in essence a police state, but also equality and rights enshrined in law. People living under Napoleonic rule had been exposed to a new concept of society.

Hence in 1830, France's king was again deposed, Belgium declared independence, and constitutional monarchies were set up in both cases. In 1848, a French king was yet again deposed, and this time the news spread instantly by telegraph, producing a domino effect of uprisings across Europe. Russian troops crushed the protesters but could not crush the spirit of the age.

The Declaration of the Rights of Man and the Citizen had claimed the "source of all sovereignty resides in the nation." The revolution had swept away feudal loyalties and replaced them with the idea of citizenship. For many people, being called to fight for the revolution had brought them beyond their local community for the first time. Often they had never heard the French language before. Yet they grasped the idea of France: an imagined community to which they belonged on equal terms with millions of strangers. This articulated the underlying idea behind republicanism and opened the door to a century of national independence movements.

First came Haiti, then, following Napoleon's invasion of Spain, two decades of revolutionary wars broke Spanish America up into independent republics. By 1832, the Greeks, encouraged to remember the glories of their ancient past, had thrown off Ottoman rule. National liberation in these cases was not delivered by Napoleon, but the idea of it was.

Across Europe, cultural movements were forming that sought to define nationality through language, shared histories, common myths, and musical traditions—increasingly disseminated by the growth of newspapers and railways. This culminated in the 1848 uprisings. After their suppression it became clear that nationalist movements alone could not create nation-states, but it was also clear they could not be ignored. From this time on, expansionist states like Prussia and Piedmont saw an opportunity and began to present themselves as the representatives of national consciousness. By 1870, both a Piedmont-led Italy and a Prussia-led Germany had come into existence as nation-states.

Gradually, established rulers realized that national sentiment need pose no threat to the old order. It could be courted by means of flags, national anthems, and so forth as a powerful new legitimizing force linked to ethnicity rather than republican ideals. By the close of the century, therefore, the great motivating idea of the French Revolution had been bent to serve the rivalries of Europe's imperial powers, now elbowing their way toward 1914 and "a war to end all wars."

A century earlier, nationalism had delivered France into the hands of its people and the French nobility had lost their heads. The real losers, however, had been the poor. Church tithes had provided poor relief and funded hospitals. Fifty years after the revolution, France possessed only half the hospitals it had had in 1789. Napoleon had saved the revolution and exported its ideals, but not quite in the way many had hoped for.

RUSSIA

Lacking clear physical boundaries, Russia became a natural territorial empire seeping ever outward from Moscow, its limits defined only by the power of the tsars. At the same time, Russia lay between East and West and over the centuries developed a split personality. In the end, victory against Napoleon made the tsars complacent, when what they needed to do was bring together a divided society.

THE THIRD ROME

In 988 CE, Vladimir I had baptized his people in the Dnieper and brought Orthodox Christianity to the Rus. The next half century was Kiev's golden age, when trade between the Black Sea and the Baltic brought wealth and cosmopolitanism, and the family of Vladimir's son Yaroslav I ("the Wise") married into royal households across Europe. With a state church on the Byzantine model, power in Kiev was more centralized than in most of Europe.

Subsequently, raiders from the south began driving people north into the forests and after Crusaders sacked Constantinople in 1204, river trade shifted from the Dnieper to the Volga. The Republic of Novgorod in the north and the Principality of Vladimir-Suzdal in the northeast began to supplant Kiev. Then, in the winter of 1240–1241, the Mongols came riding up the frozen Dnieper and Kiev was destroyed. The Mongols set up as the Golden Horde at Sarai on the lower Volga and began exacting tribute.

Novgorod was spared the threat from the east but faced two from the west—the Swedes and the crusading order of the Teutonic Knights—and sought help from Alexander, fourth son of Vladimir-Suzdal's ruler. In 1240, at the age of 19, he saw off the Swedes at the River Neva and became Alexander *Nevsky*. In 1242, he lured the Teutonic Knights onto the ice of Lake Peipus, where their horses slid around and his foot soldiers could get the better of them. Appeasing the Mongol khans brought Alexander to power in Vladimir-Suzdal, with their backing.

On a tributary of the Volga, deep in Vladimir-Suzdal's forest, lay the little trading post of Moscow. Under its first prince, Alexander Nevsky's son Daniel, Moscow began taking over its neighbors. Daniel's son Yuri married the khan's sister and was given charge of Vladimir-Suzdal. Yuri's son, Ivan I ("the Moneybag"), helped put down an uprising against the Golden Horde, became rich collecting tribute for them, and used his money to put up the first stone buildings of the *Kremlin* ("Fortress"). In 1325, Moscow's importance was confirmed when Metropolitan Peter, head of the Russian Orthodox Church, relocated there.

Moscow now had to shake off the taint of Mongol collaboration. In 1359, Dmitri Ivanovich came to power as a child and was advised by Metropolitan Alexis. At this time, a grassroots religious revival associated with St. Sergius of Radonezh was underway and new monasteries were being built, extending the church's influence. Dmitri's closeness to the metropolitan broadcast a cleaner image for Moscow. With the blessing of St. Sergius himself, Dmitri underlined the new message in 1380 by fighting off the Golden Horde at Kulikovo on the banks of the Don, after which he became Dmitri *Donskoi* and Moscow became Russia's capital.

In adopting Orthodox Christianity, Russia received the example of a church serving the interests of centralized state power. At the same time, the Russian Church began to diverge from its roots; Andrei Rublev's Trinity *(ca. 1410) is very different from a Byzantine icon.*

It was left to Ivan III ("the Great," 1462–1505) to complete the "gathering of the Russian lands." In 1478, he annexed Novgorod, gaining access to the White Sea, and, in 1480, the khans gave up their claim to tribute. From the slavic form of *Caesar*, Ivan took the title "*Tsar* of all the Russias." After the fall of Constantinople in 1453, he saw Moscow as guardian of Orthodox Christianity and, hence, as the Third Rome. In 1472, he married the last Byzantine emperor's niece and began using the Byzantine double-headed eagle, symbol of secular and spiritual power combined.

THE EAST

Ivan the Great had gathered together more than Russians, however. The far north contained countless indigenous peoples with their own languages and beliefs. From the start, the tsars ruled a widely dispersed multiethnic population and only managed it by concentrating their power. Ivan IV ("the Terrible," 1533–1584) both looked farther afield and tightened his grip.

On the Volga, the Golden Horde had splintered into the khanates of Kazan and Astrakhan, which Ivan took in the 1550s, reaching the Caspian. In 1553, Richard Chancellor of London's Company of Merchant Adventurers arrived in Moscow to begin trading, having sailed around Norway to the White Sea. In 1558, Ivan tried to open an easier route through the Baltic but this turned into a futile 25-year war that only allowed the Khanate of the Crimea to step up raids from the south, necessitating a cripplingly expensive border guard and producing civil unrest.

Meanwhile, rulers of Ivan the Terrible's annexed lands had come to his court to join the *boyars*, the old Moscow nobles. In an already tense climate, Ivan, a strong ruler but prone to paranoid mood swings, began to suspect a boyar coup. In 1565, he confiscated the best third of Russia's land to create his *Oprichnina*, a private estate run by his own secret police. *Oprichniks* dressed in black rode around on black horses attacking boyars, merchants, and peasants. The Oprichnina lasted just seven years, but from this time the tsars were feared as never before. Boyars and peasants alike fled Russia's heartland, farms were abandoned, and grain prices rose tenfold.

In the south, peasants joined previous runaways who had settled on the lower Don as the Golden Horde broke up. Their independence was tolerated as they helped hold the border and provided mercenaries. These were the Cossacks. Farther east, the powerful Stroganov family was developing land in the Urals for farming, fishing, mining, and more. The Stroganovs hired a

Cossack named Yermak Timofeyevich to deal with raids from the Khanate of Sibir beyond the Urals. In 1582, Yermak took the city of Sibir and began the colonization of Siberia.

The vast Siberian forest contained fur, particularly sable, lay beyond the reach of Moscow, and was laced by waterways. Up to the Yenisey River it was flat, then there was a plateau. The inhabitants could offer little resistance and in 60 years, Cossacks had reached the Pacific. Here they turned south looking for better farmland and met the Manchu just as they came to power in China. In 1689, with the Treaty of Nerchinsk, they agreed to stay north of the Amur river in return for trade with China.

Half a century later, in 1741, Vitus Bering, a Danish sea captain commissioned by the tsars to chart the Far East, reached Alaska. By 1812, trade in sea otter pelts had brought the Russian–American Company as far south as Fort Ross, 60 miles (95 kilometers) from San Francisco. But in the days before the Trans-Siberian Railway, transporting pelts from the Pacific back to European Russia was uneconomical and, in 1867, Russia sold Alaska to the United States for $7 million.

THE WEST

Ivan the Terrible's son died without heir and 15 years of chaos ensued until 1613, when the boyars chose Mikhail Romanov to be the first of a new ruling dynasty. In the absence of a tsar, however, the machinery of the state had kept functioning and under the Romanovs this began to grow.

In 1649, a new legal code formally sanctioned serfdom, licensed chasing runaway peasants, and forbade artisans to switch towns. This benefited the boyars but at the expense of them becoming part of the *dvoryanstvo*, an expanded nobility created by giving land and serfs in return for civil and military service. The nobility were becoming part of the tsar's bureaucracy.

A new ambivalence toward the West arose after Moscow took over Kiev following an uprising against Polish rule in 1648. Unlike Moscow, Kiev had retained contact with the Greek Orthodox Church and centuries of divergence in religious practice now came to light. In 1448, the Russian Orthodox Church had become officially independent, but now Patriarch Nikon tried to bring it back in line with Constantinople. Many saw this both as unwelcome interference from the church establishment in Moscow and as kowtowing to the West. In 1667, dissenters known as the Old Believers left the church, laying themselves open for religious persecution. It was a foretaste of the resistance to modernization Peter I ("the Great," 1682–1725) would soon face.

Peter hated Moscow. When he became tsar as a child, the Kremlin guards had revolted, killing friends and family of his. He also thought Russia needed modernizing. After studying shipbuilding in Holland, he built a navy and, by 1721, had wrested a Baltic window on the West from Sweden. Here he employed Western architects to build St. Petersburg, a new capital resembling Vienna or Paris, not Moscow. He established a new senate, appointed by himself, pushed industry, and set up technical and scientific academies, where previously there had been only religiously based education. The holy Russian beard, emblem of Orthodoxy, he ordered shaved.

As it happened, Peter's Westernization program made Russia only more autocratic and created a cultural divide. Agriculture remained unmodernized, mining companies were given serfs as development grants, and the new schools affected only the top layer of the nobility. This became a Westernized French-speaking St. Petersburg elite, increasingly divorced from the rest of society.

Focus on the West increased after Catherine II ("the Great," 1762–1796) took power by having her lover murder her husband, Peter III. Poland had been supported by France but after losing the Seven Years' War, France was too weak to protect it and between 1772 and 1795 Russia, Austria, and Prussia carved

Poland into three. Avoiding a fight for Poland left Catherine free to invade the Khanate of the Crimea in 1783 and reach the Black Sea.

Catherine was German and made a great show of being modern, founding schools and hobnobbing with French intellectuals such as Voltaire and Diderot. She wrote memoirs, fiction, and a treatise on childhood education. She also increased the powers of the nobility over their serfs, exempted them from tax, cracked down on freedom of speech, and presided over an ever-worsening series of peasant revolts.

Firearms bring Yermak's Cossacks across the Irtysh River in May 1582, overwhelming the forces of Khan Kuchum of Sibir and opening the way to lands many times Russia's size. Vasiliy Surikov, 1895.

Principality of Moscow ca. 1300
Moscow on accession of Ivan III ("the Great") in 1462
Grand Duchy of Moscow by death of Ivan the Great in 1505
Tsardom of Russia by death of Ivan IV ("the Terrible") in 1584
Tsardom of Russia on accession of Peter I ("the Great") in 1682
Russian Empire by death of Catherine II ("the Great") in 1796
Russian Empire by 1917
Territory given up
Under strong Russian influence by 1917
Routes of fur trappers, 16th and 17th centuries
Trans-Siberian Railway, built 1891–1916
Chinese Eastern Railway, built 1898–1902
Naval bases (Russian navy founded 1696 by Peter the Great)
Fur
Gold
Silver
Copper
Iron
Coal
Scale 1:50 million
1585–1586: Yermak Timofeyevich founds Tobolsk, first Russian city of Siberia, near razed capital of Khanate of Sibir
1240–1242: Alexander Nevsky holds back Swedes at River Neva and Teutonic Knights at Lake Peipus
1693: Peter the Great orders first state shipyard built
1380: Dmitri Donskoi throws off the Golden Horde at Kulikovo
1552: Khanate of Kazan falls
1556: Khanate of Astrakhan falls
Arctic Ocean
Laptev Sea
Barents Sea
Kara Sea
White Sea
Baltic Sea
Black Sea
Caspian Sea
Aral Sea
Mediterranean Sea
Lake Balkhash
Lake Baikal
Arctic Circle
NORWAY
SWEDEN
FINLAND
PRUSSIA
LITHUANIA
WHITE RUSSIA
POLAND
AUSTRIA-HUNGARY
UKRAINE
BESSARABIA
CRIMEA
OTTOMAN EMPIRE
GEORGIA
ARMENIA
PERSIA
AFGHANISTAN
TIBET
TURKESTAN
QING EMPIRE
MONGOLIA
SIBERIA
NOVGOROD (to 1478)
STROGANOV LANDS
Ural Mountains
Saami
Karelians
Komi
Samoyeds (Nenet)
Samoyeds (Enet)
Samoyeds (Tavgi)
Dolgans
Tungus (Ewenki)
Yakuts
Khantys
Mansis
Selkups
Kets
Permians
Udmurts
Maris
Chuvash
Mordvas
Tatars
Kazan Tatars
Bashkirs
Kalmyks
Cossacks
Don Cossacks
Caucasian tribes
Caucasus
Azeri
Turkmens
Uzbeks
Kazakhs
Kirghiz
Oirats
Khalkhas
Uighurs
Shors
Teleuts
Tuvans
Buryats
Altai
Yenisey
Ob
Lena
Volga
Don
Dnieper
Stockholm
Helsinki
St Petersburg
1703
Riga
Pskov
Novgorod
Vilna
Warsaw
Minsk
Smolensk
Tver
Yaroslavl
Vladimir
Moscow
Nizhny Novgorod
Perm
Kazan
Samara
Kiev
Odessa
Asov
1696
Sarai
Sevastopol
1783
Constantinople
Astrakhan
1722
Tbilisi
Yerevan
Baku
1867
Tabriz
Tehran
Baghdad
Arkhangelsk
Berezov
Tobolsk
Sibir
Yekaterinburg
Orsk
Omsk
Tomsk
Krasnoyarsk
Yeniseysk
Turukhansk
Barnaul
Semipalatinsk
Aralsk
1847
Khiva
Bukhara
Samarkand
Tashkent
Kokand
Vyerny
Kabul
Irkutsk
Kyakhta
Urga
Nerchinsk
Chita
Verkhoyansk
40°E

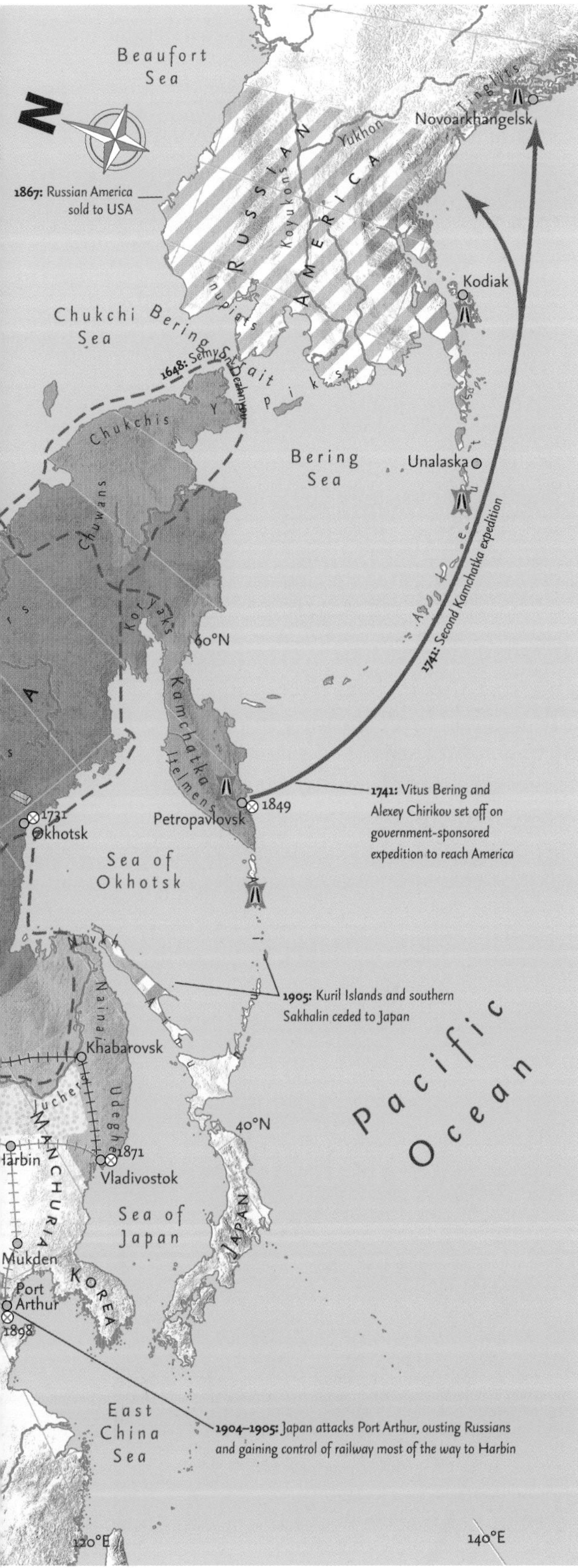

AFTER NAPOLEON

By the 19th century, Russia's tiny French-speaking elite were wondering how to reconnect with the people of Russia's heartland, to say nothing of its ethnic minorities. Some, looking to the West as Peter the Great had done, advocated educating and modernizing the peasantry. Others saw the solution in rediscovering traditional Russian culture. At the heart of these concerns lay the question of the tsar, who stood above the law and whom the peasantry looked up to as a savior whose rule was sanctioned by God. Was the tsar holding Russia back or was he Russia's strength?

Before 1812, Alexander I (1801–1825) had toyed with representative government, but, in the glow of defeating Napoleon and gaining Finland plus more of Poland, this seemed no longer necessary. The troops who chased Napoleon home, however, had returned with republican ideas and when Alexander's staunchly reactionary brother Nicholas I (1825–1855) came to power, they protested. Nicholas, who had no interest in toying with any kind of new ideas, promptly deported them to Siberia.

The memory of 1812 allowed Nicholas to stay focused on Russian glory. He pursued an ongoing Chechen war against the background of imperial designs on Persia and a broader awareness of growing British power in Asia. In 1848, Russia's greatness was confirmed for Nicholas when he marched through Europe, crushing the uprisings of that year and earning the nickname "Gendarme of Europe." But the tsar's self-image was an illusion. In 1855, moves to take the Black Sea from Ottoman control resulted in the Crimean War and humiliating defeat at the hands of Britain and France.

With this Russia's backwardness was exposed. The glaring weakness was serfdom, which motivated neither landowner nor peasant to innovate. In 1861 the serfs were granted their freedom by Alexander II—but only to find they were homeless. They now had legal status as free men and women, yet in law they owned nothing. In order to live and work as they had always done, they would have to buy back the land that had in practice been theirs all along. Luckily the nobles were willing to sell. The peasants stayed in debt for the rest of the century and

THE GROWTH OF RUSSIA *ca. 1300–1917*

Moscow began expanding under the Mongol khans, before taking over their lands plus the huge northern Republic of Novgorod. In the 17th century, Cossacks conquered Siberia. The 18th century brought access to the Baltic and the Black Sea, plus America, and the 19th century saw expansion south toward Persia.

remained without new skills and new tools. For the government, it was all too difficult, so agriculture was abandoned for industry.

From the 1880s on, Western companies drove a fast-track industrial revolution, but one that lined the pockets of the tsar and his foreign investors while exacerbating social dislocation. Peasants were in debt, factory workers were experiencing new hardships, and seasonal, casual laborers relayed grievances between the two.

In 1905, half a century since the Crimean War, the image of the tsar suffered another humiliation when Russia fought Japan for far-off Manchuria and lost. On the back of this defeat, strikes and uprisings broke out and were brutally put down. Nicholas II (1894–1917) conceded a parliament but he still stood above the law, so it was stripped of its power and soon dissolved.

The final act came when Austria-Hungary declared war on Serbia in 1914 after a Serb nationalist assassinated the heir to the Austro-Hungarian throne. The rise of national consciousness in Europe had led Russia to cast itself as the mother country for Slav states in the Balkans, so the tsar felt compelled to respond. By 1917, however, a badly run war fought for little discernable reason but claiming countless lives seemed to sum up tsarist Russia, and this time full-blown revolution followed.

Autocratic rule held on longer in Russia than anywhere else in Europe. While the rest of Europe was emerging from the medieval world and beginning to think about rule of law, Russia had been learning from the Mongols and putting its faith in an all-powerful tsar. It had taken a different path, and when all that Europe had been up to was discovered, it felt unfamiliar and brash. For 200 years Russia turned first one way, then the other, trying to pull the two sides of itself together, without ever succeeding. And all the while the pressure was building, ensuring that when change finally came it would be extreme.

But even then, something of the rule of the tsars would linger on.

Nicholas II reviews his troops, World War I.

THE AUSTRIAN HABSBURGS

Before the age of the nation-state, personal connections counted for everything and no one could network better than the Habsburgs. Knowing the right people delivered them control of most of Europe and America before they split their possessions for convenience. It then allowed them to hold together a collection of lands in eastern Europe for another three centuries—until the rise of nationalism found them unable to adapt.

COLLECTING LANDS

When Emperor Otto I died in 973 CE, Austria was part of a border province of the Holy Roman Empire. In 1246, Austria's rulers died out and, when Frederick II died in 1250, much of the empire fell into the hands of robber barons, allowing the king of Bohemia to grab Austria for his son.

Meanwhile, Frederick's godson, Rudolf of Habsburg, was busy collecting lands. In 1239 he inherited the original Habsburg Castle in Switzerland. Marriage brought him land in Swabia and his godfather gave him more within the empire. In the chaos following Frederick's death, Rudolf picked up yet more by seizing, by negotiating, and by bribing bishops. By 1273, his new wealth and power got him elected emperor as Frederick's successor, ending a 23-year interregnum. He now reclaimed for the empire lands seized by others since Frederick's death. Bohemia had to give back Austria, Styria, Carinthia, and Carniola. A few years later, Rudolph began giving these lands to members of his own family. When he died in 1291, the Holy Roman Empire was still in bad shape, but the Habsburgs now owned Austria.

For 200 years, the Habsburg lands were shared out across the family until, in 1493, they were united under Maximilian I (1493–1519). Maximilian married his family right to the top. Marrying the Duke of Burgundy's daughter in 1477 brought him the Netherlands when she died in 1482, and marrying the Duke of Milan's daughter in 1493 delivered Milan when the male line died out in 1535. In the meantime, Maximilian's son Philip married Joanna of Castile in 1496, following which Maximilian arranged to marry their children Ferdinand and Mary to Anna and Louis, children of the king of Bohemia and Hungary. In 1526, Louis, now king, was killed fighting Suleyman the Magnificent, so his lands fell to Ferdinand.

Meanwhile, in 1506, Ferdinand's elder brother Charles had inherited the Netherlands from his father and, in 1516, Spain and together with it the New World from his mother. In 1519 came the rest of the Habsburg lands from his grandfather, plus the title of Holy Roman Emperor, which the pope had made a hereditary Habsburg title in 1508.

As a result, Charles V found himself constantly traipsing across Europe. One thing he did not need was more land. So in 1556, he split his empire, giving the western and overseas part to his son Philip II and the Austrian lands, with the title of Holy Roman Emperor, to his brother Ferdinand I.

CREATING A CULTURE

Ferdinand had already been trying to manage the lands he inherited in 1526. In Hungary, he faced resistance in Transylvania on top of war with the Ottomans. After Suleyman besieged Vienna in 1529 and 1533, Ferdinand agreed to split Hungary with him.

In Bohemia there had been a tradition of religious dissent since Jan Hus was burned at the stake for heresy in 1415. From 1517 on, Protestantism found a welcome reception here and, in 1555, Charles and Ferdinand tried to appease Bohemian and German nobles by allowing them their own churches.

An interlude of peace came to Bohemia when, in 1583, Rudolf II made Prague his capital. To Prague he brought painters, astronomers, and alchemists, together with strange plants and animals, clocks, automata, scientific instruments, and curiosities of every kind. Beginning in Rudolf's time, "Bohemian" became a byword for the exotic.

By 1618, however, the capital was back in Vienna and religious tolerance had ended. When officials were sent to Prague to stop the building of Protestant churches, they were tried by an assembly of nobles and thrown out of a window into a pile of horse manure, igniting the Thirty Years' War (1618–1648). The Habsburgs started confiscating Bohemian estates and giving them to their generals, officials, and trustworthy Catholic supporters. Defeat in 1648 forced them to recognize Protestant states within the Holy Roman Empire, but by now Bohemia and the other hereditary Habsburg lands were in the hands of a new loyal Catholic aristocracy.

Under Leopold I (1657–1705) the Ottomans began to be pushed back, and the Habsburg system found its form. The great families raised taxes from their estates and staffed the Habsburg army and civil administration. In return they gained access to the Habsburg court at Vienna.

The court was the place to make contacts and receive further privileges. It was also a theater displaying the wealth and newfound confidence of Catholic Europe. Its style was ostentatious, florid, and exuberant, and held within it a desire, in the wake of religious warfare, to set the flamboyance of the Catholic mass against the dourness of the Protestant service. There was ornate church music and expensive Italian opera. Baroque palaces, built to ape the grandeur of cathedrals, dotted the Habsburg lands as testament to Vienna's creation of a common culture across what was a multiethnic aristocracy. Vienna was a club for aristocrats, whose palaces were on a par with those of the emperor himself.

This was the context in which Maria Theresa (1740–1780) came to power the same year as Frederick II ("the Great") of Protestant Prussia, who straightaway marched in to take Silesia. Maria Theresa detested Frederick but saw she had to emulate his better organization if she hoped to win Silesia back. She began taking more direct control of the provinces, increasing taxes, setting up military and engineering academies, and building up her army. She also allied herself with France. In 1756, however, Frederick became Britain's ally and, with Britain and France fighting in America, he struck first. By 1763, Frederick had fought off half of Europe and become the role model for Napoleon. A new German power had arrived and Maria Theresa had to accept Silesia's loss.

She turned instead to Hungary, encouraging German settlers to develop the economy of a country held back by centuries of war and aristocratic resistance to change. Like Frederick and Catherine the Great, Maria Theresa flirted with ideas for planning a progressive society along secular lines. She brought in state schools and abolished capital punishment. But she was cautious, both toward the church and her nobility. Her son Joseph II (1780–1790) was different.

Joseph was a one-man revolution. As soon as his mother died, he abolished serfdom, made everyone equal before the law, brought in compulsory primary-school education, and took control of the church away from Rome. But this was all too much. His program was imposed and generally resented as interference. His mother had put "decency police" in the streets of Vienna to root out unsavory behavior; Joseph charged his own secret police to stop people from baking gingerbread because he thought it was bad for them. He had to drop many of his reforms and died a disappointed man.

NATIONALISM

In 1806, having defeated both Austria and Prussia, Napoleon scrapped the Holy Roman Empire and grouped together the smaller German

The Schlosshof, on the border of Austria and Slovakia, as seen by Canaletto in 1760. Under Maria Theresa, it became an imperial Habsburg residence, but originally it was just one of the many Baroque palaces owned by members of an aristocracy tying the Habsburg lands together.

Austrian Habsburg lands in 1525
Gains by 1526
Habsburg–Ottoman frontier zone 1526–1683
Gains by 1699
Gains by 1815
Lost by 1870
Annexed in 1908
Brandenburg–Prussia in 1648
Prussian gains by 1815
Joint Austro–Prussian annexation 1864 (to Prussia 1860)
Included in German Empire 1871
Nationalist uprising 1815–1914
Austro–Hungarian Empire 1914
German Empire 1914
Russian Empire 1914
Ottoman Empire 1914
Holy Roman Empire 1648
N
White Russians
Poles
Germans
Ukranians
Czechs
Slovaks
Hungarians
Slovenes
Romanians
Croats
Serbs
Italians
Bulgarians
Albanians
Greeks
Stockholm
Sweden
Denmark
Baltic Sea
Copenhagen
North Sea
Schleswig-Holstein
Kiel
East Prussia
Danzig
Russian Empire
Netherlands
Hamburg
Amsterdam
Brandenburg
Hanover
1817–1831
Berlin
1848
1830–1831
Warsaw
1831
Brussels
Belgium
(independent 1831)
Cologne
1848
German States
(unified under Prussia 1871)
Poland
West Galicia
1795–1809
Silesia
1526–1741
Breslau
1866: Prussia defeats Habsburgs and goes on to create German state excluding Austria
1683: Last Ottoman siege fails. Habsburgs begin to push border back
Kiev
50°N
Luxembourg
(independent 1839)
Rhine
Bohemia
Prague
1848
Sadowa
1866
Krakow
1848
1847
Galicia
Lemberg
(Lviv)
Stuttgart
1848
Moravia
Kaschau
Carpathians
France
Habsburg Castle
Munich
1848
Salzburg
Vienna
1848
1683
Pressburg (Bratislava)
Austria
Switzerland
1847–1848
Innsbruck
Styria
Budapest
1848
Hungary
Geneva
Tirol
Graz
Lyon
Lombardy
1815–1866
Carinthia
Transylvania
Odessa
Venetia
1797–1866
Bessarabia
Milan
1848
Carniola
Croatia
Danube
Piedmont
Venice
1848
Fiume
Slavonia
Banat
1821
Istria
Karlowitz
Lesser Wallachia
1718–1739
Romania
(independent 1878)
Marseille
Milan
1714–1797
Parma
1735–1748
Bosnia-Herzegovina
Sarajevo
1914
Belgrade
1718–1739
1807–1833
Bucharest
1821
Black Sea
Italian States
(unified under Piedmont 1870)
Dalmatia
Adriatic Sea
Serbia
(independent 1878)
Pleven
1877
Montenegro
(independent 1878)
Corsica
Sofia
Bulgaria
(independent 1908)
Cetinje
Kosovo
Rome
1848
Kumanovo
1912
Kurdzhali
1912
Constantinople
Tirana
Sardinia
Naples
1820, 1848
Albania
(independent 1913)
Macedonia
Yanitza
1912
Thessaloniki
Ottoman Empire
40°N
0
250
500 miles
500 kms
Greece
(independent 1832)
1821, 1848
Palermo
Sicily
1821–1833
Smyrna
10°E
20°E
Athens
30°E

states within it to form the Confederation of the Rhine. The Habsburg emperor abdicated and became emperor of Austria instead. In 1814–1815, at the Congress of Vienna, Austrian Minister of State Prince Metternich restored Europe's deposed monarchs and drew the Holy Roman Empire back on the map, calling it the German Confederation. Half of Prussia's lands lay outside this boundary, however, and, in 1818, it created a customs union to link its eastern and western parts, a union soon joined by other German states.

Metternich's restoration of the old order made the uprisings of 1848–1849 more or less inevitable. Bohemians (Czechs) and Hungarians wanted to keep the Habsburg Empire but wanted a say in running it. Elsewhere, Italians and Germans wanted nation-states. The Habsburgs responded by suppressing these voices.

Others saw in them an opportunity for expansion. Piedmont, the strongest Italian state, became champion of Italian nationalism and began looking to take Lombardy and Venetia from the Habsburgs. Prussia co-opted German nationalism to help build, from its customs union, a German state that excluded Austria. In 1864–1865, Prussia and the Habsburgs jointly annexed Schleswig-Holstein, with its potential for a North Sea–Baltic canal. When the Habsburgs made the mistake of trying to run it for themselves, Prussia declared war and, thanks to its industrial strength and railways, defeated the Habsburgs in six weeks, while Piedmont invaded from the south. By 1871, both Italy and Germany were nation-states.

War with Prussia and Piedmont gave Hungary another chance to press for representation and, in 1867, the Habsburgs were forced to create the dual monarchy of the Austro-Hungarian Empire. Vienna and Budapest now housed separate governments responsible for domestic policy, with Emperor Franz Joseph (1848–1916) in charge of a joint foreign policy. It was a cumbersome compromise because recruiting, training, and supplying the army was no longer handled by a single authority, which did not bode well for a future war. There was also the problem of language. The Hungarians had their own parliament, with Magyar as the official language, but there were many other minorities within the empire. All regions were therefore given the right to use their own language for education and administration. This made running the empire far more complicated and sharpened nationalist antagonisms through arguments over which language should be used in which area.

Opposite page: main map:

THE AUSTRO-HUNGARIAN EMPIRE *in 1914*

The Habsburgs inherited Hungary when its king was killed fighting the Ottomans in 1526 and centuries of Ottoman conflict followed. As Holy Roman Emperors, a claim to German lands involved the Habsburgs first in religious wars until 1648, then in a struggle with Prussia to create a unified German state. In 1867, they were forced to share power with Hungary.

Inset map:

NATIONALITIES IN AND AROUND THE EMPIRE *in 1914.*

Vienna lay in a mostly German-speaking area, but Habsburg lands embraced an array of different peoples increasingly conscious of their national identities.

THE BALKANS

By 1700, the Habsburgs had pushed the Ottomans back to Belgrade and after Russia took the Crimea in 1783, the Balkan peoples found themselves in the crossfire of three empires, two of them jealously watching for further Ottoman decay. Shifting frontiers pricked national consciousness and by 1817 the Serbs were calling for independence.

Slav nationalism gave Russia, posing as the Slav mother country, a claim on the Balkans. In 1876, a Bulgarian uprising prompted brutal massacres by Ottoman irregulars, which shocked Europe. Serbia and Montenegro declared war and, in 1877, after trying to negotiate, Russia followed suit.

As Europe's ruling dynasties sought to marry more and more within their own circle, so physical manifestations of inbreeding emerged, such as the Habsburg jaw. The Emperor Charles V had such difficulty chewing his food he suffered chronic indigestion and ate alone for most of his life. Christoph Amberger, 1532.

At the Congress of Berlin in 1878, Britain tried to keep a lid on Balkan nationalism by getting the Ottomans to recognize Montenegro, Serbia, and Romania as independent, and allow self-government for northern Bulgaria. Russia was appeased with part of Bessarabia (Moldova), which it had lost after the Crimean War, and Bosnia came under Habsburg administration. But Bosnia was home to many Serbs.

From this time on, the European powers began trying to protect themselves from each other by scaling up industrial production and forming alliances. In 1879, worried about Russia, the Habsburgs allied with Germany. In 1892, Russia, after financial disputes with Germany, allied with France. In 1904, Britain, eyeing Kaiser Wilhelm's new German navy, also allied with France and, in 1907, with Russia, too.

This delicate balance began to tip in 1908 when the Turks themselves challenged Ottoman authority. Bulgaria declared independence and the Habsburgs formally annexed Bosnia. In the 14th century, however, before the arrival of the Ottomans, a Serbian empire had covered most of the Balkans and the Serbs had not forgotten this.

In 1912, the Balkan states combined to take almost all Ottoman lands in Europe and in 1913, fought each other for the spoils. Greece and Serbia carved up most of Macedonia, and Serbia took Kosovo. Now Bosnia was the outstanding issue.

On June 28, 1914, Archduke Franz Ferdinand and his wife, Sophie, were in Sarajevo, the Bosnian capital, on their wedding anniversary. It was also the anniversary of the Battle of Kosovo in 1389, when a Serb-led Balkan league had killed the Ottoman sultan, Murad I. On this occasion, the Habsburg heir and his wife were shot by a 19-year-old Bosnian Serb, Gavrilo Princip. When Serbia refused to allow Habsburg police in to root out conspirators, the Habsburgs declared war. Russia was forced to reciprocate and Europe's network of alliances brought the rest in to begin the First World War. Four years later, the Hapsburgs, in company with the tsars and their old adversaries the Ottoman sultans, had lost an empire they had begun assembling in the Middle Ages.

In 1914, the crowned heads of Europe were all related but the Austrian Habsburgs stood out as conspicuously unrepresentative rulers. In Maria Theresa's day it was class, not nationality, that had mattered, and so it was still for Franz Joseph. This was the truth for the old dynastic rulers of Europe, who depended on personal connections, not nationality, for their positions. But it showed a failure to see that the world had changed since the French Revolution; holding on to power meant clothing oneself in a new form of legitimacy.

By this time, even the Queen of Great Britain and Ireland and Empress of India (who was mostly German) had somehow learned to pass herself off as the figurehead of a nation.

EMPIRES OF INDUSTRIAL CAPITALISM

The British Empire / The High Age of Imperialism / The Empire of Japan

By 1750, Europeans had been in the East for 250 years, but for all this time their impact had been slight. The economies of India, China, and Japan were huge; Indian textiles and Chinese ceramics dwarfed European production and, in the 17th century, Japan exported more silver than Peru. Besides, Europeans were confined to a handful of European trading ports. After the middle of the 18th century, however, the British broke out of coastal confinement and penetrated the Indian interior.

At home, Britain was changing. While political revolution reinvented France, a technological revolution was transforming Britain from a country of farmers and traders into an industrial power. This produced a new relationship to colonial possessions.

Factories churning out textiles boosted demand for cotton from America and India. Machine production brought costs down far enough for textiles to be sold back to the cotton producers. Profits were used to build new cotton mills in Lancashire—and so the cycle continued. Once Britain became saturated with factories, profits were invested abroad, to build railroads, develop mines, and export the factory system to the colonies. A growing pool of finance began circling the globe and by the mid-19th century Britain operated its own global economy.

Toward the end of the 19th century, a second industrial revolution, replacing steam and iron with oil and steel, was underway in Germany and Continental Europe. A race to industrialize soon turned into a frantic scramble to colonize Africa, Asia, and the Pacific.

Africa became a new, safely removed playing field for the age-old jostling of European powers, in the process of which almost all of it was carved up into colonies. China, by contrast, barely hung on despite being brought to its knees; it was a developed society with too long a history to be completely subdued. Across the water, however, Japan had been watching and learning from the West.

The arrival of Western industrial power in Japan in 1853: the steam-powered USS Mississippi gunship comes to force open trade. Uniquely, the Japanese resisted colonization through imitation. By the time Tsukioka Yoshitoshi made this woodblock print in 1876, traditional dress was dying out and Japan was fast becoming a Western country.

THE BRITISH EMPIRE

The American Revolution robbed Britain of an empire in the West, but by then a new empire in the East was forming. This empire developed hand in hand with Britain's industrialization to create a new style of imperialism. Meanwhile, trade with the United States only increased after independence, calling into question the need to have formal colonies at all.

THE TURN EAST

In the 1660s, the English East India Company (EIC) began shipping tea to England and, by the 1750s, tea and teapots from China and sugar from Jamaica had combined to produce a national drink. Rising demand for tea and porcelain created a problem, however, because Britain had nothing China wanted in return—except silver.

The solution to a worrying drain of silver lay in India. Mughal power had been in decline since the early 1700s and the provinces had been independent in all but name since 1739, when the shah of Iran sacked Delhi. Now the jostlings of provincial *nawabs* and other regional rulers fed into the rivalry of the British and French, who had each established a string of trading ports.

In 1756, war between Britain and France spread beyond America to Europe. Against the request of the new nawab of Bengal, Siraj ud-Daulah, the EIC began building up its fort at Calcutta, provoking him to capture it. Lieutenant Colonel Robert Clive retook Calcutta for the EIC but trouble with the nawab continued. So Clive cut a deal with the nawab's recently demoted right-hand man, Mir Jafar, who betrayed Siraj ud-Daulah to give Clive victory at the Battle of Plassey in 1757. Mir Jafar became nawab but had to concede Clive so much in return that he could not pay his army, a vulnerability that eventually led to the EIC gaining the rights to the taxes of Bengal.

Bengal's taxes allowed the EIC to build an army of *sepoys*, Indian soldiers, armed with British muskets. Clive had brought 2,000 men to Calcutta. By the time the American colonies rebelled, there were 115,000. By 1806, sepoys had conquered India for the British—at no cost to the British taxpayer.

Access to India's interior enabled poppy plantations to be established. Now the EIC was able to exchange Bengal opium for Chinese tea. Middlemen smuggled the drug into China, where it was banned, and soon opium exports outstripped tea imports, reversing the flow of silver. When the EIC lost its monopoly on Chinese trade in 1833, it smuggled tea plants out of China and began growing its own in India.

India became the center of a second, eastern empire for the British. After Napoleon annexed Holland, protecting access to India provided the logic for seizing Dutch possessions from South Africa to the East Indies. Later, control of India allowed expansion into Burma, Malaya, and Tibet.

Farther east, Britain found a new undeveloped continent to replace America. In 1788, 717 convicts were dumped in Port Jackson, Australia: out of sight, out of mind. By 1800, however, an industrious settler colony dealing in timber, coal, seal skins, and oil had begun to emerge. Farther east still, the British began to settle New Zealand.

Britain's relationship to its new eastern colonies was now transformed by developments at home.

THE INDUSTRIAL ECONOMY

By the mid-18th century, England had largely replaced small-scale subsistence farming with commercial agriculture. Increased yields from technological improvements were now supporting a higher population than ever before.

This meant greater demand for clothing and employment, which was met by an expanding textile industry, initially based on home-produced wool but soon using imported cotton. Huge machines for faster spinning and weaving were developed, drawing workers together under one roof. By the 1760s, these machines were powered by watermills on fast-flowing rivers in the northwest of England. They were made from iron—produced cheaply since 1709 by smelting with coke instead of less plentiful charcoal. The use of coke led to the growth of coalmining, and the need to pump water out of deep mineshafts in turn produced the steam engine.

When cotton mills switched from water to steam power, output soared and prices plummeted. By the 1820s, British machine-produced textiles were being sold in India, previously the world's largest producer, and within a generation India's textile industry had collapsed.

Britain's new, insatiable demand for raw cotton led American plantations to expand. But when American planters blocked exports in 1861 to force British support for the Confederate South in the American Civil War, Britain sank money into new cotton plantations in India. A classic pattern was established whereby colonies produced raw material for Britain's factories so manufactured goods could be sold back to the colonies.

After his treachery at Plassey, Mir Jafar became a despised EIC puppet nawab, incessantly leeched for money. When he protested, the British deposed him, but installed a successor, Mir Qasim, who challenged the EIC at the Battle of Buxar in 1764, helped by the nawab of Oudh and the Mughal emperor Shah Álam II. When they lost, Shah Álam officially signed over to Clive the rights to Bengal's taxes. Benjamin West, 1774.

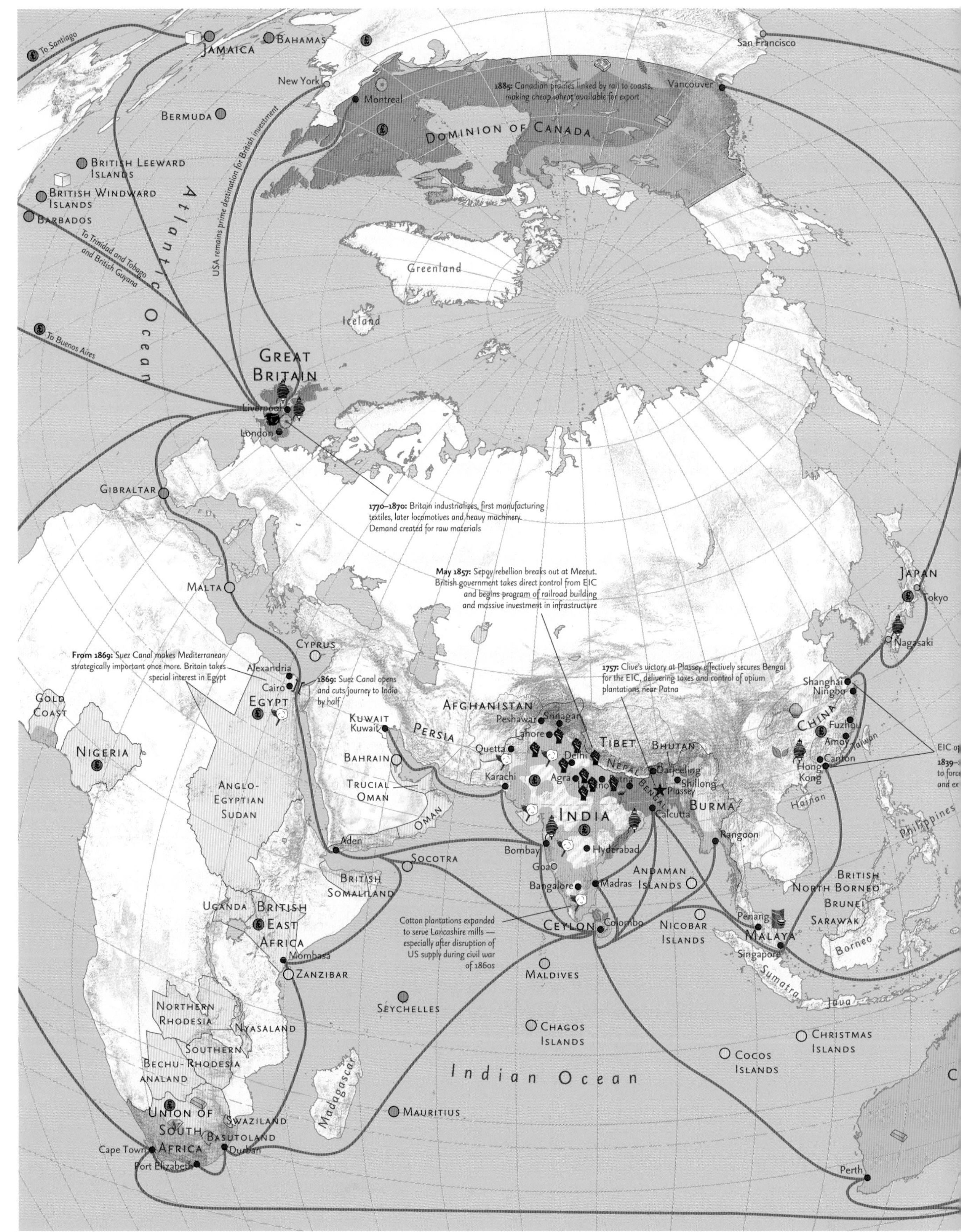

To Santiago
Jamaica
Bahamas
San Francisco
New York
Montreal
1885: Canadian prairies linked by rail to coasts, making cheap wheat available for export
Vancouver
Bermuda
Dominion of Canada
USA remains prime destination for British investment
British Leeward Islands
British Windward Islands
Barbados
To Trinidad and Tobago and British Guyana
Atlantic Ocean
Greenland
Iceland
To Buenos Aires
Great Britain
Liverpool
London
Gibraltar
1770–1870: Britain industrializes, first manufacturing textiles, later locomotives and heavy machinery. Demand created for raw materials
May 1857: Sepoy rebellion breaks out at Meerut. British government takes direct control from EIC and begins program of railroad building and massive investment in infrastructure
Japan
Tokyo
Nagasaki
Malta
Cyprus
From 1869: Suez Canal makes Mediterranean strategically important once more. Britain takes special interest in Egypt
Alexandria
Cairo
1869: Suez Canal opens and cuts journey to India by half
1757: Clive's victory at Plassey effectively secures Bengal for the EIC, delivering taxes and control of opium plantations near Patna
Shanghai
Ningbo
Gold Coast
Egypt
Afghanistan
Peshawar
Srinagar
China
Fuzhou
Amoy
Taiwan
Kuwait
Kuwait
Persia
Lahore
Tibet
Bhutan
Quetta
Delhi
Nepal
Darjeeling
Canton
Hong Kong
Nigeria
Bahrain
Karachi
Agra
Bengal
Shillong
Plassey
Trucial Oman
Anglo-Egyptian Sudan
Oman
India
Calcutta
Burma
Hainan
Philippines
Aden
Bombay
Hyderabad
Rangoon
Socotra
Goa
Andaman Islands
British Somaliland
Bangalore
Madras
British North Borneo
Brunei
Uganda
British East Africa
Cotton plantations expanded to serve Lancashire mills — especially after disruption of US supply during civil war of 1860s
Ceylon
Colombo
Nicobar Islands
Penang
Malaya
Sarawak
Borneo
Mombasa
Singapore
Zanzibar
Maldives
Sumatra
Java
Seychelles
Northern Rhodesia
Nyasaland
Chagos Islands
Christmas Islands
Cocos Islands
Southern Rhodesia
Bechuanaland
Indian Ocean
Madagascar
Union of South Africa
Mauritius
Swaziland
Basutoland
Cape Town
Durban
Port Elizabeth
Perth

By this time, canals and railroads crisscrossed Britain, linking coalmines to cotton mills to ports. Freedom from internal customs barriers had allowed Britain's industrial economy to develop and this now colored a new approach to imperial trade.

FREE TRADE

In 1819, Stamford Raffles founded Singapore for the EIC. He had been in the East Indies since 1805 and became popular for a liberal approach to colonial administration. In Singapore he outlawed slavery, set up schools teaching in indigenous languages, and resisted the temptation to charge a toll on the Strait of Singapore.

Raffles personified a new British outlook. Religious reformers and secular thinkers alike were denouncing slavery on humanitarian grounds, but there were also economic objections: slaves were less productive than paid workers, they were less skilled, and their low purchasing power made them unable to stimulate demand.

The Navigation Acts of the 1650s and 1660s had helped the navy grow by forcing colonies to trade only with England and restricting imports to those carried by English ships. This was standard behavior; all countries sought to protect themselves from the danger of bullion draining away to pay for imports. At the heart of this practice lay the idea that the buyer loses, that there must be a winner and a loser from any exchange. This was the crux of mercantilist economic theory, which had driven states to impose customs duties and vie with each other for a slice of the imperial pie for over two centuries.

But now there was a new idea in the air: instead of merely transferring wealth from buyer to seller, it might be that trade actually *creates* wealth by exchanging what each party produces most efficiently. If so, then anything that increases trade would benefit everyone—from paying workers more so they could buy more, to lifting tolls and customs duties, to fixing currency values against an international standard, such as gold. This was the idea of free trade.

Not everyone shared this attachment to free trade, however. In India, market forces had created a dependent economy. In China, they had created widespread opium addiction, plus a silver drain to pay for it. Hence, in 1839, China dumped 20,000 chests of Bengal opium into the sea at Canton. The British government, having promised to reimburse the dealers for their loss, sent in the gunships. By 1842, Hong Kong had been seized and China made to open another five ports to British trade.

THE SECOND BRITISH EMPIRE ***by 1914***

In 1757, the EIC gained a foothold in Bengal and a new empire centered on the east began to form. The Napoleonic Wars brought Singapore, and Hong Kong was seized in 1842, while new settler colonies developed in Australia, New Zealand, and South Africa. A global web of investment linked colonies and trading partners alike.

In the settler colonies of Canada, Australia, and New Zealand, a common culture produced advantageous trade with less force. Money, machines, and railroads were ploughed in, meat and dairy products returned in refrigerated steamships, and parliaments on the Westminster model were encouraged as a first step to independence. In 1867, Canada became a self-governing Dominion, saving Britain administration costs while continuing to supply cheap wheat.

A lightbulb came on when it was realized that investment alone could secure beneficial trading arrangements. With money piling up in Britain, investors began pumping it into Argentine beef, Chilean nitrates, and Brazilian rubber until the distinction between the empire and British involvement in South America became hazy.

By the mid-19th century, Britain ran an empire of free trade, in theory benefiting the world, in practice serving British interests. The navy forced open markets and policed the seas for pirates, the City provided finance. The Gold Standard plus a boom economy made sterling the strongest currency for investors and the Bank of England propped up all the world's banks.

Global economic dominance allowed a consensus to develop in Britain that the benefits of free trade made formal imperial control unnecessary. In 1857, however, this changed.

For the British, free trade meant the right to sell opium to the Chinese. Demand for Chinese goods had drained silver from the West since Roman times, but stimulating illegal demand for opium grown in British India redressed the balance. As addiction took hold, China's economy nosedived and society began to break down. The Qing government's attempts to intervene provoked two wars, ending with the British forcing China to legalize opium. US newspaper illustration, 1864.

THE WHITE MAN'S BURDEN

In 1757, India's wealth and sophistication had astonished Robert Clive. In 1773, EIC corruption prompted Westminster to appoint a governor-general, in the person of Warren Hastings, to oversee Bengal and in effect India generally. He was yet more fascinated by India and particularly aware of the need to understand its culture, speaking Urdu, founding a Muslim college to train interpreters, and hiring brahmin advisors. India was still officially under Mughal rule, local princes were largely self-governing, and Hastings worked within the traditional caste system.

In the 19th century, however, cultural sensitivity gave way to the idea that India was held back by traditions hindering efficient government and oppressing its people. James Dalhousie, governor-general from 1847 on, provoked resentment by taking direct control of various provinces and banning customs such as *suttee*, which obliged a Hindu widow to throw herself onto her husband's funeral pyre. Then, in 1857, sepoys were issued with new gun cartridges that needed biting open. These were rumored to be greased with beef and pork fat, offending both Hindus and Muslims. A mutiny broke out and spread across India, joined by peasants, landowners, and 500 princes.

Now the British government stepped in, swept both the Mughals and the EIC aside, and established formal rule. India's infrastructure was overhauled, railroads were built, and a vast bureaucracy erected. Earlier, EIC employees had been absorbed into India, marrying local women or taking concubines. Now steamships enabled the new civil servants to bring their wives with them and maintain closer contact with Britain. The British no longer tried to change India but neither did they assimilate. They lived in enclaves and ran the country as a people set apart.

In Britain, new forces were beginning to threaten the interests of free trade. The working classes were starting to organize themselves. They formed unions, protected their wages, and protested against the use of cheap immigrant labor. Businessmen grown rich from the empire now looked to protect their gains. Their children had entered the professions and cared more for preserving institutions than stimulating trade. The landowning aristocracy were preoccupied with calls for independence in Ireland, oldest of all the colonies. On the Continent, new trade tariffs were erected beginning in the 1870s as a general race to industrialize geared up and European states sought to protect their fledgling industrial economies from Britain's domination of the international market.

By the late 19th century, the free-trade consensus had collapsed in the face of competing interests. In its place, politicians tried to draw together the various sectors of British society with vague, suggestive appeals to "Britishness" and imperial glory. With this came a new championing of "formal empire" as personified by Cecil Rhodes, an English adventurer who made a fortune from South African diamonds in the 1880s, annexed huge swathes of Africa, and imagined himself charged with a mission to civilize.

For most of the 19th century, Britain posed as a benevolent uncle, keeping the peace at sea and distributing the benefits of industry and free trade around the world. But "free trade" meant trade dominated by industrial supremacy and the unchallenged power of the Royal Navy. To other eyes Britain seemed simply to be lording it over a rigged market.

Europe grew envious, and as the century drew to a close a scramble broke out for the remaining uncolonized parts of the globe.

THE HIGH AGE OF IMPERIALISM

By the 1870s, nationalism had become as much a force to serve imperial ambitions as to incite independence movements. A second industrial revolution now gave Continental powers the chance to compete with Britain, and as the 19th century drew to a close, a single global empire gave way to a feeding frenzy for colonial possessions ending in the First World War.

SECOND CHANCES

The Napoleonic Wars spread far beyond Europe and left Britain almost alone as an imperial power. The British had taken French and French-controlled Dutch colonies and incited anti-colonial uprisings in South America, which, by 1830, had wrested the continent from Spain and Portugal. Holland and France, however, now began to rebuild.

The Dutch were almost bankrupt, especially after the secession of Belgium in 1830, which had been part of the Netherlands since 1815. In 1824, however, the British had given back most Dutch possessions in the East Indies, in exchange for the Dutch recognizing their claim to Singapore. Abandoning wider imperial ambitions, the Dutch government embarked on a program to develop an extensive plantation economy on its existing holdings, pushing inland from coastal trading ports and embroiling itself in decades of local wars. After 1870, a move toward privately owned plantations and the cultivation of new crops such as rubber brought a sharp upturn in profits.

The French were more concerned with politics than economics. In 1830, Charles X lost the support of parliament. In a desperate bid to woo the nation with an act of glory, he crossed the Mediterranean and took the city of Algiers. It was not enough to save him but his successor, Louis-Philippe, thought it wise to hold onto Algiers and consolidated control by expanding into the surrounding countryside.

In 1848, Louis-Philippe was ousted and a new republic declared with Napoleon's nephew, Louis Napoleon, as president. Louis Napoleon lived in the shadow of his uncle, nurturing both republican ideals and imperial ambitions. In 1851, he staged a coup and made himself president for life. In 1852, he declared France an empire and himself Napoleon III.

In 1859, France took Saigon, ostensibly in retaliation for the persecution of French missionaries, but keen to rejoin Britain as an imperial power in the East. In the West, Napoleon III tried to resurrect French greatness by setting up a puppet monarchy in Mexico while the United States was occupied with civil war. Once the war ended, however, US-backed Mexican resistance forced him to withdraw.

NEW INDUSTRIAL POWER

While the Dutch were rebuilding their economy and France was trying to rehabilitate its self-image, Prussia was laying the ground for a national German state and for a subsequent second industrial revolution.

After the battle of Waterloo, Prussia had received land on the Rhine, including the coal-rich Ruhr Valley. Machines and steam engines were imported from Britain, and mines and engineering works were opened here. Soon railroads took over from canals and rivers as the main form of transport and Prussia was able to develop Silesia in the east, which Frederick the Great had taken from Austria. Prussia's customs union accompanied the railroads in bringing these two industrial regions together.

Britain's industrial revolution had emerged piecemeal from private experimentation but Prussia, aware it needed to catch up, drove industrialization through government sponsorship both in industry and education. Prussian universities included institutes for scientific research at a time when Oxford and Cambridge focused on classical scholarship.

In 1870, a Prussian-led German League used its railroads and greater industrial strength to humiliate Napoleon III in a brief war that ended with France conceding industrially useful Alsace and Lorraine to a new German state, unified under Prussian prime minister Otto von Bismarck in January 1871.

Other European states knew they needed to industrialize, too, but they faced economic pressures. Britain dominated the market for industrial goods and, from the 1870s on, overproduction drove prices down and a long recession set in. In addition, with the opening of the Union and

Behind the imperial rivalries of the late 19th century lay mounting industrial and military capabilities. Visitors at the 1876 World's Fair in Philadelphia admire the precision tooling of a gun manufactured by Krupp, the German company responsible for French defeat in 1870.

Central Pacific Railroad in 1869, the United States was able to flood Europe with cheap grain from the Midwest. Britain, already industrialized, accepted the loss of its agricultural sector and Denmark switched from grain to livestock, but most of the rest of Europe responded by protecting their farmers as well as their infant industrialization programs with customs duties.

The recession begun in the 1870s ended more quickly in Germany and on the Continent generally than in Britain because Germany spearheaded the development of new products. Steel replaced iron, oil replaced coal, the internal combustion engine and the electric dynamo replaced the steam engine, and a chemical industry was born, driven in the first instance by a search for textile dyes and thereafter for medicine. Although the British had produced steel in the 1850s, Britain was tied into older technology and lacked the government-funded research institutes on which Germany's new high-tech industrial sector was based.

As a result, Europe by the late 19th century was no longer so dominated by Britain. Several fast-industrializing powers now competed with each other, each looking abroad for raw materials, each protecting its economy with tariffs.

THE SCRAMBLE FOR AFRICA

Since Napoleon's Egyptian campaign of 1798, Europeans had been trying to penetrate the African interior. Africa's rivers, however, were hard to navigate and infested with malarial mosquitos. European demand for groundnuts, palm oil, and ivory for billiard balls and piano keys gave rise to inland trading empires, but these were run by African businessmen who supplied European traders at the coast.

By the mid-19th century, steamships and in particular quinine, which gave protection against malaria, began to make exploration easier. In the 1850s and 1860s, Scottish missionary David Livingstone charted the Zambezi, and British explorers Richard Burton, John Speke, and James Grant found the Great Lakes and the source of the Nile. Then, in the 1870s, Welsh journalist Henry Morton Stanley charted the River Congo and was commissioned by Leopold II of Belgium to open up the area for commercial exploitation. In the age of the steamship, the railroad, and quinine, such a venture now seemed possible.

For a while, the idea of Africa as a free-trade zone for European business was entertained, but national rivalries soon made this unworkable. In the 1860s, a French company had built a canal at Suez joining the Mediterranean and the Red Sea, but in 1875, debts forced Egypt to sell its shares to Britain. Farther west, the French Foreign Legion had begun marching inland from Senegal. There was little economic advantage here but there was an opportunity for cheap glory to offset the shame of defeat to Prussia in 1870. In 1881, France claimed territory opposite Belgium on the Congo and occupied Tunisia. In 1882, Britain occupied Egypt to protect Suez from a coup. Italy had ambitions in Eritrea and finally Portugal called for regulation.

Bismarck emerged as Europe's diplomat, motivated by a desire to create a breathing space for his new state by turning the spotlight elsewhere. In 1884, he chaired the Berlin Conference, which laid down rules for Africa's colonization. Lines were drawn on the map within which each power had initial rights to

Opposite page: main map:

THE SCRAMBLE FOR AFRICA

France annexed Algiers in 1830 but sought serious expansion only after defeat to Prussia in 1870, by which time the Suez Canal gave Britain an interest in Egypt. Belgian designs on the Congo led to the Berlin Conference of 1884, at which rules for an imperial land-grab were agreed, and an all-out race followed.

Inset map:

AFRICA CARVED-UP ***by 1914***

By the outbreak of the First World War, European powers had claimed all of Africa save Ethiopia and Liberia, a state created in 1822 for freed American slaves.

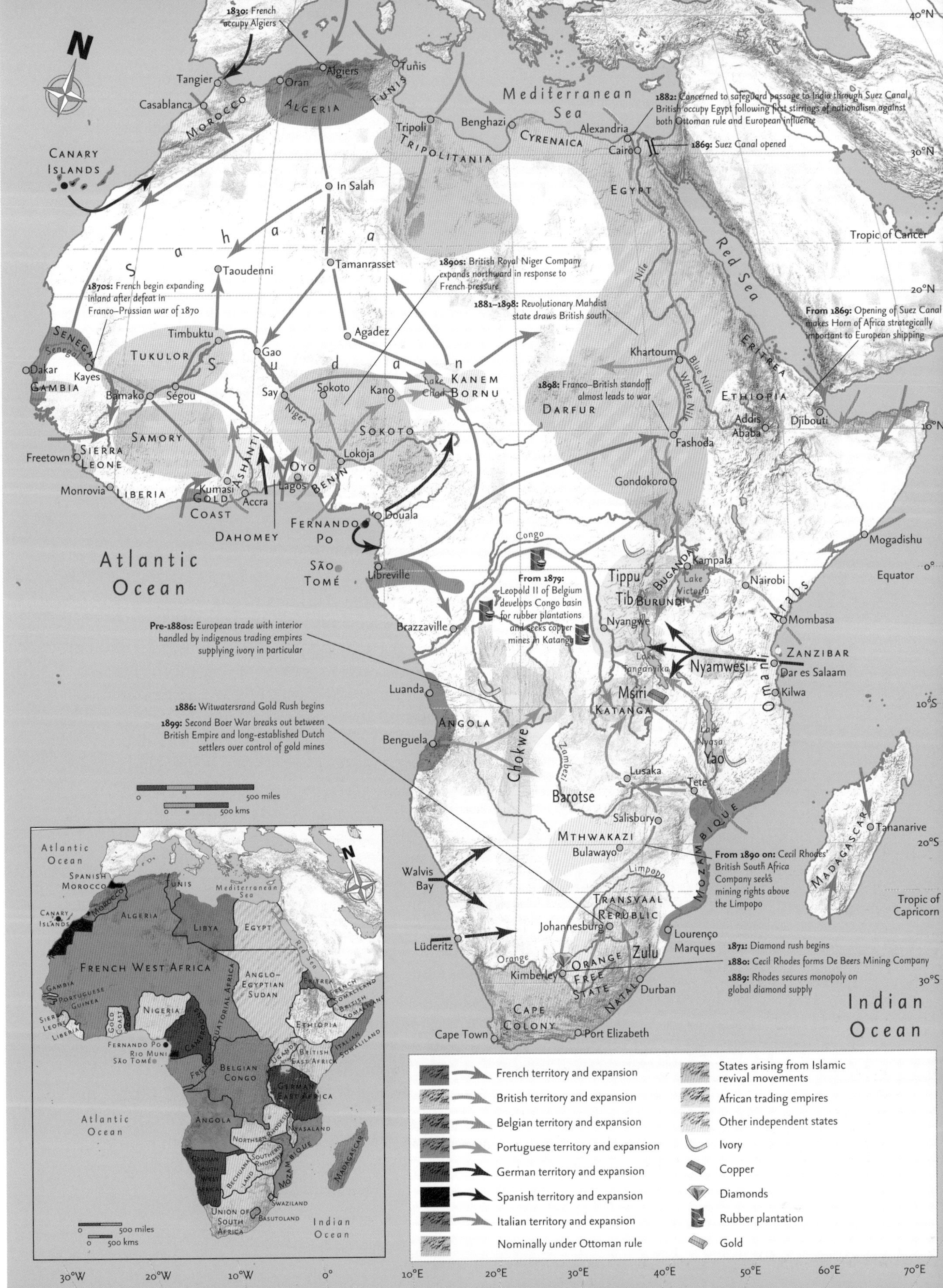

1830: French occupy Algiers
N
Tangier
Oran
Algiers
Tunis
Casablanca
MOROCCO
ALGERIA
TUNIS
Mediterranean Sea
1882: Concerned to safeguard passage to India through Suez Canal, British occupy Egypt following first stirrings of nationalism against both Ottoman rule and European influence
Tripoli
Benghazi
Alexandria
CYRENAICA
TRIPOLITANIA
Cairo
1869: Suez Canal opened
CANARY ISLANDS
In Salah
EGYPT
Sahara
Tropic of Cancer
Red Sea
Nile
Taoudenni
Tamanrasset
1890s: British Royal Niger Company expands northward in response to French pressure
1870s: French begin expanding inland after defeat in Franco–Prussian war of 1870
1881–1898: Revolutionary Mahdist state draws British south
From 1869: Opening of Suez Canal makes Horn of Africa strategically important to European shipping
SENEGAL
Senegal
Timbuktu
Agadez
Gao
TUKULOR
Sudan
Khartoum
ERITREA
Dakar
Kayes
GAMBIA
Bamako
Ségou
Say
Sokoto
Kano
Lake Chad
KANEM BORNU
1898: Franco–British standoff almost leads to war
DARFUR
Blue Nile
White Nile
ETHIOPIA
Addis Ababa
Djibouti
Niger
SOKOTO
SAMORY
Fashoda
Freetown
SIERRA LEONE
ASHANTI
OYO
Lokoja
Monrovia
LIBERIA
Kumasi
GOLD COAST
Accra
Lagos
BENIN
Gondokoro
DAHOMEY
FERNANDO PO
Douala
Atlantic Ocean
Congo
SÃO TOMÉ
Libreville
Mogadishu
Kampala
BUGANDA
Lake Victoria
Tippu Tib
BURUNDI
Nairobi
Equator
From 1879: Leopold II of Belgium develops Congo basin for rubber plantations and seeks copper mines in Katanga
Arabs
Brazzaville
Nyangwe
Mombasa
Pre-1880s: European trade with interior handled by indigenous trading empires supplying ivory in particular
ZANZIBAR
Lake Tanganyika
Nyamwesi
Dar es Salaam
Omani
Kilwa
Luanda
Msiri
KATANGA
1886: Witwatersrand Gold Rush begins
1899: Second Boer War breaks out between British Empire and long-established Dutch settlers over control of gold mines
ANGOLA
Benguela
Chokwe
Zambezi
Lake Nyasa
Yao
Lusaka
Tete
Barotse
500 miles
500 kms
Salisbury
MOZAMBIQUE
MADAGASCAR
Tananarive
MTHWAKAZI
Bulawayo
From 1890 on: Cecil Rhodes' British South Africa Company seeks mining rights above the Limpopo
Walvis Bay
Limpopo
TRANSVAAL REPUBLIC
Tropic of Capricorn
Johannesburg
Lüderitz
Lourenço Marques
1871: Diamond rush begins
Orange
ORANGE FREE STATE
Zulu
1880: Cecil Rhodes forms De Beers Mining Company
Kimberley
1889: Rhodes secures monopoly on global diamond supply
Durban
NATAL
Indian Ocean
CAPE COLONY
Cape Town
Port Elizabeth
Atlantic Ocean
SPANISH MOROCCO
TUNIS
Mediterranean Sea
MOROCCO
ALGERIA
CANARY ISLANDS
LIBYA
EGYPT
Red Sea
FRENCH WEST AFRICA
ANGLO-EGYPTIAN SUDAN
ERITREA
FRENCH SOMALILAND
BRITISH SOMALILAND
GAMBIA
PORTUGUESE GUINEA
SIERRA LEONE
LIBERIA
GOLD COAST
NIGERIA
FRENCH EQUATORIAL AFRICA
ETHIOPIA
ITALIAN SOMALILAND
CAMEROON
FERNANDO PO
RIO MUNI
SÃO TOMÉ
UGANDA
BRITISH EAST AFRICA
BELGIAN CONGO
GERMAN EAST AFRICA
Atlantic Ocean
ANGOLA
NORTHERN RHODESIA
NYASALAND
SOUTHERN RHODESIA
GERMAN SOUTH WEST AFRICA
BECHUANALAND
MOZAMBIQUE
MADAGASCAR
SWAZILAND
UNION OF SOUTH AFRICA
BASUTOLAND
Indian Ocean
500 miles
500 kms
French territory and expansion
British territory and expansion
Belgian territory and expansion
Portuguese territory and expansion
German territory and expansion
Spanish territory and expansion
Italian territory and expansion
Nominally under Ottoman rule
States arising from Islamic revival movements
African trading empires
Other independent states
Ivory
Copper
Diamonds
Rubber plantation
Gold
40°N
30°N
20°N
10°N
0°
10°S
20°S
30°S
30°W
20°W
10°W
0°
10°E
20°E
30°E
40°E
50°E
60°E
70°E

conquest—but if it failed to hold and make use of its conquests this right would fall to whoever could.

Over the next couple of years Germany played its own brief part in the inevitable scramble that followed, but Bismarck's chief interest was to encourage Britain and France to remember their traditional enmity. The British were drawn south from Egypt to deal with religious revolt in the Sudan and the French marched steadily east in their largely valueless conquest of western Africa. In 1898, they met at Fashoda on the White Nile and, for a moment, a new Anglo–French war seemed about to erupt.

The same year, however, Kaiser Wilhelm II began building a German navy, breaking from Bismarck's emphasis on diplomacy and ushering in a new overtly militaristic Germany. Within a few years, Britain had finally realized the French were no longer the threat. In the meantime, Britain had annexed the free Boer republics in Southern Africa, tens of millions had been killed or mutilated in the rubber plantations of the Belgian and French Congos, and Africa had become a patchwork of colonies slapped over traditional social and political boundaries, storing up bloodshed for the future.

THE END OF THE OLD EMPIRES

Despite brutal exploitation, much imperial ambition in Africa was motivated by political and cultural concerns rather than sound business sense. Hard economic interest had always been focused on China. After the Qing lost the First Opium War of 1839–1842 and conceded Hong Kong to the British, the continuing opium trade produced a deepening economic crisis that culminated in the Taiping Rebellion of 1850–1864, during which 25 million people died. Together, the French and British took advantage of this to take Peking (Bejing) and force further concessions, including legalizing opium, in the Second Opium War (1856–1860).

The Second Opium War enabled Russia to push south and found Vladivostok. In the 1880s, the French moved north through Indochina, and the British moved east through Burma and Tibet. In the 1890s Japan took Taiwan, and all the imperial powers began maneuvering for China's collapse. A quarter of Chinese men were now addicted to opium and in 1900–1901, anti-Western feeling erupted in the so-called Boxer Uprising, initiated by a martial arts sect called the Fists of Righteous Harmony. Western railroads were destroyed, Christians were massacred, and in the ensuing chaos, China was divided up among the imperial powers into zones of influence—China's tradition of rebellions made manipulating the government seem more attractive than taking on direct rule. After the Qing Empire finally fell in 1911, a new provisional government was able to hold off the Europeans until they had a war of their own to worry about.

The First World War brought down Russia, Austria–Hungary, the Ottomans, and the new German Empire. The empires of Britain and France increased in size with the incorporation of German and Ottoman lands, but these were unwanted gains. Britain, outwardly still the world's greatest empire, had been bankrupted by the war and could ill afford the administration of yet more overseas territories. In addition, after an imperial war that destroyed Europe, public enthusiasm for empire was waning.

SOUTHERN ENCROACHMENT ON CHINA *from 1842 on*

Aware that a British presence had been growing in China since 1842, the French joined them in a Second Opium War, during which they took Saigon. From here, they pressed north as the British spread east from India, while both penetrated China along the Yangtze. By the 1890s, the Japanese had arrived on the coast.

Decolonization, however, would have to wait until after the Second World War. Empire may have become a liability for the British, the French, and the Dutch, but their colonies represented economic and cultural investments hard to give up. When they eventually did pull out, they left power vacuums that their former colonies tore themselves apart to fill.

In the meantime, once-mighty China, brought to its knees by the West, had almost fallen to the one non-European society that resisted Western imperialism by imitation: Japan.

The Qing panic as Germany begins to cut the Chinese cake with Britain, Russia, France, and Japan each waiting for a slice. As it happened, China was too strong to succumb to Africa's fate, but the Qing Empire nevertheless fell in 1911. French cartoon, 1898.

THE EMPIRE OF JAPAN

Of all the rich pickings coveted by the West, Japan alone saved itself—by playing the Europeans at their own game. Japan transformed itself economically, politically, and even socially into a Western society, but did so while retaining an attachment to family that produced a distinctive, corporate style of capitalism, recognizably Japanese. This enabled Japan to industrialize in record time—and perhaps helped to keep it apart from the rest of the world.

THE MEIJI RESTORATION

In the 7th century CE, the Japanese, originally immigrants from the Korean peninsula, were a series of clans tied together by an emperor descended from the Shinto sun goddess Amaterasu, central diety of a pantheon of nature gods. The emperor was regarded as a father figure, but his power was far from absolute.

By the 9th century CE, clans holding the northern frontier gave rise to a *samurai* or warrior class. The samurai grew in power as protectors of noble estates and, by the end of the 12th century, a samurai ruled in the name of the emperor as *shogun* ("military commander"). Central control, however, remained elusive. Japan was a land of fiercely independent great families, a society producing Zen Buddhism, a form of mental training for samurai as well as a reflective philosophy for their noble masters.

In the 1540s, the Portuguese arrived, bringing guns. Guns enabled the Tokugawa shoguns to take power in 1603 and head the other clans in a stable feudal arrangement of reciprocal duties. The Portuguese and their Christianity were soon driven out and the Dutch were allowed restricted trade on condition they did not preach. There followed two centuries of peace and trade, mostly with China, and Japan became rich. A business class rose up, clans fell into debt with moneylenders, and samurai, with no one to fight, became officials with quaint customs rather than genuine warriors.

In 1853, Commodore Matthew Perry arrived in Edo with four US warships to force open diplomatic relations, trade, and settlement. As in India and China, "free" trade soon proved to mean destabilizing foreign control of trade. Prices rose, revolts broke out, and a formal foreign takeover was widely feared.

At this point Japan realized it needed centralized power to save itself. A new emperor acceded in 1867 and, in 1868, three young samurai, Okubo Toshimichi, Saigo Takamori, and Kido Takayoshi, staged a coup to restore power to him on condition he oversee modernization along Western lines. Tokugawa Yoshinobu, the last shogun, was forced to resign and give up his land. Other clans followed suit until all land belonged to the new Emperor Meiji. Okubo Toshimichi had already pioneered the wearing of Western clothes and now Western institutions were embraced wholesale. Newspapers appeared, as did a national education system and a parliament—one, however, the emperor's cabinet could overrule.

More significant was the establishment of a national, tax-funded conscript army. Peasants could now fight for their country and samurai found a new role as an officer class. From 1878 on, the chief of the armed forces had direct access to the emperor, bypassing parliament. Samurai army officers were sent to learn from the French and Germans, naval officers from the British.

The key political lesson Japan learned from the West was the power of nationalism. Buddhism was suppressed and Shintoism revived as a national religion. Beginning in 1870, everyone had to register at a local Shinto shrine, and in 1872 the emperor's birthday became a religious festival.

By the 1880s, the Japanese government was directly funding fast-track industrialization, but it soon found a partnership with powerful business dynasties worked better.

FROM BUSINESS TO EMPIRE

Like Britain, Japan's industry relied on foreign trade, which meant coordinating transport and international finance with industry itself. Japan achieved this through the *zaibatsu*, family-owned corporations.

In the late 17th century, Mitsui Takatoshi, son of a miso-seller, opened a kimono shop in Edo and subsequently became moneychanger to the Tokugawa shoguns. In 1876, Mitsui & Co. opened Japan's first private bank and, the following year, a Shanghai office to sell Japanese coal to British companies. Mitsui employees were sent to the United States to study business.

By the 1880s, Mitsui & Co. was buying cotton from China and using it to manufacture textiles in Japan, which it sold back to the Chinese. In the 1890s, Mitsui set up a Bombay office to buy Indian cotton. In 1902, a cotton mill was set up in Shanghai. Finally, in 1911, Mitsui & Co. began buying raw cotton from the West with the opening of an office in Texas.

From the start, Japanese industry and banking were more integrated than in the West. Where British foreign investment represented speculators looking for a return from any source, Japanese foreign investment served the development of Japanese companies abroad. Zaibatsu such as Mitsui and Mitsubishi comprised a holding company above a bank connected to several industrial and transport companies.

The zaibatsu sent employees to learn from the West but tried to operate largely as self-sufficient units, both economically and culturally—in the 1890s Kikkoman opened a soy-sauce factory in Denver to cater to expatriates. At home, they brought parts of the state within their corporate ambit. The Rikken Seiyukai, Japan's main political party between 1900 and 1921, was all but a part of Mitsui & Co., which was also tied to the army. In the late 1920s, the Rikken Minseito, which took over from the Seiyukai, was linked to Mitsubishi and the navy.

Already in 1876, Japan had copied Western practice and forced open three Korean ports to Japanese trade. By the 1890s, all the powers were positioning themselves for the Qing Empire's collapse. Russia seemed ready to pounce on the mineral resources of Manchuria—and maybe to invade Korea, too. If anyone felt history entitled them to Qing territory, however, it was Japan.

So, in 1894–1895, Japan took the Liaodong Peninsula in southern Manchuria as well as the island of Taiwan. The West, led by Russia, forced it to give back Liaodong, which made Japan resentful, especially as Russia proceeded to lease Port Arthur on the peninsula and build a railroad in Manchuria. This railroad in part provoked the Boxer Rebellion of 1900, which Russia, in concert with the other Western powers, sent in troops to quell. Afterward, Russian troops remained in Manchuria despite agreements to withdraw. By 1905, therefore, Japan felt entitled to invade again. This time it showed it had arrived as an industrial power, and no one dared ask it to give back its gains.

By now Japan had well-established business interests in Manchuria and China. There were flour mills, factories producing textiles, matches, and soybean oil, and most of Japan's materials for heavy industry, such as coal and iron ore, came from the mainland. So Japanese influence abroad continued to grow, particularly during the First World War when European powers were otherwise occupied—and when Japan was making money by supplying Britain with armaments.

THE GROWTH OF JAPAN *1868–1941*

By the 1890s, Japan's economy depended on overseas trade. War with Russia in 1905 yielded a foothold on mainland China and commercial development followed. But during the 1920s Japan became isolated from the West and in the 1930s sought an empire that would make it self-sufficient.

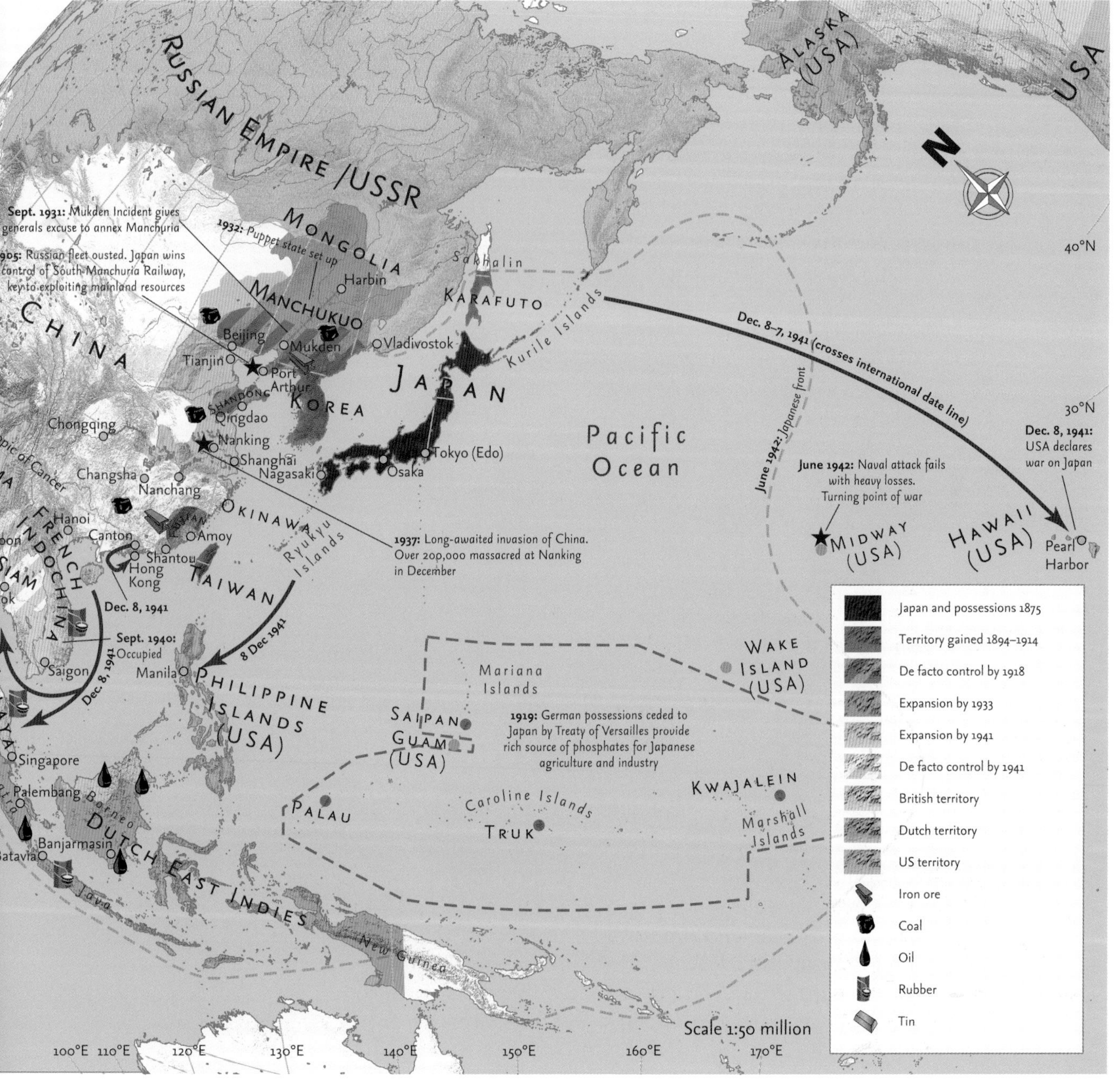

GOING IT ALONE

By the 1920s, however, the economic boom Japan had enjoyed during the First World War was over. Industrialization had created a population explosion but now the foreign trade on which it depended was suffering as relations with the West cooled. In the aftermath of war, Western governments wanted to check military buildup and viewed Japanese expansion unenthusiastically.

Then the United States barred Asian immigration and anti-Western feeling exploded. Disaffected samurai linked to the army fused Shinto nationalism with a revival of the "Way of the Warrior," the ancient samurai code of honor, to produce a strident militarism ushering in Hirohito, the Showa emperor, in 1926. Army leaders envisaged a new shogunate with the emperor once again a front for a military commander.

In 1929, the New York Stock Market crashed and, by 1931, Japan's exports had dropped by half. The idea of a Japan involved in international trade seemed to have had its day. It was time for a self-sufficient Japanese empire. In 1931, the army engineered an explosion on the Japanese railroad in Manchuria and used it as a pretext to invade and set up a puppet state. The generals had acted without consulting the government, which

In the Assault at Makungcheng Fortress, Captain Awata Fights Furiously With His Celebrated Sword—a scene from the invasion of Taiwan (1894–1895), captured by Migita Toshihide. By now the Japanese army wore Western uniforms, but the archetype of the samurai persisted.

consequently fell. The new government was dominated by the army, and voted to pull out of the League of Nations.

In 1937, the army finally launched the long-awaited, full-scale invasion of China, now conveniently split between nationalists and communists. Hundreds of thousands were massacred in Nanking (Nanjing) and by 1939 the coast and most of the important cities were under Japanese control.

Japan was now committed to a course. It needed materials, particularly oil from Southeast Asia, but this meant war with Western powers. In December 1941, a bold start was made with simultaneous attacks on British Malaya and Hong Kong, the US-held Philippines, and the US naval base at Pearl Harbor in Hawaii. British and American forces were taken completely by surprise.

For a while Japan made advances to mirror its Axis partners in Europe, spreading across the western Pacific and the East Indies, and pushing up through Southeast Asia to the border of British India. But encroaching directly on the colonial possessions of Western powers was not the same thing as invading China while the West stood by. The attack on Pearl Harbor drew America into the war and with it came the inevitable bombs, perhaps as much to send a signal to the Russians threatening to invade Japan from the north as to end the fighting.

Japan was just not rich enough to take on the United States. The zaibatsu had performed a miracle in taking Japan from feudalism to industrial capitalism in half a century, but they paid low wages and the Japanese army lived off the land. This was not well-cushioned imperialism on the British or US model. Faced with defeat, the Japanese fell back on traditional concepts of honor and glory, engaging in suicidal *banzai* charges and *kamikaze* dive-bombing, as if to deny that a new era dominated by twin superpowers many times Japan's size had arrived.

Japanese troops mark the capture of Nanking, December 1937.

9 EMPIRES AND UTOPIAS

The United States of America / The Soviet Union / The European Union

rom the beginning, empire held within it the dream of a better world. The very first empires were orn of a desire to break free from tribal warfare and achieve peace, but for a long time it seemed peace ould be imposed only by force and a better world enjoyed only by a few. Rule by force is both costly nd dangerous, however, so by the Classical Age, emperors began extending the benefits of imperial eace to more of their subjects in a bid to garner consent.

he European colonial empires brought new technology that made possible the exploitation of eople and natural resources on a far grander scale than ever before. At the same time, the discovery f a whole new continent breathed new life into the old dream of building a better world, and the idea hat liberty should be for all began to grow.

or a time, national independence seemed to be the recipe for peace and freedom. But the nation-tates of Europe eyed each other jealously and descended into war without precedent. In the New Vorld, a federation of united states had married independence with cooperation and in the Old Vorld, too, it had become obvious that some form of supranational government had to be found if he promised land were to be reached.

better world, however, meant different things to different people. For Americans, it meant a world n which each was free to acquire property. For Russians, it meant a world free from the inequalities roperty ownership produced. For Western Europeans, it meant a world in which mutual dependence revented poverty, revolution, and war. In each case, the pursuit of utopia produced something that ooked like empire.

e United States annexed Hawaii and "liberated" Cuba, the Philippines, and Puerto Rico from Spanish rule. Here, Hawaii and Puerto Rico demurely accept Uncle vised political emancipation, but Filipino leader Emilio Aguinaldo and squabbling Cubans, despite the cooperation of General Maximo Gomez, are less

UNCLE SAM'S NEW CLASS IN THE ART OF SELF-GOVERNMENT.

THE UNITED STATES OF AMERICA

The United States of America (USA) was born from revolt against empire. From the beginning it stood for liberty—liberty to acquire property before all else. Citizens of the USA came to see themselves as a chosen people, destined to take possession of what lay before them by virtue of their enterprise and their enlightened republican government. They began to think of themselves as guardians of the free world.

MANIFEST DESTINY

By 1781, the United States of America had finally thrown off the British yoke. The War of Independence, however, had emerged from fighting the French for land west of the Appalachians and, with the British defeated, the new republic claimed the Indian Reserve of 1763 and reached the Mississippi.

In 1803, Napoleon sold Louisiana for $15 million and the size of the United States doubled overnight. A second war with Britain in 1812 largely decided the border with Canada. In 1819, Spain, fighting revolution in Mexico, was pressed into selling Florida for $5 million after armed US incursions, initially to destroy a fort held by runaway US slaves.

By the 1840s, the term "Manifest Destiny" was being used to describe the idea that the United States was destined to stretch to the Pacific as bringer both of technological development and representative government—representative to some, at least. This idea seemed vindicated by Texas, having broken away from Mexico, seeking to join the United States in 1845, and by a resulting war with Mexico itself yielding lands from Texas to California. In 1846, it almost produced a third war with Britain before a compromise was reached over the Oregon Country, which separated California from Russian America (Alaska). Alaska itself was bought from Russia in 1867 for $7 million.

The continental United States, though prized from rival empires, had in practice been won from millions of Native Americans already living in each of the regions the expanding republic bought, negotiated, or wrested by force. Tribes were wiped out or moved on by war, by the fencing off of big ranches and little homesteads, and, most of all, by the Union and Central Pacific Railroad, completed in 1869, which ran to San Francisco. The railroad cleared away the buffalo herds on which the Plains Indians depended and peppered the West with new towns. After the defeat of the Sioux at Wounded Knee, South Dakota, in 1890, all lands belonged to the white conquerors.

The West was really won, however, not by ranchers and homesteaders, but by big money in the East.

LAND OF GIANTS

The West had already provoked North and South to fight for control of the continent. The United States had begun with plantations in the South and slavery had been written into the Consitution, but three quarters of the population lived in the plantation-free North, increasingly resentful of the rich planters and their disproportionate influence on government. In 1861, Abraham Lincoln became president, determined to keep new states free from slave plantations. So 11 southern states broke away and the North began four years of war to force them back into line and abolish slavery outright.

At the same time, Lincoln promoted railroad construction and, in 1863, work began on the Union and Central Pacific. Before track could be laid across the continent, however, it had to be manufactured. The United States needed to be industrialized on a scale unknown in Europe and awesome sums of money had to be found.

The government had been wary of taking on risky financial ventures since a banking failure in 1837, besides which Lincoln was fighting a civil war. So he incorporated two private companies and granted them land on either side of the track to offset their costs. As towns sprang up along the railroad, key parts of the West became in effect colonies of investors in the East.

Industrialization made America into a land of giants. Steamship and railroad tycoon Cornelius Vanderbilt, steel magnate Andrew Carnegie and his coal-mining partner Henry Frick, John D. Rockefeller, father of Standard Oil and world's richest man—these were purest capitalists, unfettered by government. They knew their enemy was free-market competition and fought each other ruthlessly for monopoly control, outmaneuvering laws to check company size by forming trusts—a trail blazed by Rockefeller in 1882.

Banking made J.P. Morgan puppetmaster in these wars. In 1901, he bought out Carnegie and various others to form the monster trust of US Steel. Then, after a battle with Rockefeller to buy control of the Northern Pacific Railway almost brought down the stockmarket, he formed a trust to unite their interests. Between them, J.P. Morgan and J.D. Rockefeller held almost all of US big business.

The US government became little more than another holding in the palms of these giants. In 1904, President Theodore Roosevelt finally took them on and broke up Morgan's railway trust—but he was happy enough to receive funding from the same sources for that year's election campaign. Theodore Roosevelt was also an enthusiastic promoter of the US entrepreneurial spirit abroad.

COLONIES

In fact, the US government had been assisting business overseas long before the West was won. In 1856, it had passed the Guano Islands Act, under which territory could be seized without needing to be brought into the Union and dispensed with when no longer needed. Under the act, US ships began taking islands mainly in the Pacific, some for guano (seabird excrement used as fertilizer), some like Midway, claimed in 1859, as refueling stops for the steamships that followed Commodore Perry's expedition to force open trade with Japan in 1853. Like several other islands, Midway was subsequently annexed.

Since the 1870s, US businessmen in Hawaii had been investing in sugar plantations. In 1887, they backed a revolt and forced a constitution giving power to white men of property. When the queen tried to change this constitution in 1893, the US government dispatched marines to overthrow the monarchy. In 1898, Hawaii was annexed.

That year was a defining one. North America had been settled, but now President William McKinley revived the term "Manifest Destiny" to justify the annexation of Hawaii. In addition, since the early 19th-century wars of independence across Latin America, the idea had grown that the United States was charged to protect the whole of the New World from other imperial powers.

In February, the *USS Maine* unaccountably blew up in Havana harbor, having been sent to safeguard US citizens during Cuba's struggle for independence from Spain. US newspapers alleged Spanish involvement and whipped up jingoistic fervor for war. The marines were sent in and by December the Spanish colonies of Cuba, the Philippines, Puerto Rico, and Guam were in US hands.

The events of 1898, particularly war in the Philippines, divided the United States. For Mark Twain, foremost critic of the Spanish-American War, the possession of colonies undermined the country's republican principles. A majority, however, accepted the claim that the United States was acting first to liberate the oppressed, second to prepare the way for responsible government.

But abroad, as at home, government was increasingly in the grip of US business interests. In the 1870s, Minor C. Keith, commissioned to build a railroad in Costa Rica, began planting bananas along the track to feed his workers. In return for bailing out the Costa Rican government in the 1880s, he received land and established some banana plantations. The railroad turned out not to be profitable, but bananas sold to the US were and Keith soon developed plantations throughout Central America.

By 1899, the investment of Keith's United Fruit Company in Honduras, the original "banana republic," was propping up the government, which allowed the company to enclose more and more land to prevent cultivation by competitors (i.e., local people). When trouble arose, US marines would show up. In Guatemala, the United Fruit Company owned the country's only port and 40 percent of the best land, and ran the postal service. In Colombia, over a thousand striking United Fruit Company workers were killed by Colombian government forces in 1928.

Theodore Roosevelt had come to prominence leading US troops in Cuba in 1898, but, as president following McKinley, he declared the role of the US government abroad was not to expand territorially but to intervene to protect US interests. In 1903, he helped Panama break away from Colombia in order to secure US rights to land on which to build a canal linking the Pacific and the Caribbean. The US later paid Colombia $25 million in reparations. Nonetheless, once the Panama Canal was opened in 1914, access had to be protected. For decades, Nicaragua, the Dominican Republic, and Haiti were variously occupied or had uprisings suppressed, puppet dictators installed, and so on.

GLOBAL MONEY, GLOBAL BRANDS

Of Europe's troubles, however, the United States wanted no part. In 1917, German submarine attacks on ships supplying Britain dragged it into the First World War, ensuring Germany's defeat, but afterward the United States turned away, raising import duties to protect business from a postwar downturn. The international dimension of the US economy was becoming unavoidable, however. The downturn reflected a bankrupt Europe and a shift in the economic center of gravity. By 1918, Britain owed the United States $8 billion. By 1924, the United States was lending Germany money so it could pay reparations to Britain and Britain could pay the United States.

During the 1920s, the US car industry took off but, in 1927, the big New York banks belatedly tried to cash in on the consumer boom by buying up stock in huge quantities. Shares kept rising until people started selling high in the hope of buying back low. On October 29, 1929, 650,000 US Steel shares were dumped on the market in the first three minutes of trading and all confidence evaporated.

Loans to Germany stopped, bringing down Kredit Anstalt, central Europe's main bank, and with it the German economy and very nearly the Bank of England. While

Germany succumbed to Nazism, small banks folded across the United States. Fields of wheat rotted in the Midwest and livestock was slaughtered and left for the buzzards because farmers unable to get credit could afford neither transportation nor feed.

In 1933, at the depth of the crisis, Franklin Delano Roosevelt became president and took over the economy. The government bought up 20 percent of the banking sector, separated investment houses from lending banks, and financed a raft of job creation schemes known as the New Deal. It was a start, but what really revived the economy was another war.

In December 1941, the Japanese bombing of Pearl Harbor, the US naval base in Hawaii, dragged the United States onto the world stage once and for all. Japan's inescapable but drawn-out defeat, which began with a pivotal battle at Midway in June 1942, ended in US occupation of the whole Pacific. The United States left Japan in 1952, Okinawa in 1972, and the Trust Territory of the Pacific Islands only in 1986, even then retaining nuclear testing rights in various parts.

With US forces came more than military occupation, however. During the war, General Eisenhower had ten Coca-Cola bottling plants set up for his men in North Africa. Locals soon developed a taste for Coke themselves. Levi jeans were first seen on off-duty servicemen. Europeans tried to swap anything they could

Buffalo and Plains Indians flee before homesteaders and railwaymen bringing a utopia of initiative, hard work, and representative government across America. The figure of "Manifest Destiny" chaperones them, an idea that became embedded in the American psyche. American Progress, *by John Gast, 1872.*

for them. US soldiers brought American cigarettes, nylon stockings, and other products associated with a lifestyle already familiar through cinema and popular song.

The continued postwar export of these US brands was engineered by a conference at Bretton Woods, New Hampshire, in 1944. Here, architects of the New Deal developed similar measures designed to stimulate and regulate international trade. Exchange rates were pegged to the dollar to keep them stable, the International Monetary Fund (IMF) was created to provide loans to countries with short-term balance of payments problems, and the World Bank was set up to lend money for postwar reconstruction.

This was not enough to rebuild war-shattered economies and by 1948, Europe was receiving huge grants rather than loans. By 1950, even larger sums were flowing into Japan as it became a US base in the Korean War. In both cases, unprecedented growth accompanied consumption of US products.

The World Bank began lending instead to the Third World, at first to build roads and ports but by the 1970s to build schools and hospitals. Improving social conditions produced less of an immediate return than road building, however, and by the 1980s, loans were increasingly made just to service previous loans. To guard against further debt, they now came with requirements to cut public spending, privatize utilities, and encourage investment in industry.

This opened poor countries up to Western business (US or US-financed business) just when managed exchange rates had been dropped as unworkable and the idea of an unregulated market had come back into vogue.

Western companies could buy water rights and outsource manufacturing to tariff-free zones. Governments would help meet setup costs, relax environmental and worker protections, and give tax breaks for an initial period, at the end of which the company could threaten to relocate unless tax breaks were extended. Subcontracting could preserve anonymity. In the 1990s, a Levi Strauss subcontractor in Micronesia was fined $9 million over pay and working conditions, while Levi Strauss themselves were able to plead ignorance.

US-led reconstruction after the Second World War created an international market for US goods and capital, but it was also deemed necessary for another reason: to keep back the tide of communism.

GUARDIAN OF LIBERTY

During the war, the Soviet Union emerged as the major Allied power alongside the United States. As US aid arrived in Berlin in 1948, however, Stalin blockaded the city, prompting the United States to airlift in supplies. The following year, the North Atlantic Treaty Organization (NATO), a new military alliance binding Western Europe to North America, was formed. In 1950, the extension to Korea of communist revolution in China galvanized NATO against a perceived global communist threat.

President Harry Truman had begun trying to "contain" this threat in 1946. Since the New Deal, the government's size had mushroomed and, in 1947, the Central Intelligence Agency (CIA) was set up. The year after, it was authorized not just to gather information but also to assist or else carry out undercover operations abroad.

Following pages:

THE GROWTH OF THE USA AND ITS INTERNATIONAL ROLE 1783-2017

After Independence, the USA expanded west, spanning the continent by rail in 1869. War with Spain in 1898 boosted colonial ambitions abroad, though most US control remained unofficial. After 1945, the USA kick-started the global economy and built an empire of military bases allowing it to adopt a role as global policeman.

As communism stood against capitalist free enterprise, so the desire to contain communism sat alongside US business interests abroad. In 1953, supposed communist fears in Iran provided a smokescreen for the CIA to topple its first government with the help of Britain's Secret Intelligence Service, MI6. A coup was orchestrated, a newly compliant shah reinstated, and the majority share of Iran's oil secured. But things rarely went this smoothly.

In 1959, a communist revolution against US-backed dictator Fulgencio Batista brought Fidel Castro to power in Cuba. President John F. Kennedy charged the CIA with overthrowing Castro's government and an invasion followed in April 1961 at the "Bay of Pigs." As it happened, Cuban intelligence had been forewarned and the campaign turned into a fiasco, only strengthening the revolution and leading to Soviet missiles being stationed on Cuba the following year.

But the biggest mistake was Vietnam. In 1945, the French returned to the south of Indochina to find the north under communist control. After eight years of war the French left, but the CIA and US armed forces took over and pursued an increasingly hopeless campaign. In 1975, the USA finally pulled out, too, and Saigon fell to the communists.

Long before this time, however, the war had taken its toll at home. The same issues divided the country now as they had done in 1898, only this time the balance of opinion had swung the other way. Vietnam drew mounting criticism at home and abroad to the United States's global influence, pursued through economic pressure, CIA operations, and overt military action. Finally, the fall of the Soviet Union in 1992 robbed the USA of its communist demon, making it hard to continue posing as "guardian of the free world."

In September 2001, however, the Twin Towers of the World Trade Center in New York were destroyed in an al-Qaeda terrorist attack and with that a new demon was delivered. Flanked by oceans thousands of miles wide, the continental United States had long been able to gaze out at the rest of the world with a sense of physical security none of the great empires of the past had known. Pearl Harbor had been a shock, Cuba had been a genuine fear, but an attack on New York surely belonged only in the movies. So when it came, it stunned the world.

Immediately, the United States sought to retaliate, launching a "War on Terror," and invading Afghanistan with ground troops, which it had been wary of deploying since Vietnam. But this new demon was vague and shadowy—it was a concept, not a state. As such it was hard to tell when the war had been won. So Afghanistan led to Iraq, and Iraq led to Syria, and the War on Terror has now become the longest war in US history and a potentially endless justification for intervention abroad.

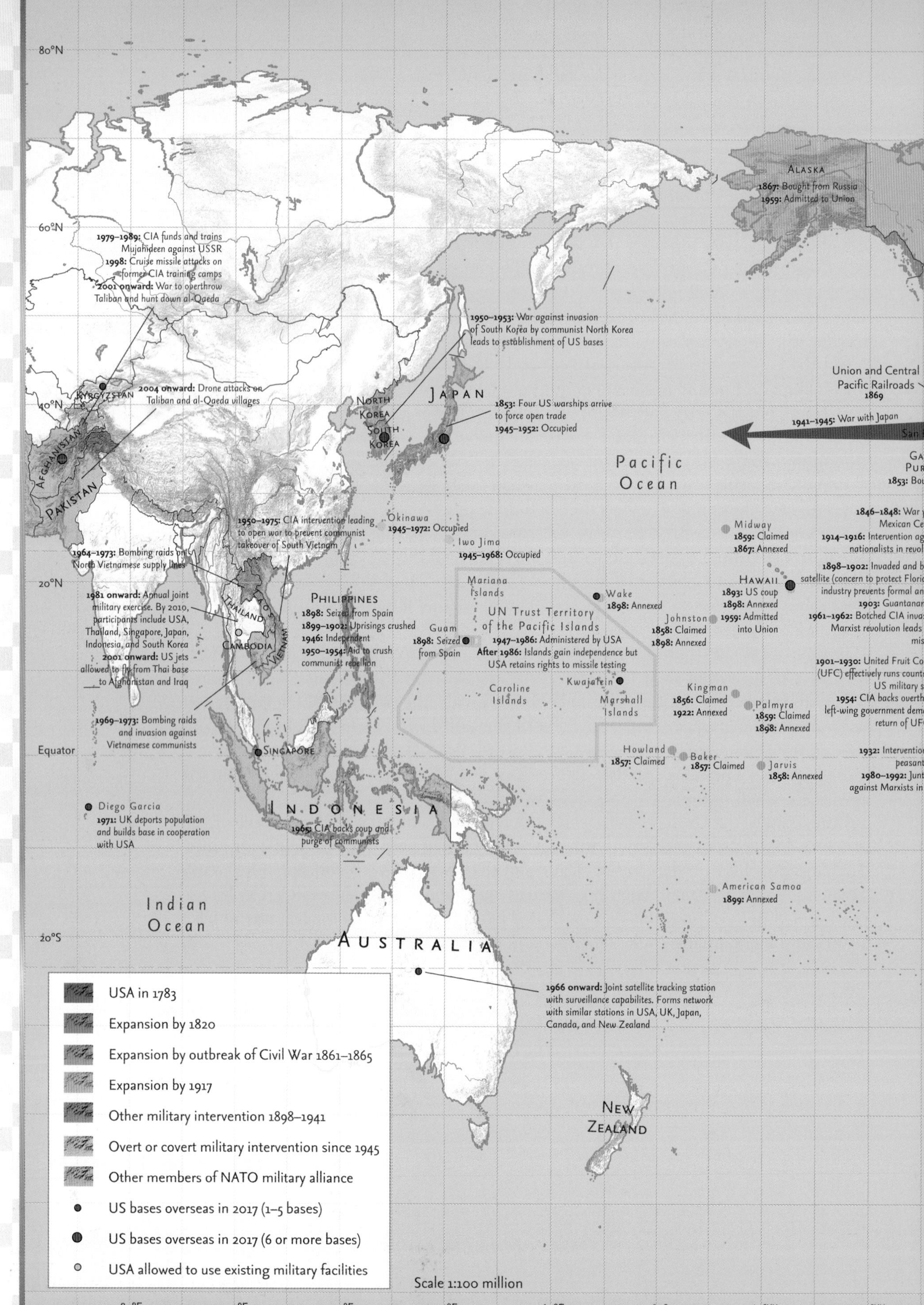

80°N
60°N
40°N
20°N
Equator
20°S
80°E
100°E
120°E
140°E
160°E
180°
160°W
140°W
Alaska
1867: Bought from Russia
1959: Admitted to Union
1979–1989: CIA funds and trains Mujahideen against USSR
1998: Cruise missile attacks on former CIA training camps
2001 onward: War to overthrow Taliban and hunt down al-Qaeda
1950–1953: War against invasion of South Korea by communist North Korea leads to establishment of US bases
Union and Central Pacific Railroads 1869
Kyrgyzstan
2004 onward: Drone attacks on Taliban and al-Qaeda villages
North Korea
South Korea
Japan
1853: Four US warships arrive to force open trade
1945–1952: Occupied
1941–1945: War with Japan
Afghanistan
Pakistan
Pacific Ocean
1853: Boug
1846–1848: War
Mexican Ces
1914–1916: Intervention aga
nationalists in revolu
Okinawa
1945–1972: Occupied
1950–1975: CIA intervention leading to open war to prevent communist takeover of South Vietnam
Iwo Jima
1945–1968: Occupied
Midway
1859: Claimed
1867: Annexed
1964–1973: Bombing raids on North Vietnamese supply lines
1898–1902: Invaded and be
satellite (concern to protect Florid
industry prevents formal ann
1903: Guantanam
1961–1962: Botched CIA invas
Marxist revolution leads t
Mariana Islands
Wake
1898: Annexed
Hawaii
1893: US coup
1898: Annexed
1959: Admitted into Union
Philippines
1898: Seized from Spain
1899–1902: Uprisings crushed
1946: Independent
1950–1954: Aid to crush communist rebellion
1981 onward: Annual joint military exercise. By 2010, participants include USA, Thailand, Singapore, Japan, Indonesia, and South Korea
2001 onward: US jets allowed to fly from Thai base to Afghanistan and Iraq
Thailand
Laos
Cambodia
Vietnam
Guam
1898: Seized from Spain
UN Trust Territory of the Pacific Islands
1947–1986: Administered by USA
After 1986: Islands gain independence but USA retains rights to missile testing
Johnston
1858: Claimed
1898: Annexed
1901–1930: United Fruit Com
(UFC) effectively runs country
US military su
1954: CIA backs overthr
left-wing government dema
return of UFC
Kwajalein
Caroline Islands
Marshall Islands
Kingman
1856: Claimed
1922: Annexed
Palmyra
1859: Claimed
1898: Annexed
1969–1973: Bombing raids and invasion against Vietnamese communists
Singapore
Howland
1857: Claimed
Baker
1857: Claimed
Jarvis
1858: Annexed
1932: Intervention
1980–1992: Junta
against Marxists in
Diego Garcia
1971: UK deports population and builds base in cooperation with USA
Indonesia
1965: CIA backs coup and purge of communists
American Samoa
1899: Annexed
Indian Ocean
Australia
1966 onward: Joint satellite tracking station with surveillance capabilites. Forms network with similar stations in USA, UK, Japan, Canada, and New Zealand
New Zealand
USA in 1783
Expansion by 1820
Expansion by outbreak of Civil War 1861–1865
Expansion by 1917
Other military intervention 1898–1941
Overt or covert military intervention since 1945
Other members of NATO military alliance
US bases overseas in 2017 (1–5 bases)
US bases overseas in 2017 (6 or more bases)
USA allowed to use existing military facilities
Scale 1:100 million

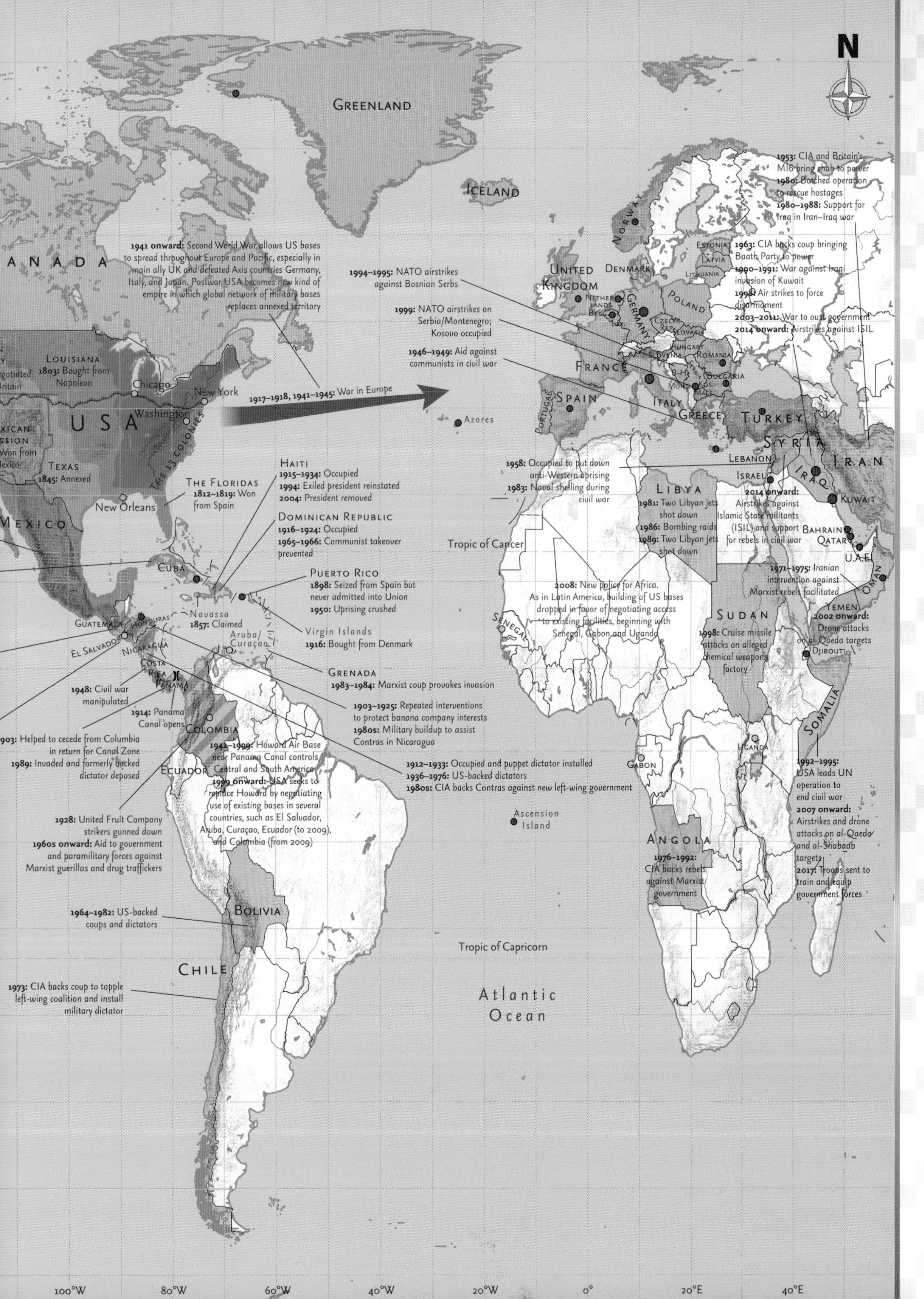

N
Greenland
Iceland
Canada
USA
Louisiana
1803: Bought from Napoleon
Chicago
New York
Washington
The 13 Colonies
Texas
1845: Annexed
The Floridas
1812–1819: Won from Spain
New Orleans
Mexico
1941 onward: Second World War allows US bases to spread throughout Europe and Pacific, especially in main ally UK and defeated Axis countries Germany, Italy, and Japan. Postwar USA becomes new kind of empire in which global network of military bases replaces annexed territory
1917–1918, 1941–1945: War in Europe
Azores
1994–1995: NATO airstrikes against Bosnian Serbs
1999: NATO airstrikes on Serbia/Montenegro; Kosovo occupied
1946–1949: Aid against communists in civil war
Norway
United Kingdom
Denmark
Estonia
Latvia
Lithuania
Poland
Germany
Czech Rep.
Slovakia
Hungary
Romania
Slovenia
Bulgaria
France
Spain
Portugal
Italy
Greece
Turkey
1953: CIA and Britain's MI6 bring shah to power
1980: Botched operation to rescue hostages
1980–1988: Support for Iraq in Iran–Iraq war
1963: CIA backs coup bringing Baath Party to power
1990–1991: War against Iraqi invasion of Kuwait
1998: Air strikes to force disarmament
2003–2011: War to oust government
2014 onward: Airstrikes against ISIL
Lebanon
Israel
Syria
Iraq
Iran
Kuwait
2014 onward: Airstrikes against Islamic State militants (ISIL) and support for rebels in civil war
Bahrain
Qatar
U.A.E.
Oman
1971–1975: Iranian intervention against Marxist rebels facilitated
Yemen
2002 onward: Drone attacks on al-Qaeda targets
Djibouti
1958: Occupied to put down anti-Western uprising
1983: Naval shelling during civil war
Libya
1981: Two Libyan jets shot down
1986: Bombing raids
1989: Two Libyan jets shot down
Tropic of Cancer
2008: New policy for Africa. As in Latin America, building of US bases dropped in favor of negotiating access to existing facilities, beginning with Senegal, Gabon and Uganda
Senegal
Sudan
1998: Cruise missile attacks on alleged chemical weapons factory
Somalia
1992–1995: USA leads UN operation to end civil war
2007 onward: Airstrikes and drone attacks on al-Qaeda and al-Shabadb targets
2017: Troops sent to train and equip government forces
Uganda
Gabon
Ascension Island
Angola
1976–1992: CIA backs rebels against Marxist government
Haiti
1915–1934: Occupied
1994: Exiled president reinstated
2004: President removed
Dominican Republic
1916–1924: Occupied
1965–1966: Communist takeover prevented
Cuba
Puerto Rico
1898: Seized from Spain but never admitted into Union
1950: Uprising crushed
Virgin Islands
1916: Bought from Denmark
Navassa
1857: Claimed
Aruba/Curaçao
Grenada
1983–1984: Marxist coup provokes invasion
Guatemala
Honduras
El Salvador
Nicaragua
Costa Rica
Panama
1948: Civil war manipulated
1914: Panama Canal opens
1903: Helped to cecede from Columbia in return for Canal Zone
1989: Invaded and formerly backed dictator deposed
1903–1925: Repeated interventions to protect banana company interests
1980s: Military buildup to assist Contras in Nicaragua
1912–1933: Occupied and puppet dictator installed
1936–1976: US-backed dictators
1980s: CIA backs Contras against new left-wing government
Colombia
Ecuador
1942–1999: Howard Air Base near Panama Canal controls Central and South America
1999 onward: USA seeks to replace Howard by negotiating use of existing bases in several countries, such as El Salvador, Aruba, Curaçao, Ecuador (to 2009), and Colombia (from 2009)
1928: United Fruit Company strikers gunned down
1960s onward: Aid to government and paramilitary forces against Marxist guerillas and drug traffickers
Bolivia
1964–1982: US-backed coups and dictators
Chile
1973: CIA backs coup to topple left-wing coalition and install military dictator
Tropic of Capricorn
Atlantic Ocean
100°W
80°W
60°W
40°W
20°W
0°
20°E
40°E

THE SOVIET UNION

During the First World War, Russia disowned its empire and all it was based on—tsar, class, capitalism, and all forms of exploitation. But the tsars had always sharply felt the danger of relaxing their grip and their autocratic style of rule was harder to disown.

NO COMPROMISE

In 1905, 1,000 members of a peaceful demonstration seeking better working conditions were gunned down outside the Winter Palace in St. Petersburg. A resulting wave of protests forced Nicholas II to set up a parliament, but this merely enabled him to marginalize radical opposition before stifling the parliament itself.

In February 1917, Nicholas tried to suppress more protests, but this time two million had died in a war effort he was directing. His troops mutinied, the rule of the tsars came to an end, and a liberal provisional government was set up in St. Petersburg ("Petrograd" since 1914). Worsening food shortages and a decision to continue the war, however, made this government increasingly unpopular.

Vladimir Lenin (1917–1924), leader of the Marxist revolutionary Bolsheviks, promised to end the war, give the peasants their land, and govern through *soviets* (workers' councils) around the country. First the Petrograd Soviet, backed by a workers' volunteer force called the Red Guards, transferred support from the government to the Bolsheviks. Then, in August, an attempted Bolshevik coup brought workers, sailors, and soldiers in and around Petrograd together. In September, Lenin refused an offer to join a new coalition government and after a second, better-planned revolution in October, he held sole power.

Immediately, he opened negotiations to pull out of the war, but Germany stalled while pushing the Russian line back. By the time a peace treaty was signed at Brest-Litovsk in March 1918, a third of the Russian Empire's agricultural land, half of its factories, and three-quarters of its coal and steel had been lost. Lenin saw these as short-term losses, expecting the October Revolution to spread. Instead, they joined his refusal to share power in provoking civil war.

In December 1917, he had formed the *Cheka*, his secret police, to control looting and sniff out dissent. In January 1918, his right-hand man and fellow Marxist theorist Leon Trotsky expanded the Red Guards into a better organized Red Army ("red" for blood shed in the name of the revolution). By summer, there was general conscription. By the end of 1918, moderate socialists had largely been suppressed, but war against anarchists and elements opposed to revolution per se continued until 1923. During this time the tsar and his family were shot, 15 million people died, and the economy was destroyed.

The civil war was mostly fought beyond Russia's heartland and reclaimed Byelorussia (Belarus), the Ukraine, and the Caucasus. With Russia, these regions became the first four republics of the 1922 Union of Soviet Socialist Republics (USSR)—nominally a federation of equal partners, within which there were further ethnically defined provinces. Political and economic autonomy were not on the agenda but non-Russian culture was able to flourish.

A NEW RUSSIA

After the devastation and requisitioning of the civil war, Lenin allowed a degree of private enterprise, mostly in agriculture and retail trade. Many farmers, businessmen, and public-sector officials did well for themselves, to the resentment of traditional Bolshevik supporters. In 1924, Lenin died and was succeeded, against his warnings, by Joseph Stalin (1924–1953), who outmaneuvered Trotsky and his other rivals on both sides of the Communist Party and sought to distance himself from both those who had benefited since the civil war and the intellectuals of the revolution. Stalin created a power base by expanding party membership and making it a vehicle through which the uneducated could move up in the world.

His vision was not world revolution but a strong socialist state. By the end of the 1920s, he predicted a new war in Europe for which the USSR had just ten years to prepare. Lenin's compromise with consumerism was dropped as Stalin took control of the whole economy. His "Five-Year Plans" set awesomely ambitious targets focused on heavy industry and agriculture. Millions died on state construction projects and from famine on state farms. Many more died in purges carried out by the People's Commissariat for Internal Affairs (NKVD), successor to the Cheka—purges targeting Stalin's potential rivals, army generals, and, in the end, just about anyone.

By these means, the USSR became an industrial power just in time for Hitler's invasion in June 1941. Hitler hated communism and despised Russians as culturally and racially inferior. This was to be a war of extermination. For Lenin, nationalism had been a gaudy veil used to obscure a class oppression that was international, but a fight for survival in the Great Patriotic War gave Russia a new national identity. It also cast Stalin as the father of a socialist nation, making him the subject of a personality cult with distinct tsarist overtones.

Stalin, however, built an empire in Europe to outshine the tsars. As Napoleon had been chased back to Paris, so the Red Army chased the Nazis back to Berlin through eastern Europe and the Balkans. After the war, Stalin held on to his newly won buffer zone. Reeducation programs begun as territory was conquered now continued and military structures were fused. National armies were given Soviet equipment and new uniforms, and officers were accepted into Soviet military academies.

Civil administration followed a similar pattern. Single-party political systems were set up to run command economies, to provide a vehicle for advancement, and to link back to the party in Moscow (Russian capital since 1918). The higher tiers of the

Comrade Lenin Cleans the World of Filth, *by V.N. Deni, 1920. Already by 1920, however, a vicious civil war was calling into question such an idealized vision of socialist utopia, as did Lenin's subsequent relaxation on free enterprise.*

Communist Party of the Soviet Union functioned, if unofficially, as an imperial administration. In addition, Russia's new eastern European satellites each had secret police organizations set up by the NKVD.

TWIN EMPIRES

Unlike the tsars, Stalin ruled an empire confronted by only one other power. In Europe, he refused the offer of US aid for postwar reconstruction, fearing US influence in Eastern Europe. Instead, he set up his own organization to counter the lure of the West, the Council for Mutual Economic Assistance (COMECON), which eventually included countries as far afield as Vietnam and Cuba.

In Berlin, which lay within the Soviet zone of a Germany partitioned by the Allies, the appearance of US aid in 1948 led Stalin to blockade the city. The West airlifted supplies in and by the time the blockade was called off a year later, Germany had become two states. By 1961, 20 percent of East Germany's population had defected to the West through Berlin and a wall was built to stem the flow.

The tension inherent in the new bipolar world was focused by nuclear weapons. The USA had dropped two atomic bombs on Japan in 1945, and Stalin tested his first device in 1949, a few months after the formation of NATO. After a communist revolution in 1959, a buildup of Soviet nuclear missiles on Cuba led to a US blockade and, in 1962, brought the world to the brink of nuclear war.

The Dawn of Our Fatherland, *by Fyodor Shurpin, 1949. By the Second World War, Stalin had completed a political, economic, and social transformation Lenin had only begun. The war galvanized a new society, but at its top stood a very traditional figure: Stalin himself as father of the nation—a new tsar.*

It was obvious that nuclear weapons could not be used in a world where more than one power possessed them. Imperial rivalry needed safe playgrounds in which to express itself, just as Africa had provided European powers with at the end of the 19th century. European decolonization, which gathered pace during the 1950s and 1960s, provided an opportunity for Soviet weapons and military expertise to fight the United States by proxy in the Third World.

But the prime displacement arena was space. The Soviet Union had launched Sputnik, the first satellite, in 1957, the same year it tested the first intercontinental ballistic missile. The connection was not lost on the United States. In 1961, Yuri Gagarin became the first man in space and thereby a hero of the Soviet Union, but US money made sure the Russians were not first on the moon. Even if they had been it would have been a pyrrhic victory; the space race, together with the arms race that lay behind it, claimed a decent chunk of the US budget—but for the USSR it took everything. Hence, by the 1970s, Russia was left trying to hold an empire together with a cleaned-out account.

LOSING GRIP

In 1956, Stalin's successor Nikita Khrushchev (1953–1964) denounced the harshness of Stalin's rule. Millions were allowed back from the *gulags* (prison camps), and there were moves toward greater freedom of speech and a relaxation toward Eastern Europe.

Protestors in Hungary now called for true independence, with an end to the one-party state and withdrawal from the Warsaw Pact, the Soviet-controlled military alliance enforced on Eastern Europe. Moscow's response was to send the tanks in but afterward to reemphasize ideology. Through joint training exercises, Russia tried to repackage itself as part of a multinational communist force rather than an imperial power. "External aggression" was defined as any anti-communist activity. In 1968, however, Czechoslovakia began to go the same way as Hungary with Czechoslovakian leader Alexander Dubček granting greater freedom of speech and lifting travel restrictions. After trying to avoid a replay of 1956, Moscow clamped down once again, and Dubček's policies were reversed.

From this time on, economic stagnation began to set in. Aside from the cost of the arms race, four decades of an economy based on government supply rather than market demand had made identifying unprofitable areas difficult. The Soviet Union was coming to rely more and more on imports and, after fears arose of a possible US–China alliance, negotiations were opened with the West.

In 1975, East and West finally recognized the legitimacy of a divided Germany, trade increased, and commitments to human rights were signed. Dissidents, however, took the opportunity a more relaxed atmosphere offered to draw the West's attention to ongoing restrictions of freedom and concerns over rule of law. Equally, weapons continued to be stockpiled and supplied to the Third World. So when the USSR invaded Afghanistan in 1979, the West cooled off. Moscow tried to respond in kind but trade had opened Eastern Europe to Western culture, and the West was now harder to demonize.

Meanwhile, in 1978 a Polish cardinal became Pope John Paul II, the first non-Italian pope in 400 years. This fact alone gave Poland a new confidence, but this was also a pope who had lived under communism and stood firmly against it. In 1979 he spoke before millions in Warsaw and made a pilgrimage to the Lenin Shipyard in Gdansk, where strikers had been gunned down in 1970.

Before long there were new strikes at the Gdansk shipyards, and Solidarność was formed, an association of independent trade unions linked to the Catholic Church. In 1981, when Soviet troops looked ready to move in, the Polish government preempted them and imposed martial law itself. Solidarność survived, and within a few years Mikhail Gorbachev (1985–1991) had arrived in the Kremlin.

The USSR was in theory a federation of republics, never an empire, but in practice Moscow made policy that the republics were expected simply to rubber-stamp. Under Gorbachev, they finally had a genuine say in their own affairs, and they used it to secede. In 1991, 14 republics from Europe to Central Asia declared their independence and by the end of December, the USSR had fallen.

Alone among its peers, Russia removed itself from the imperial farce of the First World War and the global economic system on which it fed. Twenty years later, it seemed it had merely exchanged one empire for another and one tsar for another. Russia was barely recognizable but its ruler, as before, wielded power unchecked by rule of law.

According to Marxist theory, Russia in 1917 was not ready for revolution because it was not a mature capitalist society on the European model. Lenin held that communal attitudes to property customary among the peasantry would allow Russia to "leapfrog" a capitalist stage of development and move straight from feudalism to communism. But this meant rule of law remained an unfamiliar concept, overshadowed by continued attachment to patronage.

Once the Soviet Union fell, the absence of legal checks allowed a tiny club of well-placed officials to pocket Russia's previously state-owned assets, bringing forth a desire for a new strongman to rebuild the state, and, if possible, the empire. But dwarfed by the competing attractions of making money and putting faith in a new tsar, the old dream of giving Russia to its people lives on.

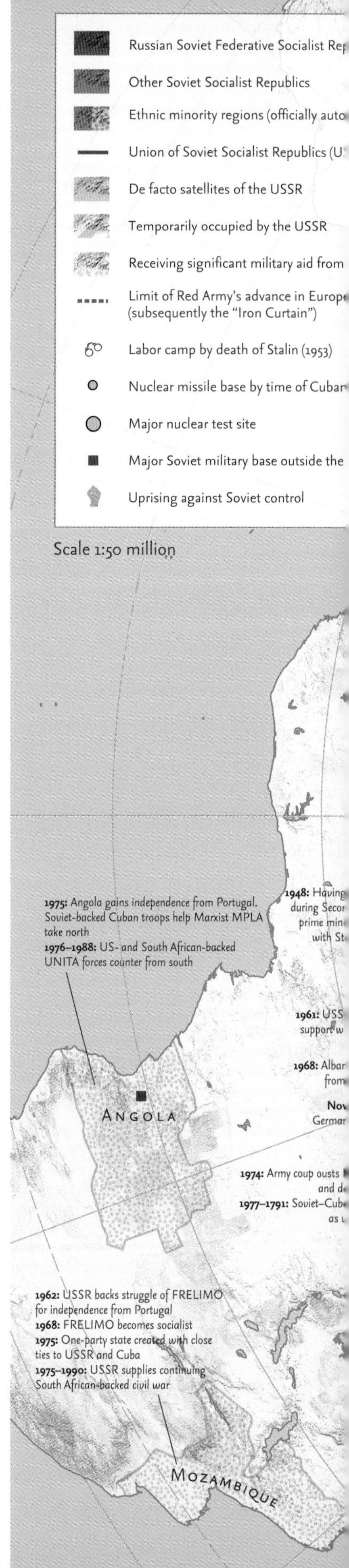

Other Soviet Socialist Republics
De facto satellites of the USSR
Temporarily occupied by the USSR
(subsequently the "Iron Curtain")
Labor camp by death of Stalin (1953)
Major nuclear test site
Uprising against Soviet control
Scale 1:50 million
1975: Angola gains independence from Portugal. Soviet-backed Cuban troops help Marxist MPLA take north
1976–1988: US- and South African-backed UNITA forces counter from south
ANGOLA
1962: USSR backs struggle of FRELIMO for independence from Portugal
1968: FRELIMO becomes socialist
1975: One-party state created with close ties to USSR and Cuba
1975–1990: USSR supplies continuing South African-backed civil war
MOZAMBIQUE

THE USSR AND ITS INFLUENCE ABROAD *1922–1991*

Revolution and civil war restored most of the Russian Empire in the shape of the Moscow-run USSR, a union of four republics in 1922, becoming 15 by 1956. War with Germany brought Eastern Europe as a group of de facto colonies and the Cold War produced global strategic interests.

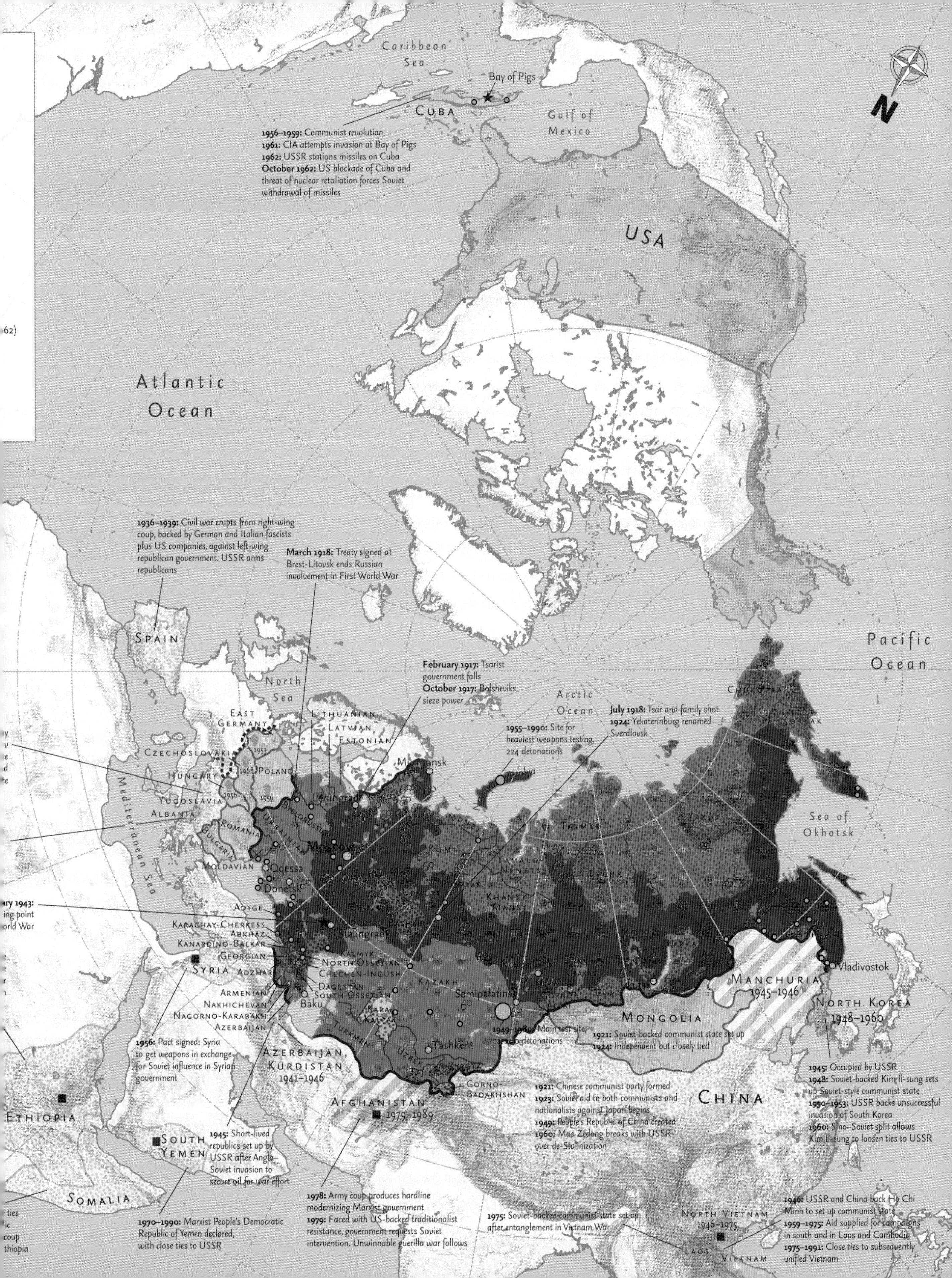

Caribbean Sea
Bay of Pigs
Cuba
Gulf of Mexico
1956–1959: Communist revolution
1961: CIA attempts invasion at Bay of Pigs
1962: USSR stations missiles on Cuba
October 1962: US blockade of Cuba and threat of nuclear retaliation forces Soviet withdrawal of missiles
USA
Atlantic Ocean
1936–1939: Civil war erupts from right-wing coup, backed by German and Italian fascists plus US companies, against left-wing republican government. USSR arms republicans
March 1918: Treaty signed at Brest-Litovsk ends Russian involvement in First World War
Spain
Pacific Ocean
February 1917: Tsarist government falls
October 1917: Bolsheviks sieze power
North Sea
Arctic Ocean
July 1918: Tsar and family shot
1924: Yekaterinburg renamed Sverdlovsk
East Germany
Lithuanian
Latvian
Estonian
Czechoslovakia
1953
1968
Poland
Hungary
1956
Yugoslavia
Albania
Romania
Bulgaria
Byelorussian
Ukrainian
Leningrad
Murmansk
Moscow
1955–1990: Site for heaviest weapons testing, 224 detonations
Chukotka
Koryak
Sea of Okhotsk
Yakut
Taymyr
Komi
Nenets
Yamalo-Nenets
Evenk
Khanty-Mansi
Mediterranean Sea
Moldavian
Odessa
Donetsk
Adyge
Karachay-Cherkess
Abkhaz
Kanardino-Balkar
Georgian
Syria
Adzhar
Armenian
Nakhichevan
Nagorno-Karabakh
Azerbaijan
Kalmyk
North Ossetian
Chechen-Ingush
Dagestan
South Ossetian
Stalingrad
Sverdlovsk
Baku
Kazakh
Semipalatinsk
Novosibirsk
Karakalpak
Turkmen
Uzbek
Kirghiz
Tashkent
Vladivostok
Manchuria 1945–1946
North Korea 1948–1960
Mongolia
1921: Soviet-backed communist state set up
1924: Independent but closely tied
1956: Pact signed: Syria to get weapons in exchange for Soviet influence in Syrian government
Azerbaijan, Kurdistan 1941–1946
Gorno-Badakhshan
1921: Chinese communist party formed
1923: Soviet aid to both communists and nationalists against Japan begins
1949: People's Republic of China created
1960: Mao Zedong breaks with USSR over de-Stalinization
China
1945: Occupied by USSR
1948: Soviet-backed Kim Il-sung sets up Soviet-style communist state
1950–1953: USSR backs unsuccessful invasion of South Korea
1960: Sino–Soviet split allows Kim Il-sung to loosen ties to USSR
Ethiopia
Afghanistan 1979–1989
1945: Short-lived republics set up by USSR after Anglo-Soviet invasion to secure oil for war effort
South Yemen
Somalia
1978: Army coup produces hardline modernizing Marxist government
1979: Faced with US-backed traditionalist resistance, government requests Soviet intervention. Unwinnable guerilla war follows
1970–1990: Marxist People's Democratic Republic of Yemen declared, with close ties to USSR
1975: Soviet-backed communist state set up after entanglement in Vietnam War
North Vietnam 1946–1975
Laos
Vietnam
1946: USSR and China back Ho Chi Minh to set up communist state
1959–1975: Aid supplied for campaigns in south and in Laos and Cambodia
1975–1991: Close ties to subsequently unified Vietnam

THE EUROPEAN UNION

In 1945 Europe lay in ruins. Its last empire had been its briefest and most destructive by far, and now the continent needed to be rebuilt—this time, for good. Europeans had to be freed once and for all from the recurring threat of violent conquest they had lived under for centuries. So in committees and assemblies across Western Europe, civil servants and politicians sat down to weave a web of interdependence.

THE LAST EMPEROR

In November 1918, Germany accepted that defeat in the First World War was now unavoidable and an armistice was signed before Germany itself was invaded. In June 1919, the Treaty of Versailles laid full blame for the war at Germany's door, redrew its borders, and imposed a crippling reparations bill.

Germany was torn apart by attempted coups and revolutions. When it could not pay its reparations, France took control of the Ruhr Valley's industry. German money became worthless. Starting in 1924, US loans kept Germany afloat and brought American culture, but the Wall Street Crash of 1929 took these away. By 1933, Adolf Hitler had come to power on a protest vote.

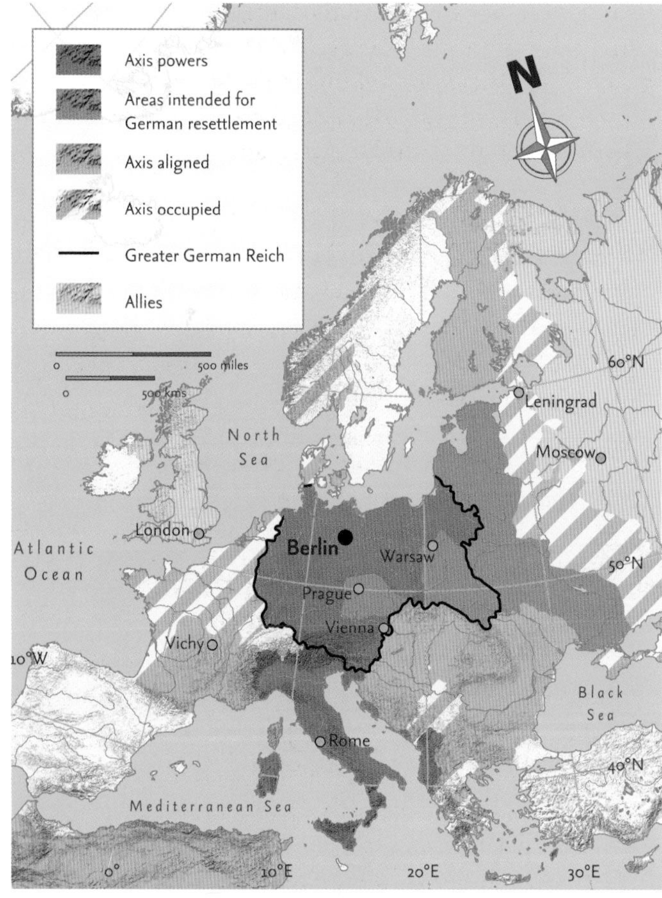

HITLER'S ATTEMPT TO UNIFY EUROPE *1942*

Hitler's empire combined several types of political entity: a Greater German state, areas for German resettlement, allied states, and states with Nazi-controlled puppet governments, as well as occupied countries.

For Hitler, signing both the Armistice and the Versailles Treaty had been betrayals. Since then, a starving Germany had seen its national identity undermined by communists touting an internationalist ideology and by liberal lapdogs for US capitalism. Behind both, Hitler believed, lurked Jewish intellectuals and Jewish businessmen.

Hitler imagined a nostalgic, homogeneous Germany of farmers and small shopkeepers freed from the need to engage in foreign trade and, from 1938 on, with the economy in better shape, he was able to pursue this vision. He began annexing German-speaking regions to form a greater Germany and removing people who did not fit his idea of Germanness: Jews, Slavs, Gypsies, communists, homosexuals, the disabled, and others—at first by deportation, later by murder.

But for Hitler's dream of agricultural self-sufficiency to be realized, Germany needed more farmland. This meant taking it from people who inhabited the vast plains of eastern Europe and Russia. As Slavs, and communists, too, in Russia, these people were worthless in Hitler's eyes; it was only right they should give up their land to a "superior culture."

Ironically, the military muscle needed to acquire this farmland depended on Germany building up its industry as never before. So in September 1939, Hitler invaded Poland, was forced thereby to invade France when Britain, much to his disappointment, declared war, and in June 1941 invaded Russia, making the same mistake as Napoleon.

For a few short years, Hitler held together a loose European empire assembled from various kinds of administration including direct rule from Berlin, puppet governments, and allied states. But Hitler's empire fed on a spiraling dynamic of manufacturing enemies and, with war on two fronts, by 1945 it was all gone.

It seemed to be the end of the line for Europe's story. National consciousness, once the call to throw off oppressive rule, had led to genocide. Industrialization, the passport for all to enjoy material comforts once reserved for the rich, had led merely to industrialized killing. The Enlightenment idea of progress itself—that scientific and technological advance leads to a better society—lay in tatters. The great innovations Europe had brought the world had led only to its own destruction.

PICKING UP THE PIECES

The immediate question for the Allies, as they stood in the rubble of Berlin, was what to do with Germany. Nothing like this could be allowed to happen again.

German industry had meant German weapons. Twenty million Russians had died and Stalin for one did not want to see Germany rebuilt as an industrial power. Neither did Roosevelt's Treasury Secretary Henry Morgenthau, who in 1944 had proposed turning Germany back into an agricultural economy—eerily close to Hitler's own vision. So, the dismantling of 1,500 industrial plants began and in 1946 France took control of German coal to build up its own steel industry.

But an agricultural Germany came with a cost. Germany had been partitioned between the Allies while the eastern Russian sector held the bulk of its farmland. In the US, French, and British sectors, Germans began to starve. With coal scarce and a hard winter in 1946–7, they also began to freeze. Italians and Dutch wanted to trade vegetables for badly needed coal and steel but on top of production limits, Germany was forbidden to trade. What hurt Germany was hurting recovery elsewhere. In this environment, support for communist parties grew, especially in France and Italy.

This was a good reason for Stalin to resist helping with produce from farmland he held in the east. His troops had taken Berlin, and he counted on the rest of Germany falling to him as economic hardship began to bite. For America, mounting tension with Stalin, now refusing to withdraw from eastern Europe as he had agreed, was supplanting fear of German rearmament as the main concern. In addition, US industry was booming and needed overseas buyers for its products.

So by 1947, the United States decided its best interests lay in a prosperous Germany within a properous Europe. Secretary of State George Marshall urged Europe's leaders to meet and draw up a collective plan for economic reconstruction, which the United States would fund. As each country receiving what became known as Marshall Aid had to agree to US scrutiny of its economy, Stalin refused the offer for the countries he held. When Marshall Aid was joined by the *deutschmark*, a new US-backed German currency, he blockaded Berlin and US planes began airlifting food into the city to keep it going for a year.

The Berlin Airlift exposed a new fault line between two Europes and set a tone for the decades to come. Berliners developed an affection for the American *rosinenbomber* ("raisin

A 1947 poster to promote the European Recovery Program, or Marshall Plan. The sails display the flags of European countries, but the US flag turns them to catch the wind. The Marshall Plan paved the way for future European integration.

bombers") that dropped food and sweets from the sky, and in turn the West softened toward Berlin. By the time the airlift ended in 1949, West Germany had been formed, a new and decidedly capitalist country.

But nationalism remained to be overcome. Marshall Aid continued until 1951, preserving political stability by kick-starting Western Europe's recovery, and in so doing pointing to the value of integrating a rebuilt Germany, but before it ran out, Europe would have to seize the initiative itself. Already in 1946, Britain's wartime prime minister Winston Churchill had called for a "United States of Europe" led by France and Germany to safeguard Europe against another war. But in this regard Britain, like the United States, saw its future role as that of an onlooker.

BEYOND THE NATION

The ball was now in France's court, but there were centuries of wounds to heal with Germany. For France to reach out would require someone able to take the long view. French Foreign Minister Robert Schuman harked back to Charlemagne to present a vision of a common Franco-German community and set in motion the stitching together of Europe through a series of treaties. As a first step, in 1949 the Treaty of London created the Council of Europe, a body charged with establishing a framework for cooperation by drawing up a bill of rights.

But as the Marshall Plan had shown, what was needed was something that went beyond an agreement that might be broken at any time to a structural interdependence all but impossible to undo. In 1950, Schuman and Planning Commissioner Jean Monnet suggested a single coal and steel industry spanning France and West Germany, open to other countries and overseen by a common and impartial authority. German Chancellor Konrad Adenauer hailed it as a breakthrough.

So in April 1951, France, West Germany, the Netherlands, Belgium, Luxembourg, and Italy all signed the Treaty of Paris, bringing into being the European Coal and Steel Community (ECSC) headed by Monnet. This Schuman termed "the first supranational institution," and it was in essence a government, with an executive, a legislature, and a judiciary, agreed to by member countries but with binding powers over them. The ECSC abolished customs duties for coal and steel traded between the six countries, and used a 1 percent tax on production to issue loans and fund better conditions for miners and steelworkers.

The balance of power in postwar Europe now began to shift, aided by subsequent events. In 1956, when Britain and France joined Israel to take back control of the Suez Canal following a revolution in Egypt, a wider war with threats of Soviet nuclear attacks on Europe looked imminent. In this context, the United States would not back the invasion and Britain, without notifying France, beat a humiliating retreat.

France saw this as proof that neither Britain nor the United States could be relied on. West Germany took it as a sign it should look to closer European integration, not to America, for its future security. So Europe's project received a push and in 1957 the Treaties of Rome created the European Economic Community (EEC), to create a customs union across member countries, and the European Atomic Energy Community (EURATOM), to do for atomic power what the ECSC was doing for coal and steel.

Suez had shown Britain it was no longer a major power, and by the early 1960s it was asking to join the EEC. But lingering French distrust blocked British membership for another decade. In the meantime, Europe's planners were moving toward a more comprehensive union. In 1967, the EEC took over the ECSC and EURATOM to form a single authority. By 1979, Members of the European Parliament (MEPs) had become elected representatives.

New countries were now joining the original six. Passport controls were largely waived in the 1980s and in 1993 the Treaty of Maastricht established the European Union (EU), together with a common currency and the concept of European citizenship. Failure to prevent nationalist fervor yet again sparking war in Europe when Yugoslavia broke up into separate republics in the 1990s prompted the EU to assemble a military force, which in the new century would be sent on peacekeeping missions within Europe and far beyond.

Half a century of meetings had produced something entirely new: a budding superpower with its own citizens, government, and central bank, whose authority derived from independent nations but whose laws could bind them. It had come about completely by consent, without drawing a sword or firing a gun.

A NEW ROME

But by the turn of the century the scope of integration had changed. The fall of the Soviet Union in 1991 had doubled the EU's potential size, presenting opportunity but also challenge. Germany had already been reunited in 1990, producing an economic powerhouse to look forward to, but in the meantime bringing huge restructuring costs for the former West German economy.

So in 1993 the Copenhagen Criteria, a set of new conditions for would-be EU members to meet, was drawn up, requiring a market economy and enough stability to guarantee democracy and the rule of law, in addition to acceptance of existing EU laws.

But a wider union brought other issues. The EU now had an elected parliament, but for people to engage with it they needed to feel part of the community it represented—they needed to feel part of a shared European culture. But that was harder now.

This became clear as people from the new member countries of eastern Europe began to seek work in the wealthier west. The skills and economic boost they brought took second stage to the sense that newcomers were putting pressure on jobs, accommodation, and public services. In the west, people from the east were seen more as foreigners than fellow Europeans.

Other problems came with the adoption of a single currency beginning in 1999. The strength of the euro rests on the economies of the original "inner six" member states, in particular on Germany. For weaker economies the euro's strength makes it harder to export goods and attract inward investment. This became a particular problem for several Mediterranean countries following the global financial crisis of 2007-2008, even affecting Italy, one of the "inner six." Tight fiscal policy directed by the European Central Bank in

Members of the European Coal and Steel Community (ECSC) 1951 and European Economic Community (EEC) 1957
Additional members by creation of the European Union (EU) 1993, with date of accession
Additional EU members by 2017, with date of accession
Accepted as members, pending adoption of EU law (as of 2017)
Applied for membership (as of 2017)
Limit of Council of Mutual Economic Assistance (COMECON) 1949–1991 (the "Iron Curtain")
Recipient of Marshall Aid 1948–1951, with amount in US$ million
Countries using the euro in 2017
N
Greenland
Joined as part of Denmark in 1973, but left in 1985 after winning home rule. May rejoin.
Other overseas territories, remnants of the empires of Denmark, Britain, France and the Netherlands, have varying relationships to the EU. All can be full members
Iceland
29
Applied to join in 2009 following financial crash but shelved application in 2013. May resume, but fears losing fishing rights
Two applications (in company with Denmark, United Kingdom, and Ireland) blocked by France in 1960s. Another two rejected by referendum in 1972 and 1994. Fears losing fishing rights within the EU, but accepts some EU laws in return for access to single market
Faroe Islands
Fears losing fishing rights if joins the EU
Finland
1995
Norway
236
Sweden
1995
107
Atlantic Ocean
North Sea
Baltic Sea
Estonia
2004
Latvia
2004
Lithuania
2004
Russian Federation
Still an intimidating presence for the EU, though in theory eligible to be considered for membership
Denmark
1973
273
Republic of Ireland
1973
148
United Kingdom
1973
3190
Voted to leave by narrow margin in 2016 referendum, triggering start of process in 2017. Negotiating withdrawal scheduled to take 2 years. Would like to retain access to single market but wants power to limit movement of EU citizens into the UK
Netherlands
1084
East Germany
1990
Belarus
Authoritarian government disliked by and uninterested in the EU
Belgium
Brussels (executive government)
Germany
Frankfurt (bank)
Poland
2004
Luxembourg (law courts)
Luxembourg
West Germany
1391
Czech Republic
2004
Ukraine
Interested in EU membership but unlikely to join for some time
Moldova
Belgium and Luxembourg receive $546 million Marshall Aid between them
France
2714
Strasbourg (parliament)
Slovakia
2004
Austria
1995
678
Hungary
2004
Switzerland
Liechtenstein
Application rejected by referendum in 1992, since when series of treaties agreed as a substitute. Euro unofficially in use
Slovenia
2004
Croatia
2013
Romania
2007
Portugal
1986
51
Spain
1986
Andorra
Monaco
San Marino
Bosnia-Herzegovina
Serbia
Black Sea
Montenegro
Kosovo
Bulgaria
2007
Microstates too small or autocratic to join, but all closely tied to EU members
Vatican City
Italy
1509
Macedonia
Albania
Turkey
225
Applied to join in 1987, but reluctance to comply with EU law set to continue delaying membership. Has customs union agreement with EU
Greece
1981
707
Ongoing political and economic effects of 1990s wars delaying membership of Balkan countries
Application rejected by Brussels on basis Morocco not part of Europe
Close economic ties with EU
Morocco
Algeria
Joined as part of France in 1951, but left after independence in 1962
Tunisia
Malta 2004
Mediterranean Sea
Cyprus
2004
500 miles
500 kms
30°W
20°W
10°W
0°
10°E
20°E
30°E
40°E
40°N
50°N
60°N

Frankfurt contributes to resentment toward a currency that benefits some countries more than others.

These issues have sharpened the image of a two-tier EU: an inner core of states driving closer union, surrounded by a compliant but less convinced periphery. This has brought with it the suspicion that the EU is a form of empire—even that its true leader may not be the President of the European Commission at all, but rather the German Chancellor Angela Merkel. Ironically, perhaps, it is not within the new eastern European countries that this idea has found most favor, nor in the economically stretched countries of the Mediterranean, but in Britain, where in 2016 a slim majority voted to leave the EU.

The issue for Britain has always been sovereignty. The principle that makes the EU possible—a body of law to stand above national law—is difficult for Britain to accept. While the early EU fathers were forming a vision of a European family, Britain was preoccupied with converting its worldwide empire into the Commonwealth of Nations. Britain had its own family, whose members still respected it as former head of the household.

The other members of Europe's family see it as a new kind of household based on consent. They accept the need for a coordinating authority and see the EU parliament as the way to voice their concerns. Britain, by contrast, cannot get beyond the fundamental status of EU law. Perhaps it is just too soon to expect the former leader of the world's largest empire to be able to see the EU as anything other than a new imperial rival.

Yet Britain has become used to the benefits brought by the common European market. Despite its long-established global links, its economy depends more and more on Europe. So the mother of the old empire finds herself caught between the past and the future.

Meanwhile, Britain's exit, or "Brexit" as it has become known, has presented the EU with a test it seems to have passed. The prospect of one of the EU's member countries choosing to secede has been voiced for decades. There has always been tension, and the fear has long existed that if one country took the plunge, a domino effect would follow and the EU would collapse.

But Britain's choice has had the opposite effect. Brexit will cost the EU, but it will cost the British far more. Britain is now facing years of Byzantine legal entanglements, far-reaching economic problems, and backward-looking social dislocation; the rest of Europe looks on with horror and incomprehension. Britain may well be right in claiming the EU to be an empire of sorts, but to those within Europe's walls, life on the outside now looks bleak and uninviting.

And so the European project, with France and Germany at its helm, moves on with increased confidence towards its new Rome.

Opposite page:

THE EUROPEAN UNION 2017

The embryo of the EU was a unified coal and steel industry, formed in 1951. By the fall of the Berlin Wall in 1989, most of Western Europe had joined the EEC. In 1993, the EU was formed, since when almost all of Europe has either joined or applied to join.

AFTERWORD

The history of empire is to a large extent everyone's history. Almost all states were at some time either cores or peripheries of empires that formed stepping stones to today's global community. The rise and fall of empires pushed people together and brought new types of society—Europe passed from the classical world to feudalism to forms of capitalism and socialism through the medium of empire.

As such, a century ago empire appeared to be an intrinsic part of civilization. Half a century later, it seemed a passing historical stage. By then, colonial subjugation had become morally unacceptable in the same way as slavery before it—and moreover, had ceased to pay. But had empire genuinely become a thing of the past?

EMPIRE BY ANY OTHER NAME

Well before the imperial finale of the First World War, the British had already abandoned the protectionism of formal empire for a global economy based on free trade. Much earlier, Rome had gradually extended citizenship of the republic to the limits of the empire. Both Rome and Britain seemed to have sailed beyond the concept of empire into uncharted waters.

Later generations, however, were able to look back on both the Romans and the British and see key features of empire persisting, albeit in altered guise. The British had exchanged the expense of formal rule for the cheaper use of informal economic pressure to achieve the same goal of controlling the market. In Rome, extending citizenship had been the classic tool for buying off resistance and also for recruiting soldiers and widening the tax base. In both cases, a familiar core–periphery relationship was preserved. Control was sufficiently absolute not just for the periphery to be exploited but also for the time-honored dream of a stable imperial peace to be realized for a while.

These two ideas, imperial exploitation on the one hand and imperial peace and stability on the other, still find expression today.

EMPIRE AS EXPLOITATION

After the fall of the old empires, exploitative core–periphery relationships lived on in varying degrees under the United States, the USSR, and maybe the EU, too—and not least in the business world. Companies seek to extend influence through the market according to an imperial pattern: sprouting branches, franchises, subsidiaries, and taking over other companies just as strong states once acquired colonies. The ambition to increase market share mirrors the ambition to conquer territory. Beyond a certain size, all businesses are empires.

In addition, international business empires have their roots in the West, growing in an industrial, mercantile, and financial loam built up over centuries of Western imperial dominance. So the cumulative effect of the spread of businesses through the world market is to reinforce a divide between a global core and a global periphery first marked out by the Spanish, the Portuguese, the East India Companies, and their successors.

But business empires, though grown from national soil, have the potential to overwhelm the nation-state. The greater interconnectedness of today's global economy means the big Western banking houses wield even more power than the East India Companies, in the sense that no state dares either regulate them or allow them to fail. When the market collapses, Western governments pay their debts, and even China is not big enough to risk losing Western investment by withholding financial aid. The nation-state is neither an antidote nor an effective check on empire.

EMPIRE AS GLOBAL GOVERNMENT

Alongside this, attempts at international cooperation between states have steadily increased. In the late 18th and early 19th centuries, the idea of the nation-state stood opposed to empire, insisting national identity should set a natural limit to a state's spread. But by the late 19th century, nationalism had become a new tool for states with traditional imperial ambitions. It could rally people more fervently than loyalty to kings or emperors alone because it brought outsiders into sharper focus. The First World War made this horrifyingly clear. So even as lumbering multinational assemblages like the Austro-Hungarian Empire breathed their last, the idea of multinational organizations found new favor.

A peace imposed by empire, however, could no longer be justified; cooperation between states had to be voluntary. So the League of Nations was formed, followed, after its failure to prevent a second world war, by the United Nations and other associations charged to promote international harmony. These bodies have all faced the problem any committee faces in trying to marry representation with effective decision making. Typically, an inner core ends up making the big decisions; only five out of 192 states make up the permanent members of the United Nations Security Council, and even then its effectiveness is questionable. The EU, a more centralized structure, relies on a single authority to orchestrate the nations of Europe, allowing some to accuse it of imperial overtones, but it is hard to imagine what a looser union could achieve.

GOOD EMPIRES AND BAD

For most of human history, people sought not an alternative to empire but simply a better empire. Being part of an empire brought increased trade and contact with other cultures. Ordinary people had little taste for the economic uncertainty and social dislocation that came with an empire's fall. Bad emperors, however, courted collapse through excessive exploitation, profligacy, divisive policies, and warmongering. Good emperors knew the importance of stability and, accordingly, distributed certain benefits to their people. They knew the value of consent.

For the moment it remains unclear what a world free of imperial ambition would look like. We still have aggressor states, insatiable business corporations, movements calling for a new caliphate, and multinational organizations seeking to direct nation-states. But some of these outfits are interested in consent, and in that lies a hope not simply to repeat past mistakes.

FURTHER READING

These books explore in greater depth topics touched on in the present volume.

GENERAL THEORETICAL WORKS

Arendt, Hannah, *The Origins of Totalitarianism*, Harcourt Brace, 1951
Hobson, J.A., *Imperialism: A Study*, Cosimo, 1902
Ibn Khaldûn, *The Muqaddimah: An Introduction to History*, abridged by N.J. Dawood, Princeton University Press, 2004
Lenin, V.I., *Imperialism: The Highest Stage of Capitalism*, International, 1939
Schumpeter, J.A., *Imperialism and Social Classes*, Blackwell, 1951
Wallerstein, Immanuel, *Historical Capitalism with Capitalist Civilization*, 2nd edition, Verso, 1996

1. WAR AND PEACE

Sumer and Akkad

Kramer, Samuel Noah, *History Begins at Sumer: Thirty-Nine Firsts in Recorded History*, University of Pennsylvania Press, 1956
Roux, Georges, *Ancient Iraq*, 3rd edition, Penguin, 1993

Egypt

Kemp, Barry J., *Ancient Egypt: Anatomy of a Civilization*, new edition, Routledge, 1991
Shaw, Ian (ed.), *The Oxford History of Ancient Egypt*, Oxford University Press, 2000

Assyria and Babylonia

Saggs, H.W.F., *The Greatness That Was Babylon*, Sidgwick & Jackson, 1962
Saggs, H.W.F., *The Might That Was Assyria*, Sidgwick & Jackson, 1984

Persia

Curtis, J.E. & Tallis, N. (eds.), *Forgotten Empire: The World of Ancient Persia*, University of California Press, 2005
Olmstead, A.T., *History of the Persian Empire*, University of Chicago Press, 1948

2. EMPIRES OF THE CLASSICAL WORLD

Athens

Fine, John V.A., *The Ancient Greeks: A Critical History*, Harvard University Press, 1985
Strassler, Robert B. (ed.), *The Landmark Thucydides: A Comprehensive Guide to the Peloponnesiann War*, Touchstone, 1998

Rome

Cary, M. & Scullard, H.H., *A History of Rome: Down to the Reign of Constantine*, 3rd edition, St Martins, 1976
Luttwak, Edward N., *The Grand Strategy of the Roman Empire from the First Century* AD *to the Third*, Johns Hopkins University Press, 1979
Mommsen, Theodor, *The History of Rome*, abridged by Dero A. Saunders & John H. Collins, Meridian, 1958

Alexander

Green, Peter, *Alexander the Great and the Hellenistic Age*, Phoenix, 2008
Mensch, Pamela & Romm, James S. (eds.), *Alexander the Great: Selections from Arrian, Diodorus, Plutarch and Quintus Curtius*, Hackett, 2005

Iran

Axworthy, Michael, *A History of Iran: Empire of the Mind*, Basic Books, 2008
Herrmann, Georgina, *The Iranian Revival*, Elsevier-Phaidon, 1977

India
Basham, A.L., *The Wonder That Was India*, 3rd edition, Sidgwick & Jackson, 2000
Sharma, R.S., *India's Ancient Past*, Oxford University Press, 2008

China
Lewis, Mark Edward, *The Early Chinese Empires: Qin and Han*, Harvard University Press, 2007
Loewe, Michael, *Everyday Life in Early Imperial China during the Han Period*, 202 BC–AD 220, Hackett, 2005

3. EMPIRES OF FAITH

The Byzantine Empire
Obolensky, Dimitri, *The Byzantine Commonwealth: Eastern Europe 500–1453*, Phoenix, 2000
Runciman, Steven, *The Byzantine Theocracy: The Weil Lectures*, Cambridge University Press, 2004

The Holy Roman Empire
Brown, Peter, *The Rise of Western Christendom: Triumph and Diversity,* AD *200–1000*, 2nd edition, Blackwell, 2003
Cantor, Norman F., *The Civilization of the Middle Ages*, Harper, 1994

The Abbasid Caliphate
Glubb, John Bagot, *The Great Arab Conquests*, Hodder & Stoughton, 1963
Kennedy, Hugh, *The Court of the Caliphs*, Weidenfeld & Nicolson, 2004

4. EMPIRES OF THE HORSE

The Mongols
Morgan, David, *The Mongols*, Blackwell, 1990
Ratchnevsky, Paul, *Genghis Khan: His Life and Legacy*, Blackwell, 1993

Chinese Empires
Ebrey, Patricia Buckley, *The Cambridge Illustrated History of China*, Cambridge University Press, 1999
Fairbank, J.K., *China: A New History*, 2nd revised edition, Harvard University Press, 2006

Muslim India
Eraly, Abraham, *The Mughal World: India's Tainted Paradise*, Phoenix, 2008
Richards, John F., *The Mughal Empire*, Cambridge University Press, 1996

The Ottoman Empire
Findley, Carter Vaughn, *The Turks in World History*, Oxford University Press, 2004
Inalcik, Halil, *The Ottoman Empire: The Classical Age 1300–1600*, Phoenix, 2001

5. EMPIRES OF ISOLATION

The Empire of Mali
Bovill, E.W., *The Golden Trade of the Moors: West African Kingdoms in the Fourteenth Century*, 2nd edition, Markus Wiener, 1995.

The Aztec Empire
Hassig, Ross, *Aztec Warfare: Imperial Expansion and Political Control*, University of Oklahoma Press, 1995
Leon-Portilla, Miguel, *Aztec Thought and Culture: A Study of the Ancient Nahuatl Mind*, University of Oklahoma Press, 1990

The Inca Empire
D'Altroy, Terence N., *The Incas*, new edition, Blackwell, 2003
Conrad, Geoffrey W. & Demarest, Arthur Andrew, *Religion and Empire: The Dynamics of Aztec and Inca Expansionism*, Cambridge University Press, 1984

6. THE FIRST GLOBAL EMPIRES

The Empires of Spain and Portugal
Boxer, C.R., *The Portuguese Seaborne Empire 1415–1825*, Hutchinson, 1969
Braudel, Fernand, *The Mediterranean and the Mediterranean World in the Age of Philip II*, Harper & Row, 1972

Parry, J.H., *The Spanish Seaborne Empire*, Hutchinson, 1966

The Dutch

Boxer, C.R., *The Dutch Seaborne Empire 1600–1800*, Hutchinson, 1965

Vries, Jan de & Woude, Ad van der, *The First Modern Economy: Success, Failure, and Perseverance of the Dutch Economy, 1500–1815*, Cambridge University Press, 1997

Britain and France in America

Parkman, Francis, *The Battle for North America*, abridged by John Tebbel, Doubleday, 1948

Taylor, Alan, *American Colonies: The Settling of America*, Penguin, 2002

7. EMPIRES AND NATIONS

Napoleon

Grab, Alexander, *Napoleon and the Transformation of Europe*, Macmillan, 2003

Hobsbawm, Eric J., *The Age of Revolution: Europe 1789–1848*, Weidenfeld & Nicholson, 1962

Russia

Pipes, Richard, *Russia Under the Old Regime*, 2nd edition, Penguin, 1997

Riasanovsky, Nicholas V. & Steinberg, Mark, *A History of Russia*, 7th edition, Oxford University Press, 2004

The Austrian Habsburgs

Evans, R.J.W., *The Making of the Habsburg Monarchy, 1550–1700: An Interpretation*, Oxford University Press, 1984

Macartney, C.A., *The Habsburg Empire 1790–1918*, Macmillan, 1969

8. EMPIRES OF INDUSTRIAL CAPITALISM

The British Empire

Porter, Andrew (ed.), *The Oxford History of the British Empire: Volume III: The Nineteenth Century*, Oxford University Press, 2001

Porter, Bernard, *The Lion's Share*, 4th edition, Longman, 2004

The High Age of Imperialism

Headrick, Daniel R., *The Tools of Empire: Technology and European Imperialism in the Nineteenth Century*, Oxford University Press, 1981

Hobsbawm, Eric, *Age of Empire: 1875–1914*, Weidenfeld & Nicholson, 1987

Wesseling, H.L., *The European Colonial Empires: 1815–1919*, Longman, 2004

The Empire of Japan

Beasley, W.G., *Japanese Imperialism 1894–1945*, Oxford University Press, 1991

McClain, James L., *Japan: A Modern History*, Norton, 2002

9. EMPIRES AND UTOPIAS

The United States of America

Johnson, Chalmers, *Nemesis: The Last Days of the American Republic*, Metropolitan, 2007

Reynolds, David, *America, Empire of Liberty: A New History*, Allen Lane, 2009

The Soviet Union

Fitzpatrick, Sheila, *The Russian Revolution*, Oxford University Press, 1982

Kort, Michael, *The Soviet Colossus: History and Aftermath*, 6th edition, M.E. Sharpe, 2006

The European Union

Moravcsik, Andrew, *The Choice for Europe: Social Purpose and State Power from Messina to Maastricht*, Routledge, 1998

Zielonka, Jan, *Europe as Empire: The Nature of the Enlarged European Union*, Oxford University Press, 2006

INDEX

Note: Page numbers in **bold** indicate maps; Page numbers in *italic* indicate illustrations/captions

ACKNOWLEDGEMENTS

My thanks to James Brown of Birkbeck College, London, and Bill Tompson of the OECD for their generous help and encouragement in the early stages of this book. Also to Julie Dunne for inspiring me at the outset. Most of all I thank Kate Parker, whose dogged optimism, endless patience, and willingness to turn her hand to whatever needed doing kept this project afloat. Without her this book would not exist. I would also like to thank Jeremy Hauck for his readiness to include, mostly at very short notice, numerous revisions designed to improve the book.

The author and publishers would like to thank the following copyright holders for allowing their photographs to be used in this book:

The Art Archive/British Museum (page 188), Bridgeman Art Library (page 99); Corbis photos: Stapleton Collection (frontispiece), page 197, Gianni Dagli Orti (pages 30, 42, 164), Araldo de Luca (page 53), Robert Harding World imagery (page 21), Royal Ontario Museum (page 71), The Gallery Collection (page 94), Asian Art & Archaeology, Inc. (page 105), Philadelphia Museum of Art (page 206), Swim Ink 2, LLC (page 226), Courtesy of Museum of Maritimo (Barcelona)/ Ramon Manent (page 129); dbimages/Alamy (page 75); Getty Images photos: The Bridgeman Art Library (page 14), Basawan and Chatai/The Bridgeman Art Library (page 117), Islamic School/The Bridgeman Art Library (page 121), National Geographic (page 91), Hulton Archive (pages 170, 220), Andrei Rublev/The Bridgeman Art Library (page 174), Christoph Amberger/The Bridgeman Art Library (page 186); iStock photos: vasiliki (page 38), fanelliphotography (page 50), millsrymer (page 9), eROMAZe (page 63), Hazlan Abdul Hakim (page 81); R. Sheridan @ Ancient Art & Architecture Collection (pages 46, 57); Shutterstock photos: Albina Tiplyashina (page 10), Everett Historical (pages 180 and 207); TopFoto photos: Charles Walker (page 146), The Granger Collection (pages 27, 35, 37, 77, 83, 86, 108, 125, 127, 135, 140, 145, 158, 162, 183, 194, 202, 209, 213, 219), RIA Novosti (page 176), The British Library/HIP (page 191).